The 15-MINUTE Chef

Patricia Mack

HPBOOKS

HPBooks
Published by The Berkley Publishing Group
A member of Penguin Putnam Inc.
375 Hudson Street,
New York, New York 10014

First edition: March 1999

Published simultaneously in Canada.

The Penguin Putnam Inc. World Wide Web site address is http://www.penguinputnam.com

Library of Congress Cataloging-in-Publication Data

Mack, Patricia.
    The 15-minute chef / Patricia Mack.—1st ed.
      p.   cm.
    ISBN 1-55788-300-9
      1. Quick and easy cookery.   2. Menus.   I. Title.   II. Title:
    Fifteen-minute chef.
    TX833.5.M34   1999
    641.5'55—dc21   98-46903
                                                        CIP

Printed in the United States of America

10 9 8 7 6 5 4 3 2 1

Contents

Preface · iv

Introduction · v

Take Five · viii

Beef & Veal · 1

Pork & Lamb · 23

Fish · 45

Shellfish · 79

Chicken · 103

Turkey · 143

Eggs · 157

Pasta · 171

Soups & Stews · 207

Main-Dish Salads · 237

Vegetable Entrees · 265

Index · 285

Preface

I do more than write about food: I cook for my family, too. And I am sad to report that more times than not they're getting short shrift. The problem is time. Our lifestyle requires efficiency in all areas, meal preparation included.

Like a number of other people, I've programmed my telephone with the number of the pizza delivery and Chinese takeout restaurants. And while these businesses are a blessing, there are many nights when guilt sets in with every bite of my moo shu pork. I like to cook, but more important, I like knowing that my family is getting a fresh, home-cooked meal.

I know a lot of other people feel the same way. One of the delicious things about the job of food editor at a major northeastern newspaper is the amazing dialogue with people who read the food section and take time to call or write. Essentially, they are the reason for *The 15-Minute Chef*. Readers and my own sense of changing priorities are driving elements.

The 15-Minute Chef provides each recipe with a menu, but the menu requires only one dish (the recipe) that needs to be cooked and that dish will go from stovetop to tabletop in fifteen minutes. Side dishes are of the ready-to-eat-when-you-bought-them variety.

Introduction

Put on your Rollerblades. We're going to cook dinner.

No time. No time. No time. It's the refrain of busy people all over America.

According to *Supermarket Business*, a food marketing trade publication, the average meal preparation declined to just thirty minutes per day in 1990. It is expected to decline to fifteen minutes per day by the year 2000.

Not too long ago, Tupperware, the master of kitchen tidiness, asked its sales representatives to talk to customers about their major kitchen concerns.

What the customers said didn't surprise me and probably won't surprise you: From washing dishes and cleaning the stove to the simplest steps in food preparation—even chopping an onion—consumers said they had no time.

Just about everyone said planning meals would be a help, but they also said they lacked the time to do even that.

Recently, Reynolds Kitchens studied the cooking habits of Generation X women. They cook at least three times a week, but when asked when they plan "tonight's dinner," 70 percent said they plan it "today." Of those who plan it "today," 27 percent said they do it that very morning; 20 percent plan it during the day, and 23 percent plan it in the car on the way home from work.

That's where *The 15-Minute Chef* can be a real help. The recipe is a shopping list.

You don't need to depend exclusively on convenience products to produce fast meals, but they do help. There are a lot of them on the market. Keep in mind that not all convenience products are good products, but the good ones are a boon. Yes, they cost money, but you're buying time.

We're all overbooked and overwhelmed these days, but I don't think the solution has to be a lifetime sentence of takeout pizza, noisy restaurants serving food you could probably make better at home, tasteless frozen dinners, or a charge account at the local Chinese restaurant.

I think the answer is a different kind of cooking for the way we live today—cooking that allows for our busy schedules and our desire to spend less time in the kitchen, but that still embraces our desire for simple, satisfying food. *The 15-Minute Chef*'s solution is to use a combination of basic ingredients and the best of what's fresh and seasonal, cooked with ease and pleasure.

SHOPPING TIPS

- Select precut fresh vegetables in the supermarket.
- Buy bagged fresh greens for salads in minutes.
- Purchase refrigerated fresh pasta. It cooks in 2 to 5 minutes instead of the dry pasta's 10 minutes.
- When purchasing red meats, choose cuts that are one inch thick or less. They'll cook quickly and easily under the broiler.

IN THE KITCHEN

Keeping a supply of favorite foodstuffs on hand in the cupboard, freezer, or refrigerator ensures that one way or another, a tasty meal will make it to the table. True, I have had to sacrifice my fantasy of being the fabulous cook who shops for fresh ingredients for every meal. Instead, I devote myself to thinking about what I have on hand that's quick to prepare and quick to clean up.

Organizing the pantry helps to put meals together with things that are on hand. Here are a few suggestions:

THE PANTRY

- Keep canned chicken and beef broth in your pantry.
- Store bottled pasta sauces in your pantry.
- Buy quantities of canned chopped tomatoes. They are an invaluable ingredient for thousands of dishes. The tomatoes are already peeled, seeded, and chopped.
- Keep packaged bread crumbs on hand for topping baked dishes such as macaroni and cheese or fried fish.
- Try instant couscous. It's ready in seconds.
- Nonstick vegetable spray is fast and healthful; it also saves calories.

THE REFRIGERATOR

- Keep chopped garlic that is packed in oil and sold in jars. Half a teaspoon of prechopped garlic equals one clove of freshly chopped garlic.
- Stock packaged grated cheeses such as Cheddar, Monterey Jack, and mozzarella. They're great for dishes such as salads or to use in a simple omelet.
- Buy several prepared salad dressings. They add variety to simple mixtures of fresh greens or cold leftover vegetables from dinner the night before.
- Containers of chopped nuts provide toppings for frozen yogurt or sliced fresh fruit for a tasty dessert.

THE FREEZER

- Keep a supply of boneless, skinless chicken breast halves in the freezer. They are convenient, cook quickly, and can be served as an entree or cut into cubes or strips and tossed into a garden salad or stir-fry. Some supermarkets sell a cut called chicken tenders, which are slices of boneless, skinless chicken breast. Because they are thin and small they cook very quickly, and can be a real time saver. Alas, they also cost a bit more than chicken breasts.
- Stock frozen vegetables such as broccoli, green beans, corn, peas, carrots, or mixed vegetables that can be tossed into soups, served as side dishes, or added to skillet meals.

· Use frozen whipped topping to dress up simple puddings or angel food cake.

· Keep pound cake in the freezer as a great dessert or a simple breakfast accompanied by fresh fruit.

KITCHEN EQUIPMENT

Aside from my stove, the single most important appliance in the preparation of a speedy meal is my microwave oven. It has more uses than defrosting or reheating leftovers. I don't usually cook whole dishes in it, but I find it invaluable for melting cheese, butter, or chocolate. I can sauté onions and bell peppers quickly. It's good for heating sauce and steaming vegetables.

Take Five

FIVE TIPS FOR THE TIRED COOK

1. Instead of putting dishes back into the cupboard after dinner, put them back on the table. It takes no extra time, and the table's already set for the next meal.

2. Set up a cooking cooperative with a friend. When preparing soups, stews, casseroles, or other dishes that reheat well, make two batches. Trade one with the friend.

3. "Doctor" prepared foods. For instance, add sautéed garlic and onion, sliced pepperoni, and ripe olives to bottled pasta sauces. Add chopped onion to canned beans. A shot of rum is great in canned black bean soup.

4. When you drain hot pasta, use the pan you cooked it in to heat the sauce. Then return the pasta to the pan and toss with the sauce. That's one less pan to clean.

5. Keep jars of strained-fruit baby food on hand as an easy topping for ice cream, angel cake, or frozen yogurt.

FIVE TIME-SAVING GADGETS

1. Kitchen shears
2. Compact food processor
3. Hand-held blender
4. Sharp eight-inch chef's knife
5. Egg slicer

FIVE DRY INGREDIENTS THAT ARE A MUST

1. Bouillon cubes
2. Raisins
3. Chocolate chips
4. Ramen noodles
5. Crackers and chips

FIVE CANNED GOODS TO KEEP ON HAND

1. Kidney beans
2. Tomato paste
3. Tomato sauce
4. Tuna
5. Pineapple

FIVE ITEMS EVERY REFRIGERATOR SHOULD HAVE

1. Prepared barbecue sauce
2. Cream cheese
3. Lemons or lemon juice
4. Grated Parmesan cheese
5. Fruit preserves

Beef & Veal

I love beef, be it hamburger or tenderloin, and I eat a fair amount of it because there are so many universally appealing dishes that can be made quickly and economically with beef. Ground beef cooks the quickest and can be used in the most diverse ways. This great-tasting meat is extremely popular in other kitchens besides mine. The National Cattlemen's Beef Association says that over 71 percent of all households in the United States have ground beef on hand.

But as wonderful as it is, it isn't the only option for quick meals. Tender beef cuts and veal that cook quickly and are cut properly are all fifteen-minute options that require little more than a few ingredients to produce fast and fabulous dinners. We have an enormous selection of beef to choose from. The U.S. Department of Agriculture monitors quality by grading meat according to the age of the animal and the amount of marbling—the more the marbling, the more tender the meat.

At home, the responsibility for safe handling shifts to you. Store raw meat in the coldest part of the refrigerator, which is generally the bottom shelf, away from cooked and ready-to-eat foods. Refrigerate uncooked meats two to three days or freeze up to six months. Ground meat won't last as long: refrigerate only one to two days or freeze up to three months.

The current USDA recommendation is not to rely on the color of ground meat to determine doneness. The USDA now urges consumers to check meat patties for proper internal temperature with an instant-read thermometer. Ground beef, veal, pork, and lamb should be cooked to 160F (71C). For more information about safe food handling and preparation, call the USDA's Meat and Poultry Hotline at 800-535-4555.

Chili-Topped Potatoes

■ A microwaved potato can be the basis for a savory dinner. Use medium russet or baking potatoes—they have good texture, contain only 110 calories, and have important vitamins and minerals, including vitamin C and potassium. Two baking potatoes can be cooked in a microwave in 8 to 10 minutes.

2 medium russet potatoes, scrubbed and
  pierced once or twice with a fork
1 (12-oz.) can beef chili with beans
¼ cup shredded Cheddar cheese

Place potatoes on a microwave-safe plate and cook on HIGH for 8 to 10 minutes or until soft. Wrap in foil and allow to stand for 2 minutes.

Meanwhile, heat canned chili in a 1-quart saucepan over medium heat until hot, about 4 minutes.

Remove foil, pierce top of potatoes, and squeeze open. Top with hot chili, then shredded cheese.

MENU: Green salad with ranch dressing. Apple slices sprinkled with lemon juice and tossed with golden raisins.

SERVINGS: Makes 2 servings.

Beef Stir-Fry

■ My supermarket deli stocks prepared sesame noodles in the refrigerated case. If they're not available, drained beef-flavored ramen noodles, which can be cooked in a matter of minutes, make a good substitute.

2 teaspoons peanut oil
¾ pound thinly sliced beef for stir-frying
2 cups broccoli florets
½ cup steak sauce
About 1 pound prepared sesame noodles or
  other cooked noodles

Heat 1 teaspoon of the oil in a wok or large frying pan over high heat. Add beef and stir-fry 2 to 3 minutes or until browned. Remove beef from pan with a slotted spoon. Add remaining oil to pan. Add broccoli and stir-fry until crisp-tender, about 2 minutes.

Add steak sauce and stir-fry about 2 minutes or until heated through. Return meat to the pan along with sesame noodles and toss until heated through.

MENU: Spinach salad with marinated mushrooms and ranch dressing. Sliced mangoes with crystallized ginger and blueberries.

SERVINGS: Makes 4 servings.

Great Steaks with Mushroom Topping

■ A lot of cooks recommend seasoning meat with salt and pepper before cooking. I don't think it's always a good idea. Salt pulls natural juices away from the meat—the opposite of what you want to happen when cooking steak. The idea is to sear the meat surface, which seals it and keeps the juices inside.

4 beef rib-eye steaks
2 tablespoons canola oil
Freshly ground black pepper
1 cup sliced mushrooms
2 teaspoons Worcestershire sauce

Preheat broiler. Rub steaks with 1 tablespoon of the oil and pepper. Place steaks on a broiler pan rack that has been sprayed with nonstick cooking spray. Broil 4 inches from source of heat for 4 minutes per side for medium-rare, turning once, or to desired doneness.

Meanwhile, heat remaining canola oil in a 10-inch skillet over medium heat. Add sliced mushrooms and sauté, stirring occasionally, until mushroom juices evaporate, about 5 minutes. Add Worcestershire sauce and toss with mushrooms. Cook 1 minute. Top steaks with mushroom mixture.

MENU: Hearts of palm on lettuce with blue cheese dressing. Canned potato sticks. Bakery cupcakes.

SERVINGS: Makes 4 servings.

Balsamic Beef

■ Beef tenderloin is naturally tender. Marinate it briefly in balsamic vinaigrette, and it will melt in your mouth.

4 sprigs fresh oregano
4 (4-oz.) beef tenderloin fillets
1 cup balsamic vinaigrette salad dressing

Preheat broiler. Place oregano and beef in a shallow glass dish. Pour vinaigrette over beef. Set aside for 5 minutes, turning once.

Place fillets on a broiler pan rack that has been sprayed with nonstick cooking spray. Broil 4 inches from source of heat for 4 minutes per side for medium-rare, turning once, or to desired doneness.

MENU: Chicory and romaine salad with ripe olives and feta cheese. Kaiser rolls. Lemon sherbet.

SERVINGS: Makes 4 servings.

Deviled Steak

■ This dish qualifies as company fare although it's a snap to prepare. The sauce has some fire, but it's more likely to leave a gentle, warm afterglow rather than scorched palates.

1 to 1½ pounds boneless beef tenderloin, cut into 1-inch-thick slices
1 tablespoon sherry
1 tablespoon butter
1 teaspoon dry mustard
1 tablespoon Worcestershire sauce
Dash of freshly ground black pepper
1 tablespoon chopped fresh parsley

Preheat broiler. Place tenderloin on a broiler pan rack that has been sprayed with nonstick cooking spray. Broil tenderloin 4 inches from source of heat for 5 minutes. Turn and grill for 4 more minutes for medium-rare or to desired doneness.

Meanwhile, combine sherry, butter, mustard, Worcestershire sauce, and pepper in a small saucepan over medium heat. Cook, stirring occasionally, until bubbly. Stir in the parsley.

Spoon sauce over broiled tenderloin.

MENU: Poppy-seed dinner rolls. Deli green bean salad. Marinated mushrooms. Apple slices with caramel dip (produce section).

SERVINGS: Makes 4 servings.

Grillades

■ This is a Creole dish that takes its name from the French word for "grilled food." Traditionally grillades are served with grits, but to save time, I serve it with corn muffins from the bakery.

Seasoned salt
4 beef round cube steaks
1 tablespoon canola oil
1 large onion, sliced
1 garlic clove, minced
2 tomatoes, chopped

Rub seasoned salt into cube steaks. Heat oil in a heavy 10-inch skillet over medium heat. Add onion and garlic and sauté until golden, about 3 minutes. Remove onion and garlic from pan with a slotted spoon and keep warm.

Increase heat to medium-high and add cube steaks. Brown on both sides, turning once, about 5 minutes. Return onion and garlic to pan; add tomatoes. Cover and cook for 2 more minutes.

MENU: Red-pepper spears drizzled with ranch dressing. Bakery corn muffins. Deli rice salad with fresh berries.

SERVINGS: Makes 4 servings.

Spicy Minute Steaks

■ Beef cube steaks are a good cut of meat to keep in the freezer. They thaw quickly and can be the basis for many meals.

4 beef round cube steaks
4 teaspoons Dijon mustard
½ teaspoon dried thyme
⅛ teaspoon cayenne pepper

Preheat broiler. Place steaks on a broiler pan rack that has been sprayed with nonstick cooking spray. Broil steaks 4 inches from source of heat for 4 minutes.

Meanwhile, mix together mustard, thyme, and cayenne. Turn cube steaks; spread mustard mixture over steak tops.

Broil steaks for 4 minutes or to desired doneness.

MENU: Deli red-potato salad. Portuguese dinner rolls. Bakery cinnamon coffeecake.

SERVINGS: Makes 4 servings.

Chili Steak

■ This is a quick way to enjoy Southwestern flavor. Inexpensive round steak cooks quickly when sliced into thin strips. The secret is to get the oil really hot before adding the meat. This sears the surface, preserving tenderness and flavor.

3 tablespoons canola oil
¾ pound beef round steak, cut into thin 3 × ½-inch strips
1 large onion, sliced
½ teaspoon chili powder
½ cup red wine
1 tablespoon flour dissolved in ½ cup cold water

Heat oil in a 10-inch skillet over high heat. Add beef, a few strips at a time, and cook for about 5 minutes or until browned on both sides but rare at the center. Lift beef from pan with a slotted spoon. Keep warm.

Add onion and chili powder to the drippings. Cook, stirring occasionally, over medium heat until tender, about 3 minutes. Add wine and flour mixture. Cook, stirring, until thickened. Return meat to gravy and heat through.

MENU: Corn chips. Deli three-bean salad. Vanilla yogurt with strawberry topping.

SERVINGS: Makes 3 or 4 servings.

Three-Pepper Steak

■ When time is more important than money, I buy the sliced mushrooms and bell peppers from the supermarket salad bar.

1 (1-lb.) beef top-sirloin steak (1 inch thick)
3 tablespoons butter
1 each green, red, and yellow bell peppers, cut into ¾-inch strips
½ cup sliced mushrooms
1 clove garlic, finely chopped
2 tablespoons dry red wine

Preheat broiler. Place steak on a broiler pan rack that has been sprayed with nonstick cooking spray. Broil steak 12 to 14 minutes, turning once, for medium, or to desired doneness.

Meanwhile, in a 10-inch skillet, melt butter over medium-high heat. Add bell peppers, mushrooms, and garlic and stir-fry for about 5 minutes or until crisp-tender. Add wine and cook 2 to 3 minutes or until liquid has evaporated. Carve steak into thin slices. Serve with bell pepper mixture.

MENU: Prepared sesame or other cooked noodles. Diced apples and arugula leaves tossed with poppy-seed dressing. Bakery oatmeal cookies.

SERVINGS: Makes 3 or 4 servings.

Garden Steak

■ This is a lovely dish to make in late summer when the temperature is perfect for grilling on the patio and the garden produce is at its peak.

2 tablespoons olive oil
3 cloves garlic, thinly sliced
1 small eggplant, diced
3 small onions, quartered
2 tablespoons white wine
1½ pounds tomatoes, peeled, seeded, and cut into ½-inch pieces
4 boneless beef loin or New York strip steaks

Preheat broiler or grill. Heat oil in a 10-inch skillet over high heat. Add garlic and cook for 30 seconds. Add eggplant, onions, and wine. Reduce heat and simmer 3 to 4 minutes. Add tomatoes and simmer 3 to 4 minutes, stirring frequently, or until vegetables are softened.

Meanwhile, place steaks on a broiler pan or grill rack that has been sprayed with nonstick cooking spray. Broil or grill steaks 3 to 4 minutes per side for medium-rare, or to desired doneness.

Transfer steaks to plates and top with vegetable mixture.

MENU: French bread loaves. Deli new-potato salad.

SERVINGS: Makes 4 servings.

Steak Bourguignonne

■ In the interest of time, I thought I would have to abandon one of my favorite dishes—beef bourguignonne—because it requires long, slow simmering. Eureka! I invented steak bourguignonne, my update on the classic. It may not compare to the original, but it has a good, satisfying flavor.

1¼ pounds boneless beef sirloin steak
2 tablespoons butter
1 large yellow onion, sliced
1 cup bottled mushroom gravy
½ cup red wine
1 (15-oz.) can whole potatoes, drained and halved

Slice steak into 3 × ½-inch strips.

Melt 1 tablespoon of the butter in a 10-inch skillet over high heat. Add steak and sauté, turning as it browns, about 5 minutes. Remove to a bowl.

Reduce heat. Melt remaining butter in skillet. Add onion and cook, stirring, until browned, about 2 minutes. Add gravy, wine, and potatoes. Cover and cook for 5 minutes. Stir in beef and cook, stirring, until beef is heated through.

MENU: Deli green bean salad. Bakery angel food cake with peaches and vanilla yogurt.

SERVINGS: Makes 6 servings.

Beef Sauté

■ This is a quick dish for a romantic occasion. It's easy to make, but it comes to the table just reeking of sophistication.

1 clove garlic, minced
¼ teaspoon cracked black pepper
2 (¾- to 1-inch thick) beef tenderloin steaks
¾ cup beef broth
2 tablespoons Madeira
1 teaspoon butter
2 small heads Belgian endive, halved lengthwise
2 plum tomatoes, cut into wedges

Combine garlic and pepper. Rub into surface of steaks. Bring broth, Madeira, and butter to a boil in a medium skillet over medium-high heat. Add endive, cut side down, in a single layer. Reduce heat and cook until endive is crisp-tender, about 5 minutes. Add tomatoes and heat through, about 1 minute.

Meanwhile, pan-broil steaks in a 10-inch nonstick skillet over medium-high heat 6 to 8 minutes, turning once, or until medium-rare. Remove vegetables and steaks to plates. Cook liquid over high heat until reduced by half. Pour sauce over steaks and vegetables.

MENU: Deli new-potato salad. Mixed baby field greens with green goddess dressing. Bakery lemon cookies.

SERVINGS: Makes 2 servings.

Lemon Flank Steak

■ Lemon juice provides the flavor and tenderizing power in this quick marinated steak dish.

½ teaspoon grated lemon peel
¼ cup fresh lemon juice
1 teaspoon salt
¼ teaspoon freshly ground black pepper
¼ teaspoon dried oregano
1 (about 1½ pounds) beef flank steak

Preheat broiler. Mix together lemon peel, juice, salt, pepper, and oregano in a shallow dish. With a sharp knife, score both sides of steak in a diamond pattern. Marinate steak in juice mixture for 5 minutes, turning once.

Place steak on a broiler pan rack that has been sprayed with nonstick cooking spray. Broil 3 inches from source of heat for 8 to 10 minutes, turning once, for medium-rare.

Slice thinly on the diagonal. Serve with pan juices.

MENU: Pumpernickel toast. Deli potato salad. Sliced mangoes with crystallized ginger.

SERVINGS: Makes 6 servings.

Pepper Steak

■ My mother's version of pepper steak and the pepper steak served in Chinese restaurants have little in common except sliced steak. Well, they also both have bell peppers, and they're both stir-fried, although no mother in America used that term back in the fifties.

3 tablespoons peanut oil
1 pound boneless beef sirloin steak, cut into thin ¾-inch-long slices
2 large green bell peppers, sliced into thin strips
1 clove garlic, minced
2 tablespoons minced fresh parsley

Heat oil in a wok or 12-inch skillet over high heat. Add steak and stir-fry until brown on all sides, about 2 minutes. Remove steak from pan with a slotted spoon; keep it warm.

Reduce heat to medium-high, add bell peppers, and stir-fry until they are translucent. Stir in garlic and parsley. Combine bell peppers with steak.

MENU: Carrot-raisin salad. Bakery chocolate chip cookies.

SERVINGS: Makes 4 servings.

Asian Beef Stir-Fry

■ Partially freezing the beef before slicing into thin strips makes the job easier, but a good sharp knife will work if the beef is frozen or not. The thinner the beef is sliced, the quicker it will cook and the more tender it will be.

½ pound beef top round steak, thinly sliced
1 tablespoon dry sherry
2 tablespoons teriyaki sauce
1 teaspoon peanut oil
1 clove garlic, crushed
4 scallions, thinly sliced
¼ cup sliced celery
½ cup sliced mushrooms
½ cup thinly sliced green bell pepper
1 cup cherry tomatoes, halved

Place beef in a medium bowl. Pour sherry and teriyaki sauce over beef and stir to combine. Allow to stand at room temperature for 5 minutes.

Heat oil and garlic in a 10-inch skillet or wok over high heat. Add scallions, beef, and marinade. Stir-fry for 1 minute. Add celery, mushrooms, and bell pepper. Stir-fry 2 minutes. Add tomatoes, reduce heat, and cover. Cook for 1 minute.

MENU: Raw broccoli and cauliflower with mustard vinaigrette. Deli fresh fruit salad with nonfat pineapple yogurt.

SERVINGS: Makes 2 servings.

Beef with Leeks and Mushrooms

■ Until recently the only kind of fresh mushrooms available were button mushrooms. Now there are more than half a dozen mushrooms on display in supermarkets that take pride in their fresh produce. This recipe calls for shiitake mushrooms. They can be quite large, but most are sold when they are 3 to 6 inches in diameter. Shiitake mushrooms are more expensive than the buttons, but they're also meatier and richer in flavor.

4 tablespoons peanut oil
1 cup thinly sliced leeks, white part only
¼ pound shiitake mushrooms
1 pound beef flank steak, thinly sliced
1 tablespoon soy sauce
1 teaspoon cornstarch
¼ cup water
Sesame oil
1 tablespoon sherry

Heat 2 tablespoons of the peanut oil in a 10-inch skillet or wok over high heat. Add leeks and mushrooms and stir-fry 1 minute. Remove from skillet with a slotted spoon. Keep warm.

Drain oil and wipe out skillet with a paper towel. Add remaining 2 tablespoons oil and the beef and stir-fry 2 minutes. Return leek mixture to skillet and add soy sauce. Stir-fry 1 minute.

Mix cornstarch with water and stir into beef mixture. Stir-fry 1 minute. Add a dash of sesame oil and the sherry. Stir-fry until heated through.

MENU: Oriental shrimp crackers. Deli rice pudding.

SERVINGS: Makes 4 servings.

Beef, Pepper, & Onion Stir-Fry

■ This popular dish is surprisingly easy to make at home with the help of the prepared stir-fry sauces available in supermarkets.

1 pound beef top round steak, sliced into very thin strips
¼ cup stir-fry sauce
2 tablespoons peanut oil
1 cup green bell pepper strips
1 onion, cut into thin wedges
1 clove garlic, minced

Combine beef and stir-fry sauce in a medium bowl. Set aside.

Heat oil in a 10-inch skillet or wok over high heat. Add bell pepper strips, onion, and garlic and stir-fry for 2 minutes. Remove from skillet with a slotted spoon. Keep warm.

Add beef mixture to skillet, ⅓ at a time, and stir-fry until brown, about 2 minutes per batch. Remove each batch and add to vegetables before adding the next batch. Return all ingredients to skillet and stir-fry 2 minutes.

MENU: Spinach salad with cherry tomatoes and mustard vinaigrette. Chow mein noodles with duck sauce.

SERVINGS: Makes 4 servings.

Beef with Asparagus

■ In this recipe it's important to drain the oil used to cook the beef and replace it with fresh oil to cook the asparagus. The reason is that there are natural substances in the meat juices that become foamy and cloud the oil. Changing the oil will ensure that all the elements in the dish keep their distinct flavors.

1 pound beef round steak, thinly sliced
2 tablespoons dry sherry
1 tablespoon teriyaki sauce
2 tablespoons beef broth
4 tablespoons peanut oil
10 thin asparagus spears, cut into 1½-inch lengths

Place beef in a medium bowl. Combine sherry, teriyaki sauce, and beef broth in a small bowl. Pour sherry mixture over beef and stir to combine. Allow to stand at room temperature for 5 minutes.

Heat 3 tablespoons of the peanut oil in a 10-inch skillet or wok over very high heat. Add beef and stir-fry 30 seconds. Remove beef from pan with a slotted spoon. Drain oil and wipe out skillet with a paper towel.

Heat remaining oil in skillet over medium-high heat. Add asparagus and stir-fry 1 minute. Return beef to pan and stir-fry 30 seconds.

MENU: Deli new potato salad. Chocolate, vanilla, and strawberry ice cream.

SERVINGS: Makes 4 servings.

Red Flannel Hash

■ Red Flannel Hash, which takes its name from a mixture of beef, potatoes, and beets, is an old-time Sunday-night supper recipe. Despite its age, it fits right into the modern world where simple, quick meals are often a necessity. Another good thing about this dish is that it is made from things you can keep on hand.

2 tablespoons butter
¼ cup finely chopped onion
1 (15-oz.) can whole potatoes, drained and chopped
1 (8.25-oz.) can sliced beets, drained
1½ cups cooked or canned corned beef chunks
Salt and freshly ground black pepper to taste
2 tablespoons milk

Melt butter in a 12-inch nonstick frying pan over medium-high heat. Add onion and cook, stirring occasionally, until tender, about 3 minutes.

Stir in potatoes, beets, and corned beef. Season with salt and pepper.

Cook over medium heat, stirring occasionally, for 8 to 10 minutes or until browned. Stir in milk and heat through, about 1 minute.

MENU: Crusty multigrain rolls. Bakery cheesecake with fresh berry topping.

SERVINGS: Makes 4 servings.

Beef Fajitas

■ Sizzling fajitas have become a popular dish at restaurants that feature Tex-Mex and Mexican cooking. This is a fast and easy way to duplicate these tasty tortilla wraps at home. Purchase the beef, salsa, and guacamole at the supermarket deli.

¾ pound thinly sliced cooked roast beef
1 tablespoon fresh lime juice
¼ teaspoon garlic powder
½ teaspoon chili powder
¼ teaspoon cayenne pepper
1 tablespoon canola oil
1 medium onion, sliced crosswise and separated into rings
4 medium green bell peppers, cut into strips
8 (about 8-inch) flour tortillas, warmed
½ cup sour cream
½ cup salsa
½ cup guacamole

Cut beef into ½-inch strips. Combine with lime juice, garlic powder, chili powder, and cayenne pepper in a medium bowl. Set aside.

Heat oil in a nonstick 10-inch skillet over medium-high heat. Add onion and stir-fry 1 minute. Add bell peppers and stir-fry 2 minutes. Add beef mixture and stir-fry 3 minutes.

Fill warm tortillas with hot beef mixture. Serve with sour cream, salsa, and guacamole.

MENU: Deli three-bean salad. Graham crackers. Melon slices.

SERVINGS: Makes 4 servings.

Meatballs with Cilantro Dipping Sauce

■ Plain yogurt mixed with herbs can be the basis for tasty dipping sauces that will add variety to your dinner menus.

1 (1-lb.) package frozen meatballs
¾ cup plain yogurt
¼ cup minced fresh cilantro leaves
Freshly ground black pepper

Prepare meatballs according to package directions.

Meanwhile, in a small bowl combine yogurt, cilantro, and pepper to taste. Serve yogurt sauce in individual ramekins with meatballs.

MENU: Whole-wheat pita bread. Citrus salad. Bakery chocolate cupcakes.

SERVINGS: Makes 4 servings.

Meatballs & Ravioli

■ There are many good convenience products on the market. Frozen meatballs are one, and fresh ravioli is another. Add a favorite bottled sauce and dinner is almost on the table.

1 tablespoon vegetable oil
1 (1-lb.) package frozen meatballs
1 (14-oz.) jar favorite pasta sauce
1 (9-oz.) package refrigerated fresh cheese-filled ravioli
Grated Parmesan cheese

Heat oil in a 10-inch large skillet over medium heat. Add meatballs and cook, stirring occasionally, until browned, about 10 minutes. Drain off fat.

Add sauce to meatballs and stir to combine. Add ravioli and cook just until heated through, about 5 minutes. Serve with Parmesan cheese.

MENU: Red-leaf lettuce, red pepper slices, diced red onion, and red cherry tomatoes tossed in red wine and olive oil salad dressing. Fresh-baked bread sticks. Bakery Italian sesame cookies.

SERVINGS: Makes 4 servings.

Meatballs with Burgundy Sauce

■ Bottled gravies have come a long way from the tinny-tasting canned gravies of the fifties and sixties. Today they are respectable convenience products that should have a place in every busy cook's kitchen.

1 (1-lb.) package frozen meatballs
1 (5¼-oz.) bottle beef gravy
2 tablespoons Burgundy wine
1 cup sliced fresh mushrooms

Prepare meatballs according to package directions.

Meanwhile, combine gravy, wine, and mushrooms in a 1-quart saucepan. Bring to a boil. Reduce heat and simmer, covered, 10 minutes.

Spoon gravy over meatballs and serve.

MENU: Tossed salad with buttermilk dressing. Soft bread sticks. Bakery chocolate cake.

SERVINGS: Makes 4 servings.

Sautéed Beef with Onions

■ Onions may be a humble kitchen staple, but they deliver pungent and aromatic flavors to a host of dishes, turning even commonplace ground beef into a gourmet treat.

1 pound lean ground beef
2 tablespoons seasoned bread crumbs
2 tablespoons chopped cilantro
¼ cup grated carrot
1 tablespoon ketchup
2 cloves garlic, minced
1 tablespoon canola oil
2 large onions, thinly sliced, separated into rings
¼ pound mushrooms, sliced
2 tablespoons sherry
¼ cup plain yogurt

Combine beef, bread crumbs, cilantro, carrot, ketchup, and half of the minced garlic in a medium bowl. Form into 4 patties. Set aside.

Heat oil in a 10-inch skillet over medium heat. Add onions, mushrooms, and remaining minced garlic and sauté, stirring occasionally, for 3 minutes or until softened but not browned. Remove from pan with a slotted spoon. Keep warm.

Increase heat to medium-high. Add patties to the pan and cook until browned on both sides, about 2 minutes. Pour off any excess fat. Return onion mixture to pan. Reduce heat and cook about 7 minutes or until onions are tender and patties are cooked through. Transfer patties to a serving plate.

Increase heat to high. Add sherry and cook, stirring rapidly, 30 seconds. Reduce heat to low. Stir in yogurt and cook just to heat through. Spoon onion and yogurt mixture over burgers.

MENU: Sesame-seed rolls. Green salad with Caesar dressing. Bakery apple turnovers.

SERVINGS: Makes 4 servings.

Sesame Burgers

■ It isn't imperative to toast the sesame seeds in this recipe; they'll still provide a nice crunch and good flavor. But sautéing them briefly in a dry skillet, just until they turn golden, gives them a lovely, mellow flavor.

1 pound ground beef
¼ cup finely chopped scallions
¼ cup soy sauce
2 tablespoons sesame seeds, toasted

Preheat broiler. Combine beef, scallions, soy sauce, and sesame seeds in a medium bowl. Shape into patties.

Place patties on a broiler pan rack that has been sprayed with nonstick cooking spray. Broil 4 to 5 inches from source of heat for 6 to 7 minutes on each side, or to desired doneness.

MENU: Sesame-seed buns. Garden salad with lemon vinaigrette. Melon cubes.

SERVINGS: Makes 4 servings.

Spur-of-the-Moment Chili

■ When time permits, I make chili with a longer list of ingredients and cook it for a longer period of time, but in a pinch, this quick cooking chili delivers some fiery Southwestern flavor.

1 pound ground beef
2 onions, chopped
3 tablespoons chili powder
1 teaspoon crushed red pepper flakes
1 teaspoon salt
1 (15-oz.) can kidney beans, drained
1 (16-oz.) can tomato puree

Cook ground beef with onions in a 3-quart saucepan over medium heat, stirring to break up beef, about 10 minutes or until browned. Drain off fat. Stir in chili powder, red pepper flakes, salt, beans, and tomato puree.

Simmer, uncovered, over medium heat for about 5 minutes to combine flavors.

MENU: Bakery corn muffins. Tossed green salad with ranch dressing. Bakery apple turnovers.

Viva Beef Salad

■ This is a quick dish, but it takes some planning because it requires a ripe avocado. If you're lucky you'll find one in the supermarket marked down for quick sale, but most of the time, a few days will be needed to bring an avocado to the buttery, perfect-for-eating stage.

½ pound ground beef
1 small onion, chopped
¼ cup taco sauce
2 teaspoons chili powder
Iceberg lettuce
1 ripe avocado
1 small tomato, chopped
½ cup (2 oz.) shredded Cheddar cheese
Sour cream
Ripe olives
Tortilla chips

Cook beef and onion in a 10-inch skillet over medium-high heat, stirring to break up beef, until beef is browned, about 6 minutes. Drain off fat. Add taco sauce and chili powder. Simmer, uncovered, for 5 minutes.

Meanwhile, shred lettuce and arrange on 2 salad plates. Halve, seed, and peel avocado.

Remove beef from pan with a slotted spoon and divide between the 2 plates. Top with tomato, cheese, sour cream, and olives. Arrange avocado slices around the plate. Serve with tortilla chips on the side.

MENU: Lemonade. Strawberry ice cream with bakery shortbread cookies.

SERVINGS: Makes 2 servings.

Beef with Cabbage & Carrots

■ This dish is very versatile and will quickly become a family favorite.

¾ pound extra-lean ground beef
4 cups shredded green cabbage
1½ cups shredded carrots (about 2 large carrots)
½ teaspoon caraway seeds
1 teaspoon sugar
3 tablespoons red wine vinegar
Salt and freshly ground black pepper

Cook ground beef in a 10-inch skillet over medium-high heat, stirring to break up beef, about 6 minutes or until browned. Drain off fat. Reduce heat to low. Stir in cabbage, carrot, and caraway seeds.

Cover, and cook 6 to 7 minutes or until vegetables are tender, stirring occasionally. Stir in sugar and vinegar (add a little water if the mix seems dry). Season to taste with salt and pepper.

MENU: Cantaloupe and honeydew melon cubes. Toasted Kaiser rolls. Vanilla frozen yogurt.

SERVINGS: Makes 4 servings.

VARIATION
Substitute Chinese cabbage for the green cabbage; sesame seeds instead of caraway; and rice wine vinegar for the red wine vinegar.

Hamburger Skillet

■ There are lots of good reasons to use lean ground beef. One is that you consume less fat, but another is that there is less shrinkage because there's less fat to melt away.

1½ pounds lean ground beef
1 onion, chopped
1 (28-oz.) can chopped plum tomatoes in puree
1 (16-oz.) package frozen mixed vegetables
Salt and pepper to taste

Cook beef and onion, stirring to break up beef, in a 10-inch nonstick skillet that has been sprayed with nonstick cooking spray, until beef is browned, about 5 minutes. Drain off any excess fat.

Add tomatoes and vegetables. Bring to a simmer and cook for 6 minutes or until heated through. Season to taste with salt and pepper.

MENU: Toasted crusty bread. Mixed field greens salad with ranch dressing. Bakery angel food cake with sliced strawberries.

SERVINGS: Makes 6 servings.

Beef with Cabbage

■ This dish is for those times when speed really counts, because it starts with a package of coleslaw from the produce section. You can make your own cabbage mixture, but it'll take more time.

¾ pound extra-lean ground beef
1 (1-lb.) package (about 5 cups) coleslaw mix
½ teaspoon celery seeds
1 tablespoon white wine vinegar
1 teaspoon sugar

Cook ground beef in a 10-inch skillet, stirring to break up beef, about 7 minutes or until browned. Drain off fat. Reduce heat to low.

Stir in coleslaw mix and celery seeds. Cover and cook 6 to 7 minutes, stirring occasionally, or until cabbage is tender. Stir in vinegar and sugar and heat through.

MENU: Pumpernickel bread. Deli new-potato salad. Bakery apple turnovers.

SERVINGS: Makes 4 servings.

Knockwurst Boiled Dinner

■ During the winter, I have an afghan in the living room. On my bed there are flannel sheets and an electric blanket. Sweaters, silk ski socks, quilted slippers—add them to the list of comforts on those cold winter nights. In the kitchen, there is hot, warming, hearty food.

Among the heartiest is a simple boiled dinner composed mostly of root vegetables and mild knockwurst sausage.

Great condiments include sour cream, mustard, and horseradish, red or white.

To save time, use canned potatoes (don't be horrified; there's a new generation of canned potatoes that are much tastier than the old ones). The cooking time won't change, because the potatoes will need the time to absorb other flavors, but no peeling will be required.

1 (10¾-oz.) can condensed chicken broth
1 (15-oz.) can whole potatoes, drained and quartered
½ cup thinly sliced carrots
1 large onion, sliced
1 pound knockwurst, slashed at 1-inch intervals
½ medium cabbage, cut into 8 wedges
1 medium apple, cored and cut into eighths
¼ teaspoon caraway seeds

Bring broth to a boil in a 3-quart saucepan or Dutch oven. Add potatoes, carrots, onion, and knockwurst. Cover and cook 5 minutes.

Add cabbage wedges and apple slices. Sprinkle with caraway seeds. Cover and cook 8 minutes. Remove vegetables and knockwurst with a slotted spoon. Serve juices on the side.

MENU: Pumpernickel bread, warmed in the oven. Bakery cinnamon coffeecake.

SERVINGS: Makes 4 servings.

Kraut Brats

■ Cincinnati was once renowned for its German food, courtesy of a large German population. This culinary legacy is embraced by just about everybody in the Queen City in the form of "brats"—better known as bratwurst, and "mets," which is not a team but another wurst—mettwurst. These two German sausages are sold in buns hot off the grill, just like hot dogs.

¾ cup (3 oz.) shredded Gruyère cheese
⅓ cup sauerkraut, well drained
4 smoked bratwurst
2 to 3 tablespoons Thousand Island dressing
4 hot dog buns

Preheat broiler. Combine cheese and sauerkraut in a small bowl. Split each bratwurst by cutting from end to end, cutting almost all the way through so they can be split open.

Spread dressing on cut edges, filling each bratwurst with about ¼ cup of sauerkraut mixture. Place bratwurst, filling side up, on a broiler pan rack that has been sprayed with nonstick cooking spray. Broil 4 inches from source of heat for 8 to 10 minutes or until heated through. Place in buns.

MENU: Canned potato sticks. Raw vegetables (carrot sticks, cucumber slices, scallions, and radishes) with ranch dressing. Peaches with sliced almonds.

SERVINGS: Makes 4 servings.

Kielbasa with Cabbage

■ Beef kielbasa, sometimes called Polish sausage, has a hearty, spicy flavor. It's very quick to cook and combines well with cabbage and sauerkraut.

¾ pound beef kielbasa, sliced into 4 pieces
1 (12-oz.) can beer
1 (8-oz.) package (about 3 cups) coleslaw mix
¾ teaspoon caraway seeds
1 teaspoon sugar
1 teaspoon salt

Place kielbasa and beer in a 3-quart saucepan or Dutch oven. Bring just to a boil over medium-high heat. Reduce heat to medium and simmer 8 minutes.

Remove kielbasa, leaving beer in saucepan. Stir coleslaw mix, caraway seeds, sugar, and salt into beer. Place kielbasa on top of cabbage mixture. Cover and simmer 6 to 7 minutes or until just tender. Drain and serve.

MENU: Caraway rye bread. Deli green bean salad. Bakery carrot cake.

SERVINGS: Makes 4 servings.

Veal Marsala

■ This is a dish that accepts no substitutions. It can be found on restaurant menus, but why not make it at home? Marsala is a fortified wine from Italy.

1 pound veal scallops
All-purpose flour
¼ cup butter
Freshly ground black pepper
1 cup small mushrooms
½ cup dry Marsala
½ cup chicken broth

With a meat mallet, pound veal scallops until thin. Dredge in flour and shake off excess.

Melt butter in a 10-inch skillet over medium heat. When butter begins to sizzle, add veal, and sauté until lightly browned on both sides, about 4 minutes total. Season with pepper, remove from pan, and keep warm on a platter.

Add mushrooms and sauté until lightly browned, about 2 minutes. Pour in Marsala and broth. Increase heat to high and boil sauce for 2 minutes. Pour sauce and mushrooms over veal.

MENU: Chicory and romaine salad with ripe olives and lemon vinaigrette. Dinner rolls. Bakery chocolate chip cookies.

SERVINGS: Makes 4 servings.

Veal with Prosciutto

■ Veal is a moist meat that does not keep well, so plan to use it within two days of purchase, or freeze it for another time.

4 veal scallops
All-purpose flour
2 tablespoons olive oil
Freshly ground black pepper
4 thin slices prosciutto
4 thin slices provolone cheese
1 tablespoon minced fresh flat-leaf parsley

With a meat mallet, pound veal scallops until thin. Dredge in flour and shake off excess.

Heat oil in a 10-inch skillet over medium-high heat. Add veal and brown lightly on one side, about 2 minutes. Turn the veal and season with pepper. Top each scallop with a slice of prosciutto and a slice of provolone. Continue cooking until veal is lightly browned on the other side and cheese is melted, 2 to 3 minutes. Sprinkle with parsley.

MENU: Sesame bread sticks. Marinated artichoke hearts. Fresh plums.

SERVINGS: Makes 4 servings.

Tarragon Veal

■ Light olive oil offers all the healthful benefits of regular olive oil but imparts no fruity taste. It's perfect for browning delicate veal cutlets.

1 pound veal cutlets
1 teaspoon seasoned salt
1 tablespoon light olive oil
1 medium onion, thinly sliced
½ pound mushrooms, sliced
1 teaspoon dried tarragon, crumbled

With a meat mallet, pound veal to ¼-inch thickness. Sprinkle veal with seasoned salt.

Heat oil in a 10-inch skillet. Add veal and cook to a deep golden brown, about 5 minutes, turning to brown all sides. Remove veal and keep warm.

Add onion and mushrooms to pan. Sauté, stirring occasionally, until tender, but not brown, about 3 minutes.

Return veal to skillet and sprinkle with tarragon. Spoon vegetables over veal. Heat through.

MENU: Sliced tomatoes and Boston lettuce drizzled with vinaigrette. Cantaloupe chunks sprinkled with lime juice and chopped fresh mint. Rye toast. Bakery lemon meringue pie.

SERVINGS: Makes 4 servings.

Garlic & Rosemary Veal Chops

■ Veal does not require a lot of seasoning or sauce to bring out its best flavors. Here, an elemental combination of garlic and rosemary works magic.

2 cloves garlic, crushed
2 teaspoons dried rosemary
Freshly ground black pepper
1 teaspoon olive oil
4 veal chops

Preheat broiler. In a small bowl, combine garlic, rosemary, pepper, and oil. Rub onto veal chops. Set aside for 5 minutes.

Place chops on a broiler pan rack that has been sprayed with nonstick cooking spray. Broil chops 4 inches from the source of heat for 4 to 6 minutes per side, turning once.

MENU: Italian bread. Green salad with sun-dried tomatoes and fresh mozzarella cheese, drizzled with Italian dressing. Coffee ice cream with chocolate sauce.

SERVINGS: Makes 4 servings.

Veal with Onions

■ This recipe calls for sweet onions, which impart a delicate flavor.

4 veal rib chops
1 tablespoon Dijon mustard
1 teaspoon mustard seeds
2 large Vidalia or Bermuda onions, cut in half crosswise
2 teaspoons butter
2 tablespoons packed brown sugar

Preheat broiler. Brush both sides of veal chops lightly with mustard. Sprinkle both sides with mustard seeds.

Place veal and onions, cut side down, on a broiler pan rack that has been sprayed with nonstick cooking spray. Broil about 3 inches from heat for about 6 minutes. Turn veal and onions.

Spread ½ teaspoon of butter over each onion half. Sprinkle onion with brown sugar. Broil about 6 minutes longer or until veal is brown and onions are tender.

MENU: Deli new-potato salad. Fruit salad. Bakery oatmeal cookies

SERVINGS: Makes 4 servings.

Veal Cutlets with Tomato Sauce

■ Using fresh plum tomatoes in cooking is relatively new to me. They are especially good for cooking, because they have a thicker skin and are less watery, which helps them hold up well.

1 tablespoon vegetable oil
1 pound veal cutlets
1 small onion, chopped
4 small plum tomatoes, chopped
¼ cup chopped fresh basil leaves or 1
    tablespoon dried
⅓ cup peppercorn or ranch dressing

Heat oil in a large skillet over medium-high heat. Add veal and cook 2 minutes on each side or until browned.

Remove veal to a serving platter; keep warm. Add onion to pan juices. Cook 2 minutes, stirring occasionally. Add tomatoes and basil; cook 5 minutes, stirring occasionally.

Stir in dressing until heated through. Spoon tomato mixture over cutlets.

MENU: Garlic bread sticks. Deli Caesar salad. Ice cream sandwiches.

SERVINGS: Makes 4 servings.

VARIATION
This dish can be made with boneless, skinless chicken breast halves.

Thyme Veal Chops

■ Thyme is one of my favorite herbs. It gives a pungent, earthy flavor that becomes more intense during cooking.

4 (about ½-inch-thick) veal loin chops
Freshly ground black pepper
1 teaspoon fresh thyme or ½ teaspoon dried
2 tablespoons oil and vinegar dressing

Preheat broiler. Sprinkle chops with pepper and thyme. Drizzle chops with some of the dressing.

Arrange chops on a broiler pan rack that has been sprayed with nonstick cooking spray. Broil about 4 inches from heat for 4 minutes. Turn and brush chops with remaining dressing. Broil until chops are cooked through, 4 to 5 minutes.

MENU: Deli three-bean salad. Oat bread. Bakery angel food cake with yogurt and fresh fruit.

SERVINGS: Makes 4 servings.

Pork & Lamb

These days pork and lamb are leaner and tastier than ever, and Mother Nature didn't have a lot to do with it. Lamb and pork producers have been working for decades to produce meat that tastes great but has less fat, and they've succeeded admirably. Contemporary pork tenderloin has become so slim that it compares with skinless chicken breast meat, and I think it has more flavor and a better texture. Pork tenderloin medallions cook very quickly and can be brought to the table in many a fifteen-minute dish.

You'll also find recipes for pork chops here, but these are not the pork chops of yesteryear that required hours of cooking. These are thinner chops that have the fat sliced away. They can be browned and cooked very quickly to be served with a light sauce, or natural pan juices enhanced with herbs and lemon juice. Even if you prefer thicker cuts that require longer cooking, there's no need to overcook fresh pork for safety. Trichinosis is now so rare that it's not a worry. Experts recommend cooking pork to an internal temperature of 160F (70C). Overcooking will cause pork to lose flavor and natural juiciness.

Lamb has never gained widespread popularity in the American kitchen, in part because of its more pronounced flavor and in part because of its high price. Both factors have changed, and public opinion about lamb could change as well. Chefs in fine restaurants feature modern, lighter, and more delicate lamb on their menus. Nothing inspires Americans to try new dishes more than celebrity chefs serving creative fare. Today's lamb is tasty and mild. The same breeding technology that mellowed the culinary attributes has also lowered the prices. So why delay? Lamb chops grilled or sautéed, ground lamb in burgers, and other ground meat dishes make for fast and satisfying dinner fare.

Pork Chops with Piquant Sauce

■ *Sauce piquante* is a classic French spicy brown sauce made with shallots and white wine, gherkins, and parsley. It takes too much time to make when you're in a hurry. My piquant sauce offers the same delicious tart bite, but in a fraction of the time.

1 tablespoon canola oil
4 (1-inch-thick) boneless pork chops
⅓ cup pineapple-orange juice blend
2 teaspoons fresh lemon juice
4 scallions, minced
2 teaspoons dried cranberries, chopped
½ teaspoon grated fresh ginger
1½ teaspoons dry sherry

Heat oil in a 10-inch skillet over medium heat. Add pork chops and cook, turning, until brown on both sides, about 4 minutes. Reduce heat and cook, turning, for about 10 minutes or until pork is cooked through.

Meanwhile, combine fruit juices, scallions, cranberries, and ginger in a 1-quart saucepan over medium heat. Bring to a simmer. Reduce heat and cook, uncovered, about 10 minutes. Stir in sherry and cook for 1 minute.

Place pork chops on plates. Spoon some sauce over pork chops. Serve remaining sauce on the side.

MENU: Deli green bean salad. Bran muffins. Vanilla pudding.

SERVINGS: Makes 4 servings.

Teriyaki Pork Chops

■ Keep teriyaki sauce in your cupboard. It's a real flavor booster, a great marinade, and an all-around good condiment.

4 (1-inch-thick) pork chops
½ cup teriyaki sauce
2 tablespoons prepared horseradish

Preheat broiler. Place chops in a shallow dish. Blend teriyaki sauce and horseradish in a small bowl; pour over chops, coating well.

Place chops on a broiler rack that has been sprayed with nonstick cooking spray. Broil chops 3 inches from source of heat, turning once and brushing with additional sauce, for 5 to 6 minutes or until no longer pink in the centers.

MENU: Red-tipped lettuce with tofu cubes and mustard vinaigrette. Rice crackers (available in international food section). Cherry sorbet.

SERVINGS: Makes 4 servings.

Lemon-Nut Pork Chops

■ Nuts are faster and easier to chop when they're warm. So pop a few macadamia nuts in the microwave and heat on high power for about 20 seconds. Then, chop away.

4 (½-inch-thick) boneless pork loin chops, trimmed
½ teaspoon garlic salt
¼ teaspoon lemon-pepper seasoning
1 tablespoon vegetable oil
2 tablespoons chopped macadamia nuts
2 tablespoons fresh lemon juice
½ teaspoon grated lemon peel

Sprinkle both sides of chops with garlic salt and lemon-pepper seasoning.

Heat oil in a 12-inch skillet over medium-high heat. Add chops; cook 5 to 7 minutes per side or until chops are browned and no longer pink in the centers. Remove chops to a serving plate. Sprinkle with nuts; keep warm.

Stir lemon juice into pan drippings. Heat for 1 minute, stirring constantly. Spoon over cooked chops; sprinkle with lemon peel.

MENU: Deli prepared sesame noodles or other cooked noodles. Water chestnuts tossed with radish slices and vinaigrette. Deli vanilla pudding.

SERVINGS: Makes 4 servings.

Lime-Cumin Pork Chops

■ Cumin is a spice that is often overlooked. What a shame, because it brings a distinctive, nutty, aromatic flavor to simple dishes.

Juice of 1 lime
¼ cup dry white wine
¼ teaspoon ground cumin
4 (1-inch-thick) boneless pork chops
Salt and freshly ground black pepper

Preheat broiler. Mix together lime juice, wine, and cumin; set aside.

Place chops on a broiler pan rack that has been sprayed with nonstick cooking spray. Broil chops 3 inches from source of heat, turning once and brushing chops with lime-cumin mixture several times, 5 to 6 minutes or until no longer pink in the centers. Season with salt and pepper.

MENU: Canned whole-kernel corn, drained and tossed with minced red bell pepper. Warm flour tortillas. Melon salad.

SERVINGS: Makes 4 servings.

Honeyed Pork Stir-Fry

■ Although stir-fry recipes say heat a wok or skillet, I personally prefer the skillet because it was designed for an American stove. The skillet sits closer to the heat, hence the pan gets hotter, and a very hot pan is one of the secrets of a successful stir-fry.

1 tablespoon chili oil (see Note, below)
1 tablespoon peanut oil
1 pound pork tenderloins, cut into 2-inch slices
1 cup fresh pineapple chunks
½ cup red bell pepper slices
3 tablespoons honey
4 cups shredded Napa (Chinese) cabbage

Heat a 12-inch skillet or wok over high heat until hot. Add oils; rotate skillet to coat sides. Add pork and stir-fry 3 to 4 minutes or until cooked through. Add pineapple, bell pepper, and honey and stir-fry 1 minute. Add cabbage and stir-fry 1 minute or until crisp-tender.

MENU: Bakery apple muffins. Deli marinated mushrooms. Bakery or frozen cheesecake.

SERVINGS: Makes 4 servings.

NOTE
Chili oil is available in Asian grocery stores or in the international food section in most supermarkets.

Chinese Pork Chops

■ Pork is as versatile as chicken; it's mild flavored enough to take on varied sauces and seasonings. This reliable, no-fuss dish was inspired by my passion for Chinese food. I call it Chinese pork chops, but the only ingredient that's Chinese is hoisin sauce, which can be found in supermarkets. While these chops are good broiled, they're even better grilled; but because they are thin, they must cook quickly or they'll dry out.

2 tablespoons hoisin sauce
½ teaspoon freshly ground black pepper
½ teaspoon cayenne pepper
½ teaspoon ground cumin
1 teaspoon salt
2 pounds (¾-inch-thick) pork chops

Preheat broiler or grill. Combine hoisin sauce with black pepper, cayenne pepper, cumin, and salt. Spread on pork chops.

Place chops on a broiler pan rack or grill rack that has been sprayed with nonstick cooking spray. Broil 3 inches from source of heat for 5 to 6 minutes on each side or until no longer pink in centers.

MENU: Red-tipped lettuce and cherry tomatoes with cucumber dressing. Prepared sesame or other cooked noodles. Bakery almond cookies.

SERVINGS: Makes 4 servings.

Pork with Orange Sauce

■ Pork tenderloin is a good, lean cut of meat that cooks very quickly. Select a tenderloin that is pink in color, with a little marbling, and white fat.

1 tablespoon canola oil
1½ pounds boneless pork tenderloin,
    trimmed and sliced into 6 equal portions
2 teaspoons finely chopped fresh ginger
½ cup orange juice
3 tablespoons soy sauce
1 tablespoon honey mustard
2 cloves garlic, crushed

Heat oil in a 10-inch skillet over medium-high heat. Add pork and cook until brown, 3 to 4 minutes on each side.

While pork cooks, combine ginger, orange juice, soy sauce, mustard, and garlic in a small bowl.

Remove pork from pan. Drain well. Wipe out skillet. Return pork to pan. Pour juice mixture over pork and simmer, uncovered, 5 minutes. Serve with pan juices.

MENU: Deli three-bean salad. Potato rolls. Gingersnaps.

SERVINGS: Makes 6 servings.

Soy-Lemon Pork Chops

■ Center-cut boneless pork chops cook quickly. This lemon-soy basting sauce adds an exotic flavor and helps seal in the natural juices.

⅓ cup soy sauce
Juice of ½ lemon
¼ teaspoon dried oregano
4 center-cut boneless pork chops

Preheat broiler. Mix together soy sauce, lemon juice, and oregano. Brush chops with juice mixture.

Place chops on a broiler pan rack that has been sprayed with nonstick cooking spray. Broil 3 inches from source of heat for 5 to 6 minutes on each side or until no longer pink in centers, turning once and brushing with more juice mixture.

MENU: Spinach salad with fresh strawberries and pignoli (pine) nuts. Deli rice and green bean salad. Chocolate ice cream sandwiches.

SERVINGS: Makes 4 servings.

Teutonic Pork Tenderloin

■ Pounding the pork helps tenderize the meat and also facilitates quick cooking. Serve this dish with a really good, grainy mustard.

1 (1½-lb.) boneless pork tenderloin, cut into 6 rounds
1 egg, slightly beaten
2 tablespoons water
½ cup crushed pretzels
1 teaspoon canola oil

Pound pork until each round is ¼ inch thick. Mix together egg and water. Dip pork into egg mixture. Coat with pretzel crumbs.

Heat oil in a 10-inch nonstick skillet over medium-high heat. Add pork and cook until brown, about 8 minutes or until cooked through, turning once.

MENU: Pumpernickel bread. Deli green bean salad. Bakery apple turnovers.

SERVINGS: Makes 6 servings.

Pork & Black Bean Sauce

■ Black bean sauce can be found on many supermarket shelves that feature international foods. It lends a deep, earthy taste to this dish.

¼ cup stir-fry sauce
2 tablespoons black bean sauce
1 tablespoon peanut oil
¾ pound pork tenderloin, cut into thin strips
1 cup frozen green peas
1 medium zucchini, cut into ¼-inch slices
1 medium red bell pepper, cut into 1-inch pieces

Mix together stir-fry sauce and bean sauce; set aside. Heat oil in a wok or 12-inch skillet over high heat. Add pork; stir-fry about 4 minutes or until no longer pink.

Add peas, zucchini, and bell pepper; stir-fry 4 minutes or until vegetables are crisp-tender. Stir in stir-fry sauce mix. Stir-fry 2 minutes to heat and combine flavors.

MENU: Toasted rye bread. Beet salad. Vanilla ice cream.

SERVINGS: Makes 4 servings.

Rum Pork Chops

■ I returned from a vacation in Puerto Rico with a bottle of rum—a delicious beverage, but also a great cooking ingredient. It adds an almost nutlike taste, rich and deep.

1 tablespoon vegetable oil
1 clove garlic, minced
4 (1-inch-thick) boneless pork chops
½ cup bottled gravy for pork
1 tablespoon dark rum

Heat oil in a 10-inch skillet over medium-high heat. Add garlic; sauté until golden, about 1 minute. Add pork chops; sauté, turning once, until brown on both sides, about 5 minutes.

Mix together gravy and rum. Pour over pork chops. Reduce heat and simmer for about 8 minutes or until pork is no longer pink.

MENU: Bakery corn muffins with apple butter. Deli potato salad. Red and green grapes.

SERVINGS: Makes 2 or 3 servings.

Pork Chops with Peppers

■ The grocery section featuring olive oil is expanding, and among the many selections are flavored oils. The benefit of having one or two of these around is that they add flavor very quickly and you don't have to mince and chop.

½ teaspoon garlic salt
1 teaspoon Worcestershire sauce
1 teaspoon white wine vinegar
1 tablespoon olive oil
4 (1-inch-thick) pork chops
4 roasted red bell peppers, cut into large pieces (see Note, below)
1 tablespoon garlic-flavored oil

Preheat broiler. Mix together garlic salt, Worcestershire sauce, vinegar, and olive oil in a small bowl. Rub seasoning mixture into chops.

Place chops on a broiler pan rack that has been sprayed with nonstick cooking spray. Broil chops 3 inches from source of heat for 5 to 6 minutes, turning once, or until no longer pink in the centers.

Meanwhile, toss bell peppers with garlic-flavored oil. Add to broiler pan and broil until heated through.

MENU: Deli kidney bean salad. Bakery bran muffins. Sliced peaches with peach ice cream.

SERVINGS: Makes 4 servings.

NOTE
Roasted bell peppers are available in jars at most supermarkets.

Browned Pork with Capers

■ I changed the name of this dish from sautéed pork to browned pork when my daughter, then a college student, said she wouldn't try to make this simple dish because she didn't know how to sauté. "But you know how to brown something," I said. "Oh, sure," she replied. Hence the name. Basically, what browning and sautéing have in common is cooking something quickly in a small amount of oil or butter in a skillet or shallow pan over direct heat.

1 tablespoon unsalted butter
4 (3-oz.) slices pork tenderloin
1 small onion, minced
½ small red bell pepper, diced
½ cup dry white wine
2 teaspoons capers, drained
1 teaspoon Dijon mustard
Pinch of dried thyme

Melt butter in a 12-inch skillet over medium heat. Add pork and onion and cook, stirring occasionally, until brown, about 5 minutes. Turn pork and add bell pepper. Cook until pork is cooked through, 5 to 7 minutes. Remove pork to a plate and keep warm.

Stir wine, capers, mustard, and thyme into vegetables in skillet. Cook, stirring occasionally, over medium-high heat until sauce is slightly reduced, about 3 minutes. Spoon sauce over pork.

MENU: Applesauce dusted with cinnamon. French bread. Bakery angel food cake.

SERVINGS: Makes 2 servings.

Winter Pork with Fruit

■ I love the intense flavors of dried fruits, and winter is the best time to cook with them.

2 tablespoons butter
1 pound pork tenderloin, cut into 1-inch-thick slices
¼ cup chopped dried apricots
¼ cup golden raisins
1 shallot, diced
1 teaspoon grated ginger root
1 teaspoon white wine vinegar
2 teaspoons light brown sugar

Melt 1 tablespoon of the butter in a 12-inch skillet over medium-high heat. Add pork and sauté about 2 minutes per side or until golden brown.

Add remaining butter and other ingredients. Reduce heat, cover, and simmer 3 to 4 minutes, stirring occasionally.

Transfer pork to 4 plates. Spoon fruit mixture over pork.

MENU: Applesauce. Rye bread.

SERVINGS: Makes 4 servings.

Braised Pork Chops

■ Braising is one of the most common forms of cooking. First, food is browned in a little fat to seal in its juices, then liquid is added for simmering until the food is tender. In this recipe the liquid I added was apple cider, which melds beautifully with the natural flavors of the pork. Then, when the chops are finished cooking, I use the cooking liquid to make a sauce with a little apple jelly for sweetness and a tad of tart cider vinegar.

1 tablespoon vegetable oil
4 (about ½-inch-thick) pork chops
½ teaspoon dried sage leaf
¾ cup apple cider
¼ cup apple jelly
½ teaspoon cider vinegar

Heat oil in a nonstick 10-inch skillet over medium-high heat. Add chops and cook until brown, about 6 minutes, turning once. Pour off fat.

Sprinkle chops with sage. Pour cider over chops. Cover, reduce heat to low, and simmer about 8 minutes or until chops are just cooked through.

Remove chops to a platter; keep warm. Stir jelly and vinegar into liquid in skillet. Cook, stirring constantly, until jelly melts, about 1 minute. Spoon over chops and serve.

MENU: Spinach and mushroom salad with ranch dressing. Pumpernickel bread. Bakery brownies with frozen vanilla yogurt.

SERVINGS: Makes 3 or 4 servings.

Pork Chops & Red Onions

■ I was introduced to cardamom in a Indian restaurant where I enjoyed it in what I considered an exotic dessert—*kulfi*, a rich pistachio-and-almond-flavored ice cream. When I looked for cardamom the next time I shopped, I was astonished at the price of a few ounces of it ground. But considering how much I had enjoyed the flavor in the *kulfi*, I thought it worth the cost. I found many ways to use it in cakes, cookies, and rice dishes and sprinkled over fruit with a little coconut. I also found that it goes quite nicely with meats.

2 tablespoons vegetable oil
1 large or 2 medium red onions
½ teaspoon sugar
4 (about 1-inch-thick) boneless pork chops
¼ teaspoon ground cardamom

Heat 1 tablespoon of the oil in a 10-inch nonstick frying pan over medium-low heat. Add onion and cook, stirring, for 5 minutes. Add sugar and cook, stirring often, until onion is a deep golden brown, about 3 minutes more.

Meanwhile, heat remaining oil in another 10-inch frying pan over medium-high heat. Add chops and cook until well browned on both sides, about 4 minutes, turning once. Reduce heat and continue cooking, turning once, until no longer pink in centers, about 10 minutes. Spoon out onion into a serving dish. Top with chops and sprinkle with cardamom.

MENU: Cottage cheese on lettuce leaves topped with fresh fruit and chopped mint leaves. Marbled rye bread. Deli rice pudding.

SERVINGS: Makes 3 or 4 servings.

Pork Chops with Gravy

■ The good news about pork is that not only is it generally less expensive than beef but it's leaner, too. Even though it's trim and inexpensive, it is still delicious. Pork is as versatile as chicken. You can braise it, salt it, smoke it, fry it, roast it, or stir-fry it.

1 tablespoon vegetable oil
4 (¾- to 1-inch-thick) pork loin chops
½ cup water
2 teaspoons chopped parsley
¼ teaspoon salt
2 scallions, chopped
¼ teaspoon Worcestershire sauce
2 tablespoons instant flour (see Note, below)
⅓ cup milk

Heat oil in a 12-inch skillet over medium-high heat. Add chops and cook until browned on both sides, about 4 minutes, turning once. Add water, parsley, salt, scallions, and Worcestershire sauce. Cover, reduce heat to low, and simmer 10 minutes.

Meanwhile, combine flour and milk in a small bowl, stirring until smooth. Remove chops from pan and keep warm. Gradually add flour mixture to pan; cook, stirring, until thickened to a gravy consistency, about 1 minute. Serve with chops.

MENU: Canned potato sticks. Applesauce dusted with cinnamon. Bakery pecan sandies.

SERVINGS: Makes 4 servings.

NOTE

Instant flour is a granular flour that will dissolve quickly in both hot and cold liquids without lumping. Wondra is the usual brand that is available and it is sold in a can.

Peppered Pork

■ Freshly ground whole peppercorns deliver more flavor than does preground pepper, which I believe loses its flavor and bite long before it gets to my kitchen. This dish is easy to make and full of flavor, courtesy of my trusty pepper mill.

2 teaspoons freshly ground black pepper
½ teaspoon dried thyme
4 (¾- to 1-inch-thick) boneless pork loin chops
2 teaspoons vegetable oil
2 teaspoons Worcestershire sauce

Mix together pepper and thyme. Coat chops with pepper mixture. Heat oil in 10-inch skillet over medium-high heat. Add chops and cook until browned on both sides, about 4 minutes, turning once. Reduce heat and cook for 10 minutes or until chops are no longer pink in centers. Remove chops from pan to a dish; keep warm.

Add Worcestershire sauce to the hot skillet; stir constantly to remove browned juices from the bottom of the skillet. Pour accumulated juices on the chops dish back into the pan. Stir, then pour pan juices over chops and serve.

MENU: Dinner rolls. Carrot-raisin salad. Ice-cream sandwiches.

SERVINGS: Makes 4 servings.

One-Dish German Dinner

■ My simple version of a German dinner seems to fit into a more modern lifestyle. The pork chops are braised, not fried. Any fat on the meat can be cut away before cooking. The red cabbage, onion, and caraway seeds will add flavor without hefty calorie counts.

1 (1-lb.) jar red cabbage (2 cups), drained
¼ cup chopped onion
1 teaspoon caraway seeds
4 to 6 smoked pork chops

Combine cabbage, onion, and caraway seeds in a nonstick 10-inch frying pan that has been sprayed with nonstick cooking spray. Place chops on top. Cover and simmer over medium-low heat for 10 minutes or until onion is tender.

MENU: Rye bread. Apple and pear slices dusted with cinnamon. Gingersnaps.

SERVINGS: Makes 4 to 6 servings.

Chinese Burgers

■ One day I was dismayed to find that I had purchased a package of ground pork instead of ground beef. I do like pork—chops, pork roast, and barbecued pork—but the merits of ground pork had eluded me. The contents of my refrigerator provided inspiration: a jar of black bean paste and another of hoisin sauce. Eureka! I decided to make Chinese burgers.

3 tablespoons soy sauce
3 tablespoons rice wine vinegar
2 tablespoons black bean paste (see Note, below)
1 teaspoon grated ginger
2 garlic cloves, minced
1 pound ground pork
4 sesame-seed hamburger buns
Hoisin sauce (optional)

In a large bowl, combine soy sauce, vinegar, bean paste, ginger, and garlic. Mix well. Combine all but 3 tablespoons of mix with pork. Form pork into 4 patties.

Heat a large frying pan over medium-high heat. Add patties and cook until brown on both sides, turning once. Reduce heat and cook about 8 minutes more or until no longer pink in centers. Pour the reserved 3 tablespoons of liquid mixture into the pan and bring to a simmer with pan juices.

Serve on buns. Top with hoisin sauce, if desired.

MENU: Spinach salad dressed with marinated mushrooms. Raw scallions. Fresh pineapple slices.

SERVINGS: Makes 4 servings.

NOTE
It can be a problem to find black bean paste in some supermarkets. If it is not available, just use 4 tablespoons of hoisin sauce.

Bavarian Dinner

■ I used canned sauerkraut for years until one day I noticed fresh refrigerated kraut in plastic bags. The fresh kraut has a far superior taste and crunch.

1 tablespoon canola oil
1 pound knockwurst, cut in half lengthwise
½ cup chopped onion
1 cup grated carrots
1 cup diced celery
½ cup beer
Freshly ground black pepper
3¼ cups drained fresh sauerkraut

Heat oil in a 10-inch skillet over medium heat. Add knockwurst and cook until brown, turning often, about 5 minutes. Remove from pan; set aside.

Add onion, carrots, and celery; cook, stirring occasionally, until crisp-tender, about 2 minutes. Add beer, pepper, and sauerkraut. Toss ingredients to combine. Add knockwurst, lower heat, cover, and cook 7 minutes.

MENU: Deli potato salad. Dark rye bread. Bakery apple turnovers.

SERVINGS: Makes 6 servings.

Ham Skillet

■ This is a great dish for leftover ham, but my family likes it so much I sometimes make it with boiled ham purchased in a pound block at the deli counter.

1 tablespoon canola oil
1 cup finely chopped sweet onion
1 (8-oz.) package (3 cups) coleslaw mix
¼ cup apple juice
½ teaspoon fennel seeds
1½ cups cubed cooked ham

Heat oil in a 12-inch skillet over medium-high heat. Add onion; stir-fry 1 to 2 minutes or until crisp-tender.

Add coleslaw mix, apple juice, and fennel seeds. Bring to a boil. Reduce heat to low, cover, and simmer 5 minutes or until slaw is crisp-tender, stirring occasionally. Stir in ham, cook 5 minutes more or until ham is thoroughly heated.

MENU: Applesauce. Bakery corn muffins. Vanilla frozen yogurt with walnuts.

SERVINGS: Makes 4 servings.

Ham Steak

■ Ham steak is a hurry-up dinner standby, but just because it's the old reliable doesn't mean it can't be versatile. A simple glaze or sauce or the addition of fruit can give fresh appeal to a ham steak. Labels on ham steak packages usually say fully cooked, but ham steaks require more cooking for the best flavor.

I've also found that ham steaks vary in taste; some are sweeter than others and some saltier. The best way to discover the ham you like is to experiment with different brands or different stores. I like tender ham, sweet or briny, so I never go wrong as long as it is tender.

1 (about 1¼-lb.) fully cooked ham steak, ¾ inch thick
1 tablespoon canola oil
1 medium onion, coarsely chopped
1 cup canned or frozen whole-kernel corn
1 (6-oz.) package cornbread stuffing mix
¾ cup water
¼ cup apricot jam
1 teaspoon prepared mustard

Preheat broiler. Place ham on a broiler pan rack that has been sprayed with nonstick cooking spray. Broil 4 inches from source of heat for 8 minutes, turning once.

Meanwhile, heat oil in a 10-inch nonstick frying pan. Add onion and sauté 2 minutes. Add corn, seasoning packet from stuffing mix, and water. Simmer for 3 minutes. Add bread stuffing. Toss to mix.

Transfer ham to a platter. Spoon stuffing around ham.

Heat apricot jam and mustard in a small saucepan over medium-low heat, stirring to combine. Remove from heat. Spread over ham.

MENU: Bakery bran muffins. Strawberries with ricotta cheese.

SERVINGS: Makes 4 servings.

Ham with Red-Eye Gravy

■ A family for whom I worked as an occasional baby-sitter and house-sitter during my struggling student days in Kentucky always had a strange object on the kitchen counter. Its odd shape was loosely concealed beneath a clean dish towel.

When I finally caught a glimpse, I was totally unprepared for the sight of country ham. "It's gone bad," I told the cook. "It's all moldy!" This was a cause of great hilarity for everyone but me. "You Northerners," the cook said. "Let me fix you some." She made an open-faced sandwich of leaf lettuce and thinly sliced pieces of ham topped with a hot, thin sauce that she whipped up in a flash. With my young charges and the cook urging me on, I took a bite. I've never forgotten it.

Country ham with red-eye gravy is one of America's great dishes. Salty and deeply flavorful, it is wonderful. Country ham is a great deal more famous than the red-eye gravy—an amazing sauce made with black coffee—and a lot more expensive. I sometimes substitute regular ham sliced paper thin.

2 tablespoons rendered drippings from baked ham or vegetable oil
1 pound baked ham, thinly sliced
¼ cup firmly packed dark brown sugar
½ cup strong black coffee

Heat drippings in a heavy 12-inch skillet over medium-high heat. Add ham slices and cook, turning several times, until lightly browned on both sides, about 5 minutes.

Remove ham from pan with a slotted spoon; keep warm. Stir sugar into pan juices and cook over low heat, stirring constantly, until sugar dissolves, about 1 minute. Add coffee and simmer until gravy turns a rich brown, about 5 minutes; do not boil. Pour gravy over ham and serve.

MENU: Toasted English muffins. Deli potato salad. Pear slices.

SERVINGS: Makes 4 servings.

Fusion Sausages

■ Italian sausage, Chinese chili sauce, and Japanese teriyaki sauce—mix them together and you have a delicious dish.

2 garlic cloves, finely chopped
2 tablespoons teriyaki sauce
1 tablespoon olive oil
2 tablespoons Chinese chili sauce
4 large hot Italian sausages
2 lemon wedges

Preheat broiler. Mix together garlic, teriyaki sauce, oil, and chili sauce in a 1-quart saucepan. Cook over low heat, stirring, until hot.

Prick sausages and place on a broiler pan rack that has been sprayed with nonstick cooking spray. Brush with sauce. Broil 4 inches from source of heat, brushing with sauce occasionally, about 5 minutes on each side or until cooked through.

Squeeze lemon wedges over sausages.

MENU: Oriental shrimp crackers. Spinach salad with favorite dressing. Sugar doughnuts.

SERVINGS: Makes 4 servings.

Ham Steaks with Cabbage & Apples

■ Ham steaks are a quick dinner option. Besides great flavor, they also have a real down-home, comforting appeal.

1⅓ (8-oz.) packages (4 cups) coleslaw mix
½ cup chopped onion
1 tablespoon packed brown sugar
1 tablespoon cider vinegar
1 large Granny Smith apple, peeled, cored, and cut into rings
4 (3-oz.) fully cooked ham steaks

Combine coleslaw mix, onion, brown sugar, vinegar, and apple rings in an 11 × 7-inch microwave-safe dish.

Cover loosely and microwave on HIGH 5 to 7 minutes, stirring after 2 minutes, until apple is crisp-tender.

Place ham on top of slaw mixture. Cover loosely and microwave on HIGH, about 5 minutes, rotating dish ½ turn after 2 minutes, until ham is heated through.

MENU: Deli potato salad. Rye toast. Bakery brownies with vanilla ice cream.

SERVINGS: Makes 4 servings.

German Sausage & Red Cabbage Skillet

■ This is hearty fare perfect for cold nights. The flavor is the sweet-sour combination that is featured in many traditional German dishes.

2 teaspoons corn oil
1 pound ground pork sausage
1⅓ (8-oz.) packages (about 4 cups) shredded red cabbage
1 cup coarsely chopped onion
½ cup water
3 tablespoons apple cider vinegar
2 tablespoons grape jelly
Salt and freshly ground pepper
2½ cups sliced McIntosh or Granny Smith apples

Heat oil in a 12-inch skillet over medium-high heat. Add sausage and cook, stirring to break up sausage, until brown, about 5 minutes. Drain all but 1 tablespoon of oil and drippings.

Add cabbage and onion and sauté 5 minutes, stirring often.

Stir in water, vinegar, jelly, salt, and pepper. Reduce heat to medium; cover and simmer 2 minutes. Add apples. Simmer, uncovered, about 2 minutes or until cabbage and apples are tender.

MENU: Pumpernickel bread. Bakery Black Forest Cake.

SERVINGS: Makes 4 servings.

Southern Ham & Vegetable Dinner

■ The best dietary advice is to eat a variety of foods in moderation. If you're eating the same old thing, try something new. If you live in the South, this may seem old hat, but anywhere else, okra is thought of as exotic. It's now available fresh in season in my market in New Jersey, and there's always a supply of frozen. A 10-ounce package of frozen okra will work in this recipe.

3 tablespoons corn oil
½ cup minced onion
½ cup chopped green bell pepper
½ pound fresh okra, cut into 1-inch chunks
1 (11-oz.) can whole-kernel corn, drained
2 cups cubed cooked ham
1 (14-oz.) can stewed tomatoes
Salt and freshly ground black pepper
½ teaspoon fresh thyme or a pinch of dried

Heat oil in a 12-inch skillet over medium heat. Add onion and pepper and sauté 2 minutes, stirring occasionally. Add okra and sauté 5 minutes, stirring occasionally. Stir in corn, ham, tomatoes, salt, pepper, and thyme. Cook, stirring occasionally, for about 5 minutes.

MENU: Bakery bran muffins. Sliced peaches and cream.

SERVINGS: Makes 4 servings.

Scented Lamb Chops

■ Loin lamb chops are usually more than an inch thick and ideally suited to broiling. They don't require much more care then seasoning with salt and pepper. But, I love to experiment, hence this recipe for a lovely orange-scented marinade.

8 lamb chops
2 teaspoons grated ginger
3 garlic cloves, crushed
¼ cup fresh orange juice
2 tablespoons canola oil
Orange wedges

Preheat broiler. Place chops in a shallow glass dish. Combine ginger, garlic, orange juice, and oil in a medium bowl. Pour juice mixture over lamb. Set aside for 5 minutes, turning once.

Place chops on a broiler pan that has been sprayed with nonstick cooking spray. Broil 4 inches from source of heat for 5 minutes on each side or to desired doneness, brushing once or twice during cooking with orange marinade. Serve garnished with orange wedges.

MENU: Deli marinated mushrooms on Bibb lettuce leaves. Dinner rolls. Deli rice pudding.

SERVINGS: Makes 4 servings.

Armenian Patties

■ The versatility of ground meats is amazing. Ground lamb works best in these Middle Eastern–inspired patties.

1 small onion, minced
1 pound lean ground lamb
1 egg, slightly beaten
4 tablespoons chopped fresh flat-leaf parsley
Salt and freshly ground black pepper
1 tablespoon olive oil
½ cup plain yogurt

Mix together onion, lamb, egg, 2 tablespoons of the parsley, salt, and pepper in a medium bowl. Shape into 4 patties.

Heat oil in a 10-inch skillet over medium-high heat. Add patties and cook until brown, about 2 minutes on each side. Reduce heat, and cook 8 more minutes or until lamb reaches desired degree of doneness.

Meanwhile, mix together remaining parsley and yogurt. Serve patties with yogurt-parsley mixture on the side.

MENU: Pita bread. Red and green pepper spears. Fig bars.

SERVINGS: Makes 4 servings.

Lemon & Garlic Lamb Chops

■ Lamb has never been very popular in America, but I sense that is changing, because of the artistry of restaurant chefs who feature this delicious and delicate meat on their menus. I like it prepared simply.

1 tablespoon all-purpose flour
1 tablespoon grated lemon peel
1 clove garlic, minced
Salt and freshly ground black pepper
4 lamb chops
2 tablespoons canola oil

Mix flour, lemon peel, garlic, and salt and pepper in a paper bag. Add chops. Shake to coat. Set aside.

Heat oil in a large skillet. Add chops. Fry over medium-high heat about 10 minutes or until chops are golden brown, turning once. Drain on paper towels.

MENU: Deli Mediterranean lentil salad. Fruit chutney. Frozen yogurt.

SERVINGS: Makes 4 servings.

Spicy Lamb Chops

■ Spice lovers will love this sauce. It has everything in it but the kitchen sink. Positively addictive.

⅓ teaspoon ground ginger
¼ teaspoon ground allspice
1 teaspoon curry powder
1 teaspoon dried oregano
1 cup barbecue sauce
8 lamb chops

Preheat broiler. Combine seasonings and barbecue sauce in a small bowl.

Place lamb chops on a broiler pan rack that has been sprayed with nonstick cooking spray. Brush with sauce mixture. Broil about 4 inches from source of heat for 6 to 7 minutes on each side or to desired doneness, brushing with sauce as chops cook.

MENU: Deli new-potato salad. Carrot and celery sticks with ranch dressing dip. Pear slices.

SERVINGS: Makes 4 servings.

Lamb with Yogurt Mint Sauce

■ Mint is the classic accompaniment for lamb in the United Kingdom and America. I confess to a preference for mint. But when thinking about cooking lamb, consider what other countries do—Algerians pair it with prunes and almonds, Moroccans with lemons and olives, the Belgians with endives, the Swedes with dill.

⅔ cup plain yogurt
¼ cup fresh mint leaves
2 tablespoons sugar
4 (about 1-inch-thick) lamb loin chops

Preheat broiler. Place yogurt, mint, and sugar in a blender or food processor. Process until smooth.

Place lamb chops on a broiler pan rack that has been sprayed with nonstick cooking spray. Broil chops about 3 inches from source of heat for 5 to 6 minutes on each side or to desired doneness. Serve with yogurt sauce.

MENU: Deli rice salad. Whole-wheat rolls. Sliced strawberries with slivers of candied ginger.

SERVINGS: Makes 4 servings.

Orange-Ginger Lamb Chops

■ I'm a part-time resident of Florida; you might have guessed it by counting all the recipes with oranges, limes, or grapefruit. I think they offer endless possibilities.

¼ cup frozen orange juice concentrate
¼ cup soy sauce
1 teaspoon crushed fresh ginger
6 (½-inch-thick) lamb shoulder chops

Preheat broiler. Combine orange juice, soy sauce, and ginger in a small bowl. Set aside.

Place lamb chops on a broiler pan rack that has been sprayed with nonstick cooking spray. Broil chops about 4 inches from source of heat for 5 to 6 minutes on each side, brushing two or three times with orange sauce, or to desired degree of doneness.

MENU: Whole-wheat toast. Deli green bean salad. Nectarine slices with a dollop of ricotta cheese and sliced almonds.

SERVINGS: Makes 6 servings.

Hawaiian Lamb Chops

■ When I was growing up, I remember turning up my nose at the very mention of lamb. When or how I finally developed a taste for it is lost in the mists of time, but currently I am passionate about it. Why do I love it? Because it's light, tender, and luscious. Although leg of lamb and lamb roast are great, chops have the advantage of cooking quickly and easily.

When buying lamb chops, look for bright pink and fine-grained flesh, creamy white fat, and spongy pink bones.

1 (8-oz.) can crushed pineapple in juice, undrained
½ cup orange marmalade
¼ cup fresh lemon juice
1 tablespoon Dijon mustard
½ teaspoon salt
4 (1-inch-thick) lamb shoulder chops

Preheat broiler or grill. Combine pineapple, marmalade, lemon juice, mustard, and salt in a small saucepan. Bring to a boil and cook, stirring, until marmalade is melted.

Place lamb chops on a broiler pan rack or grill rack that has been sprayed with nonstick cooking spray. Broil chops about 4 inches from source of heat for 4 to 5 minutes on each side, brushing with orange sauce the last 3 to 4 minutes, or to desired degree of doneness.

MENU: Carrot and celery sticks. Deli rice salad. Rum-raisin ice cream.

SERVINGS: Makes 4 servings.

Thyme Lamb Chops

■ This recipe calls for lamb loin chops, which include part of the backbone. They're very tender and broil very nicely and quickly.

6 (1-inch-thick) lamb loin chops
2 tablespoons butter, softened
½ teaspoon dried thyme, crumbled

Preheat broiler. Score fat around chops. Place chops on a broiler rack that has been sprayed with nonstick cooking spray. Broil 4 inches from source of heat for 5 minutes on each side, or to desired doneness. Place on a heated platter.

Meanwhile, combine butter and thyme in a small bowl. Spread about a teaspoon over each hot chop.

MENU: Deli red-potato salad. Bakery Portuguese rolls. Bakery cinnamon buns.

SERVINGS: Makes 6 servings.

Lamb Patties

■ This is a love story. I love lamb; he does not. He doesn't even like it. Usually this dilemma is solved when we dine out. I order lamb; he orders something else. I'm happy and he's happy. Every once in a while, though, I become a sneaky cook and try a lamb dish I'm sure he will not recognize and will love. I will reveal the truth, he will come to love lamb, and we, meaning me, will get to eat more of it.

No matter how I smother it, sauce it, disguise it, he detects the deceit. I've come to believe there's just no way to disguise the taste of lamb, and why would anyone want to, unless she were, like me, trying to deceive a lamb hater? So, if I cook it at home, now I cook just enough for me.

But if your family likes lamb, broiled lamb patties are simple, delicious, and incredibly quick to make.

1 pound ground lamb
2 tablespoons seasoned bread crumbs
1 egg, slightly beaten
1 clove garlic, minced
4 slices bacon

Preheat broiler. Mix together all ingredients except bacon. Shape into 4 patties, each about 1 inch thick. Wrap bacon around each patty. Secure with a wooden pick.

Place patties on a broiler pan rack that has been sprayed with nonstick cooking spray. Broil patties 3 inches from source of heat, turning once, until desired doneness, about 10 minutes.

MENU: Deli carrot-raisin salad. Jewish rye bread. Bakery brownies.

SERVINGS: Makes 4 servings.

Fish

If ever there was an ingredient made for the 15-minute chef, it's fish. It can be cooked in a flash in endless and delicious ways. Unfortunately, many home cooks, who love eating fish in a restaurant, are hesitant to cook it at home. I don't know why. Nothing could be simpler—certainly simpler than cooking chicken and simpler than cooking meat. An added incentive is that fish is very lean; even so-called fatty fish are low in fat, and the kind of fat they have contains omega-3 fatty acids, a substance that helps protect against heart disease.

If you're not familiar with cooking fish, introduce yourself to a local fishmonger. He or she can help with tips, advice, even recipes.

Most quick dishes will require fish fillets or steaks rather than whole fish. When you select these, check to be sure that the fish has a fresh odor, the meat is firm, and the appearance is moist, not dry.

If you buy fish from a frozen food case, check to see that it's solidly frozen and its wrapping is undamaged. Packages with lots of ice crystals mean there's been defrosting and refreezing.

Although many of my recipes call for a specific kind of fish, a lot of fish varieties can be used interchangeably as long as they're within the same group of fish. This is a boon when one variety is on sale and another is not.

There are three general groups: lean; moderate-fat fish; and high-fat fish. Lean refers to fish that have a fat content of less than 2.5 percent, which would include those such as flounder, haddock, halibut, perch, and pollack. Moderate-fat fish, which have less than 6 percent fat but more than 2.5, include varieties like catfish, striped bass, swordfish, trout, and whiting. High-fat fish generally contain about 12 percent fat, and these include bluefish, mackerel, salmon, sablefish, shad, smelt, and yellowtail.

TIPS FOR COOKING FISH

When I set out to learn how to cook, fish was not in my study plan. I assumed that what everybody said about it was true: Home cooks can't hope to create satisfying seafood dishes. Fish is what you order when you are out.

As I learned to cook, this tenet became more and more implausible. Why should fish be so hard to cook? As a matter of fact, cooking fish is one of the easiest things a home chef can do. Fish cooks quickly and adapts well to a variety of seasonings and sauces that contribute their flavors and textures to the table.

HERE ARE A FEW TIPS:
- Dry-heat methods like baking, broiling, or grilling are best for higher-fat fish like salmon, bluefish, or tuna.
- Frying, sautéing, or poaching are best for lean fish. These moist-heat cooking techniques allow fish such as scrod or sole to remain firm during cooking.
- Fish is fully cooked when the translucent flesh becomes opaque and flakes easily with a fork, but extended cooking toughens it and makes it dry.

Deviled Catfish

■ There is no secret about cooking fish properly: it is all in the timing. Fish is done when the flesh has just begun to turn from translucent to opaque or white and is firm but still moist.

½ cup chili sauce
2 tablespoons canola oil
2 tablespoons prepared mustard
2 tablespoons prepared horseradish
1 tablespoon Worcestershire sauce
½ teaspoon sea salt
2 pounds catfish fillets, rinsed and patted dry

Preheat broiler. Combine all ingredients except catfish in a small bowl.

Place fish on a broiler pan rack that has been sprayed with nonstick cooking spray. Spread chili sauce mixture evenly over fish.

Broil fish 4 inches from source of heat for 5 to 8 minutes or until fish flakes easily when tested with a fork.

MENU: Bakery corn muffins and apple butter. Tossed salad with Thousand Island dressing. Toasted pound cake slices with fresh berries.

SERVINGS: Makes 6 servings.

Pecan Catfish

■ Born and raised in New Jersey, I grew up on "shore dinners"—saltwater fish extravaganzas. I have no memory of ever eating a freshwater fish until I first visited my in-laws in the Midwest. They introduced me to catfish.

I'd heard bad things about catfish—the worst being that they had a "muddy" taste. Happily, the farm-raised varieties lack that unfortunate characteristic. Better diet and a controlled environment have yielded a reliably fine-textured, mild-tasting, and very versatile fish.

I've devoted myself to learning how to cook them and was greatly helped by the Catfish Institute, an industry organization. This is its recipe for easy but elegant catfish with pecans.

2 tablespoons milk
3 tablespoons Dijon mustard
4 catfish fillets, rinsed and patted dry
1 cup ground pecans (see Note, below)

Preheat oven to 500F (260C). Combine milk and Dijon mustard in a small bowl. Dip fillets into mustard mixture. Then dip into ground pecans, shaking off excess. Place coated fillets on a greased baking sheet. Oven-fry for 10 to 12 minutes or until catfish flakes easily when tested with a fork.

MENU: Grated summer squash dressed with yogurt, minced mint, and a touch of lime juice. Toasted sourdough bread. Bakery peach crumb pie.

SERVINGS: Makes 4 servings.

NOTE
Pecans can be ground in a small food processor or in a rotary nut grater. Be careful, though; if overprocessed, they become pecan butter.

Cod with Parsley Butter

■ Just a little cayenne pepper adds a lot of piquancy to any dish. I put it in sauces, chili, stews, egg dishes, pizza, soups—anything that could use a little lift.

Most cayenne pepper is blended from pungent Chinese, Indian, African, and Mexican chilies. Restraint in its use is essential, because cayenne is very hot. The degree of hotness, though, can vary from brand to brand.

To keep it spicy, store cayenne in an airtight container in a cool, dark, dry place. Replace it every six months and buy its replacement from a busy store that restocks its spice section fairly often.

This simple dish is a quick, flavorful supper with uncomplicated tastes and a little bite from cayenne.

¼ cup butter
1 tablespoon chopped fresh parsley
1 tablespoon fresh lemon juice
¼ teaspoon salt
⅛ teaspoon cayenne pepper
1 pound cod fillets, cut into 4 servings, rinsed, and patted dry

Preheat broiler. Melt butter in a 1-quart saucepan over low heat. Add parsley, lemon juice, salt, and cayenne. Remove from heat.

Arrange fish on a broiler pan rack that has been sprayed with nonstick cooking spray. Spoon half of the butter mixture over fish. Broil 4 inches from source of heat for 7 minutes or until fish flakes easily when tested with a fork. Spoon remaining butter sauce over fish. Broil 1 minute more.

MENU: Bakery corn muffins. Carrot strips and deli marinated mushrooms. Seedless grape halves and fresh blueberries topped with vanilla yogurt.

SERVINGS: Makes 4 servings.

Cod, Asian Style

■ Coastal dwellers in Asia have been found to have a lower incidence of heart disease than their farming neighbors. The conclusion seems pretty clear: fish is healthy to eat. This cod dish borrows some Asian flavors.

¾ cup soy sauce
3 tablespoons sugar
1 teaspoon sesame oil
1 clove garlic, minced
⅛ teaspoon cayenne pepper
6 (about 6-oz.) cod steaks, rinsed and patted dry
1 red bell pepper, cut into 6 spears

Preheat broiler. Combine soy sauce, sugar, sesame oil, garlic, and cayenne pepper in a small bowl.

Place fish and bell pepper on a broiler rack that has been sprayed with nonstick cooking spray. Brush fish and bell pepper with soy sauce mixture. Broil fish and bell pepper 4 inches from source of heat for 10 minutes, basting with mixture and turning several times, or until fish flakes when tested with a fork.

MENU: Rice cakes. Mixed greens with bamboo shoots and lemon vinaigrette. Angel food cake with fresh pineapple.

SERVINGS: Makes 6 servings.

Garlic Lovers' Cod

■ Garlic lovers are a special breed. The lasting garlic breath means not a whit. I know a couple who have a pact; when one eats garlic, so does the other—that way, there's no problem about kissing. They'd love this dish, redolent with their favorite flavor.

1 pound cod fillets, rinsed and patted dry
4 cloves garlic, coarsely chopped
1 tablespoon butter
1 tablespoon olive oil
2 tablespoons fresh lemon juice
½ teaspoon salt
Snipped fresh cilantro

Preheat broiler. Cut fish fillets into 4 serving pieces and place on a broiler pan rack that has been sprayed with nonstick cooking spray. Broil 4 inches from source of heat until fish flakes easily with a fork, 10 to 12 minutes.

Meanwhile, combine garlic, butter, and olive oil in a 1-quart saucepan over medium heat. Cook, stirring, until garlic is golden brown, about 2 minutes. Remove garlic with a slotted spoon; reserve.

Transfer fish from rack to a serving dish. Add lemon juice to butter mixture and ladle over fish. Sprinkle with salt, cilantro, and reserved garlic.

MENU: Whole-wheat bread. Tossed salad with Russian dressing. Banana slices tossed with lemon juice and coconut.

SERVINGS: Makes 4 servings.

Red Pepper Cod

■ Red bell peppers are more expensive than green peppers, but what you get for your money is a sweeter taste.

1 pound cod fillets, rinsed and patted dry
2 tablespoons stir-fry sauce
2 medium red bell peppers, cut into 1-inch pieces
1 cup mushrooms, cut in half

Arrange fish in an 8-inch-square microwave-safe dish. Brush with stir-fry sauce. Top with bell peppers and mushrooms.

Cover loosely and microwave on HIGH 8 to 12 minutes, rotating at 4-minute intervals, or until fish flakes when tested with a fork. Let sit, covered, for 3 minutes before serving.

MENU: Deli prepared sesame or other noodles with chopped scallions. Pineapple spears. Bakery almond cookies.

SERVINGS: Makes 4 servings.

Greek Fish

■ I know only one Greek phrase, which I can say but cannot write. Translated it means "Your kitchen looks nice." I learned it from my best friend in high school's mother, who kept a traditional Greek home and cooked traditional Greek food.

My Greek fish recipe is created from the memory of a dish my friend's mother made. I remember it especially well because I went shopping with her and my friend to buy the cod from a Greek fishmonger who was a member of their church. She and the proprietor briefed my friend and me on the proper selection of fresh fish. My friend and I, both sixteen, had a propensity for laughing at everything, and the instruction to smell the fish hit us as especially silly.

I may have giggled then, but the truth is, I learned, and I take great care in picking fresh fish. It's true, you know; your nose will know.

¼ cup fresh lemon juice
2 teaspoons olive oil
¼ teaspoon dried oregano
1 pound cod fillets, rinsed and patted dry
Spinach leaves
¼ cup kalamata olives
Lemon wedges

Combine lemon juice, olive oil, and oregano in a small bowl.

Place fish in a 10-inch skillet. Pour oil mixture over fish. Bring to a boil. Reduce heat, cover, and simmer 5 to 10 minutes or until fish flakes when pierced with a fork.

Meanwhile, line a serving plate with spinach leaves. Remove fish with a slotted spoon and place atop spinach leaves. Spoon some cooking liquid over fish. Garnish with olives and lemon wedges.

MENU: Deli curly pasta salad. Broccoli florets and red pepper strips with Caesar salad dressing. Deli marinated mushrooms. Fig bars.

SERVINGS: Makes 4 servings.

Limey Fillets

■ This is a recipe for the so-called lean fish: cod, orange roughy, catfish, flounder, sole, haddock, halibut, and red snapper to name a few. Take your pick.

1 pound fish fillets, rinsed and patted dry
¼ cup prepared tartar sauce
Juice of 1 lime
⅔ cup dry bread crumbs
Lime wedges

Cut fish into 4 servings.

Combine tartar sauce and lime juice in a flat bowl. Dip fillets in tartar sauce mixture, then in crumbs, being sure to coat evenly. Place fish in a greased 12 × 8-inch microwave-safe baking dish. Loosely cover.

Microwave on HIGH 5 to 7 minutes or until fish flakes easily with a fork. Garnish with lime wedges.

MENU: Deli potato chips. Deli coleslaw. Bakery pecan sandies.

SERVINGS: Makes 4 servings.

Flounder with Cilantro Sauce

■ It's easy to mistake flat-leaf parsley for cilantro and vice versa. Visually they may be similar, but when it comes to taste—there's no mistaking cilantro for anything but cilantro. It's a wonderful aromatic herb but it must be used sparingly, because it is very strong and can easily dominate all other flavors.

1½ pounds flounder fillets, rinsed and patted dry
2 tablespoons fresh lime juice
Salt
3 tablespoons canola oil
⅔ cup heavy cream
2 tablespoons chopped fresh cilantro

Cut fillets into 1-inch strips. Sprinkle with lime juice and salt. Heat oil in a 10-inch skillet over medium-high heat. Add fillets in a single layer (do not crowd pan or fish will steam instead of frying) and sauté the fillets, turning frequently and carefully, for 4 to 5 minutes or until opaque.

Remove fish with a slotted spoon. Pour off oil and wipe skillet clean with paper towels.

Pour cream into skillet and add cilantro. Bring to a boil, reduce heat, and simmer 2 minutes. Return fish to pan and heat through.

MENU: Onion rolls. Cauliflower and broccoli salad. Bakery pecan pie.

SERVINGS: Makes 4 servings.

Sunshine Fish

■ This is a dish I made recently when, in my eagerness for it to be orange season, I bought a bag of oranges that weren't at their best.

I hate to throw anything away—especially food. The oranges just sat in the fruit basket for a day or two staring at me, until I decided I'd try to do something with them. This is what I came up with—sunshine fish. It was quite simple and good enough that I'll make it again when oranges are in season.

1 pound flounder fillets, rinsed and patted dry
Juice of 1 lemon
Juice of 2 oranges
3 tablespoons canola oil
1 small red onion, chopped
1 clove garlic, minced

Place fish in a glass dish. Combine juices and pour over fish. Set aside for 5 minutes.

Heat oil in 10-inch frying pan over medium-high heat. Add onion and stir-fry about 2 minutes or until softened but not browned. Add garlic.

Reduce heat and add fish in a single layer. Cook fish over low heat, with cover slightly ajar, until fish flakes when tested with a fork, 5 to 8 minutes.

MENU: Potato dinner rolls. Deli green bean salad. Pound cake with vanilla frozen yogurt.

SERVINGS: Makes 4 servings.

Flounder with Cilantro Butter

■ Flounder is sometimes sold as sole, but like the rose, whatever its name, it will still be great. Although this is a lean fish, it can be baked, broiled, pan-fried, or poached. In this recipe, broiled works best.

4 flounder fillets (1 to 1½ pounds), rinsed and patted dry
¼ cup butter
2 tablespoons fresh cilantro leaves
2 teaspoons fresh lime juice

Preheat broiler. Place fish, skin side up, on a broiler pan rack that has been sprayed with nonstick cooking spray. Broil 4 to 6 inches from source of heat for 3 minutes. Turn carefully and broil 2 to 4 minutes more or until fish flakes when tested with a fork.

Meanwhile, melt butter in small saucepan. Remove from heat; stir in cilantro and lime juice. Spoon over fish.

MENU: Carrot and celery sticks. Bakery corn muffins with apple butter. Raspberry sherbet.

SERVINGS: Makes 4 servings.

Marjoram-Scented Flounder Fillets

■ I prefer using fresh herbs to dried. Many dried herbs have all the taste and flavor of dust, but this is not true of marjoram. Even in its dried state, it retains good flavor, which it imparts to dishes made with tomatoes, egg, cheese, fish, and roasted meat. Dried marjoram is worth putting in the spice rack.

1½ pounds flounder fillets, rinsed and patted dry
1 onion, grated
Juice of 1 lemon
2 tablespoons butter, melted
Salt and freshly ground black pepper
½ teaspoon dried marjoram
2 teaspoons minced fresh chives
1 tablespoon minced fresh parsley

Preheat broiler. Arrange fish on a broiler rack that has been sprayed with nonstick cooking spray. Mix together remaining ingredients in a small bowl and pour over fish.

Broil fish 4 inches from source of heat for 6 minutes or until fish flakes easily when tested with a fork.

Remove to a hot platter; pour drippings from pan over top and garnish with parsley.

MENU: Kaiser rolls. Deli marinated vegetable salad. Pear slices.

SERVINGS: Makes 4 servings.

Curried Flounder

■ This recipe calls for flounder, but feel free to substitute any firm-fleshed white fish that's on sale.

Instant rice
2 tablespoons raisins
1 pound flounder fillets, rinsed and patted dry
Salt and freshly ground black pepper
1 tablespoon canola oil
1 medium onion, chopped
1 teaspoon curry powder

Prepare rice according to package directions for 4 servings. Stir in raisins; set aside.

Meanwhile, season fish with salt and pepper. Heat oil in a 10-inch skillet over medium heat. Add onion and curry powder and cook, stirring occasionally, for 2 minutes or until onion is soft.

Add fish, cook over medium heat, 4 minutes per side or until fish flakes when tested with a fork.

Place rice and raisin mix on a serving platter. Top with fish and onions.

MENU: Pita bread. Banana slices with honey and coconut.

SERVINGS: Makes 4 servings.

Flounder with Chives

■ Fish is great when you're in a hurry, because it cooks so quickly. As long as you don't overcook it, you don't really need a recipe. Just improvise with a few flavor notes—add lemon, herbs, and vegetables. Too busy to think about it? Let me help.

1 pound flounder fillets, rinsed and patted dry
Salt and freshly ground black pepper
1 tablespoon olive oil
1 teaspoon fresh lemon juice
3 tablespoons chopped fresh chives

Season fish with salt and pepper.

Heat oil in a 10-inch skillet over medium-high heat. Add fish and sauté until brown, turning carefully, about 4 minutes per side. Drizzle with lemon juice. Sprinkle with chives.

MENU: Vinegar potato chips. Broccoli florets with ranch dressing. Strawberry ice cream with fresh strawberries.

SERVINGS: Makes 4 servings.

Fish Mexicano

■ Like chicken, seafood lends itself to many different preparations and flavorings. This dish takes its inspiration from south of the border.

1 pound haddock fillets, rinsed and patted dry
1 medium tomato, chopped
4 scallions, chopped
2 jalapeño chiles, seeded and minced
2 tablespoons chopped fresh cilantro
Juice of 1 lime
1 teaspoon chili powder
1 tablespoon mayonnaise
¼ cup salsa

Cut fish into 4 serving-size pieces. Place in a greased 12 × 8-inch microwave-safe baking dish. Combine tomato, scallions, chiles, cilantro, lime juice, and chili powder in a medium bowl. Spoon tomato mixture over fish fillets.

Cover loosely with microwave-safe plastic wrap. Microwave on HIGH 7 to 8 minutes or until fish flakes easily with a fork.

Meanwhile, in a small bowl, combine mayonnaise and salsa. Serve with fish and vegetables.

MENU: Corn chips. Bakery cinnamon cookies.

SERVINGS: Makes 4 servings.

Haddock with Olives

■ I don't know who thought up olive bars in supermarkets, but I'd like to shake his or her hand. I love olives—not the kind that come in cans and jars, but the kind that can be ladled out of bins. Of course, this requires pitting and pitting takes some time.

Substitute canned olives in a pinch, but if you have an extra few minutes you're willing to spend, here's how to pit olives quickly: Lay an olive on a work surface, hold the flat side of a chef's knife on top of it, and give the knife a gentle but firm whack with your other palm or fist. The pit should slip out easily.

1½ pounds haddock fillets, rinsed and patted dry
Salt and freshly ground black pepper
2 tablespoons vegetable oil
1 small onion, quartered
1 tablespoon white wine vinegar
⅓ cup ripe olives, pits removed

Season fish with salt and pepper. Heat oil in a heavy 10-inch skillet. Add fish in a single layer; sauté 5 minutes.

Meanwhile, place onion, vinegar, and olives in a food processor. Pulse until finely chopped.

Turn fish and spread olive mixture over fish. Cover and simmer for 5 minutes or until fish flakes when tested with a fork.

MENU: Whole-wheat bread. Deli mushroom salad. Fresh berries with rice pudding.

SERVINGS: Makes 4 servings.

Halibut Broil

■ Pineapple juice has a lovely sweetness, which not only imparts great flavor to the halibut but also helps create a wonderful crust over the cooked fish.

½ cup pineapple juice
¼ cup steak sauce
1 teaspoon lemon-pepper seasoning
2 pounds halibut fillets, rinsed and patted dry

Combine all ingredients except fish in a small bowl; set aside.

Preheat broiler. Place fish on a broiler pan rack that has been sprayed with nonstick cooking spray. Broil fish 4 inches from the source of heat for 4 to 6 minutes. Turn fish, brush with sauce. Broil 4 to 6 minutes more or until fish flakes when tested with a fork.

Serve with remaining sauce on the side.

MENU: Deli three-bean salad. Deli-style potato chips. Deli rice pudding.

SERVINGS: Makes 6 servings.

Lemon-Basil Halibut

■ Basil has become a year-round herb, so it's possible to avoid using dried basil which has little flavor. Fresh basil doesn't have the staying power of parsley, but it will keep pretty well for several days if it's wrapped loosely in a plastic bag and kept in the refrigerator.

¼ cup olive oil
Juice of 1 lemon
1 tablespoon chopped fresh basil
1 teaspoon Hungarian paprika
4 (about 6-oz.) halibut steaks, rinsed and patted dry

Preheat broiler. Combine olive oil, lemon juice, basil, and paprika in a small bowl.

Place halibut steaks on a broiler pan rack that has been sprayed with nonstick cooking spray. Broil fish 4 inches from source of heat 5 minutes. Turn fish and baste with lemon-basil mixture. Broil about 10 minutes or until fish flakes when tested with a fork.

MENU: Deli new-potato salad. French baguette. Peaches in cream, dusted with cinnamon.

SERVINGS: Makes 4 servings.

Halibut in Wine

■ Words like "subtle but assertive, with elegant color and a fresh, crisp taste" describe wines, not fish, but when I want to describe halibut, those are the words I use.

The Atlantic halibut, which ranges from Labrador to the New Jersey coast and to Greenland, is a member of the flounder family. Its meat is clear white, and when it's finished cooking, the meat breaks off in large white flakes that are tender and naturally lean. Atlantic halibut can be found year-round in frozen form, and from April to December fresh.

4 (about 6-oz.) halibut steaks, rinsed and
   patted dry
⅓ cup dry white wine
4 tablespoons butter
½ cup chopped scallions
½ cup sliced celery
1 tablespoon chopped fresh parsley
1 teaspoon Worcestershire sauce
Cherry tomatoes

Place fish in a shallow glass dish. Add wine and set aside.

Melt butter in a 10-inch skillet over medium heat. Add scallions and celery; cook, stirring occasionally, until tender, about 2 minutes. Stir in parsley and Worcestershire sauce.

Add fish and wine. Cover and cook over low heat until fish is opaque, about 8 minutes. Add cherry tomatoes. Cover and cook 2 minutes or until tomatoes are just hot.

MENU: Cucumbers with sour cream. Deli three-bean salad on lettuce leaves. Bakery peach pie.

SERVINGS: Makes 4 servings.

Halibut Ragu

■ High-quality imported plum tomatoes are what gives this dish its authentic Italian flavor. Essentially it is a simple fish stew—satisfying and delicious.

1 tablespoon olive oil
1 green bell pepper, cut into thin strips
1 onion, chopped
2 garlic cloves, minced
1 tablespoon chopped fresh basil or
   1 teaspoon dried
1 (28-oz.) can imported crushed plum
   tomatoes.
1 pound halibut fillets, rinsed, patted dry,
   and cut into cubes

Heat oil in a 3-quart saucepan or Dutch oven. Add bell pepper, onion, and garlic. Sauté until onion is soft, about 2 minutes. Add basil and plum tomatoes. Bring to a simmer.

Add halibut, cover, and simmer for 10 minutes or until fish flakes when tested with a fork.

MENU: Garlic bread. Romaine leaves with sliced fresh mozzarella and sun-dried tomatoes dressed with red-wine vinaigrette. Lemon sherbet.

SERVINGS: Makes 4 servings.

Southwestern Halibut

■ I want to recommend sea salt if you haven't ever tried it. It used to be a commodity found in gourmet stores, but now it's being stocked in supermarkets. I find a noticeable difference in taste, but that's just one of the reasons I like to use it. It's a coarse-ground salt that I don't bother to measure because a pinch or two is plenty. I think I end up using less salt this way but extract more flavor.

1 to 1½ pounds halibut, rinsed and patted
  dry
Sea salt
⅔ cup spicy hot salsa
½ cup chopped red onion
1 clove garlic, minced
1 medium green bell pepper, chopped
6 cherry tomatoes, halved

Lightly sprinkle fish with salt and set aside.
Combine salsa, onion, and garlic in a 10-inch skillet. Bring to a boil over medium heat, stirring constantly.
Reduce heat. Add fish and bell pepper. Cover and simmer gently for 10 minutes or until fish flakes easily when tested with a fork. Remove fish to serving plate; keep warm.
Cook and stir pan juices until slightly thickened, 1 to 2 minutes. Stir in tomatoes; heat through. Spoon some sauce over fish. Serve extra sauce on the side.

MENU: Mesclun salad with green goddess dressing. Corn chips. Bakery cinnamon coffeecake.

SERVINGS: Makes 4 servings.

Mahi-Mahi in Fennel Sauce

■ The single most important factor in cooking fish is to buy good-quality fish. There's a way to recognize it: if the fish is whole, look for eyes that are bright and clear, not cloudy. The gills should be deep red, not pink or brownish. If it's fillets, smell them. Don't worry about propriety, just let your nose tell the tale. Fresh fish don't smell fishy. They smell like the ocean.

2 tablespoons olive oil
2 tablespoons butter
½ cup chopped fennel bulb
¼ cup chopped scallions
6 (about 6-oz.) mahi-mahi fillets, rinsed and
  patted dry

Preheat broiler. Heat oil and butter in a 1-quart saucepan over medium-high heat. Add fennel and scallions. Sauté for 2 minutes; set aside.
Arrange fish on a broiler rack that has been sprayed with nonstick cooking spray. Broil 4 inches from source of heat for 5 minutes. Turn fish and brush with butter-oil mixture from vegetables and broil about 5 minutes or until fish flakes with a fork. Spoon scallions and fennel over fish.

MENU: French bread. Sliced pears with farmer cheese. Bakery pecan pie.

SERVINGS: Makes 6 servings.

Salmon Teriyaki

■ Teriyaki sauce is a soy-based cooking sauce from Japan that also contains sake or sherry, sugar, and ginger. It's a handy condiment to keep in the pantry as an instant flavoring agent.

4 (abut 6-oz.) salmon steaks, rinsed and
  patted dry
2 tablespoons minced fresh parsley
½ cup teriyaki sauce
¼ teaspoon hot pepper sauce

Preheat broiler. Place salmon steaks in a shallow pan. Combine 1 tablespoon of the parsley with teriyaki sauce and hot pepper sauce. Pour over fish. Let sit for 3 minutes, turn, and let sit for 3 more minutes.

Remove fish from pan, place on a broiler pan that has been sprayed with nonstick cooking spray. Broil 4 inches from source of heat for 3 to 4 minutes on each side or until fish flakes easily with a fork, brushing with sauce mixture 2 or 3 times. Discard remaining sauce. Sprinkle remaining parsley over fish.

MENU: Fresh fruit salad. Broccoli florets and cauliflower with cucumber dip. Deli rice pudding.

SERVINGS: Makes 4 servings.

Salmon with Salsa

■ There are many varieties of salsa available on the international foods shelves—some of them quite good. Their labels tell whether they are mild or hot, and, in some cases, incendiary.

I always keep a jar of mild and a jar of hot salsa on hand. The mild is for guests who don't share my family's passion for hotter-than-heck food. The uses for salsa extend far beyond the standard dip: it's great on hamburgers, hot dogs, and steaks. I've added it to chili and chili soup with great results.

I have also used salsa as a sauce for salmon steaks with gratifying results. Adding a squeeze of lime juice to the salsa gives an additional spark.

Juice of 1 lime
1 cup salsa
4 (about 6-oz.) salmon steaks, rinsed and
  patted dry

Preheat broiler. In a small bowl, stir together lime juice and salsa. Set aside.

Place fish on a broiler pan rack that has been sprayed with nonstick cooking spray. Broil fish 5 inches from heat source for about 5 minutes. Turn fish and spoon half of the salsa on top of salmon steaks. Broil for 5 to 7 minutes more or until fish flakes easily when tested with a fork. Serve with remaining salsa.

MENU: Corn chips. Sliced peaches on leaf lettuce with a squeeze of orange juice. Chocolate brownies.

SERVINGS: Makes 4 servings.

Mustard & Dill-Basted Salmon

■ Some fish, including salmon, contains significant amounts of omega-3 fatty acids, a type of highly polyunsaturated fat. These fatty acids provide many protective benefits in relation to heart disease, including reducing serum cholesterol levels and favorably changing the ratio of certain types of cholesterol in the blood.

1 tablespoon olive oil
1 clove garlic, minced
1½ teaspoons Dijon mustard
⅛ teaspoon dried dill
4½ tablespoons fresh lemon juice
1½ pounds salmon steaks, rinsed and patted dry

Preheat broiler. Heat oil in a 1-quart saucepan over medium heat. Add garlic and sauté 1 minute. Stir in mustard, dill, and lemon juice; remove from heat.

Place salmon on a broiler pan rack that has been sprayed with nonstick cooking spray. Broil 4 inches from source of heat for 10 minutes, turning once and basting frequently with mustard mixture, or until fish turns from translucent to opaque.

MENU: Deli three-bean salad. Whole-wheat rolls. Bakery peanut butter cookies.

SERVINGS: Makes 4 servings.

Salmon with Cucumber Sauce

■ Because of the wide availability of farm-raised salmon, it's a fish that's often found at bargain prices.

4 (about 6-oz.) salmon steaks, rinsed and patted dry
4 tablespoons olive oil
1 tablespoon fresh lemon juice
½ teaspoon crushed dried tarragon leaves
1 teaspoon minced capers
⅛ teaspoon white pepper
1 cucumber, peeled, seeded, and coarsely chopped
½ cup plain yogurt

Preheat broiler. Place salmon on a broiler pan rack that has been sprayed with nonstick cooking spray; brush with 1 tablespoon of the olive oil. Broil about 6 inches from heat source for 2 minutes.

Turn salmon, brush with another tablespoon of the olive oil. Broil an additional 5 to 7 minutes or until fish flakes easily with a fork.

Meanwhile, add lemon juice, tarragon, capers, pepper, and cucumber to a food processor. Process about 30 seconds or until chunky, slowly adding remaining olive oil. Stir cucumber mixture into yogurt and serve with salmon.

MENU: Deli coleslaw. Kaiser rolls. Fresh fruit salad.

SERVINGS: Makes 4 servings.

Salmon with Chive Butter

■ Weather conditions, time, and the rabbit population make the herbs in my garden thrive or die during various springs and summers. If there is one constant in this ever-changing little patch of land, it is my chives. Year after year, I can count on them to fill the center of the garden with long, green stems, which I happily snip to add to eggs, salads, cream-cheese dips, sauces, and soups. By late summer, their lavender flowers appear—pleasing to the eye and delicious when tossed into a fresh green salad.

Chives are a member of the onion family, but far more delicate in taste and aroma. They don't stand up to long cooking, which makes them great for salmon with chive butter.

1 stick (½ cup) butter
1 tablespoon fresh lemon juice
2 teaspoons minced fresh chives
¼ teaspoon salt
1 clove garlic, minced
⅛ teaspoon white pepper
4 (about 6-oz.) salmon steaks, rinsed and
    patted dry

Preheat broiler. Melt butter in a 1-quart saucepan over low heat. Remove from heat. Stir in lemon juice, chives, salt, garlic, and pepper.

Place salmon on an ungreased broiler pan; brush with half of the butter mix. Broil about 6 inches from heat for 6 minutes. Turn salmon; brush with remaining butter mixture. Broil for 5 minutes more or until fish flakes easily when tested with a fork.

MENU: Canned potato sticks. Deli three-bean salad. Cantaloupe with a scoop of frozen yogurt.

SERVINGS: Makes 4 servings.

Salmon in Apricot Sauce

■ I have a problem with the apricot sauce for Salmon in Apricot Sauce: it contains dried apricots—a food I hate to stop eating. It takes enormous self-control for me not to eat the entire package. I rationalize by saying that dried apricots are rich in vitamin A and a valuable source of iron and calcium. Please don't ask about the calorie count.

Besides being eaten out of hand, dried apricots can be used in a lot of ways, but this sauce is my favorite. I think the sauce pairs especially well with chicken and salmon because the orange juice and apricot in combination provide such a dramatic tangy contrast.

4 (about 6-oz.) salmon steaks, rinsed and
    patted dry
⅓ cup firmly packed brown sugar
2 tablespoons cornstarch
1 teaspoon grated orange peel
2 cups orange juice
1 cup snipped dried apricots
1 tablespoon sliced scallion
1 teaspoon cider vinegar

Preheat broiler. Place fish on a broiler pan rack that has been sprayed with nonstick cooking spray. Broil fish 4 inches from source of heat for 5 minutes per side.

Meanwhile, combine brown sugar, cornstarch, and orange peel in a medium saucepan. Blend together juice and apricots and stir into dry mixture. Bring mixture to a boil and cook, stirring, until it thickens, about 5 minutes.

Stir in scallion and vinegar. Spoon sauce over fish and broil 2 minutes or until fish flakes when tested with a fork.

MENU: Sliced cucumbers. Deli prepared sesame or other noodles. Bakery chocolate cake.

SERVINGS: Makes 4 servings.

Broiled Salmon Steaks

■ Current studies on how Americans eat are indicating a renewed interest in broiling. This is probably because it is a healthful and quick way to cook. Think of it like grilling indoors, only the heat usually comes from above instead of below.

1 tablespoon fresh lemon juice
1½ teaspoons soy sauce
1 teaspoon Worcestershire sauce
1 garlic clove, minced
Dash of hot pepper sauce
4 (6-oz.) salmon steaks, rinsed and patted dry

Preheat broiler. Combine lemon juice, soy sauce, Worcestershire, garlic, and hot pepper sauce in a small bowl.

Brush salmon generously with lemon juice mixture. Place salmon steaks on a broiler rack that has been sprayed with nonstick cooking spray.

Broil 4 inches from source of heat for 5 minutes per side, turning once and basting frequently during cooking, or until fish flakes easily when tested with a fork.

MENU: Deli olive salad. Potato rolls. Bakery apple pie.

SERVINGS: Makes 4 servings.

Orange-Scented Salmon

■ The flamingo color of the fish and the orange of the oranges make this a Florida dish, no dispute.

2 cups water
¼ cup sliced scallions
1 orange, sliced into 8 wedges
Salt and freshly ground black pepper
4 (6-oz.) salmon steaks, rinsed and patted dry
Orange wedges for garnish

Combine water, scallions, orange wedges, salt, and pepper in a deep 12-inch frying pan. Bring to a boil. Reduce heat and simmer 5 minutes.

Add salmon. Cover and simmer 7 minutes or until salmon flakes easily when tested with a fork. Remove salmon with a slotted spoon to a serving platter. Garnish with orange wedges.

MENU: Deli artichoke salad. Kaiser rolls. Fresh strawberries with half-and-half and a sprinkling of sugar.

SERVINGS: Makes 4 servings.

Sesame Salmon

■ Fish is delicious, very quick, and easy to cook. And while reveling in its great taste, consider what a good thing you're doing for yourself: you're eating a food that is nutrient dense, meaning that it offers large quantities of protein and significant amounts of vitamins and minerals, without high levels of saturated fats and calories.

1 cup rice wine vinegar
¼ cup teriyaki sauce
1 teaspoon sesame oil
1 teaspoon olive oil
2 teaspoons sesame seeds
6 (6-oz.) salmon fillets, rinsed and patted dry

Preheat broiler. In a medium bowl, combine vinegar, teriyaki sauce, sesame oil, olive oil, and 1 teaspoon of the sesame seeds. Place salmon fillets in a shallow glass dish. Pour teriyaki mixture over salmon. Set aside for 5 minutes.

Arrange salmon fillets on a broiler pan rack that has been sprayed with nonstick cooking spray. Broil 4 inches from source of heat for 2 minutes on each side and brush both sides with marinade. Broil another 4 minutes or until salmon flakes when tested with a fork. Sprinkle top with remaining sesame seeds during last minute.

MENU: Shredded Napa (Chinese) cabbage tossed with shredded carrots and mustard vinaigrette. Buttered onion rolls. Lime sherbet with toasted coconut.

SERVINGS: Makes 6 servings.

Salmon on Leeks

■ Leeks look like scallions on steroids. Unlike scallions, they aren't great for munching. For one thing, the green tops taste like hemp. The garden-variety leek is onionlike but hot, slightly bitter, and complex. It is also very coarse and chewy.

As leeks cook, they develop a warm, oniony, and almost buttery flavor. That's the characteristic I'm looking for when I pair salmon and leeks. In this dish, the leeks are cooked until they are soft and can form a bed for the salmon fillets. Then steamed together, the salmon and leeks exchange wondrous flavors. The result is a slightly sweet and soft layered dish.

3 or 4 leeks
1 tablespoon butter
¾ cup dry white wine
4 (6-oz.) salmon fillets, rinsed and patted dry
4 tablespoons grated Gruyère cheese

Trim green top and root ends from leeks. Slit vertically into quarters almost to root end. Separate sections, wash under running cold water, and drain well.

Melt butter in a 10-inch sauté pan over medium heat. Add leeks and cook 2 to 3 minutes, stirring often, until leeks are wilted. Stir in wine. Arrange salmon on leeks. Reduce heat to low, cover, and cook for about 5 minutes.

Sprinkle 1 tablespoon of cheese over each salmon fillet, cover, and cook another 3 to 4 minutes or until salmon is opaque.

MENU: Brown-and-serve rolls. Italian salad mixture with Italian dressing. Raspberry sherbet.

SERVINGS: Makes 4 servings.

Lemon Teriyaki Salmon

■ I make this dish on the grill during the warm months when we cook out a lot. Grilling is broiling upside down, or is it that broiling is grilling upside down? Well, grilling out is more than grilling in if you count the wonderful aroma that charcoal or hardwood imparts. But the flavors of this dish are good enough to be enjoyed inside or out.

⅓ cup teriyaki sauce
½ teaspoon grated lemon zest
2 tablespoons fresh lemon juice
1 tablespoon fresh basil leaves, chopped, or
    1 teaspoon dried
4 (1-inch-thick) salmon steaks, rinsed and
    patted dry

Preheat broiler. Combine teriyaki sauce, lemon zest, lemon juice, and basil in a small bowl.

Place fish on a broiler pan rack that has been sprayed with nonstick cooking spray. Brush with teriyaki mixture.

Broil 4 to 5 inches from source of heat for 4 minutes. Turn. Brush with teriyaki mixture. Broil 4 minutes longer or until fish flakes easily when tested with a fork.

MENU: Romaine lettuce and cherry tomato halves with Caesar dressing. Toasted Kaiser rolls. Honeydew melon wedges.

SERVINGS: Makes 4 servings.

Salmon with Ginger Glaze

■ Oily fish were made for broiling; they require no fat or sauce and are delicious basted with a simple lemon, lime, or herb mixture.

Salmon, which qualifies as an oily fish, has a naturally sweet and succulent quality that stands up well under the intense, dry heat of broiling.

If the skin is still on the fillet you are cooking, place it skin side down, on the rack. If the fillets are less than 1 inch thick, they don't have to be turned. If they're thicker, it's a good idea to turn them to be sure they are thoroughly cooked.

3 (about 6-oz.) salmon fillets, rinsed and
    patted dry
2 tablespoons soy sauce
2 tablespoons cream sherry
½ teaspoon dried sage
1 teaspoon sugar
1 tablespoon minced fresh ginger
1 clove garlic, minced

Preheat broiler. Arrange salmon in a single layer in a glass dish. Combine soy, sherry, sage, and sugar in a small saucepan; cook, stirring, only until sugar dissolves. Stir in ginger and garlic and cook for 1 minute. Pour mixture over salmon, coating all sides. Set aside for 5 minutes.

Place salmon on a broiler pan rack that has been sprayed with nonstick cooking spray. Broil fish 4 inches from source of heat for 5 minutes. Turn, baste with marinade, broil for 3 minutes or until salmon flakes easily when pierced with a fork.

MENU: Deli new-potato salad. Lettuce wedges, pimientos, and Russian dressing. Bakery custard pie.

SERVINGS: Makes 3 servings.

Sardine Raclette

■ After sampling raclette, the dish, at a local Swiss restaurant, I decided that I had found the perfect fast and fabulous dinner. It seemed so simple—melted cheese with tiny boiled potatoes, pickled onions, and cornichons. Little did I know.

Raclette is both a cheese and a cheese dish. The cheese is made in Switzerland from cow's milk and is similar to Gruyère. I was sure that if I could find raclette, the cheese, at my supermarket, I could make raclette, the dish. I consulted a Swiss cookbook. Here's what it takes: "Light a good fire. Buy yourself a half wheel of raclette. Scrape off the rind, top and bottom, so that the cheese can melt more easily. When the fire has died to a mass of glowing embers, procure yourself a large stone and put it before the fire. Set the half cheese on top, its cut surface exposed to the heat. Nearby, have a supply of plates. As the cheese melts, scrape it off onto a plate and serve at once. Continue in this way until everyone is full."

Lacking a fireplace, glowing embers, a large stone, and a supermarket that stocks raclette, I came up with a substitute dish.

1 (15-oz.) can whole potatoes, drained
¼ cup butter
3 tablespoons fresh lemon juice
1 (1½-lb.) Gruyère cheese
2 (3.75-oz.) cans oil-packed sardines, drained
Gherkins
Chopped scallions

Halve potatoes; set aside. Heat butter and lemon juice in a 8-inch sauté pan. Pour over potatoes; keep warm.

Place cheese in shallow, ovenproof pan. Broil 5 inches from the heat source until melting begins (watch carefully). Remove from oven.

Surround the cheese with potatoes. Serve immediately with sardines, gherkins, and chopped scallions.

MENU: Spinach salad. Pretzels. Sliced apples.

SERVINGS: Makes 6 servings.

Scrod with Tarragon

■ Tarragon is a pungent herb with an anise-like flavor. It works beautifully with fish, shellfish, and poultry, but use a light touch. Too much, and the flavor will overwhelm.

1 pound scrod fillets, rinsed and patted dry
¼ teaspoon salt
1 tablespoon butter, melted
½ teaspoon minced fresh tarragon

Preheat broiler. Place fish on a broiler pan rack that has been sprayed with nonstick cooking spray; sprinkle with salt and drizzle with butter.

Broil fish 4 inches from the source of heat until fish flakes easily with a fork and is opaque in the center, 5 to 6 minutes. Sprinkle with tarragon. Broil 1 minute more.

MENU: French baguettes. Deli Waldorf salad. Bakery lemon meringue pie.

SERVINGS: Makes 4 servings.

Tomato & Cheese Fillets

■ Scrod are young cod and haddock that weigh less than 2½ pounds. The flavor is very delicate. Scrod cook beautifully in a microwave oven, and in no time at all.

1 tablespoon butter
1 pound scrod fillets, rinsed and patted dry
Salt and freshly ground black pepper
1 tablespoon finely chopped scallion
1 cup plum tomatoes, chopped
¼ cup shredded Gruyère cheese

Microwave butter, uncovered, in a microwave-safe dish on HIGH until melted, 30 to 40 seconds.

Place scrod in dish and turn to coat with butter. Sprinkle with salt and pepper; top with scallion, tomatoes, and cheese. Cover loosely and microwave on HIGH until fish flakes easily when tested with a fork, 2½ to 3 minutes.

MENU: Canned potato sticks. Green salad with cucumber dressing. Bakery cupcakes.

SERVINGS: Makes 4 servings.

Mustard Scrod

■ Dry mustard is very pungent. Its flavor starts to develop when it's mixed with a liquid. In this case, the liquid is the scrod's own juices. It's a potent combo, so be prepared.

2 tablespoons butter, softened
1½ teaspoons dry mustard
½ teaspoon lemon-pepper seasoning
1½ pounds (½-inch-thick) scrod fillets,
   rinsed and patted dry

Preheat broiler. Mix together butter, mustard, and lemon-pepper seasoning. Set aside.

Place fillets on a broiler pan rack that has been sprayed with nonstick cooking spray. Broil 4 inches from source of heat for 5 minutes. Turn fish and brush with butter-mustard mixture and broil about 5 minutes or until fish flakes with a fork.

MENU: Pumpernickel toast. Deli three-bean salad. Frozen strawberry yogurt.

SERVINGS: Makes 6 servings.

Red Snapper with Anchovies

■ My friendly neighborhood pizzeria never asks my name or gives me a number. The conversation every Friday night for twenty-five years has been the same: Pizzeria: "Bella's." Me: "I'd like to order a large combo with extra cheese and anchovies." Pizzeria: "It's you." Me: "Yes." Pizzeria: "Twenty minutes."

I try to call the same time every week because there is one pizza maker who takes great pains with the anchovies, adding them just before the pie comes out of the oven so that they are cooked through but not incinerated. I always know when he makes my pizza, and I always call back to tell him it was great. He always asks why I like those slimy, ugly things. I just do.

I like anchovies in Caesar salad. I like them out of the can. I like them broiled with Muenster cheese on a hero roll. I like them in Snapper with Anchovies, a dish so simple and quick it will please any 15-minute chef.

2 cups marinara sauce
6 anchovy fillets, chopped
Pinch of sugar
2 tablespoons chopped fresh flat-leaf parsley
4 (1-lb.) pan-ready whole red snappers,
   rinsed and patted dry
4 anchovy fillets

Preheat broiler. Heat sauce in a 1-quart saucepan over medium heat. Add chopped anchovies, sugar, and parsley. Bring to a boil. Reduce heat and simmer while fish cooks.

Meanwhile, make 2 shallow diagonal cuts on each side of fish. Place fish on a broiler pan rack that has been sprayed with nonstick cooking spray. Broil fish 4 inches from source of heat for 7 minutes per side or until fish is opaque when tested with a fork at thickest point. Place on a warm serving dish. Spoon ¼ cup of sauce over each fish. Garnish each fish with an anchovy fillet. Serve remaining sauce separately.

MENU: Garlic bread. Arugula with thin-sliced red onion dressed with oil and vinegar. Bakery pignoli (pine nut) cookies.

SERVINGS: Makes 4 servings.

Tomato Snapper

■ If you're not in the habit of using Italian plum or Roma tomatoes, give them a try. They are not as juicy as regular tomatoes, which makes them especially good for cooking because they don't lose as much moisture and retain more of their texture when they're heated.

3 tablespoons olive oil
1½ to 2 pounds red snapper fillets, rinsed and patted dry
¾ pound plum tomatoes, seeded and chopped
1 large scallion, chopped
1 tablespoon balsamic vinegar
1 tablespoon chopped fresh basil or ½ teaspoon dried

Heat 1 tablespoon of the oil in a 10-inch skillet over medium-high heat. Add fish and cook for 4 to 5 minutes on each side or until fish flakes easily when tested with a fork. Remove from skillet and keep warm on a serving plate.

Add the remaining 2 tablespoons of oil to skillet along with tomatoes and scallion. Cook over medium-high heat for 3 to 4 minutes or until tomatoes are softened. Add vinegar and cook for 1 minute. Stir in basil. Spoon tomato mixture over fish.

MENU: Whole-wheat Italian rolls. Deli three-bean salad. Frozen strawberry yogurt.

SERVINGS: Makes 4 servings.

Mediterranean Snapper

■ Basil, tomatoes, fennel, garlic, olive oil, olives, oregano, and red bell peppers are just a few of the wonderful ingredients used in simple Mediterranean cooking. All of them remind me of sunshine.

½ cup marinara sauce
2 tablespoons fresh lime juice
1 teaspoon dried oregano
1 to 2 cloves garlic, crushed
1 (1½-lb.) pan-ready whole red snapper, rinsed and patted dry

Preheat broiler. Mix sauce, lime juice, oregano, and garlic together in a 1-quart saucepan. Heat until hot over medium heat, stirring occasionally.

Meanwhile, place fish on a broiler pan rack that has been sprayed with nonstick cooking spray. Broil fish 4 inches from source of heat for 10 minutes, turning once and brushing 2 or 3 times with sauce.

Cut fish into serving-size pieces and serve with remaining sauce.

MENU: Hot Italian bread. Roasted red peppers, ripe olives, and slices of mozzarella cheese. Bakery chocolate cream pie.

SERVINGS: Makes 4 servings.

Poached Red Snapper

■ Poaching is a simple and delicious method for cooking fish. Just lay the fillets in a single layer in skillet with 1½ inches of water. Add sliced onion, a slice of lemon, salt, and pepper. You can embellish with white wine, bay leaf, or any herb, but for this dish, I kept things pretty simple and let lemon-pepper seasoning do the heavy work.

2 tablespoons butter
1½ pounds skinless red snapper fillets, rinsed and patted dry
1 small lemon, sliced
¼ teaspoon lemon-pepper seasoning
¼ cup minced onion
2 tablespoons minced parsley

Melt the butter in a 12-inch covered frying pan over medium heat. Arrange the snapper fillets one layer deep in pan. Place a lemon slice on each fillet. Sprinkle seasoning, onion, and parsley over the fillets. Add enough water to cover and bring to a boil. Reduce heat, cover, and simmer for 10 minutes or until fish flakes when tested with a fork.

Remove fish from pan with a slotted spoon and keep warm. Bring pan juices to a boil over high heat until reduced, 4 to 5 minutes. Serve fish with reduced pan juices.

MENU: Garlic toast. Salad bar greens with ranch dressing. Fresh fruit with strawberry yogurt.

SERVINGS: Makes 4 servings.

Red Snapper Fillets

■ I find the combined flavors of lime, cilantro, and chili to be among my favorites whether these three flavor boosters are on fish, chicken, or meat.

1½ pounds skinless red snapper fillets, rinsed and patted dry
½ medium lime
1 tablespoon chopped fresh cilantro
½ teaspoon chili powder
½ cup salsa

Arrange fish in an 8-inch-square microwave-safe dish. Squeeze lime juice over fish. Sprinkle with cilantro and chili powder.

Cover loosely and microwave on HIGH for 3 to 7 minutes, rotating dish a half turn after 3 minutes, or until fish flakes easily when tested with a fork. Let stand covered for 2 minutes before serving.

Serve with salsa.

MENU: Corn chips with bean dip. Tossed salad with ranch dressing. Blueberries over nonfat coffee yogurt.

SERVINGS: Makes 4 servings.

Garlic-Lemon Fillets

■ I usually make this with red snapper, because I'm fond of its taste and texture, but other fish, such as cod, flounder, sole, and grouper, can be substituted—especially if they're on sale and red snapper is not.

I cook the fish in a deep frying pan or a wok until it's crispy, and then drench it in garlic, lemon, and butter. I spoon some of the sauce over new-potato salad that I purchase at the deli to serve along with the fish. And to assuage my conscience for the butter, I use light mayonnaise in a Waldorf salad that I also usually serve. I have no excuse for the eclairs.

About 1 pound red snapper fillets, rinsed and
    patted dry
All-purpose flour
2 tablespoons vegetable oil
4 tablespoons butter
1 clove garlic, minced
¼ cup chopped fresh parsley
Juice of 1 lemon

Cut fish into 1½-inch pieces. Dredge pieces in flour, shaking off excess.

Heat oil and butter in a wok or a deep 10-inch skillet over medium-high heat. When butter begins to sizzle, add a few pieces of fish at a time. Cook quickly, turning until pieces are lightly browned on both sides. Remove and drain on paper towels.

Reduce heat to medium and add garlic to oil and butter. Stir-fry about 15 seconds. Add fish, parsley, and lemon juice and heat through.

MENU: Deli new-potato salad. Waldorf salad. Chocolate eclairs.

SERVINGS: Makes 4 servings.

Five-Spice Snapper

■ I'll never know everything there is to know about Chinese cooking. The subject is vast beyond my comprehending. But I do know a little, learned in small measures and with great appreciation for willing teachers.

One of the first lessons I learned was about a flavor I had enjoyed in many Chinese dishes but could not recognize. It was familiar, but I just couldn't place it. The flavor was five-spice powder—a pungent mixture of five ground spices usually consisting of equal parts of Sichuan peppercorns, star anise, cassia, fennel seeds, and cloves, but it's possible to come close to this mix with a homemade blend of equal parts of cinnamon, cloves, fennel seeds, star anise, and Sichuan peppercorns.

Five-spice powder was once hard to find in supermarkets, but I've noticed that many stores now stock it on the international foods shelves.

¼ cup vegetable juice, such as V-8
2 tablespoons fresh lime juice
2 tablespoons stir-fry sauce
1 tablespoon vegetable oil
2 teaspoons five-spice powder
1 pound red snapper fillets, rinsed and patted
    dry

Preheat broiler. Mix all ingredients except fish in a medium bowl.

Place fillets on a broiler pan rack that has been sprayed with nonstick cooking spray. Brush or spoon a little of the five-spice mixture over both sides of fish. Broil fish 4 inches from source of heat for 10 minutes, basting with sauce occasionally so the fish does not dry out or until fish flakes when tested with a fork. Do not turn fish.

MENU: Stir-fried rice. Steamed broccoli. Bakery almond cookies.

SERVINGS: Makes 4 servings.

Peppers with Sole

■ I know red peppers are more expensive than green, but they're also milder and sweeter. I wait until they're in good supply, in early fall, when the prices are the best, and then I buy them to make this dish.

4 (4-oz.) sole fillets, rinsed and patted dry
3 tablespoons tamari sauce
½ teaspoon grated fresh ginger
1 clove garlic, finely chopped
2 medium red bell peppers, cut into 1-inch pieces
½ pound mushrooms, cut in half

Arrange fillets in an 8-inch-square microwave-safe dish.

Mix together tamari sauce, ginger, and garlic in a small bowl; pour over fish. Top with peppers and mushrooms.

Cover with plastic wrap and fold back one corner to vent. Microwave on HIGH for 4 minutes and rotate dish ½ turn. Microwave 3 to 5 minutes or until fish flakes when tested with a fork.

MENU: Deli prepared sesame or other noodles with chopped cucumbers. Fresh spinach salad dressed with lemon vinaigrette. Bakery peanut butter cookies.

SERVINGS: Makes 4 servings.

Sole with Lemon Sauce

■ I always specify fresh fish in seafood recipes to save time. If I had to wait for fish to thaw, preparing dinner would take considerably longer. But I also prefer everything fresh. However, fish is one food that freezes very well. I've even had frozen fish that tasted better than fresh fish—probably because the fresh fish was not handled properly.

1 large lemon
2 tablespoons olive oil
1 small clove garlic, crushed through a press
½ teaspoon salt
8 (4-oz.) sole fillets, rinsed and patted dry
¼ cup dry fine bread crumbs
2 teaspoons vegetable oil plus additional for frying

Using a vegetable peeler, cut a strip of lemon zest about 2 inches by ½ inch; cut strip into very fine slivers.

Juice lemon. Whisk olive oil, 1 tablespoon of the lemon juice, garlic, and ½ teaspoon salt in a small bowl. Set aside.

Cut sole fillets diagonally into 2-inch strips. Sprinkle strips with 1 tablespoon of the lemon juice and lightly coat with bread crumbs.

Heat about ½ inch vegetable oil in 10-inch skillet over medium-high heat. Add as many pieces of fish as will fit into a single layer and fry, turning once, until strips are golden, about 3 minutes or until browned and cooked through.

Drain fish on paper towels. Fry remaining fish. Serve with reserved lemon-garlic sauce.

MENU: Carrot sticks, scallions, and cucumber wedges with ranch dressing dip. Kaiser rolls. Pineapple spears.

SERVINGS: Makes 4 servings.

Sole Vinaigrette

■ Vinegar goes in salad dressing, right? Right, but no need to stop there. Vinegar is great to cook with, too, but you need to take a little care.

Sole vinaigrette is the perfect illustration of how to cook with vinegar. The sole is steamed over water, vinegar, and lemon juice. When vinegar is heated, it loses some of its pungency; however, in this dish, the steam carries the milder vinegar flavor into the flesh of the fish.

The lesson: If you want to take some of the punch out of vinegar, warm it. If you want to take a vinegary hit, serve it cold.

Just before serving the sole, put about 3 tablespoons of your favorite vinaigrette dressing onto the serving plate for a nice jolt of tart flavor.

4 (4-oz.) sole fillets, rinsed and patted dry
Salt and freshly ground black pepper
2 tablespoons white wine vinegar
½ lemon, cut into quarters
Vinaigrette
Flat-leaf parsley

Season fish with salt and pepper.
Bring 2 to 3 inches of water to a boil in a pot with a steamer insert. Add the vinegar and the lemon half. Spray steamer insert with non-stick cooking spray. Place fish over the boiling water. Cover and steam for about 5 minutes.

While fish is cooking, place about 3 tablespoons of your favorite vinaigrette on each of 4 plates. Place 1 fillet on each plate. Top each fillet with a teaspoon of vinaigrette. Garnish with parsley.

MENU: Deli-style potato chips. Cucumber spears. Bakery chocolate chip cookies.

SERVINGS: Makes 4 servings.

Green Fish

■ I have a passion for greens, especially bitter ones. I love arugula, chard, spinach, and my favorite, watercress. It has small, crisp, dark green leaves with a pungent flavor that's a little less bitter than other bitter greens, yet it has a peppery bite. It is also more delicate than the rest. Whereas one might get a bunch of spinach, one gets a bouquet of watercress. I find that watercress imparts a very special flavor to a simple dish I call Green Fish.

You don't have to remove the leaves from the stems to make the dish. Just wash the watercress and shake it dry, then spread it around in a greased baking dish to form a thick bed for the fish.

1 bouquet watercress
4 sole fillets (about 1 pound), rinsed and
    patted dry
4 tomatoes, sliced ½ inch thick
1 tablespoon minced scallion
2 tablespoons olive oil
1 teaspoon instant flour (see Note, page 33)
1 teaspoon sugar

Make a thick bed of watercress, including stems, in the bottom of a greased shallow microwave-safe baking dish. Place fish on top. Cover with tomato slices. Sprinkle with scallion.

Mix oil with flour and sugar with a fork in a small bowl. Pour over fish. Cover with microwave-safe plastic wrap, turning back one corner. Microwave on HIGH 10 minutes or until fish flakes when tested with a fork.

MENU: Deli marinated mushrooms on Bibb lettuce leaves. Hot Italian bread. Bakery anisette cookies and lemon sherbet.

SERVINGS: Makes 4 servings.

Citrus Fish

■ When I was experimenting with seafood cookery I read a lot of cookbook recipes. When I gained confidence, I experimented with this lemony dish. It's proved to be a tasty and reliable quick dinner that I depend on quite often.

1 pound sole fillets, rinsed and patted dry
¼ cup tartar sauce, plus additional for
  serving
2 tablespoons fresh lemon juice
⅔ cup Italian-style seasoned dry bread
  crumbs
1 tablespoon canola oil

Cut fish into 4 serving-size pieces. Set aside. Combine tartar sauce and lemon juice in a shallow bowl. Dip fish pieces in mixture, then into crumbs.

Heat oil in a 10-inch frying pan over medium-high heat. Add fish and sauté 5 minutes per side or until fish flakes easily when tested with a fork. Serve with additional tartar sauce.

MENU: Pear-walnut salad. Carrot sticks. Deli rice pudding.

SERVINGS: Makes 4 servings.

Hearts & Sole

■ This recipe was created when I found an aging can of artichoke bottoms hiding behind a bag of sugar. It was either eat it up or throw it out. I ate it up.

4 tablespoons butter
1 (15-oz.) can whole potatoes, drained,
  diced
1 (13.75-oz.) can artichoke bottoms, drained
  and diced
¼ teaspoon salt
4 (4-oz.) sole fillets, rinsed and patted dry
⅓ cup flour mixed with ½ teaspoon salt and
  a dash of pepper
1 lemon, cut into 6 wedges

Melt 2 tablespoons of the butter in a 10-inch skillet over medium heat. Add potatoes, artichokes, and ¼ teaspoon salt. Cook, stirring occasionally, until golden, about 4 minutes.

Meanwhile, dredge fish in flour mixture, shaking off excess. Remove potatoes and artichoke hearts from the skillet with a slotted spoon. Keep warm on a serving platter.

Wipe out skillet with a paper towel. Melt remaining 2 tablespoons of butter over medium-high heat. Add fish and cook until golden, about 5 minutes on each side.

Arrange fish on platter with potatoes and artichokes. Squeeze a lemon wedge over fish. Use remaining wedges for garnish.

MENU: Kaiser rolls. Sliced tomato and romaine lettuce salad. Chocolate chip cookies.

SERVINGS: Makes 4 servings.

Broiled Lemon Sole

■ A fast way to make fresh bread crumbs is in the food processor using lightly toasted bread slices. Quick on/off pulses will do the trick.

1 stick (½ cup) butter, melted
¼ cup fresh lemon juice
2 cups fresh bread crumbs (4 slices of bread)
1 tablespoon chopped fresh parsley
½ teaspoon cayenne pepper
1 pound sole fillets, rinsed and patted dry

Preheat broiler. Combine butter and lemon juice in a small bowl. Combine bread crumbs, parsley, and ¼ cup of lemon-butter mixture in a medium bowl. Add cayenne to remaining lemon-butter mix.

Dip fish into cayenne–lemon-butter mixture. Place fish on a broiler pan rack that has been sprayed with nonstick cooking spray. Broil 4 inches from source of heat about 8 minutes or until fish flakes when tested with a fork. Top with seasoned bread crumbs. Broil until crumbs brown.

MENU: Zucchini slices with yogurt-mint dip. Toasted bran muffins. Bakery peach pie.

SERVINGS: Makes 4 servings.

Sole Amandine

■ Sole amandine takes its name from the slivered almonds that contribute so much to taste and texture.

1 to 1½ pounds sole fillets, rinsed and patted dry
Salt and freshly ground black pepper
Paprika
1 cup all-purpose flour
2 tablespoons butter
1 teaspoon vegetable oil
3 tablespoons slivered almonds
1 tablespoon chopped fresh parsley
Juice of 1 lemon

Season fish with salt, pepper, and paprika. Dredge fillets in flour to coat. Heat butter and oil in a 10-inch frying pan over high heat. Add fish and cook 2 to 3 minutes or until golden brown. Turn fillets and cook 2 to 3 minutes more or until golden brown. Transfer fish to a heated serving platter.

Add almonds, parsley, and lemon juice to pan; cook, stirring occasionally, 1 minute over high heat. Spoon over fish.

MENU: Tossed salad with favorite dressing. Poppy-seed rolls. Vanilla ice cream with chocolate chip cookies.

SERVINGS: Makes 4 servings.

Sole in Tomato Sauce

■ Here's another dish where bottled pasta sauce comes to the rescue. Only don't pour it over pasta, pour it over fish.

1 pound sole fillets, rinsed and patted dry
1¼ cups marinara sauce
¼ cup finely chopped celery
1 small onion, sliced
½ small unpeeled lemon, thinly sliced
   crosswise

Place fish in a microwave-safe dish.

Mix together marinara sauce and celery. Pour over fish. Top fish with onion and lemon slices.

Cover and microwave on HIGH 2 to 3 minutes or until fish flakes when tested with a fork.

MENU: Salad bar crudités with ranch dressing. Sesame bread sticks. Fig bars.

SERVINGS: Makes 4 servings.

Pineapple Swordfish

■ The sweet-sour taste of pineapple is a natural accompaniment to swordfish.

¼ cup chopped scallions
2 tablespoons fresh lemon juice
1 tablespoon sunflower oil
1 tablespoon honey
1 (1-inch) piece fresh ginger, peeled and
   chopped
1 (8-oz.) can crushed pineapple, undrained
4 swordfish steaks, rinsed and patted dry

Preheat broiler. Combine all ingredients except swordfish steaks in a 2-quart saucepan. Bring to a boil over medium heat, stirring occasionally. Reduce heat; simmer, uncovered, for 3 minutes. Remove from heat.

Meanwhile, place fish steaks on a broiler pan rack that has been sprayed with nonstick cooking spray. Broil 4 inches from source of heat, turning once, and occasionally brushing with pineapple mixture, until fish flakes easily, about 10 minutes. Serve with additional sauce.

MENU: Orange and onion salad with lemon vinaigrette. Green bean salad. Bakery carrot cake.

SERVINGS: Makes 4 servings.

Trout with Fennel

■ Small whole trout have a firm flesh that holds up well with quick cooking. I emphasize the word "quick" because that's how this luscious fish stays moist, by getting into and out of the pan quickly.

4 small pan-ready trout with heads and tails
2 small fennel bulbs, thickly sliced
¼ cup olive oil
¼ cup dry white wine
1 clove garlic, chopped
1 teaspoon crushed red pepper flakes
2 tablespoons chopped fresh flat-leaf parsley

Preheat broiler. Rinse trout inside and out. Pat dry with paper towels. Cut 3 small slashes through the skin of the fish on both sides, and place in a large, shallow dish. Add the fennel slices.

Mix together the oil, wine, garlic, pepper flakes, and parsley in a small bowl. Pour over fish and fennel. Set aside for 5 minutes, turning once.

Remove trout and fennel from marinade. Place on a broiler pan rack that has been sprayed with nonstick cooking spray. Broil 4 inches from source of heat for 4 to 5 minutes per side for the fish, 2 to 3 minutes per side for the fennel, or until fish flakes when tested with a fork.

MENU: Tomato and olive oil brushetta. Crisp green salad with creamy Italian dressing. Nectarines tossed with lemon juice and honey.

SERVINGS: Makes 4 servings.

Trout with Dill

■ "More dill? Everybody's buying dill. What's so great about this stuff?" asked my supermarket checker, who is of high-school age.

It was a mistake to ask me, because I am dill's No. 1 fan. I launched into a paean on its joys and uses that would have gone on long after my groceries were bagged had I not taken note of the expression on the hapless youngster's face. "Well, it's really good; try it," I concluded.

In a nutshell, dill is great in soups, potato salads, cream cheese, egg dishes, salmon (especially salmon), grilled meats, vegetables, and sauces.

I love it in this trout recipe. And while I am not an expert at cooking trout, I've had excellent results with this preparation.

6 to 8 small pan-ready trout with heads and
    tails, rinsed and patted dry
¼ cup olive oil
1 bunch fresh dill
4 scallions
Lemon-pepper seasoning

Preheat broiler. Score the trout twice on each side, and brush them with olive oil. Stuff the cavity of each fish with a small branch of dill and scallions. Season the skin with lemon-pepper seasoning.

Place trout on a broiler pan rack that has been sprayed with nonstick cooking spray. Broil about 4 inches from the source of heat 5 to 7 minutes on each side or until fish flakes when tested with a fork.

MENU: Deli macaroni salad tossed with chopped sun-dried tomatoes and minced flat-leaf parsley. Pineapple slices glazed with brown sugar.

SERVINGS: Makes 4 to 8 servings.

Trout with Caper Sauce

■ The odd thing about capers is that even though I didn't know what they were, I always had them on hand. This was not intentional. They were left over from some recipe that required a teaspoon or so.

Here's the lowdown on capers: They are the flower bud of a bush native to the Mediterranean and part of Asia. The buds are picked, sun-dried, and then pickled in vinegar brine. They range in size from the petite non-pareil variety from Southern France to those from Italy that can be as large as the tip of your little finger.

½ cup tarragon vinegar
½ cup chicken broth
1 small bay leaf
6 (6- to 9-inch) pan-ready trout, split down
  the back, rinsed, and patted dry
⅓ cup butter, melted
Juice of ½ lemon
⅓ cup capers, drained

Combine vinegar and broth in a 10-inch skillet over medium heat. Add bay leaf and fish and bring to a simmer. Simmer 10 to 12 minutes or until fish flakes when tested with a fork.

Meanwhile, combine butter, lemon juice, and drained capers in a small bowl.

With a slotted spoon, remove fish to a platter. Spoon butter-caper sauce over fish or serve alongside.

MENU: Italian flat bread topped with sun-dried tomatoes. Lettuce wedges with Russian dressing. Bakery cupcakes.

SERVINGS: Makes 6 servings.

Garden-Style Tuna Steak

■ Tuna is America's favorite fish. Most of it is consumed from cans, but fresh tuna steak, especially albacore tuna, is much better. It's usually in markets in late summer and early fall. Because it is sold as steaks, there's almost no waste.

4 (6- to 8-oz.) albacore tuna steaks, rinsed
  and patted dry
¼ cup olive oil
1 clove garlic, chopped
1 small shallot, chopped
1 tablespoon fresh lemon juice
¼ cup dry white wine
1 tablespoon chopped fresh flat-leaf parsley
1 large tomato, chopped
½ cup sliced mushrooms

Preheat broiler. Brush tuna steaks with a little olive oil and place on a broiler pan rack that has been sprayed with nonstick cooking spray.

Broil tuna 4 inches from source of heat 5 minutes. Turn and brush with more olive oil and broil 5 minutes or until just cooked through or to desired doneness.

Meanwhile, heat remaining oil in a 10-inch skillet over medium-high heat. Add garlic and shallot and sauté until vegetables start to soften, about 2 minutes. Reduce heat, stir in lemon juice, wine, parsley, tomato, and mushrooms. Simmer about 5 minutes or until tuna steaks are ready.

Place steaks on a serving platter. Top with sautéed vegetables.

MENU: Deli potato salad. Rye bread. Frozen fruit bars.

SERVINGS: Makes 4 servings.

Broiled Whitefish

■ There is whitefish the species, and there is white fish—the term used to refer to any fish with white flesh. This recipes calls for the species. It's an oily or fatty fish, which means it provides omega-3 fatty acids.

1¼ pounds whitefish fillets, rinsed and
   patted dry
¼ cup butter, melted
¼ cup fresh lemon juice
1 tablespoon minced shallots
1 tablespoon chopped fresh parsley
1 tablespoon sugar
2 teaspoons salt
Lemon wedges for garnish

Preheat broiler. Place fish on a foil-lined baking sheet or broiler pan. Combine butter, lemon juice, shallots, parsley, sugar, and salt in a small bowl. Generously brush fish with butter mixture.

Broil fish 4 inches from source of heat about 8 minutes or until fish flakes when tested with a fork, basting occasionally. Garnish with lemon wedges.

MENU: Deli Greek salad. Toasted pita bread. Pear slices and grapes.

SERVINGS: Makes 6 servings.

Shellfish

The one thing you have to be careful about when preparing shellfish for dinner is not to overcook. That's something we speedy cooks don't worry about, but with shellfish we should because fifteen minutes is way too long. That's music to my ears!

The nicest thing about shellfish cookery is that it includes some of the world's best-loved foods—shrimp scampi, crawfish boil, steamed mussels with white wine, clam sauce, oyster roast, crab cakes. Oh, yes, the list is very long.

Shellfish are marketed live, fresh, and frozen. The live category includes clams, oysters, mussels, crabs, and lobsters. The reason these are marketed live is because they have a very primitive tissue, which deteriorates quickly when they are killed. So for both safety and taste, they are best cooked soon after purchase.

Pasteurized crabmeat sold in refrigerated tins does differ a bit from the others. It retains its good taste even though canned.

Scallops are almost never sold live because they die quickly when removed from seawater. The edible part is the sweet white muscle that holds together the two fan-shaped hinged shells. There are two types usually found at markets: the smaller bay scallop and the larger sea scallop. The Florida calico scallop is the same size as the bay scallop, but it is a deep-sea scallop. However, it tends to be drier and less flavorful than the other two varieties.

Shrimp is probably the most popular shellfish in America. It is sold as frozen thawed shrimp, frozen, or canned. Frozen-thawed shrimp should be cooked as soon as possible after purchase.

A real boon to the 15-minute cook is shrimp that is deveined. Deveining can be accomplished very quickly, and a shrimp dish prepared in less than a quarter of an hour, but it's so much better not to have to do the chore at all. Deveining is optional with small shrimp, but with large shrimp, it's imperative. The black sand vein, as it is called, is really the shrimp's intestinal tract, and its contents can be gritty. The grittiness can really ruin a perfectly delectable dish.

Spanish Clams

■ During three visits to Spain and many visits to the fine Spanish restaurants in New Jersey, I've developed a taste for Spanish food. I especially like the way Spanish cooks use a little bit of ham to flavor salads, vegetables, and, in this case, shellfish.

2 dozen cherrystone clams
3 tablespoons olive oil
1 large onion, finely chopped
1 red bell pepper, finely chopped
¼ pound smoked ham, cut into thin strips
2 garlic cloves, finely chopped
2 tablespoons chopped fresh flat-leaf parsley
⅓ cup dry sherry

Scrub clams well under cold running water.

Heat oil in a 5-quart saucepan or Dutch oven over medium heat. Add onion, bell pepper, and ham. Cook, stirring occasionally, until vegetables are tender, about 3 minutes.

Stir in garlic and parsley. Add sherry and clams. Cover, increase heat to medium-high, and cook until clams open, about 5 minutes. Discard any clams that do not open. Serve in soup bowls with lots of the broth.

MENU: Crusty bread. White cheese slices. Orange slices drizzled with honey.

SERVINGS: Makes 4 servings.

Clams with Scallions & Parsley

■ The taste of scallions is more delicate than that of onion, although scallions are technically members of the onion family. They can be stored in the refrigerator, in a plastic bag, for about five days. They go into soups, stews, salads, and stir-fries. To use, slice off the root section and slip off the tough outer skin before chopping.

4 dozen cherrystone clams
¼ cup olive oil
2 tablespoons butter
¼ cup chopped scallions
¼ cup chopped fresh parsley
3 tablespoons chopped capers
1 cup dry white wine or 1 cup water

Scrub clams well under cold running water.

In a 3-quart saucepan, heat oil and butter over medium-high heat. Add scallions and cook, stirring frequently, 2 to 3 minutes.

Stir in parsley, capers, and wine. Bring to a simmer. Add the clams and cover. Cook for 5 minutes or just until clams open; transfer open clams to individual serving bowls and keep warm. Continue cooking the unopened clams a few minutes longer. Discard any clams that do not open. Divide pan juices among clam bowls and serve.

MENU: Hot crusty bread for dipping. Deli new-potato salad. Brownies.

SERVINGS: Makes 4 servings.

Clams Italiano

■ Littleneck, cherrystone, and quahog clams are the same; they are just at different stages of their lives. The littlenecks are the youngest. As they get older they get tougher, so for this dish, select the smallest littlenecks you can find. In Italian they would be called *vongole*.

2 dozen littleneck clams
¼ cup dry white wine
1 cup marinara sauce
2 tablespoons chopped fresh flat-leaf parsley
2 tablespoons chopped scallion

Scrub clams well under cold running water. Place in a microwave-safe dish with wine. Cover loosely. Microwave on HIGH 3 to 5 minutes or until shells open. Discard any unopened clams.

Meanwhile, combine marinara sauce, parsley, and scallion in a bowl. Spoon over clams. Cover loosely. Microwave on MEDIUM-HIGH for 2 minutes or until hot.

MENU: Garlic bread. Tossed green salad with oil-and-vinegar dressing. Chocolate-covered doughnuts.

SERVINGS: Makes 2 servings.

Chinese Hot Clams

■ If there were a competition for which of the world's cuisines had the hottest of hot and spicy foods, I think Chinese (or maybe Thai) would win. The hottest hot chili I ever ate was in a Chinese restaurant. I didn't mean to do it, but somehow one of those tiny incendiary devices found its way onto my fork. I literally stood up as the fiery oils took hold of my taste buds, my tongue, my throat. A normal person would have sworn off the asterisked dishes noted as hot and spicy on the menu forever. I recovered, and wanted more.

The hot chiles in Chinese cooking aren't meant for eating. They're for flavoring, and what wonderful flavor they impart.

I borrowed a bit from this philosophy in making my own version of a Chinese hot sauce to spike steamed clams. I use fresh jalapeños, because I can't find fresh hot Chinese chiles at my supermarket. For people who are not as hotheaded as I, tone the sauce down (just a bit) by using plain sesame oil instead of the hot sesame oil called for in my recipe.

2 tablespoons peanut oil
½ cup soy sauce
2 tablespoons chopped jalapeño chiles
1 tablespoon hot sesame oil
1 tablespoon white vinegar
2 dozen littleneck clams

Whisk together peanut oil, soy sauce, chiles, sesame oil, and white vinegar in a small bowl. Set aside.

Scrub clams well under cold running water. Bring about ½ inch of water to a boil in a large pot. Add clams. Cover and steam until clams open, shaking the pot once or twice during cooking, about 5 minutes. Discard any unopened clams.

With a slotted spoon, remove clams to 2 bowls. Spoon some sauce onto open clams. Serve with remaining sauce on the side.

MENU: Deli rice salad. Spinach salad with red-pepper strips. Lemon ice.

SERVINGS: Makes 2 servings.

Mussels Steamed in Wine

■ Summer in New Jersey is always steamy. My family loves clams, mussels, crabs, and lobsters—seafood I associate with summer and at its best when steamed.

Of these, mussels are probably the best buy, although they take a little more work. Here's a primer on the care and cooking of mussels:

· When you bring live mussels home from the seafood market, always store them in open containers that allow for draining; never store them in direct contact with melted ice or water.

· Before you steam the mussels, be sure they are alive. The shells should be tightly closed and resist opening or close when tapped. Clean and remove the beard (byssus threads) just before cooking.

· Did you ever wonder why some mussels have orange meat and others have white meat? I found the answer: The orange-tinted meats are mature females, while the ivory meats are males and immature females.

1 ½ pounds mussels in shells
1 tablespoon butter
1 small onion, finely chopped
1 clove garlic, minced
½ cup white wine

Clean and scrub mussels carefully, discarding any with broken or open shells.

Melt butter in a 12-inch frying pan over medium-high heat. Add onion and garlic and sauté until soft, but not browned, about 2 minutes. Add wine and bring to a boil. Add mussels, cover, and steam 5 to 6 minutes or just until mussels are open. Discard any unopened mussels.

Transfer mussels from pan with slotted spoon into serving bowls. Pour pan juices into smaller bowls for dipping.

MENU: Boston lettuce and thin-sliced red onion with honey-mustard vinaigrette. Crusty bread for dipping. Berries and bakery sponge cake with whipped cream.

SERVINGS: Makes 2 servings.

Steamed Mussels & Herbs

■ Mussels are not universally loved. Don't ask me why. They're delicious, low in fat, generally available, and they're inexpensive.

In this recipe, they're steamed in a liquid containing herbs, seasonings, and wine. The result is a broth that is heavenly.

When shopping for mussels, remember that smaller mussels are generally more tender than larger ones. Often mussels are sold with beards, which must be scrubbed off with a stiff brush under cold running water.

3 pounds mussels in shells
2 tablespoons unsalted butter
6 cloves garlic, finely chopped
1 cup chopped scallions
¼ cup chopped fresh parsley
½ teaspoon dried tarragon
¾ cup dry white wine
¼ cup water

Clean and scrub mussels carefully, discarding any with broken or open shells.

Melt butter in a 3-quart saucepan over medium heat. Add garlic, scallions, parsley, and tarragon. Cook until scallions are tender but not browned, 2 to 3 minutes.

Add wine and water. Simmer 5 minutes. Increase heat to high and bring to a boil. Add mussels, cover pan, and steam until mussels open, about 5 minutes. Discard any unopened mussels. Transfer mussels and juices to a warm platter.

MENU: Romaine lettuce with Caesar salad dressing. Crusty Italian bread. Bakery strawberry pie.

SERVINGS: Makes 4 servings.

Mussels with Mustard Sauce

■ Mussels are very inexpensive and very delicious, but not as popular as clams. I can't imagine why. Mussels are often on the menu at our house.

3 pounds mussels in shells
1 teaspoon olive oil
2 cloves garlic, chopped
½ cup dry red wine
¼ cup chopped fresh flat-leaf parsley
½ cup sour cream
3 tablespoons honey Dijon mustard

Clean and scrub mussels carefully, discarding any with broken or open shells. Heat oil in a 5-quart saucepan or Dutch oven over medium-high heat. Add garlic and stir-fry 1 minute. Add mussels, wine, and parsley. Cover; bring to a boil. Simmer for 5 to 7 minutes or until mussels open. Discard any mussels that do not open.

Meanwhile, combine sour cream and mustard in a small saucepan. Heat just until warm (do not boil).

Ladle mussels and juices into individual soup bowls. Serve with sauce on the side.

MENU: Italian bread. Romaine lettuce leaves with lemon vinaigrette. Chocolate pudding.

SERVINGS: Makes 4 servings.

Mussels Marinière

■ Steaming food has been a popular cooking method throughout the world for a long time. Foods cooked with steam retain their natural flavors and, best of all, cook quickly.

3 pounds mussels in shells
1 teaspoon olive oil
⅓ cup chopped scallions
1½ teaspoons instant flour (see Note, page 33)
½ cup dry white wine
Salt and freshly ground black pepper
1½ teaspoons chopped fresh flat-leaf parsley

Clean and scrub mussels carefully, discarding any with broken or open shells. Place mussels in a microwave-safe soufflé dish with ½ cup water. Cover and microwave on HIGH 4 minutes. Stir and microwave on HIGH 3 minutes or until shells open. Discard any unopened mussels. Divide mussels among 4 individual soup bowls and keep warm. Strain juices from the dish through a sieve to remove any grit. Reserve liquid.

Heat oil in a 1-quart saucepan over medium-high heat. Add scallions and cook for 2 minutes or until tender. Stir in flour until blended. Stir in reserved liquid and wine. Cook, stirring constantly, for 3 minutes or until thickened. Season with salt and pepper; stir in chopped parsley. Divide sauce over mussels.

MENU: Warm hard rolls. Green salad with mustard vinaigrette. Bakery blueberry cheesecake.

SERVINGS: Makes 4 servings.

Thyme Shrimp & Broccoli Stir-Fry

■ This is a lively and lovely stir-fry that comes to the table in minutes. Fresh lemon juice makes all the difference.

1 tablespoon cornstarch
1 teaspoon dried thyme
½ cup clam juice
3 tablespoons white wine
1 teaspoon fresh lemon juice
1 tablespoon canola oil
1 pound shrimp, peeled and deveined
2 cups broccoli florets
1 medium yellow bell pepper, cut into thin strips
1 medium shallot, chopped

Combine cornstarch, thyme, clam juice, wine, and lemon juice in a small bowl until smooth. Set aside.

Heat oil in a 12-inch skillet or wok over medium-high heat. Add shrimp and stir-fry for 4 minutes or until light pink. Remove from skillet with a slotted spoon.

Add broccoli and bell pepper to skillet and stir-fry for 4 minutes. Add shallot and cornstarch mixture and cook, stirring constantly, until thickened. Return shrimp to pan and stir-fry until heated through, about 1 minute.

MENU: Bean sprouts. Blueberry sorbet.

SERVINGS: Makes 4 servings.

Golden Shrimp

■ Garlic and shredded carrots give a new flavor to shrimp. I buy the carrots already shredded to save time.

1 tablespoon sunflower oil
3 large cloves garlic, finely chopped
1 pound medium shrimp, peeled and
    deveined
1 cup shredded carrots
2 tablespoons chopped fresh flat-leaf parsley

Heat oil in a wok or 12-inch skillet over medium-high heat. Add garlic; stir-fry 1 minute. Add shrimp; stir-fry 2 minutes. Add carrots and parsley; stir-fry 3 minutes or until shrimp is pink and carrots are crisp-tender.

MENU: French rolls. Sliced zucchini and mushrooms tossed with vinaigrette. Grapefruit segments tossed with coconut and honey.

SERVINGS: Makes 4 servings.

Garlic Shrimp

■ Here's a quick way to peel garlic: Place the flat side of a chef's knife on top of the clove and hit it with your fist. The smack will separate the skin from the clove.

2 tablespoons olive oil
4 medium cloves garlic, crushed
1 bay leaf
1½ pounds peeled medium shrimp, deveined
¼ cup chopped cappicola (Italian ham)
Hot pepper sauce (optional)

Heat oil in a 12-inch nonstick skillet over medium heat. Add garlic and bay leaf and sauté until garlic starts to turn golden, about 1 minute.

Add shrimp and ham and cook, tossing in pan, for 1 to 2 minutes. Continue cooking until shrimp turns pink, about 5 minutes. Add hot sauce to taste, if desired. Remove bay leaf and serve.

MENU: Onion focaccia bread. Red-leaf lettuce with fresh mozzarella cheese and sun-dried tomatoes. Bakery chocolate biscotti.

SERVINGS: Makes 4 servings.

Sherry Shrimp

■ At my supermarket they've started selling shrimp that have been deveined, but still in the shells. So all I have to do before I cook them is pop them out of the shells. You can also cook these shrimp in their shells, and serve them in the sauce. The sauce seeps under the shells to delicious effect. Everybody can shell their own at the table.

2 tablespoons canola oil
5 garlic cloves, crushed
1½ pounds medium shrimp, peeled and
    deveined
¼ cup fresh lemon juice
1 cup sherry
2 tablespoons flat-leaf parsley
2 tablespoons chopped chives

Heat oil in a 10-inch skillet over medium heat. Add garlic, shrimp, and lemon juice. Cook, stirring until shrimp turn pink, about 5 minutes.

Add sherry, parsley, and chives. Bring to a boil.

MENU: Swedish flat bread. Citrus salad. Vanilla fudge ice cream.

SERVINGS: Makes 4 servings.

Shrimp Scampi

■ *Scampi* means shrimp in Italian, so Shrimp Scampi is actually scampi scampi or shrimp shrimp. Shrimp scampi sounds better. It has earned a place in American cookery, being a popular dish at restaurants and when cooked at home.

¼ cup unsalted butter
¼ cup olive oil
1 tablespoon finely chopped garlic
½ cup dry white wine
2 tablespoons fresh lemon juice
2 tablespoons chopped fresh flat-leaf parsley
1 pound medium shrimp, peeled and
    deveined

Preheat broiler. Melt butter and oil in a 10-inch skillet over medium heat. Add the garlic and sauté 30 seconds. Stir in wine and lemon juice; cook for 1 minute. Remove from heat and stir in parsley.

Spread shrimp in a single layer on broiler pan rack that has been sprayed with nonstick cooking spray. Broil 4 inches from source of heat or just until pink, about 3 minutes. Ladle some lemon-wine sauce on a serving platter. Add shrimp. Serve with additional sauce on the side.

MENU: Soft bread sticks. Deli green bean and red onion salad. Chocolate ice cream.

SERVINGS: Makes 4 servings.

Tequila Shrimp

■ Tequila—the Mexican liquor that is the basis of the popular Margarita cocktail—adds a nutty, slightly sweet taste to shrimp.

2 tablespoons butter
1 tablespoon olive oil
2 large cloves garlic, minced
1 pound medium shrimp, peeled and deveined
2 tablespoons tequila
1 tablespoon fresh lime juice
¼ teaspoon crushed red pepper flakes

Heat butter and oil in a 10-inch skillet over medium heat. Add garlic and cook for 30 seconds. Add shrimp and cook, stirring occasionally, 2 minutes. Stir in tequila, lime juice, and pepper flakes. Cook 2 minutes or until most of liquid evaporates and shrimp are pink and glazed.

MENU: Warm tortillas with melted butter. Deli three-bean salad with fresh chopped cilantro. Blueberries with nondairy whipped topping.

SERVINGS: Makes 4 servings.

Curried Scampi

■ I'm always amazed at how a little of this or a little of that can completely change an old standard into something fresh and new.

I took some liberties with an old standby, shrimp scampi, which is cooked with lots of garlic and butter. I added a little curry—just a little, since curry is a powerful spice that can easily be overpowering. The result was a wonderful surprise that quickly makes a slightly exotic dinner.

2 tablespoons butter
1 teaspoon curry powder
¼ teaspoon garlic salt
8 jumbo shrimp, peeled and deveined

Preheat broiler. Melt butter in a 1-quart saucepan over medium heat. Stir in curry powder and garlic salt and cook 30 seconds.

Arrange shrimp on a broiler pan rack that has been sprayed with nonstick cooking spray. Brush the curry butter over the shrimp. Broil shrimp 4 inches from the source of heat for 3 to 4 minutes. Brush again with curry butter, turn, and broil 3 minutes or until shrimp turn pink. Serve in remaining butter.

MENU: Rice cakes topped with slices of chopped pimiento, cucumber, onion slices, and a dab of plain yogurt. Bakery coconut cream pie.

SERVINGS: Makes 2 servings.

Ginger Shrimp

■ There are always limes and ginger root in my refrigerator and heads of garlic in the garlic jar. I would not know how to cook without these flavorful staples. They can always be called upon to make the simplest dish sparkle with good taste.

In Ginger Shrimp, I add all three, and to great advantage. This simple dish is a breeze to prepare and good enough to serve to company. Simple side dishes are in order so as not to compromise the zingy taste of the shrimp.

⅓ cup corn oil
2 cloves garlic, 1 mashed, 1 minced
1 pound medium shrimp, peeled and
  deveined
1½ tablespoons minced peeled fresh ginger
¼ cup thinly sliced scallions
½ teaspoon salt
1 tablespoon fresh lime juice

Heat oil in a 12-inch skillet or wok over low heat. Add mashed garlic clove and gently stir so that garlic flavors the oil, 3 to 5 minutes. Remove garlic and increase heat to high.

Add shrimp; cook, turning once or twice until pink, 3 to 4 minutes. Remove shrimp with a slotted spoon and drain shrimp on paper towels. Pour off all but 1 tablespoon of oil. Add ginger, scallions, minced garlic, and salt. Cook over medium heat, about 1 minute. Return shrimp to pan. Toss to mix ingredients. Remove from heat, add lime juice, and toss again.

MENU: Deli marinated mushrooms on Bibb lettuce. Fresh peach slices topped with macaroon crumbs.

SERVINGS: Makes 4 servings.

Beer-Battered Shrimp

■ As with most shellfish, cooking time, which depends on the size of the shrimp and whether it's thawed or frozen, should be as short as possible to assure a tender result. This is especially true of beer-battered shrimp, a classic American preparation and my personal favorite.

To make this recipe, choose large or extra-large shrimp; smaller varieties get lost under the batter. Any kind of beer will do to mix into the batter, but I'm partial to dark Mexican beer. The batter and the shrimp should be very cold when placed in the hot oil. This gives the batter a very nice puffy texture.

Vegetable oil for frying
1 pound large shrimp, peeled and deveined
1 cup baking mix
3 to 4 tablespoons milk
½ cup dark beer
¼ teaspoon salt
1 egg

Heat 1½ inches of oil in 3-quart heavy saucepan over medium heat or in a deep-fryer set to 350F (175C).

Lightly coat shrimp with 3 to 4 tablespoons baking mix.

Whisk together remaining ingredients with the remaining baking mix until smooth. If the batter is thick, stir in additional beer, 1 tablespoon at a time, until it reaches the consistency of whipping cream.

Dip shrimp into batter, letting excess drip into bowl. Fry shrimp, in batches, about 2 minutes on each side or until golden. Drain and serve hot.

MENU: Deli carrot-raisin salad. Brown-rice cakes with deli marinated mushrooms. Pineapple chunks mixed with low-fat lemon yogurt.

SERVINGS: Makes 4 servings.

Shrimp with Rosemary

■ Even on sale, shrimp may not be as inexpensive as chicken at the regular price, but it is affordable. And like chicken, shrimp has a wonderful mild flavor that allows for variation. You could cook a shrimp dish every night and never run out of new ways to try.

This one turned out especially well. It's made in a flash and, other than the peeling and deveining, which get easier with practice, requires no chopping, slicing, or blending of other ingredients except the parsley, which is added at the last minute.

Chopping parsley has never posed much of a problem for me. I simply snip off the desired amount of leaves with kitchen scissors. The task is even easier if you cut the parsley into a measuring cup. No mess to clean up, either.

3 tablespoons butter
1½ pounds medium shrimp, peeled and
    deveined
1½ teaspoons dried rosemary
2 tablespoons Pickapeppa sauce (see Note,
    below)
1 teaspoon fresh lemon juice
2 tablespoons chopped fresh parsley

Heat 1 tablespoon of the butter in a 12-inch frying pan over medium-high heat. Add the shrimp and rosemary and stir-fry until the shrimp begin to be tinged with pink, about 3 minutes.

Add the Pickapeppa sauce and lemon juice. Sauté until shrimp are deep pink. Remove shrimp from pan with a slotted spoon and place in a serving dish. Add remaining butter and parsley and cook over medium-high heat until butter is melted. Pour sauce over shrimp.

MENU: Red-leaf lettuce with paper-thin slices of red onion, dressed with mustard vinaigrette. Bakery Portuguese bread. Bakery carrot cake.

SERVINGS: Makes 4 servings.

NOTE
Pickapeppa sauce is a fiery condiment from the Caribbean and is available at many supermarkets. However, any hot sauce will work in this recipe.

Down & Dirty Shrimp

■ I still have the cookbook given to me at my wedding shower in 1962. It's more a curiosity than a help. This is true for many cookbooks and recipes I collected over the years.

Food preparation and our tastes for many fatty, greasy, and complicated foods have changed. For the most part, I don't feel deprived. Anything that is too salty, too sweet, or too heavy no longer tastes good. Still, there are glaring exceptions. I don't eat these dishes every night, so I don't feel guilty when I indulge.

I offer here one of those exceptions from my recipe files that has been restricted to a once-a-year treat. It is still a pleasure—albeit a guilty pleasure—to eat.

2 pounds medium shrimp
2 sticks (1 cup) butter
¼ cup hot pepper sauce
½ teaspoon barbecue spice (see Note, following)
Juice of 1 lemon
Sea salt
2 loaves Italian bread

Rinse and pat-dry shrimp, leaving shells on.

Melt butter in a 12-inch skillet over low heat. Add sauce, spice, and lemon juice. Increase heat to medium-high. Add shrimp and cook just until shrimp turn pink, 3 to 4 minutes. Be careful not to overcook. Add salt to taste.

Serve shrimp in bowls with butter sauce. Slice or tear thick pieces of bread to serve on the side to mop up the drippings.

MENU: Mixed green salad with vinaigrette. Sliced strawberries and apricots.

SERVINGS: Makes 4 servings.

NOTE

To make your own barbecue spice, mix together ½ teaspoon each garlic salt and black pepper with 1 teaspoon each dried oregano and dried basil.

Shrimp Casserole

■ I tend not to make casseroles during my workweek because they take too long to cook. First you have to assemble the ingredients, then you have to bake them for about an hour.

My shrimp casserole takes out the last step—bake for an hour—but I usually serve it in a casserole dish because it tends to be juicy.

2 tablespoons olive oil
1 garlic clove, crushed
1 medium onion, finely chopped
1 small red bell pepper, chopped
¾ pound medium shrimp, peeled and deveined
6 cherry tomatoes, halved
½ cup white wine
½ cup sliced mushrooms

Heat olive oil in a 2-quart saucepan over medium heat. Add garlic and onion; sauté, stirring occasionally, until soft, about 2 minutes.

Add bell pepper; sauté 2 minutes. Stir in shrimp. Add tomatoes, wine, and mushrooms and bring to a boil. Simmer 6 to 8 minutes or until shrimp turn pink.

MENU: Fresh fruit salad. Toasted French bread. Ice cream bars.

SERVINGS: Makes 4 servings.

Shrimp Quesadilla

■ Among the world's easiest-to-prepare foods are quesadillas. They are a cross between a turnover and a grilled sandwich, with a filling usually made with some type of cheese. They can be a snack as well as the basis of a meal.

There are a lot of filling combinations, but I like shrimp and Monterey Jack cheese. It is very mild by itself, so I usually serve the filling with two sauces: a fiery hot salsa and a cool and luscious guacamole.

Bright, fresh flavor is the hallmark of Mexican cooking. But with a busy lifestyle, it isn't always practical to make fresh salsa, so I usually pump up commercially prepared jarred salsas by adding lime juice or chopped cilantro. Guacamole is also available in refrigerated supermarket cases. If you're lucky enough to find a marked-down-for-quick-sale soft avocado in the produce section, buy it instead, and then mash it with the back of a fork. Add a little chopped tomato, lemon juice, salt, and chopped onion—delicious!

2 tablespoons butter
8 large shrimp, peeled, deveined, and cut
    into thirds
½ cup dry white wine
¼ cup chopped scallions
4 (about 7-inch) flour tortillas
1 cup (4 ounces) shredded Monterey Jack
    cheese
About ¼ cup salsa, plus extra for serving
Guacamole, shredded lettuce, and ripe olives
    to serve

Preheat oven to 325F (165C). Melt butter in a 10-inch skillet over medium-high heat. Add shrimp and sauté until the shrimp start to turn pink, about 2 minutes. Add wine and scallions; cook until wine evaporates, about 2 minutes.

Place 2 tortillas on a baking sheet. Sprinkle cheese evenly over the tortillas. Drizzle with salsa. Arrange shrimp evenly on top of salsa. Top with remaining 2 tortillas.

Bake until cheese melts, 5 to 7 minutes. Cut into wedges. Serve with salsa, guacamole, shredded lettuce, and ripe olives on the side.

MENU: Deli roasted pepper and black-bean salad. Mango slices.

SERVINGS: Makes 2 or 3 servings.

Hot Shrimp

■ Sometimes the success of a recipe depends on one little ingredient. My Hot Shrimp contains one of these. You can make it without the teaspoon of orange zest and you get a decent shrimp dish, even a good shrimp dish. But with the orange zest, it's a great shrimp dish.

"What is zest?" more than one person has asked me. Its the perfumey outermost skin of citrus fruits—usually lemon, lime, or orange—that has been grated or removed with a culinary tool called a zester. Zest adds flavor and piquancy, gusto, pleasure, punch, oomph . . . Well, I could go on.

Orange and lemon zest can usually be found, in dried form, in the spice section of supermarkets, but it's easy enough to make. Just grate an orange or a lemon on a fine grater. Be sure not to grate down to the pith or white inner skin, which tends to be bitter.

1 tablespoon olive oil
2 cloves garlic, crushed
1 teaspoon grated orange zest
1 teaspoon crushed red pepper flakes
½ teaspoon dried oregano
1 pound (about 24) large shrimp, peeled and deveined

Combine olive oil, garlic, zest, pepper flakes, and oregano in a shallow bowl or pie plate. Add the shrimp and toss to mix.

Place a 10-inch skillet over high heat. Add the shrimp, a few at a time (to prevent the pan from cooling down and steaming the shrimp). Turn the shrimp and cook until browned and crusty outside and opaque at the center, 3 to 4 minutes.

MENU: Tossed green salad with prepared dressing. Crusty bread. Lemon ice.

SERVINGS: Makes 4 servings.

Shrimp Egg Scramble

■ A few Christmases ago, my granddaughter and I shared breakfast with Santa courtesy of our town's Kiwanis Club. The menu was simple—juice, bacon, pancakes, and scrambled eggs.

Maybe it was because I hadn't had scrambled eggs in a very long time, or maybe it was because Santa's helpers cooked them a special way, but these scrambled eggs tasted great. So, inspired by the soft fluffy texture and mild taste of the eggs, I made them at home with a few sophisticated touches.

Here are some secrets to making great scrambled eggs: For lighter scrambled eggs, add a teaspoon of water per egg. For fluffier eggs, add ¼ teaspoon of cornstarch per egg. And for creamier eggs, add 1 tablespoon of sour cream for every 2 eggs.

2 tablespoons olive oil
2 tablespoons butter
½ cup chopped scallions
½ pound small shrimp, shelled and deveined
8 eggs
2½ tablespoons water
Salt and freshly ground black pepper

Heat oil and butter in a 10-inch skillet over medium-high heat. Add scallions and shrimp and stir-fry until shrimp are just pink.

In a large bowl, beat eggs and water with a fork. Lightly season with salt and pepper to taste. Pour eggs into skillet and cook, stirring constantly, until eggs are set.

MENU: Deli pasta salad. Garlic bread. Fresh-cut orange quarters.

SERVINGS: Makes 4 servings.

Lettuce Stir-Fry

■ A recent supermarket "buy-one, get-one-free" offer applied to heads of iceberg lettuce. Never one to pass up something for nothing, I took two. One head was eaten as usual, but the other stared at me from the crisper. Could we eat it before it turned to rust?

I tried giving the extra head away, but every one of my kith and kin had also taken advantage of the deal. They, too, were wondering what to do with the excess. "Can you freeze it?" my sister asked. NO!!!

I came up with a lettuce stir-fry. Lettuce contains a lot of water, and prolonged cooking will reduce it to mush. Cook it very quickly, no more than 5 minutes, so that it just wilts a bit.

2 tablespoons peanut oil
¾ cup chopped green or red bell pepper, or a mixture
¼ cup chopped onion
4 cups (1 small head) shredded iceberg lettuce
1 teaspoon fresh lemon juice
½ teaspoon dried basil
¼ teaspoon salt
⅛ teaspoon freshly ground pepper
½ pound cooked peeled shrimp

In a wok or 12-inch skillet, heat oil over medium heat. Add bell peppers and onion. Stir-fry until tender, about 4 minutes. Stir in lettuce, lemon juice, basil, salt, and pepper. Stir-fry 3 minutes. Add shrimp and stir-fry 1 to 2 minutes or until heated through.

MENU: Sesame rice cakes. Fresh orange slices and shredded coconut.

SERVINGS: Makes 4 servings.

Tarragon Crab

■ This dish requires no cooking skill whatsoever, and it's delicious.

1 pound lump crabmeat, picked over to remove any cartilage
½ cup melted butter
2 tablespoons tarragon vinegar

Preheat broiler. Place crabmeat in a shallow casserole dish.

Combine butter and vinegar. Pour over crabmeat. Toss well to combine. Broil 5 inches from source of heat for 10 minutes or until lightly browned.

MENU: Toasted pita triangles. Spinach salad with sliced strawberries and ranch dressing. Bakery lemon meringue pie.

SERVINGS: Makes 4 servings.

Crab Imperial

■ I've been using my microwave oven to cook fish and shellfish for years, but I want to caution anyone who is not experienced that microwave ovens can vary in power. Experiment a bit to find the right cooking time for a particular recipe. It's better to use less time initially; you can always cook more if needed.

½ cup mayonnaise
1 egg, beaten
1 tablespoon chopped pimiento
1 scallion, chopped
1½ teaspoons Worcestershire sauce
1 teaspoon fresh lemon juice
1 teaspoon dry mustard
Hot pepper sauce
Salt and freshly ground black pepper
1 pound crabmeat, picked over to remove
    any cartilage

Combine mayonnaise, egg, pimiento, scallion, Worcestershire sauce, lemon juice, mustard, hot pepper sauce, salt, and pepper in a medium bowl. Gently stir in crabmeat. Spoon into 4 individual microwave-safe ramekins.

Microwave, uncovered, on HIGH 7 to 9 minutes or until thoroughly heated.

MENU: Vinegar-flavored potato chips. Red-tipped leaf lettuce with sun-dried tomato vinaigrette. Bakery crumb buns.

SERVINGS: Makes 4 servings.

VARIATION
Surimi, imitation crabmeat, can be substituted.

Crab Salad with Mushrooms

■ I lead a very busy life. That's not a complaint but an explanation of why I cook and clean on a schedule that suits me. For instance, family and friends may telephone at 9 P.M. and be surprised that I'm cooking dinner. They'll drop by on Sunday afternoon and I'm scrubbing the floor. I do laundry as late as midnight.

I'm sure they think I'm frantic, but the truth is I've planned it. I think about time all the time. For instance, I measure things like flour and coffee over the sink, so I can rinse them away instead of risking spilling them on the floor or counter (major cleanup).

I mention this because this quick recipe for Crab Salad with Mushrooms calls for ¼ cup of oil and vinegar dressing. Why take a chance? Shake it over the sink and rinse away any mess.

Romaine lettuce
¼ pound small mushrooms
1 (6-oz.) package frozen snow crab, thawed
¼ cup oil-and-vinegar dressing
1 ripe avocado
3 hard-cooked eggs
Russian dressing

Arrange lettuce on a platter. Wash and trim mushrooms. Slice lengthwise into thin slices. Toss crabmeat with mushrooms and oil-and-vinegar dressing. Mound crab mixture in center of a platter. Peel and pit avocado. Slice avocado and arrange around crab mixture.

Peel and quarter hard-cooked eggs. Arrange between avocado slices. Serve Russian dressing on the side.

MENU: Sliced tomato and cucumbers with dill. Buttered oatmeal toast points. Lemon ice.

SERVINGS: Makes 4 servings.

Scallops with Lemon Mustard

■ The first step in selecting scallops is to buy them from a reliable fishmonger. Examine the scallops for a creamy white or light pinkish color and a mild, sweet odor. Make sure prewrapped packages of scallops are practically free of liquid. They are best used the day of purchase but can be held for two days.

I keep a variety of mustards on hand: standard, ballpark, grainy, honey, Dijon. Each adds a different touch.

1 pound bay scallops
1 cup white wine
1 tablespoon grated lemon peel
4 teaspoons Dijon mustard
4 tablespoons butter
1 tablespoon chopped chives

Rinse scallops with cold water, drain, and pat dry with paper towels. Bring wine and lemon peel to a simmer in a 12-inch skillet over medium heat. Add scallops and cook for 2 minutes. Remove from pan; keep warm.

Increase heat and bring wine and lemon peel to a boil. Cook for 5 minutes. Whisk in mustard and butter 1 tablespoon at a time until it is all incorporated. Return scallops to the pan. Sprinkle with chives.

MENU: Deli olive salad. French bread. Banana slices sprinkled with brown sugar.

SERVINGS: Makes 4 servings.

Sichuan Scallops

■ The spelling of Sichuan varies from place to place; you may see it as Szechuan, Sichuan, Szechwan. It means the same—the dish is from a region in China where hot and spicy is appreciated.

1 pound bay scallops
2 tablespoons corn oil
1 tablespoon minced garlic
1 tablespoon minced fresh ginger root
2 tablespoons soy sauce
3 scallions, cut into ½-inch slices
2 teaspoons Chinese chili paste
2 teaspoons cornstarch dissolved in 3 tablespoons cold water

Rinse scallops with cold water, drain, and pat dry with paper towels.

In a large skillet or wok, heat the oil over high heat. Add garlic and ginger root and cook, stirring constantly, for 30 seconds.

Add the scallops, soy sauce, and scallions, and cook, stirring, for 2 to 3 minutes or until the scallops become opaque.

Stir in chili paste. Stir cornstarch and water mixture into the scallops. Cook, stirring, until liquid is thickened, about 1 minute.

MENU: Deli marinated vegetable salad. Rice cakes. Vanilla ice cream.

SERVINGS: Makes 4 servings.

Cilantro Scallops

■ Unlike clams and oysters, scallops are not sold in their shells, which is a shame because their shells are very pretty. The reason for this is that the scallop is so delicate that it dies soon after being removed from the ocean.

¾ pound bay scallops
Red-tipped lettuce leaves
⅓ cup oil-and-vinegar dressing
3 tablespoons minced fresh cilantro
1 clove garlic, finely chopped

Rinse scallops with cold water, drain, and pat dry with paper towels. Bring ⅓ cup water to a boil in a 10-inch skillet. Reduce heat. Place scallops in a single layer in skillet. Simmer, uncovered, until scallops can be pierced easily with fork, about 3 minutes. Drain and place in a bowl.

Meanwhile, line two plates with lettuce leaves. Set aside.

Mix together dressing, cilantro, and garlic; pour over scallops. Stir well. Spoon scallops and dressing over lettuce leaves.

MENU: Deli rice salad. Deli citrus salad. Bakery brownies.

SERVINGS: Makes 2 or 3 servings.

Ginger Scallops

■ Fresh ginger is an essential item in almost all Asian cooking. It gives a refreshing, clean flavor to a wide variety of dishes.

1 pound bay scallops
¼ cup soy sauce
2 tablespoons finely chopped fresh ginger
¼ cup fresh lemon juice
2 tablespoons vegetable oil
1 tablespoon honey

Preheat broiler. Rinse scallops with cold water, drain, and pat dry with paper towels. Arrange scallops in a single layer in an 8-inch-square dish. Heat soy sauce to boiling in a small saucepan. Add ginger; reduce heat. Simmer, uncovered, for 5 minutes. Stir in remaining ingredients.

Pour sauce over scallops. Let stand for 5 minutes. Remove scallops from marinade. Arrange in a single layer on a broiler pan rack that has been sprayed with nonstick cooking oil. Broil 3 to 4 inches from source of heat for about 5 minutes or until scallops are opaque.

MENU: Deli prepared sesame or other cooked noodles. Cucumber sticks and scallions with duck sauce for dipping. Vanilla ice cream.

SERVINGS: Makes 4 servings.

Scallops Provençal

■ Provençal refers to the region of Southern France where wonderful Mediterranean foods are enjoyed—tomatoes, garlic, eggplant, and herbs. Delicious!

1½ pounds bay scallops
½ cup all-purpose flour
2 tablespoons olive oil
2 tablespoons butter
1 clove garlic, finely minced
2 tablespoons fresh lemon juice
½ cup chopped fresh flat-leaf parsley
Salt and freshly ground black pepper

Rinse scallops with cold water, drain, and pat dry with paper towels. Roll scallops in flour. Heat oil and butter in a 10-inch skillet over medium heat. Add garlic and scallops and stir-fry until scallops are opaque, about 3 minutes. Stir in lemon juice and parsley. Season with salt and pepper.

MENU: Deli marinated vegetable salad. Sliced cucumbers with cucumber dressing. Frozen strawberry yogurt with fresh sliced strawberries.

SERVINGS: Makes 6 servings.

Broiled Scallops

■ A friend who avoids cooking as much as possible called me at dinnertime recently, perplexed about what to do with a pound of scallops her husband had brought home.

"Do you boil, broil, fry, or bake these things?" she asked. "And is it too late to start cooking them tonight?" The last question was the most important one to answer. They can and should be cooked in a matter of minutes.

Fresh scallops are wonderfully succulent and delicious, but their tenderness has to be protected by quick-cooking methods. No matter which method you pick—broil, fry, or stir-fry—you can't go wrong.

1 pound bay scallops
1 clove garlic, minced
¼ cup butter
1 tablespoon fresh lemon juice
Salt and freshly ground black pepper
Paprika

Preheat broiler. Rinse scallops with cold water, drain, and pat dry with paper towels. Place scallops in a single layer in a shallow baking dish.

Cook garlic in butter over very low heat for 2 to 3 minutes. Add lemon juice, salt, and pepper. Pour butter mixture over scallops. Stir to coat.

Broil about 4 inches from source of heat for 2 minutes, then stir. Broil 2 minutes more or until scallops are opaque. Sprinkle with paprika.

MENU: Deli macaroni salad. Whole-wheat rolls. Toasted pound cake topped with frozen yogurt and fresh cherries.

SERVINGS: Makes 4 servings.

Scallops with Lime Sauce

■ I keep a supply of instant rice and noodle preparations in the cupboard, not only because they can make a handy ingredient in a quick-cooking dish, but also because my husband and children can make them on nights I'm not there to cook dinner.

1 pound bay scallops
1⅔ cups water
2 tablespoons butter
1 (4.5-oz.) package instant rice with herb butter sauce mix
2 tablespoons fresh lime juice
1 red bell pepper, cut into thin strips
Dash of freshly ground black pepper
4 scallions, sliced

Rinse scallops with cold water, drain, and pat dry with paper towels. Slice scallops.

Combine water, butter, rice and sauce mix, lime juice, bell pepper, and black pepper in a medium saucepan. Bring to a boil over medium heat. Reduce heat to low, cover, and simmer for 5 minutes, stirring occasionally.

Stir in scallions and scallops. Cook 5 minutes or until rice is tender and scallops are opaque.

MENU: Whole-wheat toast. Deli olive salad. Bakery coconut cookies.

SERVINGS: Makes 4 servings.

Scallops Amandine

■ Here's an amazing fact: An almond is not a nut; it's an edible fruit kernel. Somehow, the advertising jingle wouldn't sound right if the lyrics were: "Sometimes you feel like an edible fruit kernel/sometimes you don't."

Almond trees are related to peach trees, which explains the resemblance between the kernel inside a peach pit and an almond.

I use slivered almonds with scallops for a fast, easy kind of special entree. The almonds provide just the right texture, appearance, and flavor to pair with the mild silkiness of the scallops.

2 pounds calico or bay scallops
½ cup all-purpose flour
½ cup butter
½ cup slivered almonds
2 tablespoons chopped fresh parsley

Rinse scallops with cold water, drain, and pat dry with paper towels. Roll scallops in flour.

Melt butter in a medium skillet over medium-high heat. Add almonds and cook until lightly browned on one side, about 1 minute. Remove from pan with a slotted spoon. Drain almonds on paper towels. Set aside.

Add scallops to skillet and cook, turning carefully, so that all sides of scallops turn a light golden brown, about 3 minutes. Return almonds to the skillet. Sprinkle with parsley and turn scallops carefully to combine. Serve immediately.

MENU: Orange and red-onion salad with balsamic vinaigrette. Whole-wheat pitas. Bakery sugar cookies.

SERVINGS: Makes 6 to 8 servings.

Parsley Scallops

■ Parsley has come into its own, and flat-leaf parsley in particular is in the news. Marketing reports show that it outsells curly-leaf parsley. Both types are a rich source of vitamins and minerals. But the flat-leaf parsley, with its dark green foliage, is best for cooking as it is more flavorful and stands up better to heat.

I find both are especially good to add to sauces during the last minutes of cooking. They retain much of their texture and impart a bright, fresh flavor and add a vivid touch of green. Unlike other herbs, parsley keeps well under refrigeration.

This simple parsley dish cooks in no time, making it perfect for hot, steamy days. I serve it as a salad on a bed of butter lettuce leaves.

¾ pound bay scallops
½ cup water
⅓ cup oil-and-vinegar salad dressing
¼ cup chopped fresh parsley
1 clove garlic, minced
Butter lettuce leaves

Rinse scallops with cold water and drain. Bring water to a boil in a 10-inch skillet over high heat. Add scallops. Reduce heat to low, cover, and simmer until scallops are opaque, about 3 minutes. Drain scallops and place in a bowl.

Mix salad dressing, parsley, and garlic in a small bowl. Pour over hot scallops. Serve on a bed of lettuce leaves.

MENU: Toasted multigrain bread. Carrot, cucumber, and celery spears. Strawberry shortcake.

SERVINGS: Makes 2 or 3 servings.

Scallops & Peppers

■ Produce departments have become a bell pepper lover's heaven. The green pepper has lots of colorful cousins: red, black, orange, chocolate, and yellow.

I love the way they look, mixed and matched. No matter how mundane the dish, suddenly there's drama courtesy of a rainbow of peppers. I haven't mentioned the taste, which is great too.

Scallops & Peppers calls for three kinds of peppers. Take your pick, but I think green and red have to be in there.

¾ pounds bay scallops
All-purpose flour
1 *each* green, red, and yellow bell peppers
1 tablespoon olive oil
1 tablespoon butter
1 teaspoon crushed pepper flakes

Rinse scallops with cold water, drain, and pat dry with paper towels. Roll scallops in flour; set aside. Cut bell peppers into 1-inch squares.

Heat oil and butter in a 10-inch frying pan over medium-high heat. Add scallops, bell peppers, and pepper flakes. Cook, turning often, for 3 to 4 minutes, until scallops are opaque and firm.

MENU: Garlic bread. Deli Caesar salad. Bakery coconut layer cake.

SERVINGS: Makes 2 or 3 servings.

Scallops Dijon

■ Here's a little mustard history: The Romans introduced mustard seeds to France, and the French began mixing them into a paste using unfermented grape juice. Ever since, France has been one of the world's major producers of mustard, and the capital of the mustard world is Dijon. In 1634, the town was granted the exclusive right to make mustard. Today, Dijon accounts for more than half the world's mustard production. Its mustard carries an *appellation controlée;* only mustard made to specific standards can carry the name "Dijon."

From this global perspective, it is easier to understand why my humble little seafood dish, Scallops Dijon, tastes so good.

½ pound bay scallops
2 tablespoons butter
1 tablespoon fresh lemon juice
1 teaspoon Dijon mustard
2 teaspoons chopped fresh parsley
3 tablespoons bread crumbs

Rinse scallops with cold water, drain, and pat dry with paper towels. Melt butter in a medium saucepan over medium heat; stir in lemon juice and mustard until smooth. Add scallops and cook until scallops are opaque, about 3 minutes.

Remove scallops to a serving dish or individual plates. Add parsley and bread crumbs to the pan and cook, stirring, until bread crumbs are golden. Spoon over scallops.

MENU: Salad of bitter greens and toasted walnuts. Toasted English muffins. Pound cake topped with canned apple pie filling.

SERVINGS: Makes 2 servings.

Chicken

Because I write the 15-Minute Chef column, I am constantly trying new dishes. When they're perfected, I move on to developing other recipes. Essentially this means that I almost never make exactly the same dish twice (Christmas is the one exception).

There was one night when I cooked a new fifteen-minute recipe that turned out so great that I just beamed. "This is wonderful," my husband said after the first bite. "This is terrific!" he said, after the next. Then he put his fork down, dabbed at his lips with his napkin, looked me in the eye and said: "I'm never going to have this again, am I?" "No," I replied.

This particular dish was a chicken dish, and chicken is his favorite meal. "You could serve chicken every night, and I'd never complain," he tells me whenever I place a chicken dish before him. The beauty of chicken is that it never has to be the same. Chicken's tender, mild taste pairs beautifully with everything from tomato sauce to pears.

For the chef in a hurry, there are many choices of cuts from boneless, skinless chicken breast to rotisserie-roasted chicken. There are ground chicken and chicken wings; breaded chicken; oven-ready chicken; cooked and sliced chicken; deli chicken.

DONENESS TESTS FOR CHICKEN

An instant-read or oven thermometer is usually used to test whole or quartered chickens for doneness. For thinner cuts of chicken, there are two easy tests that can be used. The chicken is done when the juices run clear when the meat is pierced with a fork or knife or when the center of the piece of chicken is no longer pink.

MARINADE FOOD SAFETY

Any remaining marinade or sauce that is used for basting or marinating chicken must be brought to a full, rolling boil before serving as a sauce with the cooked chicken.

Any-Day Chicken

■ I always have the basic ingredients on hand—Worcestershire sauce and lemon. I usually combine them to make a quick chicken dish, but the lemon-and-Worcestershire-sauce combination works well with minute steaks, pork chops, or turkey tenderloins as well. Take your pick.

2 tablespoons butter
4 boneless, skinless chicken breast halves, rinsed
1½ tablespoons fresh lemon juice
1½ tablespoons Worcestershire sauce
½ teaspoon salt
1 teaspoon chopped fresh chives
Lemon wedges

Melt butter in a 10-inch skillet over medium heat. Add chicken and cook, turning once, until golden brown on both sides, about 4 minutes per side. Reduce heat and cook about 5 minutes. Transfer to a platter. Keep warm.

Add lemon juice, Worcestershire sauce, and salt to skillet and cook, stirring, to bring up the brown bits, about 1 minute. Stir in chives; heat through, about 30 seconds. Spoon over chicken.

MENU: Hot garlic bread. Curly endive with cucumber slices and red-wine vinaigrette. Bakery pignoli (pine nut) cookies.

SERVINGS: Makes 4 servings.

Chicken in Caper Sauce

■ Capers (see page 76) add a salty, piquant taste that can liven up many sauces. Here they really shine.

4 boneless, skinless chicken breast halves, rinsed
½ cup all-purpose flour
3 tablespoons butter
2 cloves garlic, minced
¼ cup chicken broth
1 tablespoon fresh lemon juice
1 tablespoon large capers, drained

Dredge chicken in flour, taking care to coat completely.

Melt butter in a 12-inch skillet over medium-high heat. Add chicken and garlic; cook, turning once, until chicken is golden brown, about 4 minutes per side. Add broth and lemon juice. Reduce heat and cook 5 minutes. Sprinkle with capers. Heat through, about 1 minute.

MENU: Deli marinated mushrooms on Bibb lettuce leaves. Kaiser rolls. Pear slices with purple grapes.

SERVINGS: Makes 4 servings.

Orange-Onion Chicken with Couscous

■ The first time I saw the combination of oranges and onions, I balked. Then I tasted it, and now, it is one of my favorite combinations.

Instant couscous
2 teaspoons canola oil
1 small onion, thinly sliced
1 pound boneless, skinless chicken breast halves, rinsed
⅓ cup orange juice
3 tablespoons chicken broth
2 tablespoons orange marmalade

Prepare couscous according to package directions for 4 servings.

Meanwhile, heat oil in a 10-inch skillet over medium heat. Add onion and sauté 2 minutes. Remove onion from skillet with a slotted spoon and set aside. Add chicken to skillet; cook for 8 to 10 minutes, turning once, or until golden brown and interior is no longer pink. Remove chicken from skillet; set aside.

Add orange juice, broth, and marmalade to the skillet. Bring to a boil, reduce heat to medium-high, and cook, stirring, 3 minutes. Return chicken and onion to skillet; heat through, about 1 minute. Serve with couscous.

MENU: Raisin bread. Escarole with cherry tomatoes and vinaigrette. Butter pecan ice cream.

SERVINGS: Makes 4 servings.

Apple-Dapple Chicken

■ I found an unlikely product to help with quick-cooking methods: jelly. I make a great sauce of melted pineapple jelly and horseradish; I add Damson plum jelly to my party meatball recipe. In this dish, apple jelly adds flavor and a shiny glaze. Because of the sugar content it tends to burn, so you'll have to keep an eye on it, but just for a little while.

4 boneless, skinless chicken breast halves, rinsed
½ cup butter
2 tablespoons apple jelly
½ cup apple juice
Sea salt

Preheat broiler. Place chicken on a boiler pan rack that has been sprayed with nonstick cooking spray. Broil 4 inches from source of heat for 10 minutes, turning once, or until interior is no longer pink.

Meanwhile, combine butter, jelly, and apple juice in a 1-quart saucepan over medium heat. Cook, stirring, until jelly melts.

Season chicken with salt. Brush jelly mixture over chicken. Broil 1 minute, turn. Sprinkle chicken with salt. Brush jelly mixture over chicken; broil 1 minute. Brush with jelly again and broil 1 minute to glaze.

MENU: Bakery biscuits. Deli three-bean salad. Ice-cream sandwiches.

SERVINGS: Makes 4 servings.

Macadamia Chicken

■ I had a dish something like this at a restaurant one evening and loved it. I experimented with ways to make it at home. It's quick, but the macadamia nuts, buttery rich and slightly sweet, cost a pretty penny. They're worth it.

2 tablespoons instant flour (see Note, page 33)
Salt and freshly ground black pepper
1 egg
1 tablespoon cold water
¾ cup chopped macadamia nuts
2 tablespoons canola oil
4 boneless, skinless chicken breast halves, rinsed
1 cup crushed pineapple, drained
½ teaspoon crushed red pepper flakes

Combine flour, salt, and pepper on a plate. Beat egg and water in a shallow bowl with a fork. Sprinkle nuts on another plate.

Heat oil in a 10-inch skillet over medium-high heat. Dip chicken into flour, then into egg mixture, and finally into nuts, taking care to get a good, even coating of nuts.

Add chicken to pan; cook 2 minutes or until brown on each side. Reduce heat to medium-low and cook 3 to 4 minutes more on each side or until cooked through.

Mix together crushed pineapple and red pepper flakes. Serve as a sauce, on the side.

MENU: Cinnamon bread. Carrot-raisin salad. Lemon sorbet.

SERVINGS: Makes 4 servings.

Chicken Italiano

■ The bright flavors of this dish come from the fresh tomato sauce.

¼ cup olive oil
1 teaspoon dried oregano
1 pound boneless, skinless chicken breast halves, rinsed
1 large green bell pepper, thinly sliced into rings
⅓ pound prosciutto, thinly sliced
¼ pound provolone cheese, thinly sliced
4 Italian plum tomatoes, chopped
¼ cup chopped scallions

Heat oil and oregano in a 10-inch skillet over medium-high heat. Add chicken and cook, turning once, until brown on both sides, about 4 minutes.

Add bell pepper to the pan and sauté 1 minute. Turn chicken and top each piece with prosciutto, then provolone. Sprinkle tomatoes and scallions over all. Cover pan, reduce heat, and simmer 5 to 7 minutes or until chicken is tender and cheese melts.

MENU: Salad of field greens with mustard vinaigrette. Vanilla ice cream with caramel topping.

SERVINGS: Makes 4 servings.

Stir-Fried Apples & Chicken

■ Chicken combines beautifully with fruit flavors. I like Granny Smith apples with chicken in this dish because they are tart and firm—a nice contrast to the mild flavor of the chicken.

2 tablespoons canola oil
3 boneless, skinless chicken breast halves, rinsed and cut into 2½ × ¼-inch strips
2 Granny Smith apples, cored and sliced
½ cup sliced canned water chestnuts, drained
½ cup vertically sliced scallions
1 (8-oz.) can sliced bamboo shoots, drained
1 cup snow peas
½ cup chicken broth
1 tablespoon soy sauce
1 tablespoon cornstarch
1 teaspoon sugar

Heat oil in a 12-inch skillet or wok over high heat. Add chicken; stir-fry 3 to 4 minutes or until chicken turns white. Add apples; stir-fry 30 seconds. Add water chestnuts, scallions, bamboo shoots, and snow peas; stir-fry 2 minutes or until vegetables are crisp-tender.

Combine chicken broth, soy sauce, cornstarch, and sugar in a cup and add to skillet. Stir-fry 1 to 2 minutes or until thickened and clear. Simmer 1 minute.

MENU: Rice cakes spread with scallion cheese and topped with bean sprouts. Orange wedges.

SERVINGS: Makes 4 servings.

Maple Chicken

■ Maple syrup tends to be far more expensive than maple-flavored corn syrup—which is what most pancake syrups are. I've lost my taste for imitations, so I keep a small bottle of the real thing in the refrigerator.

1 tablespoon vegetable oil
1½ pounds boneless, skinless chicken breast halves, rinsed
Fresh coarsely ground black pepper
¼ to ½ cup maple syrup, at room temperature

Preheat broiler. Rub oil into chicken. Press black pepper into chicken. Place chicken on a broiler pan rack that has been sprayed with nonstick cooking spray.

Broil chicken 4 inches from source of heat 5 minutes. Turn and, baste with maple syrup. Broil about 5 minutes or until chicken is no longer pink in center, basting and turning frequently to prevent burning.

MENU: Deli potato salad. Strawberries and vanilla yogurt.

SERVINGS: Makes 6 servings.

Chicken with Walnuts

■ Walnuts provide a nice crunch and delicate flavor in this easy-to-prepare dish that is elegant enough to serve to company.

⅓ cup soy sauce
1½ tablespoons dry sherry
¾ teaspoon ground ginger
1½ pounds boneless, skinless chicken breast
    halves, rinsed and sliced into 1-inch
    cubes
7 tablespoons peanut oil
½ cup sliced scallions
1 large garlic clove, crushed
1½ cups walnut halves

Combine soy sauce, sherry, ginger, and chicken in a medium bowl.

Heat 4 tablespoons of the oil in a wok or 10-inch skillet over medium-high heat. Add scallions, garlic, and walnuts; stir-fry 3 minutes. Discard garlic and remove scallions and walnuts to a small bowl.

Add remaining oil and heat over high heat. Add chicken mixture and stir-fry 6 minutes or until chicken is cooked through. Reduce heat; return scallions and walnuts to pan. Stir-fry 1 minute or until heated through.

MENU: Deli prepared sesame or other noodles with chopped cucumber. Pineapple spears.

SERVINGS: Makes 6 servings.

Stir-Fried Chicken Burritos

■ An Asian cooking technique works well with Mexican ingredients in this quick-to-make dinner.

2 tablespoons corn oil
1 pound boneless, skinless chicken breast
    halves, rinsed and cut into 1-inch cubes
1 cup diced green bell pepper
½ cup chopped onion
1 garlic clove, crushed
2 medium tomatoes, chopped
1 tablespoon chili powder
½ teaspoon ground cumin
8 (7-inch) warm flour tortillas
Sour cream

Heat oil in a 12-inch skillet over medium-high heat. Add chicken and stir-fry about 4 minutes or until white. Remove from pan with a slotted spoon; cover to keep warm.

Add bell pepper, onion, and garlic to skillet; stir-fry 2 minutes. Add tomatoes, chili powder, and cumin; stir-fry 1 minute or until heated through.

Divide vegetable mixture among tortillas. Divide chicken among tortillas. Fold over to enclose filling. Serve with sour cream.

MENU: Red-leaf lettuce with ranch dressing. Coffee ice cream with chocolate sauce.

SERVINGS: Makes 4 servings.

Garlic Lovers' Chicken

■ This is a dish for people who love the pungent taste and smell of garlic. The smell of it cooking makes my mouth water.

6 tablespoons soy sauce
1 tablespoon safflower oil
2 large cloves garlic, pressed
½ teaspoon dried sage
⅛ teaspoon cayenne pepper
4 boneless, skinless chicken breast halves,
   rinsed

Preheat broiler. Mix together soy sauce, oil, garlic, sage, and cayenne in a small saucepan over medium heat. Simmer for about 5 minutes or until slightly thickened.

Meanwhile, place chicken on a broiler pan rack that has been sprayed with nonstick cooking spray. Broil 4 inches from source of heat for 5 minutes per side or until chicken is no longer pink in center.

Brush with soy mixture and broil 1 minute. Turn, brush with more soy mixture, and broil 1 minute more.

Serve chicken with remaining sauce on the side.

MENU: Bakery corn muffins with currant jelly. Deli new-potato salad. Melon slices with blueberries.

SERVINGS: Makes 4 servings.

15-Minute Chicken Molé

■ A real molé sauce is much more complicated than this, but simplicity must rule if you want dinner on the table fast. What a fifteen-minute molé lacks in complexity it makes up for in direct and honest flavors.

1 (15-oz.) can tomato sauce
½ cup salsa
4 teaspoons unsweetened cocoa powder
1 teaspoon ground cumin
½ teaspoon garlic salt
2 tablespoons corn oil
1½ pounds boneless, skinless chicken breast
   halves, rinsed and cut into 1-inch strips

Combine tomato sauce, salsa, cocoa powder, cumin, and garlic salt in a medium bowl. Set aside.

Heat oil in a 12-inch skillet over medium-high heat. Add chicken and brown on both sides, about 3 minutes. Drain oil from skillet. Pour tomato sauce mixture over chicken; bring to a boil. Reduce heat, cover, and simmer for 10 minutes. Remove chicken to a platter and keep warm.

Increase heat to high, and cook, stirring, until sauce is slightly thickened, about 2 minutes. Spoon over chicken.

MENU: Corn chips. Iceberg lettuce with cherry tomato halves and shredded Monterey Jack cheese. Cinnamon doughnuts.

SERVINGS: Makes 6 servings.

Deviled Chicken

■ The culinary term "deviled" means that food has been combined with hot or spicy seasonings such as red pepper, mustard, or hot pepper sauce. Deviled eggs are probably the best-known deviled dish; however, the technique can be applied to other foods such as broiled chicken.

1 to 1½ pounds boneless, skinless chicken
   breast halves, rinsed
1 stick (½ cup) unsalted butter
1 tablespoon dry mustard
1½ tablespoons fresh lemon juice
1 teaspoon Worcestershire sauce
⅛ teaspoon hot pepper sauce

Preheat broiler. Place chicken on a broiler pan rack that has been sprayed with nonstick cooking spray. Broil 4 inches from source of heat for 8 to 9 minutes, turning once, or until chicken is no longer pink in center.

Meanwhile, blend remaining ingredients. Spread 1 teaspoon of deviled butter mixture over each piece of chicken. Return to broiler for 1 more minute.

MENU: Salad of canned corn niblets and pinto beans tossed with chopped scallions. Bakery Key lime pie.

SERVINGS: Makes 4 to 6 servings.

Easy Chicken Supper

■ Skillet suppers are a dream for a busy cook. They're not only easy and fast to fix; they also require only one pan. That means speedy cleanup. This recipe is one of my favorites because although all the ingredients are combined, their flavors are kept separate because they are added at different times.

2 tablespoons vegetable oil
2 large carrots, thinly sliced
1 small onion, sliced into rings
1 clove garlic, minced
1 teaspoon fresh thyme
4 cooked breaded boneless, skinless chicken
   breast halves
Salt and freshly ground black pepper

Heat oil in 12-inch skillet over medium heat. Add carrots, onion, garlic, and thyme and cook, stirring occasionally, for about 5 minutes or until carrots are crisp-tender.

Push vegetables to the edge of the skillet. Add chicken; cook 3 to 5 minutes on each side or until heated through.

To serve, top chicken with vegetables. Season with salt and pepper to taste.

MENU: Sliced zucchini and fresh tomato chunks tossed with creamy Italian dressing. Cantaloupe quarters.

SERVINGS: Makes 4 servings.

Raisin-Almond Chicken

■ This is simple enough to serve in the middle of the week and special enough to serve to company.

3 tablespoons golden raisins
3 tablespoons light rum
¼ cup butter
¼ cup slivered almonds
4 boneless, skinless chicken breast halves,
   rinsed
¾ cup bottled chicken gravy

Soak raisins in rum in a small dish; set aside.

Melt butter in a 12-inch skillet over medium heat. Add almonds and cook, stirring constantly, until almonds are toasted, about 1 minute. Remove almonds with a slotted spoon and drain on paper towels.

Add chicken to skillet. Cook over medium heat, turning, until golden brown, about 10 minutes. Remove from pan; keep warm.

Add gravy to skillet and cook, stirring constantly, about 1 minute. Add raisins with rum and cook, stirring, until heated through. Ladle 3 tablespoons of raisin gravy over each chicken piece. Sprinkle chicken with almonds. Serve remaining gravy on the side.

MENU: Kaiser rolls. Deli green bean salad. Chocolate wafers with lemon sherbet.

SERVINGS: Makes 4 servings.

Hot, Hot Chicken with Cashews

■ In addition to regular sesame oil, there's also hot sesame oil. This adds not only flavor but also fire. Keep it handy to add near the end of the cooking time.

2 tablespoons peanut oil
½ cup cashews
4 boneless, skinless chicken breast halves,
   rinsed and cut into ½-inch strips
½ cup sliced scallions
1 teaspoon grated fresh ginger
½ teaspoon crushed red pepper flakes
2 tablespoons teriyaki sauce
½ teaspoon hot sesame oil
¼ cup chopped fresh cilantro

Heat peanut oil in a 12-inch skillet or wok over medium-high heat. Add cashews; stir-fry for 30 to 60 seconds or until golden brown. Remove with a slotted spoon and drain on paper towels.

Add chicken, scallions, ginger, and pepper flakes to skillet. Stir-fry 6 minutes or until chicken is white. Stir in teriyaki sauce and sesame oil. Stir-fry 1 minute. Top with cashews and cilantro.

MENU: Deli prepared sesame or other noodles. Mandarin orange slices.

SERVINGS: Makes 4 servings.

Chicken Cacciatore

■ The preparation of chicken cacciatore varies from chef to chef. You'll never get anyone to agree on a recipe. This one is especially easy because it requires so few ingredients, and those ingredients don't require much work.

1 pound boneless, skinless chicken breast halves, rinsed
All-purpose flour
2 tablespoons canola oil
1 (14-oz.) jar spaghetti sauce with mushrooms
1 onion, chopped
2 small zucchini, sliced into rounds and quartered

Dredge chicken in flour, shaking off excess.

Heat oil in a 12-inch skillet over medium-high heat. Add chicken and cook until brown, 2 minutes per side. Reduce heat. Drain excess oil from pan.

Add sauce and onion. Cover and simmer for 5 minutes. Add zucchini. Cover and simmer for 6 minutes or until chicken and zucchini are tender.

MENU: Hot garlic bread. Deli Caesar salad. Bakery devil's food cake.

SERVINGS: Makes 4 servings.

Chicken Piccata

■ This is a popular restaurant dish that's very easy to make at home. The thing that makes it taste so good is the wine and butter mixture.

2 tablespoons butter
1 pound boneless, skinless chicken breast halves, rinsed
⅓ cup dry white wine
Juice of 1 lemon
Chopped fresh flat-leaf parsley

Melt butter in a 10-inch nonreactive skillet over medium heat. Add chicken and sauté until golden brown on both sides, about 4 minutes. Add wine and lemon juice; simmer 8 minutes or until tender.

Remove chicken from pan with a slotted spoon and place on a serving platter. Add parsley to pan and cook, stirring, to pick up any browned bits. Ladle pan juices over chicken.

MENU: Dinner rolls. Tossed salad with Italian dressing. Nonfat frozen chocolate yogurt with fresh strawberries.

SERVINGS: Makes 4 servings.

Honeyed Chicken

■ When time is of the essence, I forgo grating ginger and settle for instant (well, almost instant) minced ginger root. Just put a peeled chunk of ginger into a garlic press and squeeze.

3 tablespoons vegetable oil
1¼ pounds boneless, skinless chicken breast
   halves, rinsed
½ cup orange juice
2 tablespoons honey
2 teaspoons grated peeled ginger
½ teaspoon ground cinnamon

Heat oil in a 10-inch nonstick skillet over medium-high heat. Add chicken and cook for 5 to 7 minutes or until brown on all sides, turning often.

Meanwhile, combine orange juice, honey, ginger, and cinnamon in a small bowl.

Add orange juice mixture to the skillet; reduce heat to medium-low. Cover and cook 5 minutes or until chicken is tender and glazed. Serve chicken with pan sauce.

MENU: Fresh spinach leaves with sliced, fresh mushrooms and cucumber dressing. Kaiser rolls. Bakery apple turnovers.

SERVINGS: Makes 4 or 5 servings.

Chicken Parmesan

■ Varieties of prepared pasta sauces present infinite possibilities to the hurried cook. I used spaghetti sauce with mushrooms in this recipe because it contains another ingredient—mushrooms—that requires no additional work by me.

2 tablespoons vegetable oil
1 to 1¼ pounds boneless, skinless chicken
   breast halves, rinsed
1 (14-oz.) jar spaghetti sauce with
   mushrooms
¼ cup sliced ripe olives
2 tablespoons grated Parmesan cheese

Heat oil in a 10-inch frying pan over medium-high heat. Add chicken and cook, turning, about 6 minutes or until chicken is brown on both sides. Drain off excess oil.

Spoon spaghetti sauce over chicken. Top with olives. Cook over medium heat for about 5 minutes or until chicken is tender and sauce is bubbly.

Sprinkle Parmesan cheese over all. Remove from heat, cover, and let sit until cheese melts, about 2 minutes.

MENU: Hot garlic bread. Tossed salad with Italian dressing. Fruit-topped cheesecake.

SERVINGS: Makes 4 servings.

Sherry Chicken

■ Sherry is a fortified wine that is an excellent cooking ingredient. It has a mellow sweetness that provides contrast to slightly tart flavors like lemon or apricot.

½ cup sherry
½ cup chopped dried apricots
2 tablespoons corn oil
1 medium onion, sliced
1 pound boneless, skinless chicken breast
    halves, rinsed
½ teaspoon chopped fresh basil

Combine sherry and apricots in a small bowl; set aside.

Heat oil in an 8-inch frying pan over medium-high heat. Add onion and sauté, stirring occasionally, until golden, about 2 minutes. Remove onion from pan with a slotted spoon. Set aside.

Add chicken and cook until browned, about 4 to 6 minutes per side. Add reserved onion, apricot-sherry mixture, and basil. When sherry sizzles, cover pan. Remove from heat and allow to sit for 2 minutes.

MENU: Deli new-potato salad. Bakery pineapple cheesecake.

SERVINGS: Makes 4 servings.

Chicken & Olives

■ This dish, inspired by the flavors of the Iberian Peninsula—Spain and Portugal—comes together very quickly. As it cooks, the tomatoes, garlic, olives, and sherry fuse into a lively sauce full of flavor.

2 tablespoons olive oil
1 pound boneless, skinless chicken breast
    halves, rinsed
1½ cups chopped tomatoes
1 clove garlic, minced
1 cup pitted pimiento-stuffed green olives
3 tablespoons sherry

Heat oil in a 10-inch heavy skillet over medium heat. Add chicken and cook until brown, about 5 minutes.

Add tomatoes, garlic, olives, and sherry. Cover and simmer, stirring occasionally, for 10 minutes or until chicken is tender.

MENU: Portuguese bread. Mixed greens with goat cheese cubes and green goddess dressing. Orange slices.

SERVINGS: Makes 4 servings.

Chicken with Broccoli

■ Broccoli florets now can be purchased ready to use in the produce section. They're perfect for this usually tame dish that packs a wallop courtesy of a sour cream sauce spiked with horseradish.

3 cups broccoli florets
¼ cup water
½ cup sour cream or light sour cream
1 tablespoon prepared horseradish
1 tablespoon vegetable oil
1 pound boneless, skinless chicken breast
    halves, rinsed

Place broccoli and water in a 1½-quart microwave-safe casserole. Cover and microwave on HIGH 4 to 5 minutes or until crisp-tender; drain.

Meanwhile, mix together sour cream and horseradish. Set aside.

Heat oil in a large skillet. Add chicken and sauté 6 to 8 minutes, turning, or until chicken is golden and is no longer pink in center. Top chicken with broccoli. Spoon sour cream mixture over all.

MENU: Canned potato sticks. Deli coleslaw. Italian ice.

SERVINGS: Makes 4 servings.

Chicken Stir-Fry

■ Stir-fries are great time-savers, providing the recipe doesn't call for a lot of chopping and cutting. Using already-sliced mushrooms will save time, making this a chicken stir-fry that can be cooked in the blink of an eye.

2 teaspoons vegetable oil
2 large cloves garlic, finely chopped
1 pound boneless, skinless chicken breast
    halves, rinsed and cut into 2-inch squares
3 cups sliced mushrooms
1 cup 1-inch scallion pieces
¼ cup dry white wine

Heat oil in 10-inch nonstick skillet or wok over medium-high heat. Add garlic and stir-fry for 1 minute. Add chicken; stir-fry 3 to 4 minutes or until chicken is white.

Add mushrooms, scallions, and wine; stir-fry about 2 minutes or until vegetables are crisp-tender.

MENU: Field greens with Thousand Island dressing. Fresh figs. Rice crackers.

SERVINGS: Makes 4 servings.

Teriyaki Honey Chicken

■ Marinating meat for a short period of time in an intensely flavored liquid imparts a great deal of flavor. Bottled teriyaki sauce is one of the best commercially prepared marinades, and it works quickly. In this recipe, the honey helps to keep it attached to the chicken.

¼ cup minced scallions
2 cloves garlic, minced
1 tablespoon honey
2 tablespoons dry sherry
½ cup teriyaki sauce
4 boneless, skinless chicken breast halves, rinsed

Preheat broiler. Combine scallions, garlic, honey, sherry, and teriyaki sauce in a small saucepan. Dip chicken in sauce. Place chicken on a broiler pan rack that has been sprayed with nonstick cooking spray.

Broil chicken 4 inches from source of heat, brushing with sauce as chicken cooks, 8 to 10 minutes or until chicken is no longer pink in center. Remove from heat, but keep warm.

Bring remaining sauce to a boil. Strain sauce and serve with the chicken.

MENU: Deli prepared sesame or other noodles. Fruit salad topped with lemon yogurt.

SERVINGS: Makes 4 servings.

Orange Chicken Salad

■ This warm salad makes a great, quick dinner entree. If Mandarin or Clementine oranges are in season, substitute them for the canned ones. The fresh oranges will provide a major taste boost, and peeling them is as easy as opening a can.

Juice of 1 orange (about ½ cup)
¼ cup apple cider vinegar
Grated peel of 1 orange
½ cup extra-virgin olive oil
Salt and freshly ground black pepper
1 pound boneless, skinless chicken breast halves, rinsed and cut into strips
1 small head red-leaf lettuce
1 (8-oz.) can Mandarin orange sections, drained

Preheat broiler. In a medium bowl, combine orange juice, vinegar, orange peel, oil, salt, and pepper for a marinade. Place chicken in another medium bowl. Reserve 3 tablespoons of the marinade. Pour remaining marinade over the chicken. Toss to coat. Set aside.

Wash lettuce, dry, and tear into bite-size pieces. Place in a large bowl.

Drain chicken. Place chicken on a broiler pan rack that has been sprayed with nonstick cooking spray. Broil chicken 4 inches from source of heat 3 to 4 minutes on each side or until no longer pink on the inside. Pour remaining 3 tablespoons marinade over the greens. Toss and divide greens evenly among 4 plates. Divide chicken among plates. Garnish with Mandarin orange sections. Season with black pepper.

MENU: Broccoli and cauliflower florets with ranch dressing for dipping. Canned potato sticks. Prepared vanilla pudding with granola topping.

SERVINGS: Makes 4 servings.

Chicken with Zinfandel Baste

■ The fruity flavor and slightly sweet taste of white Zinfandel lends a pleasant new taste to chicken. Garlic salt provides the needed punch, and the oil prevents the chicken from drying out.

½ cup vegetable oil
½ cup white Zinfandel wine
½ teaspoon garlic salt
4 boneless, skinless chicken breast halves, rinsed

Preheat broiler. Combine oil, wine, and garlic salt in a small saucepan over medium heat. Bring to a boil. Reduce heat and simmer for 5 minutes.

Place chicken on a broiler pan rack that has been sprayed with nonstick cooking spray. Broil chicken 4 inches from source of heat, brushing with wine sauce as chicken cooks, 8 to 10 minutes or until chicken is no longer pink in center.

MENU: French baguettes. Spinach salad with blue-cheese dressing. Deli rice pudding with fresh berries.

SERVINGS: Makes 4 servings.

Five-Spice Chicken with Walnuts

■ I often buy boneless, skinless chicken tenders or cutlets because they cook quickly, but when they're not available or if boneless, skinless chicken breasts are on sale, I buy them and cut in half diagonally.

1 pound boneless, skinless chicken breast halves, rinsed and cut into ¼-inch thick strips
2 tablespoons sesame oil
1 tablespoon soy sauce
1 teaspoon honey
½ teaspoon five-spice powder
2 tablespoons peanut oil
6 scallions, chopped
½ cup walnuts

Put chicken into a bowl. Add sesame oil, soy sauce, honey, and five-spice powder. Mix to coat chicken.

Heat peanut oil in a wok or 10-inch skillet over high heat. Add the chicken with marinade and stir-fry for 5 minutes or until chicken is brown on all sides. Add scallions and walnuts and stir-fry for about 1 minute more.

MENU: Baby shrimp and Boston lettuce salad. Sesame rice cakes. Pineapple and banana cubes sprinkled with shredded coconut.

SERVINGS: Makes 4 servings.

Sweet & Sour Chicken

■ Sugar and vinegar are the point, counter-point, that create the irresistible sweet-and-sour taste that makes this dish a perennial favorite at Chinese restaurants. High-quality sweet-and-sour sauce speeds up preparation.

1 tablespoon peanut oil
1 pound boneless, skinless chicken breast
  halves, rinsed and cut into 1-inch pieces
2 cups red and green bell pepper strips
1 (8-oz.) can pineapple chunks in juice,
  drained
½ cup sweet-and-sour sauce

  Heat wok or a 12-inch skillet over high heat until hot. Add oil and rotate wok to coat sides. Add chicken; stir-fry about 3 minutes or until chicken is white.
  Add pepper strips; stir-fry about 2 minutes or until crisp-tender. Stir in pineapple and sweet-and-sour sauce; stir-fry 1 minute.

MENU: Field greens salad with mustard vinaigrette. Deli prepared sesame or other noodles. Frozen cherry-vanilla yogurt.

SERVINGS: Makes 4 servings.

Chicken with Peanuts

■ Because peanuts are so great for nibbling, they're often overlooked as an ingredient in cooked dishes. That's a shame because peanuts impart a lovely, mellow flavor. Unsalted peanuts sold in vacuum-packed jars are not only the fastest to use; their taste is also very fresh.

2 tablespoons peanut oil
1 pound boneless, skinless chicken breast
  halves, rinsed
1 cup unsalted peanuts
½ cup chicken broth
¼ cup dry sherry

  Heat oil in a 10-inch skillet. Add chicken and cook until golden and no longer pink in center, 6 to 8 minutes. Remove chicken from skillet with a slotted spoon. Keep warm.
  Add peanuts to skillet. Sauté 2 minutes, stirring occasionally. Add broth and sherry and stir-fry to heat through. Puree peanut mixture in a food processor or blender. Spoon over chicken.

MENU: Broccoli and cauliflower florets with soy-and-sliced-scallion dipping sauce. Strawberry ice cream with fresh strawberries.

SERVINGS: Makes 4 servings.

Zesty Lemon Chicken

■ Fresh lemons are a year-round kitchen mainstay. Their bright color is as refreshing as their taste. They keep in the refrigerator for two weeks, providing a reliable ingredient in a myriad of dishes.

2 tablespoons butter or margarine
1 pound boneless, skinless chicken breast
 halves, rinsed
1 large lemon, halved
1 cup sliced mushrooms
1 tablespoon chopped scallion
2 tablespoons dry sherry

Melt butter in a 10-inch skillet over medium-high heat. Add chicken and cook until golden brown, about 5 minutes. Reduce heat to low and cook 5 minutes or until tender. Remove chicken to a serving platter with a slotted spoon. Keep warm.

Juice one lemon half; thinly slice the other.

Add mushrooms and scallion to skillet and sauté until soft, about 2 minutes. Stir in sherry, stirring up all the cooked bits; bring to a boil. Add lemon juice and lemon slices. Simmer for 2 minutes. Pour over chicken.

MENU: Warm French baguettes. Watercress and sliced tomato salad with poppy-seed dressing. Nonfat vanilla yogurt with granola topping.

SERVINGS: Makes 4 servings.

Chili Chicken Stir-Fry

■ Frozen vegetable combinations make stir-fries quick work. They're easy to keep on hand and come in a variety of pleasing combinations. I used Chinese hot chili oil as a flavoring ingredient in this dish. It must be used sparingly, because its delicious fire is all-consuming.

1 tablespoon peanut oil
1 teaspoon hot chili oil
1 pound boneless, skinless chicken breast
 halves, rinsed and cut into 1-inch cubes
1 (16-oz.) package frozen broccoli, carrots,
 water chestnuts, and red pepper
1/3 cup stir-fry sauce
1/4 cup cashews

Heat a wok or 12-inch skillet over high heat. Add oils and rotate pan to coat sides. Add chicken and stir-fry 3 minutes. Add vegetables and stir-fry 5 to 7 minutes or until vegetables are crisp-tender and chicken is no longer pink in center.

Add stir-fry sauce; stir-fry about 1 minute or until heated through. Sprinkle with cashews.

MENU: Deli green bean salad. Cucumber and celery spears in rice vinegar. Pound cake with blueberry pie filling spooned on top.

SERVINGS: Makes 4 servings.

Chicken & Zucchini

■ When selecting zucchini for this dish, choose the smallest—they will be the most tender and easiest to cook. The nice thing about zucchini is that the skin is edible, so you only have to wash them, not peel them.

2 tablespoons olive oil
4 boneless, skinless chicken breast halves, rinsed
2 small zucchini, cut into ¼-inch slices
1 cup chunky pasta sauce
1 teaspoon chopped fresh oregano or ½ teaspoon dried
Salt and freshly ground black pepper

Heat oil in a 10-inch frying pan over medium-high heat. Add chicken and sauté, turning, until golden brown on both sides, 8 to 10 minutes. Drain off fat.

Add zucchini, pasta sauce, oregano, salt, and pepper. Reduce heat to medium-low. Cover and cook about 5 minutes or until zucchini are tender.

MENU: Focaccia. Romaine lettuce with sliced mushrooms and radishes. Strawberry sorbet.

SERVINGS: Makes 4 servings.

Chinese Barbecue Chicken

■ The flavor of Chinese barbecue is very different from what is served in the American South. This sauce is made with spicy hoisin sauce, sesame oil, and ginger. What it does have in common with southern barbecue is that it's finger-lickin' good.

4 skinless, boneless chicken breast halves, rinsed and sliced in half lengthwise
½ cup hoisin sauce
1 teaspoon sesame oil
1 tablespoon tomato-based chili sauce, such as Heinz
1 teaspoon grated fresh ginger
2 cloves garlic, crushed

Preheat broiler. Place chicken on a broiler pan rack that has been sprayed with nonstick cooking spray. Mix together remaining ingredients in a small saucepan; brush on chicken.

Broil chicken 4 inches from the source of heat for 8 to 10 minutes or until golden brown; turn and brush once with sauce.

Bring remaining sauce to a boil. Serve with chicken.

MENU: Sliced cucumbers in vinegar with a generous grind of black pepper. Carrot-raisin salad. Deli rice pudding with sliced fresh peaches.

SERVINGS: Makes 4 servings.

Tarragon Chicken

■ Tarragon is widely used in French cooking and is prized for its aniselike flavor. A teaspoon works to my taste in this dish, but be careful about adding more—tarragon can easily dominate.

1 pound boneless, skinless chicken breast
   halves, rinsed
1 teaspoon seasoned salt
3 tablespoons peanut oil
1 medium onion, thinly sliced
½ pound mushrooms, sliced
1 teaspoon dried tarragon, crumbled

Sprinkle chicken with seasoned salt. Heat oil in a 10-inch skillet over medium-high heat. Add chicken and cook about 4 minutes per side, turning to brown all sides. Remove chicken with a slotted spoon; keep warm.

Add onion and mushrooms to skillet. Sprinkle with tarragon. Reduce heat, cover, and simmer until vegetables are softened, about 5 minutes. Return chicken to skillet. Toss with vegetables and cook about 2 minutes.

MENU: Pear, apple, and raisin salad. Rye toast. Bakery lemon meringue pie.

SERVINGS: Makes 4 servings.

Cajun Chicken

■ A few years back, when the Cajun craze died down, southern Louisiana–style foods were firmly entrenched among American classics. I first made Cajun Chicken using a blend of seasonings from my spice shelf, but now there are good prepared Cajun spice mixes that can be substituted.

1 teaspoon vegetable oil
1 pound boneless, skinless chicken breast
   halves, rinsed and sliced in half lengthwise
1 medium onion, chopped
1 green bell pepper, chopped
1 (14-oz.) can stewed tomatoes
¼ teaspoon *each* cayenne pepper, thyme,
   black pepper, garlic salt, ground cloves,
   and ground allspice

Heat oil in heavy 10-inch skillet over medium-high heat. Add chicken and cook, turning, until browned, about 8 minutes. Remove to a platter; keep warm.

Reduce heat to medium. Add onion and bell pepper and cook, stirring occasionally, until soft, about 2 minutes. Add stewed tomatoes and seasonings, return chicken to pan, and simmer, uncovered, for about 5 minutes or until chicken is tender.

MENU: Green salad with lemon vinaigrette. French bread. Butter pecan ice cream.

SERVINGS: Makes 4 servings.

Red Pepper Stir-Fry

■ It's always good to shop with a list, but it's also true that a good cook lets what is freshest and best in the marketplace inspire meals. When they're at the height of their season, red bell peppers inspire me. The mountains of them at my supermarket are irresistible.

1 pound boneless, skinless chicken breast
   halves, rinsed and cubed
2 tablespoons cornstarch
3 tablespoons soy sauce
5 tablespoons vegetable oil
1 clove garlic, minced
2 red bell peppers, sliced
1 tablespoon slivered blanched almonds

Combine chicken and cornstarch in a medium bowl. Stir in 2 tablespoons of the soy sauce and 2 tablespoons of the oil.

Heat remaining oil in a wok or heavy 12-inch skillet over high heat. Add garlic, bell peppers, and almonds and stir-fry 3 minutes. Remove with a slotted spoon.

Drain chicken. Add to oil in wok. Stir-fry over high heat 4 to 5 minutes or until chicken is golden brown. Reduce heat. Return pepper mixture to wok. Add remaining soy sauce. Stir-fry until uniformly heated through.

MENU: Rice cakes with sesame seeds. Trimmed watercress tossed with paper-thin slices of red onion and dressed with oil, vinegar, and freshly ground black pepper. Cantaloupe wedges.

SERVINGS: Makes 4 servings.

Garlic Chicken

■ Chopped garlic in a jar is a time-saver, but I prefer fresh. It only takes a few seconds to pop the clove out of its papery shell and chop, press, mince, or mash.

4 cloves garlic, peeled
1½ teaspoons salt
1 tablespoon olive oil
¼ teaspoon freshly ground black pepper
4 boneless, skinless chicken breast halves,
   rinsed
2 cups salsa
8 romaine lettuce leaves

Preheat broiler. Mash garlic and salt to a paste in a small bowl. Stir in oil and pepper. Coat chicken with garlic mixture. Place chicken on a broiler pan rack that has been sprayed with nonstick cooking spray.

Broil chicken about 4 inches away from source of heat for about 8 minutes, turning once or twice, or until no longer pink in center.

Meanwhile, heat salsa in a pan until just warm.

Arrange 2 lettuce leaves on each plate. Place chicken on lettuce and spoon about ½ cup salsa over each piece.

MENU: Deli three-bean salad. Corn chips. Bananas drizzled with honey and dusted with grated coconut.

SERVINGS: Makes 4 servings.

Chili Chicken

■ Unless labeled "pure chili powder," most chili powder sold in supermarkets is a combination of ground chilies mixed with cumin, oregano, garlic, salt, or other spices. Some will indicate a level of heat. I like the hot best in this recipe, but any chili powder, pure or not, will work well.

4 tablespoons all-purpose flour
1 teaspoon dry mustard
1 teaspoon freshly ground black pepper
1 teaspoon dried oregano
1 teaspoon chili powder
1 pound boneless, skinless chicken breast
   halves, rinsed
¼ cup vegetable oil

Combine flour, mustard, pepper, oregano, and chili powder in a shallow bowl. Dredge chicken in seasoned flour, coating well.

Heat oil in 10-inch frying pan over medium-high heat. Add chicken, a few pieces at a time, keeping them sizzling, and cook about 3 minutes on each side or until golden brown. Drain on paper towels. Serve hot.

MENU: Salsa with corn chips. Orange and grapefruit slices sprinkled with lemon juice and sugar.

SERVINGS: Makes 4 servings.

Lemon Chicken

■ Broiling is an easy way to cook poultry, but I had to experiment several times before mastering it. Here are the tips I've learned:

· If chicken pieces are small, set the rack 4 to 5 inches from the heat. If they are large, set the rack 5 to 6 inches from the heat.
· Use a pan with low sides. Coat the inside rack with shortening or spray with nonstick cooking spray to prevent sticking.

4 tablespoons butter, melted
3 tablespoons fresh lemon juice
4 tablespoons dry sherry
2 cloves garlic, minced
1 teaspoon chopped parsley
1 pound boneless, skinless chicken breast
   halves, rinsed

Preheat broiler. Combine butter, lemon juice, sherry, garlic, and parsley in a small bowl; mix well.

Place chicken on a broiler pan rack sprayed with nonstick cooking spray. Broil 4 to 5 inches from source of heat, turning once and basting frequently with lemon mixture, for 8 to 10 minutes.

MENU: Deli macaroni salad. Cheddar cheese with grapes, apple slices, and assorted crackers.

SERVINGS: Makes 4 servings.

Chicken with Mushrooms

■ I live by the list. If I write it down, it will be done. Lists also have another function: managing time spent in food preparation. By jotting down things I need to restock or buy for a dish I plan to make, I cut down on the number of trips I make to the store. There's no formal organization to my list, just a series of words, but when the item is essential such as basil for pesto or sherry for this dish, I add an asterisk.

1 to 1½ pounds boneless, skinless chicken
   breast halves, rinsed
Seasoned salt
All-purpose flour
¼ cup butter or margarine
½ cup dry sherry
½ cup minced shallots
½ pound mushrooms, sliced

Sprinkle chicken lightly with seasoned salt. Coat with flour. Melt butter or margarine in a 12-inch skillet over medium heat. Add chicken and cook for 5 to 6 minutes, turning, or until lightly browned on each side.

Add sherry and bring to a boil. Reduce heat, cover, and simmer 5 minutes. Remove chicken to a serving platter. Keep warm. Add shallots and mushrooms to skillet and cook, stirring occasionally, about 4 minutes. Drain and spoon mushrooms and shallots over chicken.

MENU: French bread. Zucchini slices, cherry tomatoes, and carrot sticks with cucumber dressing for dipping. Deli rice pudding dusted with cinnamon.

SERVINGS: Makes 4 to 6 servings.

Herbed Chicken

■ I make this dish when my herb garden has rosemary, thyme, and chives. These ingredients are also available in produce sections. If fresh are not available, use half the amount of dried herbs.

1 pound boneless, skinless chicken breast
   halves, rinsed
6 tablespoons fresh lemon juice
2 tablespoons olive oil
2 teaspoons fresh rosemary, crushed
½ teaspoon fresh thyme leaves
½ teaspoon minced garlic chives

Preheat broiler. Arrange chicken on a broiler pan rack that has been sprayed with nonstick cooking spray.

Combine lemon juice, olive oil, rosemary, thyme, and chives in a small bowl; brush over chicken.

Broil chicken 4 to 5 inches from source of heat, turning once and basting frequently with herb mixture, for 8 to 10 minutes or until no longer pink in center.

MENU: Soft bread sticks. Spinach salad with cherry tomato halves and French dressing. Fresh blueberries with nonfat blueberry yogurt.

SERVINGS: Makes 4 servings.

Chicken Scampi

■ *Scampi* is the Italian word for shrimp. This dish combines chicken and shrimp, so it really is "chicken scampi."

⅓ cup butter
⅓ cup corn oil
2 cloves garlic, minced
3 boneless, skinless chicken breast halves, rinsed and cut into 1-inch cubes
1 pound shrimp, peeled and deveined
Juice of 1 lemon
Chopped fresh flat-leaf parsley

Heat butter and oil in a 12-inch skillet over medium-high heat. Add garlic and sauté for 2 minutes. Add chicken; stir-fry until brown, about 3 minutes. Push chicken to one side, add shrimp. Stir-fry until shrimp turn pink, about 2 minutes. Sprinkle with lemon juice and parsley and serve.

MENU: Garlic bread sticks. Sliced tomato, mozzarella cheese, and red onion drizzled with olive oil. Bakery chocolate chip cookies.

SERVINGS: Makes 6 servings.

Mandarin Chicken

■ The aroma and appearance of this dish, especially in the winter when we need a little sunshine, is divine.

½ cup orange juice
¼ cup orange marmalade
2 teaspoons prepared horseradish
½ teaspoon grated ginger root
1 tablespoon cornstarch
1 tablespoon canola oil
4 boneless, skinless chicken breasts halves, rinsed and each cut lengthwise into 8 strips
1 (10-oz.) can mandarin orange segments, drained

Combine orange juice, marmalade, horseradish, ginger root, and cornstarch in a small bowl; set aside.

Heat oil in a wok or heavy 10-inch skillet over medium-high heat. Add chicken to skillet and stir-fry until golden brown, about 3 minutes.

Stir orange juice mixture and add to wok. Stir-fry until sauce thickens, 3 to 4 minutes. Transfer to a serving dish and garnish with orange segments.

MENU: Deli sesame or other prepared noodles with scallions.

SERVINGS: Makes 4 servings.

Summer Chicken

■ This is great to make when there's an excess of ripe and juicy summer tomatoes.

4 boneless, skinless chicken breast halves, rinsed
1 egg whisked with 1 tablespoon water
Seasoned bread crumbs
2 tablespoons sunflower oil
1 tablespoon butter
4 slices Gruyère cheese
4 thick tomato slices

Dip chicken in egg-water mixture, then into seasoned bread crumbs, coating completely.

Heat oil in a 10-inch skillet over medium-high heat. Add chicken and sauté until golden on both sides, about 8 minutes. Add butter. Turn chicken and continue to cook, 1 minute.

Place a cheese slice on each chicken piece. Reduce heat and cook for 2 minutes or until cheese begins to melt. Top each one with a tomato slice. Cook 1 minute more.

MENU: Cucumber spears with green goddess dressing. Whole-wheat toast. Melon cubes.

SERVINGS: Makes 4 servings.

Chicken from the Orient

■ The crushed red pepper flakes give this dish a substantial bite. Warn partakers in advance.

1 pound boneless, skinless chicken breast halves, rinsed and sliced in half lengthwise
2 tablespoons hoisin sauce
2 teaspoons dry sherry
1 tablespoon dark soy sauce
2 tablespoons peanut oil
1 teaspoon crushed red pepper flakes
¼ cup chicken broth
4 scallions, cut on the diagonal into ½-inch slices

Combine chicken with hoisin, sherry, and soy sauce in a medium bowl; set aside.

Heat oil in a wok or 12-inch skillet over high heat. Add pepper flakes; stir-fry 1 minute. Add chicken and marinade; stir-fry 2 minutes.

Stir in chicken broth. Cover and cook 2 minutes. Uncover and cook 2 minutes more. Add scallions and stir-fry until heated through.

MENU: Spinach salad with mandarin orange slices and poppy-seed dressing. Chinese noodles. Vanilla ice cream with fresh raspberries.

SERVINGS: Makes 4 servings.

Guilty Chicken in Mushroom Sauce

■ This is a dish to put on the occasional treat list. It's loaded with delicious but high-fat topping. Yummy!

1 tablespoon canola oil
1 pound boneless, skinless chicken breast halves, rinsed and cut into 2-inch long strips
1 tablespoon butter
½ cup sliced mushrooms
½ cup sour cream
1 tablespoon dry sherry

Heat oil in a 10-inch skillet over medium heat. Add chicken and sauté until golden brown, about 4 minutes per side.

Meanwhile, place butter in a 2-cup microwave-safe bowl; microwave on HIGH for 15 seconds. Toss mushrooms with melted butter. Microwave on HIGH for 30 seconds. Stir in sour cream and dry sherry.

Reduce heat and spoon mushroom-sour cream mixture over chicken. Heat through but do not boil or sour cream will curdle.

MENU: Baguettes. Tossed salad with French dressing. Nectarine slices.

SERVINGS: Makes 3 or 4 servings.

Spicy Yogurt Chicken

■ Yogurt's culinary uses go beyond a breakfast food or a midday snack. It can be used in a variety of cooked dishes. Just be careful not to let it come to a boil or it will curdle.

½ cup plain low-fat yogurt, plus additional for serving
1½ teaspoons minced ginger
½ teaspoon paprika
¼ teaspoon ground cumin
¼ teaspoon cayenne pepper
1 clove garlic, minced
2 boneless, skinless chicken breast halves, rinsed and sliced in half lengthwise
Paprika

Preheat broiler. Combine yogurt, ginger, paprika, cumin, cayenne, and garlic in a glass dish. Cut three deep slits in each chicken breast; add to yogurt mixture, turning to coat. Marinate 5 minutes.

Remove chicken from yogurt. Place chicken on a broiler pan rack that has been sprayed with nonstick cooking spray. Broil chicken 4 inches from heat source for 10 minutes, turning once, or until chicken is no longer pink in center.

To serve, top each breast with a teaspoon of fresh yogurt sprinkled with paprika.

MENU: Whole-grain pitas. Tossed salad with marinated artichoke hearts. Berries and shortbread cookies.

SERVINGS: Makes 4 servings.

Curried Chicken

■ Originally, I marinated the chicken for 15 minutes, and then baked for 35, but it took so long, I rarely made it. So I compressed the process, using sliced chicken breast instead of chicken breast on the bone, and cooked it on top of the stove instead of in the oven. The result was different, but still delicious.

¼ cup orange juice
2 tablespoons fresh lime juice
1 medium clove garlic, minced
1 teaspoon curry powder
¼ teaspoon salt
6 boneless, skinless chicken breast halves, rinsed and sliced in half lengthwise
1 tablespoon butter

Combine the orange and lime juices, garlic, curry powder, and salt in a glass pan. Add chicken and stir to coat.

Melt butter in a 10-inch skillet over medium-high heat. Drain chicken, reserving marinade. Add chicken and sauté 6 minutes, turning frequently, until golden brown. Add marinade. Reduce heat, and cook 5 minutes or until chicken is tender.

MENU: Sliced cucumbers with sour cream–chive dipping sauce. Bakery coconut macaroons.

SERVINGS: Makes 6 servings.

Chicken & Peppers

■ My favorite kitchen gadget is the extra-long, coiled, wall telephone cord. When the phone rings, it goes to work. As I talk, I walk, and I do chores. I put away the dishes. I crumb stale bread in the food processor. I chop onions or bell peppers to keep on hand in the freezer. If the hour's near a mealtime, I set the table. I peel the vegetables. I turn on the oven.

In other words, I do a lot of mindless tasks as I talk, which saves me time because I don't have to set aside other blocks of time to do them.

I save double the time when I cook chicken and peppers. I retrieve the already chopped onions and sliced bell peppers from the freezer and toss them into the pot.

1 tablespoon vegetable oil
2 medium red bell peppers, cut into ¼-inch strips
¼ cup chopped onion
1 clove garlic, finely chopped
1 pound boneless, skinless chicken breast halves, rinsed and cut into 1-inch pieces
½ teaspoon salt
⅛ teaspoon freshly ground pepper

Heat oil in 10-inch skillet over medium-high heat. Add bell peppers, onion, and garlic and stir-fry for about 3 minutes. Add chicken. Stir-fry for 6 to 8 minutes or until chicken is no longer pink in the center. Add salt and pepper and toss to combine.

MENU: Romaine lettuce with marinated mushrooms. Nectarine slices tossed with blueberries.

SERVINGS: Makes 4 servings.

Herbed Chicken with Lemon

■ Open my refrigerator and you'll find lemons. I can't cook without them, and I've learned a thing or two about working with them in the kitchen. For instance, a lemon at room temperature will give you more juice than one that is cold. When I need just a few drops of lemon juice, I prick one with a fork and squeeze, then put it in a plastic bag and return it to the refrigerator. This recipes calls for the juice of 1 large lemon, which is 4 to 5 tablespoons.

2 tablespoons olive oil
1 large clove garlic, minced
1 sprig rosemary or a pinch of dried
1 fresh sage leaf or a pinch of dried
1 pound boneless, skinless chicken breasts, rinsed
Juice of 1 large lemon

Heat oil in a 10-inch skillet over medium-high heat. Add garlic, rosemary, and sage. Cook until garlic is soft, about 1 minute.

With a slotted spoon, remove and discard herbs. Add chicken and cook until brown on both sides, about 4 minutes. Add lemon juice. Reduce heat, cover, and simmer for 10 minutes or until chicken is tender. Spoon juices over chicken to serve.

MENU: Deli pasta salad. Arugula, sliced tomatoes, and slices of fresh mozzarella dressed in oil and vinegar. Fig bars.

SERVINGS: Makes 4 servings.

Mediterranean Chicken

■ Crushed red pepper flakes are a handy condiment—one dash and a simple dish is filled with flavor. Great restraint is needed, however, because just a little is just enough.

3 tablespoons white Worcestershire sauce
1 tablespoon olive oil
1 clove garlic, minced
½ teaspoon dried oregano or 1 teaspoon chopped fresh
½ teaspoon crushed red pepper flakes
6 boneless, skinless chicken breast halves, rinsed

Preheat broiler. Mix together Worcestershire sauce, oil, garlic, oregano, and red pepper flakes. Add chicken and stir to coat.

Place chicken on a broiler pan rack that has been sprayed with nonstick cooking spray. Broil chicken 4 to 5 inches from source of heat for about 5 minutes per side or until the chicken is no longer pink in the centers.

MENU: Toasted pita bread. Deli three-bean salad. Frozen strawberry yogurt.

SERVINGS: Makes 6 servings.

Salsa Chicken

■ There's a good reason salsa has become so popular—it's delicious and it's versatile. Think beyond a dip for corn chips. Salsa makes a great base for a savory cooking sauce.

⅓ cup all-purpose flour
⅛ teaspoon garlic powder
⅛ teaspoon chili powder
2 skinless, boneless chicken breast halves, rinsed and split into 4 pieces
1 tablespoon vegetable oil
¼ cup salsa plus additional for serving
4 ounces shredded Monterey Jack cheese with chiles

Combine flour, garlic powder, and chili powder in a shallow dish. Coat chicken with flour mixture.

Heat oil in a 10-inch nonstick skillet over medium-high heat. Add chicken and cook 3 to 4 minutes on each side or until lightly browned and chicken is no longer pink in center. Reduce heat. Spoon 1 tablespoon salsa in the center of each chicken piece. Sprinkle with cheese. Cover and cook until cheese is melted, about 1 minute.

Serve with additional salsa.

MENU: Warm tortillas. Vegetable sticks, such as carrot and celery, and cucumber spears. Deli chocolate pudding with banana slices.

SERVINGS: Makes 4 servings.

Spicy Chicken with Hoisin Sauce

■ Hoisin sauce, also called Peking sauce, used to be exotic. Now it can be found in most supermarkets' international foods aisle. This thick, reddish-brown sauce is sweet, spicy, and widely used in Chinese cooking.

2 tablespoons hoisin sauce
2 teaspoons dry sherry
1 tablespoon soy sauce
1 pound boneless, skinless chicken breast halves, rinsed and cut into ½-inch squares
2 tablespoons peanut oil
½ teaspoon crushed red pepper flakes
¼ cup chicken broth

Combine hoisin sauce, sherry, and soy sauce in a medium bowl. Add chicken and coat well with sauce. Let chicken marinate for about five minutes.

Heat wok or a 10-inch skillet over high heat. Add oil and red pepper flakes. When oil is hot, add chicken and marinade. Stir-fry for 3 to 4 minutes or until chicken is no longer pink. Stir in chicken broth. Cover and cook 3 to 4 minutes more or until chicken is tender.

MENU: Shredded bok choy with lemon vinaigrette dressing. Rice cakes. Kiwi slices tossed with grated coconut.

SERVINGS: Makes 4 servings.

Basil Chicken

■ My youngest daughter gave me a compact knife block for the kitchen. It was a luxury I thought I didn't need. I was wrong. Instead of wasting time going through drawers to find the knife I wanted for some specific carving, cutting, or paring job, now just the right knife is always at hand. I don't know who invented this simple but effective storage unit, but he or she has brought new meaning to the old rule: a place for everything, and everything in its place. It even has a place for the kitchen shears which I need when I go out into the garden to cut basil for Basil Chicken.

¼ cup white wine vinegar
¼ cup vegetable oil
2 tablespoons finely chopped scallions
2 tablespoons chopped fresh basil
1 to 1½ pounds boneless, skinless chicken
    thighs, rinsed

Preheat broiler. Combine vinegar, oil, scallion, and basil in a glass baking dish or plastic bag. Add chicken, turning to coat. Let sit at room temperature for 5 minutes.

Drain chicken; reserve the marinade. Place chicken on a broiler pan rack that has been sprayed with nonstick cooking spray.

Broil chicken 4 inches from source of heat, turning once and basting 2 or 3 times with marinade, for 8 to 10 minutes or until no longer pink in center.

MENU: Deli new-potato salad. Bakery corn muffins. Escarole and cherry tomatoes with ranch dressing. Peach ice cream with fresh peaches.

SERVINGS: Makes 4 or 5 servings.

Hungarian Chicken Thighs

■ Boneless, skinless chicken thighs are among the many kinds of quick-cooking poultry cuts you can find in refrigerated cases these days. Cooked thighs are dark, moist, and delicious.

2 teaspoons Hungarian hot paprika
Salt and freshly ground pepper
1 pound boneless, skinless chicken thighs,
    rinsed
2 tablespoons butter
2 tablespoons Dijon mustard
2 teaspoons white Worcestershire sauce
Fresh flat-leaf parsley, chopped

Preheat broiler. Combine paprika, salt, and pepper in a small bowl. Rub mixture into chicken thighs.

Melt butter in a 1-quart saucepan over low heat. Whisk in mustard and Worcestershire sauce; bring to a boil. Remove from heat.

Place chicken thighs on a broiler pan rack that has been sprayed with nonstick cooking spray. Spread with mustard mixture. Broil thighs 4 inches from source of heat, turning once or twice, for 10 minutes or until juices run clear when pierced with a fork. Serve with a sprinkling of parsley.

MENU: Rye bread. Deli macaroni salad. Applesauce dusted with cinnamon.

SERVINGS: Makes 4 servings.

Hot Sherried Chicken Thighs

■ This method of cooking creates intense flavors that penetrate the meat and keep it tender and moist.

¼ cup dry sherry
3 tablespoons soy sauce
1 large garlic clove, minced
1 large slice fresh ginger
⅛ teaspoon cayenne pepper
½ cup chicken broth
1 pound boneless, skinless chicken thighs, rinsed

Combine sherry, soy sauce, garlic, ginger, cayenne, and broth in a 10-inch skillet. Add chicken; turn to coat. Bring to a boil. Reduce heat, cover, and simmer 8 minutes. Remove cover. Increase heat to medium and bring broth to a rolling boil. Cook, turning chicken occasionally, until liquid evaporates, about 5 minutes.

MENU: Toasted French bread slices. Cucumbers in yogurt sprinkled with chopped parsley. Pear and apple slices drizzled with honey.

SERVINGS: Makes 4 servings.

Chicken & Spinach Italiano

■ A quick way to shred or slice the spinach is with a pair of kitchen shears.

2 tablespoons olive oil
1 pound boneless, skinless chicken thighs, rinsed
1 small onion, sliced
1 garlic clove, pressed
4 ounces spinach, sliced into thin strips or shredded
¼ cup grated Parmesan cheese

Heat oil in a hot 10-inch skillet; add chicken thighs. Cook 5 minutes or until golden brown.

Add onion and garlic. Lower heat, continuing to cook, covered, for 5 minutes. Push chicken to one side of pan. Add spinach. Cover, and continue to cook until spinach is wilted, about 2 minutes. Turn chicken. Sprinkle with cheese.

MENU: Garlic bagels. Olive or marinated vegetable salad. Italian sesame cookies.

SERVINGS: Makes 4 servings.

Lime-Soy Chicken

■ Although supermarkets put soy sauce on the international foods shelves with Japanese and Chinese foodstuffs, it can be used to season everything from burgers to salad dressings. I use it for grilling chicken thighs.

1 pound boneless, skinless chicken thighs
½ cup fresh lime juice
¼ cup margarine or butter
2 teaspoons soy sauce

Preheat broiler. Place chicken thighs in a medium bowl. Pour half of the lime juice over chicken. Set aside.

Melt margarine or butter in a small saucepan. Stir in remaining lime juice and soy sauce. Remove from heat.

Place chicken thighs on a broiler pan rack that has been sprayed with nonstick cooking spray. Broil thighs 4 inches from source of heat, turning once and basting with lime-soy sauce, for about 10 minutes or until juices run clear when pierced with a fork.

MENU: Crusty peasant bread. Romaine lettuce salad with cucumber dressing. Strawberries with frozen vanilla yogurt.

SERVINGS: Makes 4 servings.

Buffalo Drumsticks

■ With me and Buffalo chicken wings, it was love at first sight. The sequence was intriguing: hot, cold, snap. Yum! It occurred to me, since I never seem to get enough of this dish, that I could make it as a dinner, not with Lilliputian wings, but with drumsticks.

1 tablespoon margarine, melted
2 tablespoons cider vinegar
1 teaspoon hot pepper sauce
¼ teaspoon salt
12 chicken drumsticks
Blue cheese dressing
Celery sticks

Preheat broiler. Mix melted margarine, vinegar, pepper sauce, and salt in a glass or plastic bowl. Add drumsticks and toss and turn to coat evenly.

Drain chicken, reserving marinade. Place chicken on a broiler pan rack that has been sprayed with nonstick cooking spray. Broil about 6 inches from source of heat, turning often and brushing with more marinade, for 10 to 12 minutes or until juices run clear when pierced with a fork.

Serve with dressing and celery sticks.

MENU: Deli new-potato salad. Sliced tomatoes with fresh basil and extra-virgin olive oil. Cantaloupe slices.

SERVINGS: Makes 6 servings.

Red-Wine Barbecued Chicken

■ I make this dish on the grill in the summer and in the broiler in the winter. In any season, it's sensational.

½ cup favorite barbecue sauce
2 tablespoons dry red wine
Dash of garlic salt
Dash of freshly ground black pepper
4 chicken drumsticks

Preheat broiler. Combine sauce, wine, garlic salt, and black pepper in a saucepan. Set aside.

Place drumsticks on a broiler pan rack that has been sprayed with nonstick cooking spray. Broil 4 inches from source of heat for 7 minutes. Turn drumsticks and broil for 4 minutes. Brush with barbecue sauce and broil for 1 minute. Turn, brush with barbecue sauce, and broil for 1 minute or until juices run clear when pierced with a fork.

Bring remaining barbecue sauce to a full rolling boil. Serve drumsticks with barbecue sauce.

MENU: Bakery corn muffins. Tossed salad with thinly sliced zucchini rounds. Bakery vanilla cake.

SERVINGS: Makes 4 servings.

Apple-Wine Chicken

■ This recipe is not markedly different, complicated, or especially innovative. It's a concentration on my personal chicken preferences: crispy exterior, with a slightly sweet taste, but no gooey, thick sauce.

¼ cup butter
2 tablespoons apple jelly
¼ cup dry white wine
½ teaspoon salt
10 boneless chicken thighs, rinsed

Preheat broiler. Combine butter and jelly in a small saucepan over low heat, stirring until jelly melts. Stir in wine and salt and heat until hot.

Place chicken, skin side down, on a broiler pan rack that has been sprayed with nonstick cooking spray. Broil about 6 inches from heat source for 5 to 6 minutes. Turn and baste chicken with wine mixture. Broil 5 or 6 minutes or until juices run clear when chicken is pierced with a fork.

MENU: Deli carrot-raisin salad. Kaiser rolls. Bakery chocolate brownies.

SERVINGS: Makes 4 or 5 servings.

Down-Mexico-Way Chicken

■ Usually I don't cook chicken in a microwave oven, but this dish made with chicken thighs and lots of vegetables turns out just great.

4 boneless, skinless chicken thighs (about 1 pound), rinsed
½ cup dry red wine
2 tablespoons barbecue sauce
1 jalapeño chile, seeded and chopped
1 green bell pepper, cut into ¼-inch strips
1 red bell pepper, cut into ¼-inch strips
4 scallions, cut into 2-inch pieces

Place chicken thighs in a shallow, microwave-safe dish. Mix together remaining ingredients in a medium bowl. Spread vegetable mixture over chicken.

Cover with waxed paper; microwave on MEDIUM-HIGH 4 to 6 minutes or until juices run clear when the thickest parts of chicken are pierced with a fork.

MENU: Corn chips with bean dip. Plain yogurt dusted with cinnamon and drizzled with honey.

SERVINGS: Makes 4 servings.

Sunshine-Glazed Chicken Thighs

■ Cooking with honey takes a little care. Because it is a sugar, it can burn very quickly. Not only does it add flavor; it also keeps the sauce on the chicken.

½ cup orange juice
¼ cup honey
¼ cup butter
2 tablespoons grated orange peel
4 (about 1 pound) boneless, skinless chicken thighs
Salt and freshly ground black pepper

Preheat broiler. Combine orange juice, honey, butter, and orange peel in a small saucepan over medium heat. Cook, stirring, until butter melts and ingredients are blended. Remove from heat.

Place chicken thighs on a broiler pan rack that has been sprayed with nonstick cooking spray. Broil about 6 inches from heat source for 5 to 6 minutes. Turn and baste chicken with juice mixture. Broil 5 or 6 minutes or until juices run clear when chicken is pierced with a fork. Season with salt and pepper to taste.

MENU: Green salad with fresh papaya slices. Bakery bran muffins. Frozen vanilla yogurt.

SERVINGS: Makes 4 servings.

Chicken & Eggplant Italiano

■ It used to be the practice to drain eggplant for hours in the belief that its liquid would lend a bitter taste to any dish. I don't find that is true, especially in a quick-to-cook dish with lots of pasta sauce.

1 egg, beaten
¼ cup seasoned bread crumbs
2 tablespoons milk
1 garlic clove, minced
1 pound ground chicken
1 tablespoon cooking oil
1 (14-oz.) jar chunky spaghetti sauce
1 small eggplant, cut into ½-inch cubes
4 slices provolone cheese

Mix together the egg, bread crumbs, milk, and garlic in a medium bowl. Mix in chicken until evenly combined. Shape mixture into 4 (¾-inch-thick) patties.

Heat oil in a 12-inch nonstick skillet over medium-high heat. Add patties and cook for 10 minutes or until lightly browned on the outside and no longer pink inside, turning once. Remove from skillet and drain patties on paper towels.

Meanwhile, cook sauce and eggplant in a medium skillet over medium heat for 5 minutes or until eggplant is tender, stirring often. Top with chicken patties and provolone slices. Cook 1 or 2 minutes more or until cheese begins to melt.

MENU: Herbed bread sticks. Deli marinated mushrooms on leaf lettuce. Neapolitan ice cream.

SERVINGS: Makes 4 servings.

Chili con Pollo

■ I learned long ago that one of the best ways to save time in the kitchen is to work with a sharp knife. It will make quick work of the onion in this recipe.

1 tablespoon vegetable oil
1 medium onion, chopped
1 pound ground chicken
1 tablespoon chili powder
1 (14-oz.) can Mexican-style stewed tomatoes
1 (15-oz.) can kidney beans, drained and rinsed
1 cup (4 ounces) grated Monterey Jack cheese

Heat oil in a 10-inch frying pan over medium heat. Add onion and sauté, stirring occasionally, until soft, about 2 minutes. Add chicken and cook, stirring to break up chicken until no longer pink, about 3 minutes. Drain off fat.

Stir in chili powder, tomatoes, and beans. Bring to a boil. Reduce heat, cover, and simmer about 8 minutes or until onion is tender. Top with cheese.

MENU: Corn chips with guacamole dip and chopped tomatoes. Bakery cinnamon cookies.

SERVINGS: Makes 8 servings.

Chicken with Apples

■ Ground chicken is a good alternative to ground beef. It makes great meat patties.

1 pound ground chicken
¼ cup fresh bread crumbs
⅛ teaspoon cayenne pepper
2 teaspoons chopped fresh parsley
1 tablespoon canola oil
⅓ cup chicken broth
⅛ teaspoon ground cloves
1 large Granny Smith or McIntosh apple, peeled, cored, and thickly sliced

Place chicken, bread crumbs, cayenne, and parsley in a medium bowl; blend well. Form into 4 patties.

Heat oil in a 12-inch nonstick skillet over medium heat. Add chicken patties and cook for 10 minutes or until lightly browned on the outside and no longer pink inside, turning once.

Meanwhile, heat chicken broth, cloves, and apple slices in a 1-quart saucepan over medium heat. Simmer, covered, for 5 minutes. Remove cover and cook, stirring occasionally, for 5 to 7 minutes or until sauce is thickened. Pour over chicken patties.

MENU: Potato rolls. Field greens salad with favorite dressing. Vanilla ice cream with chocolate sauce.

SERVINGS: Makes 4 servings.

Dipper's Chicken

■ Chicken nuggets are a boon to the busy cook. They're widely available. Everybody in the family likes them. They cook in no time. The dipping sauce gives them some extra piz-zazz.

1 (1-lb.) package breaded, oven-ready chicken nuggets
1 (12-oz.) jar apricot preserves
¼ cup prepared mustard
¼ cup prepared horseradish

Prepare chicken nuggets according to package directions.

Meanwhile, combine remaining ingredients in a small saucepan. Cook, stirring, over low heat for 5 minutes or until preserves are melted. Remove from heat and pour into a serving bowl or individual dipping bowls. Serve nuggets with apricot sauce.

MENU: Cucumber slices and cherry tomatoes. Shoestring potatoes. Angel food cake with sliced fresh strawberries and nondairy whipped topping.

SERVINGS: Makes 4 servings; 1½ cups dipping sauce.

Chicken Tidbits with Pineapple Sauce

■ We have McDonald's to thank for bringing chicken nuggets to our attention. Now these tasty little morsels can be purchased already breaded and ready for the oven in either fresh or frozen form at grocery stores. I buy them often because my granddaughter adores them. "Adore" might be too strong a word to describe them, but I find they make a satisfying, quick meal when served with a really good dipping sauce.

1 (1-lb.) package breaded, oven-ready
   chicken nuggets
⅔ cup pineapple jelly
¼ cup orange juice
1 teaspoon prepared horseradish
¼ teaspoon ground ginger

Prepare chicken nuggets according to package directions.

Meanwhile, combine jelly, orange juice, horseradish, and ginger in a 1-quart saucepan. Cook, stirring, over low heat until jelly melts. Serve nuggets with pineapple sauce.

MENU: Canned onion rings. Kaiser rolls. Tossed salad with peppercorn dressing. Bakery layer cake.

SERVINGS: Makes 4 servings.

Chicken Mozzarella

■ My children so loved this dish that it was all they would order at a local Italian restaurant. I tried to duplicate what the restaurant served with fresh chicken breasts and a homemade sauce, but my children said that my dish just didn't compare. So I put together this simple four-ingredient, convenience product–driven version. They ask for it all the time. Can you believe it?

1 (12-oz.) package breaded chicken breast
   patties (see Note, below)
4 slices mozzarella cheese
2 cups marinara sauce
Grated Parmesan cheese

Prepare patties according to package directions. Place mozzarella cheese slices on top of patties 1 to 2 minutes before baking time is complete.

While chicken cooks, heat marinara sauce in a small saucepan over low heat, stirring occasionally. Spoon warm sauce over patties and cheese. Sprinkle with Parmesan cheese.

MENU: Marinated artichoke hearts on escarole leaves. Bakery sticky buns.

SERVINGS: Makes 4 servings.

NOTE
Frozen chicken breast patties can be used but will take longer to bake.

Chicken & Bean Burritos

■ The ingredients list looks long, but there's nothing exotic to collect and everything comes together with very little trouble.

1 tablespoon corn oil
2 tablespoons chopped green bell pepper
2 tablespoons chopped onion
1 teaspoon chili powder
1 (15-oz.) can red kidney beans, rinsed and drained
½ cup taco sauce
½ pound shredded cooked chicken
4 (8-inch) flour tortillas, warmed
½ cup (2 ounces) shredded Monterey Jack cheese with chiles
Sour cream

Heat oil in an 10-inch skillet over medium heat. Add bell pepper and onion and cook until soft, about 2 minutes. Stir in chili powder and cook 1 minute.

Stir in beans and taco sauce; heat through, about 1 minute. Gently stir in chicken; heat through, about 3 minutes.

Spoon ⅓ cup of chicken-bean filling in center of each tortilla. Add 2 tablespoons cheese to each burrito. Fold over and roll up to make burritos. Serve with sour cream.

MENU: Lettuce-and-tomato salad with lemon vinaigrette. Cinnamon toast.

SERVINGS: Makes 4 servings.

Creamed Chicken

■ This is comfort food. Serve it over bakery biscuits that can be warmed in the oven.

¼ cup butter
¼ cup chopped scallions
⅛ teaspoon dried sage
¼ cup instant flour (see Note, page 33)
1 (14.5-oz.) can chicken broth
1 pound cooked chicken, cut into bite-size pieces

Melt butter with scallions and sage in a 2-quart saucepan over medium heat. Stir in flour and cook, stirring, 2 minutes. Gradually stir in broth. Cook, stirring constantly, until mixture boils and thickens, about 3 minutes. Stir in chicken; heat through.

MENU: Bakery biscuits. Deli green bean salad. Chocolate ice cream with marshmallow topping.

SERVINGS: Makes 4 servings.

Hot Chicken Salad

■ This is a very pretty main dish salad that's full of crunchy good taste. I use the grating disc of my food processor to shred the squash and carrot.

2 tablespoons vegetable oil
⅔ (8-oz.) package (2 cups) coleslaw mix
2 cups chopped cooked chicken breast
¼ cup ranch dressing
1 small yellow squash, shredded
1 carrot, peeled and shredded

Heat 1 tablespoon of the oil in a 10-inch skillet over medium heat. Add coleslaw mix and stir-fry until tender, about 6 minutes. Spoon coleslaw mixture into a large bowl. Wipe skillet clean with a paper towel.

Heat remaining 1 tablespoon of oil in skillet over medium heat. Add chicken and stir-fry until heated through, about 4 minutes. Remove chicken from pan with a slotted spoon; add chicken to coleslaw mix. Pour ranch dressing into the skillet and cook, stirring, just to warm, about 1 minute. Pour dressing over chicken and coleslaw. Toss to blend. Top with shredded squash and carrots.

MENU: Toasted multigrain bread. Bakery peanut butter cookies.

SERVINGS: Makes 4 servings.

Chicken Quesadillas

■ This is how you pronounce quesadilla—key-sah-DEE-yah. Originally a snack food, sometimes an appetizer, they also make a great entree. I used leftover chicken to make mine, but if there were no leftover chicken, roasted chicken from the supermarket or fast-food restaurant works fine.

½ pound cooked chicken, shredded
½ cup shredded Monterey Jack cheese with chiles
¼ teaspoon chili powder
4 (about 8-inch) flour tortillas
1 tablespoon vegetable oil
Salsa

Preheat broiler. Combine chicken, cheese, and chili powder in a medium bowl.

Place 2 tortillas on a baking sheet sprayed with nonstick cooking spray. Divide chicken mixture between the 2 tortillas. Top with remaining 2 tortillas. Brush tortillas with a little oil.

Broil 3 inches from source of heat for 3 minutes or until browned. With a large pancake turner, carefully turn tortillas over. Brush with remaining oil. Broil until browned.

Cut each tortilla into 3 wedges.

MENU: Sliced tomato and Bibb lettuce. Vanilla pudding.

SERVINGS: Makes 2 servings.

Hot & Spicy Chicken

■ This is an unusual way to serve an already cooked roasted chicken. The corn muffins are good for helping sop up the extra sauce. If you have time to cook rice, it makes a nice side dish.

1 (2½-lb.) cooked rotisserie chicken
2 tablespoons vegetable oil
⅓ cup chopped onion
1 tablespoon chili powder
1 teaspoon cayenne pepper
1 (14-oz.) jar thick spaghetti sauce
¼ cup red wine vinegar

Heat chicken according to package directions.

Meanwhile, heat oil in a Dutch oven or a large saucepan over medium heat. Add onion, chili powder, and cayenne. Cook, stirring occasionally, until onion is tender, about 5 minutes.

Stir in spaghetti sauce and vinegar. Reduce heat to low. Cover and simmer 8 minutes, stirring occasionally.

Remove chicken to a platter. Cut into serving pieces. Spoon some sauce over chicken pieces. Serve the remaining sauce on the side.

MENU: Bakery corn muffins. Diced apples and cucumbers with ranch dressing. Frozen yogurt.

SERVINGS: Makes 4 servings.

Turkey

When I was growing up, turkey and all the trimmings was a twice-a-year treat—Thanksgiving and Christmas. As wonderful as roasted turkey is, I'm so glad the turkey industry found a way for consumers to enjoy turkey meat with less epic meals than those.

Today there is a variety of turkey cuts that lend themselves to quick, home-cooked meals. Turkey can be a quick, inexpensive, and low-calorie meat that can be prepared in dozens of ways.

In addition to turkey parts—drumsticks, breast, wings, thighs—there are tenderloins, which are long cuts of turkey breast; turkey cutlets, which are thinner medallions of turkey breast; and ground turkey. I've put all of them to use one way or the other in my kitchen. I have broiled, pan-fried, grilled, braised, and stir-fried them all.

I still find it amazing that turkey prepared in these ways doesn't taste like the roasted turkey with stuffing that we serve on Thanksgiving. Turkey has a mild taste that works well when cooked with herbs, spices, or savory sauces.

Turkey Tenderloins Dijon

■ Seasoned bread crumbs help me a lot in the kitchen. They mean I don't have to add the herbs.

About ¼ cup all-purpose flour
1 egg
3 tablespoons milk
1 tablespoon Dijon mustard
½ cup seasoned bread crumbs
4 turkey tenderloins, rinsed and patted dry
2 tablespoons canola oil

Sprinkle flour onto a large plate. Combine egg, milk, and mustard in a shallow bowl and beat well with a fork. Sprinkle bread crumbs onto a large plate.

Dredge turkey in flour, then dip into egg-milk mixture. Dip into bread crumbs, coating all sides of turkey.

Heat oil in a 10-inch skillet over medium-high heat. Add turkey and sauté for 5 minutes per side or until crispy and turkey is no longer pink in center.

MENU: Spinach and mushroom salad with lemon vinaigrette. Kaiser rolls. Strawberries with whipped cream.

SERVINGS: Makes 4 servings.

Broiled Turkey Tenderloins

■ Turkey tenderloins are a real treat in our house, especially since the budget doesn't always permit veal. Turkey tenderloins are a good substitute—honestly, I can barely tell the difference.

½ cup red-wine-vinegar-and-oil salad
   dressing
1 teaspoon chopped fresh oregano or
   ½ teaspoon dried
1 pound turkey tenderloins, rinsed and
   patted dry

Preheat broiler. Combine salad dressing and oregano in a shallow glass pan. Mix well. Add turkey tenderloins.

Drain turkey, reserving marinade. Place turkey on a broiler pan rack that has been sprayed with nonstick cooking spray and broil 4 inches from source of heat for 10 to 13 minutes or until turkey is no longer pink in center, brushing with dressing mixture throughout cooking time.

MENU: Cucumber slices with dill in cucumber salad dressing. Marbled rye bread. Bakery lemon meringue pie.

SERVINGS: Makes 4 servings.

End-of-Summer Stir-Fry

■ This is a favorite way to use up extra zucchini.

1 turkey cutlet (about 1 pound), rinsed, patted dry, and cut into ¾-inch squares
5 tablespoons stir-fry sauce
3 tablespoons vegetable oil
1 medium onion, cut into eight wedges
5 cups zucchini slices
1 large clove garlic, minced
8 cherry tomatoes, halved

Combine turkey with 2 tablespoons of the stir-fry sauce in a medium bowl.

Heat 1 tablespoon of the oil in a wok or 10-inch skillet over high heat. Add turkey and stir-fry 2 minutes. Remove turkey with a slotted spoon and keep warm.

Heat remaining oil in same pan. Add onion; stir-fry 2 minutes. Add zucchini and garlic; stir-fry 4 minutes. Stir in turkey and remaining stir-fry sauce.

Cook, stirring, until turkey and vegetables are coated with sauce. Add tomato halves and heat through.

MENU: Chinese sesame noodles. Pineapple spears. Bakery almond cookies.

SERVINGS: Makes 4 servings.

Mexican Turkey

■ I once suggested that parsley would be a reasonable substitute for fresh cilantro (sometimes called coriander). A lot of readers complained that the two look-alike herbs are not taste-alike herbs.

I knew that. And while I still think parsley will work as a substitute, I also agree with their sentiments 100 percent. There's nothing like fresh cilantro—nothing.

Pungent and bitter, cilantro is perhaps an acquired, but not disagreeable, taste. When chopped and minced like parsley, it can be mixed with cheese and sour cream in Mexican turkey for an extraordinary taste.

¼ pound shredded Monterey Jack cheese with chiles
2 tablespoons chopped fresh cilantro
½ cup sour cream
1 tablespoon unsalted butter
1 tablespoon canola oil
4 turkey breast fillets, rinsed and patted dry

Preheat broiler. Combine cheese, cilantro, and sour cream in a small bowl. Set aside.

Heat butter and oil in a 10-inch skillet over medium-high heat. Add turkey fillets 2 at a time and cook until browned, about 5 minutes per side.

Transfer turkey to a broiler pan rack that has been sprayed with nonstick cooking spray. Top each turkey fillet with a generous spoonful of sour cream mixture. Broil 4 inches from source of heat for about 2 minutes or until topping bubbles.

MENU: Rice salad. Orange-spinach salad with honey-mustard vinaigrette. Coffee ice cream.

SERVINGS: Makes 4 servings.

Sherry Turkey

■ "Deglazing" is a term that might stop novice cooks dead in their tracks. No need for fear. Deglazing is a relatively simple procedure performed after meat has been browned and the food and excess fat removed from the pan.

Deglazing is done by heating a small amount of liquid in the pan and stirring to loosen the browned bits of food on the bottom. The liquid used is most often wine or stock. I use sherry for deglazing after browning and cooking turkey cutlets. The resulting mixture makes a delicious sauce.

1 pound turkey cutlets, rinsed and patted dry
About ¼ cup all-purpose flour
⅓ cup butter
½ cup dry sherry
½ cup chopped fresh parsley

Flatten turkey with a meat mallet to about ¼-inch thickness. Dredge turkey in flour. Melt butter in large skillet over medium heat.

Add turkey and sauté 4 to 5 minutes on each side or until no longer pink in center. Remove from pan and keep warm. Add sherry to pan and boil 1 minute, stirring to loosen browned bits. Spoon over turkey.

Garnish with parsley.

MENU: Crudités with peppercorn salad dressing. Oat-bran muffins. Lime sherbet with fresh fruit.

SERVINGS: Makes 4 servings.

Sage Turkey

■ It wouldn't seem like Thanksgiving without the combined aroma of roasting turkey and sage. I never thought of sage and turkey together in any other way until one summer when my herb garden was overrun by an aggressive sage plant. Not that I minded; I'm a great fan of fresh sage. I find the aroma extremely pleasing and the soft grayish green, downy leaves nice to touch.

I found lots of ways to use sage leaves, including threading them onto kebabs. I used this recipe on the outdoor grill and liked it so much I adapted it for inside cooking.

Sage is great with turkey, Thanksgiving or not. For the grill, I use a mix of oil, sage, and garlic as a marinade; for inside cooking, I use oil for frying and the sage and garlic as seasonings. You'll be surprised by the new taste.

Instant rice
2 teaspoons olive oil
1 pound turkey cutlets, rinsed, patted dry, and halved
5 fresh sage leaves, minced
2 cloves garlic, minced

Prepare instant rice according to package directions for 4 servings.

Meanwhile, heat oil in a 10-inch frying pan over medium-high heat. Add turkey and cook until browned, about 2 minutes per side.

Sprinkle turkey with sage and garlic. Reduce heat to medium-low, cover pan, and simmer for 10 minutes or until turkey is no longer pink in center.

MENU: Deli green bean salad. Spinach salad with strawberries and poppy-seed dressing. Assorted bakery cupcakes.

SERVINGS: Makes 4 servings.

Turkey Pizza

■ I don't make a lot of pizza at home, despite the abundance of precooked pizza shells and Italian flat breads such as foccacia that are readily available, because pizza is one of those foods that I call to be delivered. But there are delectable variations on pizza that aren't sold at pizzerias.

In order to keep the time less than 15 minutes from stove to table, turn the oven on a.s.a.p. It will take at least 10 minutes to reach the proper temperature, but this pizza needs only 5 minutes so we're under the deadline.

1 tablespoon olive oil
¼ cup thinly sliced onion
¼ cup sliced mushrooms
¾ cup pizza sauce
1 (about 12-inch) prebaked pizza shell
½ pound deli roasted turkey breast slices, cut into strips
½ cup (2 ounces) shredded mozzarella cheese

Preheat oven to 375F (190C). Heat olive oil in an 8-inch skillet over medium-high heat. Add onion and mushrooms and sauté until softened, about 4 minutes.

Meanwhile, spread pizza sauce over pizza shell. Top sauce with onion and mushrooms. Arrange turkey slices over vegetables. Sprinkle with cheese.

Bake until cheese melts, about 7 minutes. Cut into wedges to serve.

MENU: Tossed salad with Italian dressing. Black olives. Honeydew melon.

SERVINGS: Makes 6 servings.

Curried Turkey

■ This is a slightly exotic dish that can be made either in the broiler or, in fair weather, on the grill.

1 cup honey
½ cup olive oil
5 tablespoons curry powder
2 teaspoons chopped fresh flat-leaf parsley
¼ teaspoon freshly ground black pepper
6 garlic cloves, minced
1 pound turkey tenderloins, rinsed, patted dry, and cut into 2-inch strips
Onion wedges
Unpeeled apple wedges, brushed with lemon juice

Preheat broiler. Combine honey, olive oil, curry powder, parsley, black pepper, and garlic in a shallow bowl. Add turkey strips and set aside for 5 minutes.

Drain turkey strips, reserving marinade, and thread onto 4 metal skewers alternating with onion wedges. Place skewers on a preheated broiler pan that has been sprayed with nonstick cooking spray. Broil 4 inches from source of heat for 6 to 10 minutes, turning and brushing with more marinade as the strips and onion cook. Serve skewers with apple wedges.

MENU: Pita bread. Cucumber slices in yogurt with chopped flat-leaf parsley. Mango with candied ginger.

SERVINGS: Makes 4 servings.

Turkey Cutlets with Sun-Dried Tomatoes

■ I usually add sun-dried tomatoes to salads. They add a wonderful tangy spark to dark green salads. But when I do cook with them, I find that I like the contrast they provide for mild-flavored poultry. I use them here to great advantage in this simple but festive-looking dish.

¼ cup instant flour (see Note, page 33)
Dash of hot Hungarian paprika
1¼ pounds turkey cutlets, rinsed
2 tablespoons olive oil
1 green bell pepper, thinly sliced
1 cup mushroom slices
½ cup oil-packed sun-dried tomato strips, drained
1 teaspoon chopped fresh basil
¼ teaspoon salt
⅛ teaspoon freshly ground black pepper

Combine flour and paprika in a shallow bowl. Press turkey cutlets with your palms to flatten slightly. Dredge turkey in flour mixture.

Heat oil in a 10-inch skillet over medium-high heat. Add bell pepper and mushrooms and sauté until softened, about 2 minutes. Add turkey and sauté, turning, until golden brown, about 5 minutes per side. Add sun-dried tomatoes and basil and cook until heated through, about 2 minutes. Season with salt and black pepper.

MENU: Hard rolls. Lettuce-and-tomato salad with ranch dressing. Angel food cake with light nondairy whipped topping and fresh strawberries.

SERVINGS: Makes 4 or 5 servings.

Oktoberfest Turkey Burgers

■ All you'll need is an oom-pah band when you serve this German-inspired hot sandwich. Ground turkey incorporates the flavors beautifully.

1 pound ground turkey
1 tablespoon canola oil
4 slices Muenster cheese
3 tablespoons butter
1½ cups thinly sliced onion
⅔ cup chopped unpeeled apple
8 slices dark rye bread, toasted
Whole-grain mustard

Form turkey into 4 patties. Heat oil in a 10-inch skillet over medium heat. Add turkey patties and cook, turning once, about 10 minutes or until no longer pink in centers. Top each patty with a slice of Muenster cheese and cook until cheese starts to melt, about 1 minute.

Meanwhile, melt butter in an 8-inch skillet over medium heat. Add onions and stir-fry 5 minutes. Add apple and stir-fry 4 minutes or until softened.

Spread 4 slices of rye toast with mustard. Top with onion and apple mixture, then a patty. Top with remaining toasted bread slices.

MENU: Deli-style potato chips. Deli coleslaw. Bakery apple strudel.

SERVINGS: Makes 4 servings.

Turkey & Chanterelles

■ Chanterelle mushrooms are trumpet shaped and come in colors ranging from yellow to orange. They have a lovely delicate and nutty flavor. Their texture is somewhat chewy, and they need a little attention during cooking because they can become tough. If fresh chanterelles are not available, substitute regular mushrooms, but promise to make this dish again when chanterelle time—summer and winter—comes again.

¼ cup plus 2 tablespoons instant flour (see Note, page 33)
¼ teaspoon salt
Dash of paprika
1 to 1¼ pounds turkey tenderloins, rinsed, patted dry, and cut into 2-by-¾-inch strips
¼ cup butter
1 cup chanterelle mushrooms
2 cups half-and-half
2 ounces (½ cup) shredded Swiss cheese
3 tablespoons dry sherry
Salt and fresh black pepper

Combine ¼ cup flour with salt and paprika in a shallow bowl. Dredge turkey in flour mixture.

Melt butter in a 10-inch skillet over medium-high heat. Add turkey and stir-fry until browned, about 2 minutes. Remove turkey with a slotted spoon and keep warm.

Add the chanterelles; sauté 1 minute. Add the remaining 2 tablespoons of flour and cook, stirring constantly, until bubbly. Add half-and-half and cook, stirring, until thickened, about 5 minutes.

Add turkey and cheese and cook, stirring, until cheese melts, about 2 minutes. Stir in sherry and cook 1 minute. Season with salt and pepper to taste.

MENU: French baguettes. Deli green bean salad. Bakery chocolate cake with vanilla icing.

SERVINGS: Makes 4 servings.

Quick Turkey à L'Orange

■ The culinary phrase "l'orange" means cooked with orange juice. It sounds kind of fancy, and the wine called for in the ingredient list makes it a kind of grown-ups-only dish, but if you want to serve this lovely citrusy turkey dish to the whole family, simply eliminate the wine and use more orange juice instead.

Instant rice
¼ cup instant flour (see note, page 33)
1 teaspoon salt
Dash of paprika
1 to 1½ pounds turkey tenderloins, rinsed, patted dry, and sliced lengthwise
3 tablespoons butter
½ cup orange juice
½ cup white wine
Orange rounds

Prepare instant rice according to package directions for 4 servings.

Meanwhile, combine flour with salt and paprika in a shallow bowl. Dredge turkey in flour mixture.

Melt butter in a 10-inch skillet over

medium-high heat. Add turkey and sauté until browned, about 4 minutes. Add orange juice and wine, cover, and simmer for 5 minutes. Remove cover and simmer until liquid is slightly thickened, 3 to 4 minutes.

Spoon turkey on top of rice on a platter. Garnish with orange rounds. Serve pan juices on the side.

MENU: French bread. Spinach salad with cherry tomatoes and French dressing. Bakery pirouette cookies.

SERVINGS: Makes 4 servings.

Mediterranean Turkey with Olives

■ Have you ever stood in a grove of olive trees? Doing so is something akin to a spiritual experience. Some of the trees are hundreds of years old, and they still produce the fruit that drives the lifestyle and food of the Mediterranean. In recent years, a wider variety of olives has become available in grocery stores. They're not as convenient as the canned or bottled variety, but they taste wonderful. If you simply don't have time to pit the olives called for in this recipe, then substitute pitted canned or bottled olives. The recipe will work well, and taste good, but it won't be sublime.

About ¼ cup all-purpose flour
1 teaspoon seasoned salt
Freshly ground black pepper
2 pounds turkey tenderloins, rinsed, patted dry, and cut into 1½-inch cubes
2 tablespoons light olive oil
1 clove garlic, minced
2 shallots, thinly sliced
⅓ teaspoon crushed rosemary
¼ cup marinara sauce
½ cup chicken broth
½ cup chopped fresh flat-leaf parsley
15 pitted and sliced ripe olives

Combine flour with seasoned salt and pepper in a shallow bowl. Dredge turkey in flour mixture.

Heat olive oil in a deep 10-inch skillet over medium-high heat. Add turkey and cook, turning, until golden, about 6 minutes. Add garlic and shallots and cook 2 minutes. Add rosemary, marinara sauce, and chicken broth.

Cover and simmer 5 minutes. Uncover and stir in parsley and olives. Simmer 2 minutes.

MENU: Portuguese bread. Mixed field greens with light Italian dressing. Bakery sugar cookies.

SERVINGS: Makes 6 servings.

Turkey Piquant

▪ I buy lemons every time I shop for groceries so that I never run out. I use them in many ways to enliven salads and salad dressings, cooked dishes, beverages—What is iced tea without a lemon? I even add lemon to colas for a change of pace. In this quick turkey dish, they put the "p" in piquant.

1 to 1½ pounds turkey tenderloins, rinsed
   and cut in half lengthwise
¼ cup all-purpose flour
½ teaspoon seasoned salt
¼ teaspoon coarsely ground black pepper
⅓ cup butter
1 tablespoon canola oil
1 teaspoon minced shallots
1 clove garlic, minced
Juice of 2 lemons
¼ cup chopped fresh flat-leaf parsley

Flatten turkey with a meat mallet to about ¼-inch thickness. Combine flour with seasoned salt and pepper in a shallow bowl. Dredge turkey in flour mixture.

Heat butter with oil in a 10-inch skillet over medium-high heat. Add shallots and garlic and sauté until soft, about 1 minute. Add turkey and sauté, turning until browned, about 8 minutes. Remove from pan; keep warm on a platter.

Add lemon juice to pan and stir to dissolve any cooked brown bits. Boil 1 minute. Add parsley and pour over turkey.

MENU: Dark rye bread. Packaged Caesar salad. Bakery blueberry pie.

SERVINGS: Makes 4 servings.

Turkey & Peppers, Italian Style

▪ Turkey is not a dish served much in Italy. However, turkey works very well with Italian-style cooking, which is simple and direct with great flavors developed from fresh ingredients.

1½ pounds turkey tenderloins, rinsed, patted
   dry, and cut in half lengthwise
All-purpose flour
2 tablespoons light olive oil
4 green bell peppers, cut into thin strips
2 cloves garlic, chopped
1 medium tomato, chopped
1 cup marinara sauce
1 tablespoon fresh basil, chopped
Salt and freshly ground black pepper

Flatten turkey with a meat mallet to about ¼-inch thickness. Dredge in flour to coat evenly.

Heat olive oil in a 10-inch skillet over medium-high heat. Add turkey and cook, turning, until browned, about 5 minutes.

Add bell peppers and garlic and cook until bell peppers are tender, about 4 minutes. Stir in tomato and marinara sauce. Simmer 2 minutes, stirring occasionally. Add basil, salt, and black pepper to taste.

MENU: Italian bread. Endive and cucumbers with black-pepper vinaigrette. Lemon sherbet.

SERVINGS: Makes 4 servings.

Spanish Rice

- I have an old recipe for Spanish rice that takes 1½ hours to cook.

It also requires a lot of pans—first to brown the meat, another to bake, and another to fill with water to put under the baking pan to give the Spanish rice just the right moisture and texture. I don't make it very often.

After sampling canned Spanish rice, boxed Spanish rice, and envelopes of dehydrated Spanish rice, I decided to create a shorter version of the classic dish. When I'm in a rush, I use quick-cooking rice; if I have more time, I'll put real rice on to cook while I prepare the sauce.

1½ cups quick-cooking rice
2 tablespoons corn oil
½ pound ground turkey
1 (14-oz) jar garden-style chunky pasta sauce
1 (4-oz.) jar chopped pimientos, drained
1½ teaspoons salt
1 clove garlic, minced
1 cup Cheddar cheese cubes

Cook rice according to directions.

Meanwhile, heat corn oil in a 10-inch skillet over medium-high heat. Add turkey and cook, stirring to break up turkey, until browned. Add sauce, pimientos, salt, and garlic. Reduce heat and bring to a simmer.

Stir cooked rice into sauce and simmer until liquid thickens slightly. Stir in cheese and simmer until cheese melts.

MENU: Salad of curly endive, pitted olives, and red onion with lemon vinaigrette. Bakery coconut macaroons.

SERVINGS: Makes 4 servings.

Teriyaki Burgers

- Teriyaki sauce, the ever-helpful kitchen staple, gives these burgers an Asian twist.

1 pound ground turkey
⅓ cup chopped canned water chestnuts
⅓ cup teriyaki sauce, plus additional sauce
    for basting
4 sesame-seed buns

Preheat broiler. Mix together turkey, water chestnuts, and teriyaki sauce in a medium bowl. Form into 4 patties.

Place patties on a broiler pan rack that has been sprayed with nonstick cooking spray. Broil 4 inches from source of heat 10 minutes or until no longer pink in centers, turning once and basting with additional sauce. Serve on buns.

MENU: Scallion potato chips. Green salad with cherry tomatoes. Vanilla ice cream with blueberries.

SERVINGS: Makes 4 servings.

Mexican Rice & Turkey

■ Where have I been? I can now find white shoepeg corn in markets both frozen and canned. What a boon!

1 tablespoon sunflower oil
1 pound ground turkey
1 (16-oz.) jar salsa
1 (11-oz.) can white shoepeg corn, drained
¼ cup chopped red bell pepper
1 jalapeño chile, seeded and chopped
1½ cups water
1 teaspoon hot Mexican chili powder
1½ cups instant rice
1 cup shredded Monterey Jack cheese

Heat oil in a 12-inch skillet over medium heat. Add turkey and cook until browned, about 5 minutes, stirring to break up turkey. Stir in salsa, corn, bell pepper, chile, water, and chili powder. Bring to a boil.

Stir in rice. Cover and remove from heat. Let stand 5 to 7 minutes, or until liquid is absorbed. Fluff with a fork. Sprinkle with cheese.

MENU: Corn chips. Chocolate ice cream.

SERVINGS: Makes 6 servings.

Herbal Turkey Patties

■ If you have an herb garden, this is a dish to make at the height of the growing season. Fresh herbs make this into much more than a burger.

1 pound ground turkey
½ red bell pepper, minced
¼ cup minced fresh chives
Seasoned salt
1 tablespoon chopped fresh lemon thyme
1½ teaspoons chopped fresh sage
2 tablespoons chopped fresh parsley
1 egg

Combine all ingredients in a large bowl. Form mixture into 4 patties.

Spray a nonstick 10-inch skillet with non-stick cooking spray. Add patties and cook about 5 minutes per side or until no longer pink in centers.

MENU: Sesame-seed rolls. Lettuce, tomato, and red onion slices. Fresh peaches with bakery coconut macaroons.

SERVINGS: Makes 4 servings.

Turkey Chow Mein

■ Fresh ground turkey is best if used within two days of purchase. Lean ground turkey (without skin) is a good choice for anyone who is watching his or her calories and fat intake, because it has less fat than other ground meats.

1 pound ground turkey
1 small onion, chopped
2 stalks celery, sliced
2 tablespoons stir-fry sauce
1 cup vegetable juice, such as V8
1 cup sliced mushrooms
1 cup bean sprouts

Cook ground turkey in a 12-inch skillet or wok over medium-high heat until browned, stirring to break up turkey. Add onion and celery; cook until onion is tender, about 2 minutes. Stir in stir-fry sauce, juice, and mushrooms.

Reduce heat, cover, and simmer 10 minutes. Top with bean sprouts.

MENU: Chow mein noodles. Pineapple spears.

SERVINGS: Makes 4 servings.

Turkey Stir-Fry with Tofu

■ Nobody smiles when I announce we're having tofu for dinner—even when I chide about how tofu is an excellent vegetarian source of high-quality protein and iron. A good source of B vitamins. Calcium, potassium, zinc. No? Studies show that soy products may protect against heart disease and some forms of cancer. If your family doesn't want to know, just announce that we're having a turkey stir-fry for dinner.

2 tablespoons peanut oil
1 tablespoon Chinese black bean sauce
2 tablespoons chopped scallions
1 garlic clove, minced
½ pound ground turkey
1 tablespoon soy sauce
⅓ cup chicken broth
½ cup 1-inch tofu cubes, drained

Heat oil in a 10-inch skillet or wok over high heat. Add bean sauce, scallions, garlic, and turkey. Stir-fry until turkey is no longer pink, about 5 minutes, stirring to break up turkey.

Add soy sauce and broth. Cook 1 minute. Carefully stir in tofu cubes. Reduce heat to a simmer and cook about 5 minutes.

MENU: Deli coleslaw. Deli marinated mushrooms. Pineapple spears.

SERVINGS: Makes 2 servings.

Eggs

Remember when eggs were bad for us? I never stopped buying them, because I needed them for baking, but I stopped eating eggs as a food because of health warnings—first about cholesterol content, and then, safety warnings about salmonella.

Today, scientists are telling us that eggs are not the bad guys they thought, either as a cause of high cholesterol or as a worry for salmonella poisoning for people in good health. Which is great news because eggs are wonderful for eating and a good and inexpensive source of protein.

The rule of thumb to follow in eating eggs is basically what it is for eating other foodstuffs: Eggs can be consumed in moderation as part of a healthful eating regimen.

I'm doing that. I dusted off my omelet recipes, experimented with new combinations, and brought to the table some enticing dishes made in a flash, courtesy of a hardworking hen.

I keep eggs on hand as part of a 15-minute chef pantry. They have saved me in the worst of time crunches.

BUYING & STORING EGGS

Just a note about buying and storing eggs: Always check the date on the carton to be sure they are the freshest available eggs. Store eggs in the refrigerator. According to the American Egg Board, fresh eggs in the shell can be stored in their carton in the refrigerator for 4 to 5 weeks beyond the pack date without significant quality loss.

EGG SAFETY

Never eat raw or cracked eggs and cook egg yolks until set. Casseroles and custards containing eggs should be cooked to 160F (70C) on an instant-read thermometer.

India Eggs

■ Here are the things I know about making omelets: It takes a good amount of butter or margarine to make the pan slick enough so that the eggs are easily maneuvered. The second thing is to use a nonstick pan. My success rate is better when those two rules are followed.

The third thing is to make sure that the butter really sizzles in the pan before you add the eggs, then reduce the heat so it is low and steady. When the eggs look like a pancake that needs to be flipped, add the filling and proceed as the recipe directs.

The recipe for India eggs yields one omelet—it's better to make one at a time.

2 large eggs
2 tablespoons water
¼ teaspoon curry powder
1 to 2 teaspoons unsalted margarine or
   butter
2 tablespoons cream cheese
2 tablespoons apricot chutney

Lightly beat eggs, water, and curry powder in a small bowl.

Place a small frying pan over medium heat for 1 minute. Add margarine or butter and swirl to coat bottom and sides. When margarine sizzles, add egg mixture. Tilt pan so that egg covers the bottom.

When egg looks like a pancake that needs to be flipped (and eggs are moist and just about set), drop pieces of cream cheese over half the omelet. Fold other half of omelet over top.

Slide omelet onto a plate. Spoon chutney on top.

MENU: Lentil soup. Orange and kiwi slices.

SERVINGS: Makes 1 serving.

Gruyère Omelet

■ Eggs are back, restored to their rightful place to be consumed in moderation as part of a well-balanced diet. Cooks in a hurry thank the scientists who researched their nutritious qualities.

4 large eggs
¼ cup half-and-half
Salt and freshly ground black pepper
2 tablespoons butter
1¼ cups (5 ounces) grated Gruyère cheese
Chopped red onion for garnish

Whisk together eggs, half-and-half, salt, and pepper in a medium bowl.

Melt butter in an 8-inch nonstick sauté pan or skillet over medium heat. When butter begins to sizzle, add egg mixture. During cooking, lift edges of eggs to allow liquid to run under the cooked portion. As eggs start to set, add grated cheese in an even layer.

As cheese begins to melt, loosen edges with a spatula, turning one half over the other. Cook until egg mixture is set, about 1 minute.

Slide omelet onto a serving plate. Garnish with red onions.

MENU: Sausage-stuffed bread. Bakery chocolate eclairs.

SERVINGS: Makes 2 servings.

Florentine Frittata

■ A frittata is an Italian omelet that is usually made with ingredients mixed with the eggs rather than folded inside, and unlike an omelet, it is not turned but the top is cooked under the broiler. It is also a quick meal. Buy the mushrooms already sliced in the produce section.

3 tablespoons butter
¼ cup minced onion
1¼ cups (1½ pound) sliced mushrooms
1½ cups chopped spinach leaves
8 large eggs, lightly beaten
½ teaspoon seasoned salt
½ cup grated Parmesan cheese

Preheat broiler. Melt butter in a 10-inch cast-iron or flameproof skillet over medium heat. Add onion and mushrooms and sauté until softened, about 2 minutes. Add spinach and cook for 1 minute.

Pour eggs into pan. Cook over low heat until eggs are set, about 7 minutes. Sprinkle with seasoned salt.

Place frittata about 6 inches from source of heat and broil for 3 minutes or until top is set. Sprinkle with grated Parmesan cheese. Cut into wedges.

MENU: Sausage-stuffed bread. Artichoke hearts in oil and vinegar. Tapioca pudding.

SERVINGS: Makes 4 servings.

Spinach Tortilla

■ A *tortilla* in Spain is not a *tortilla* in Mexico. Spanish tortillas are omelets, quick and easy to make.

1 tablespoon olive oil
1 small onion, chopped
1 (15-oz.) can whole potatoes, drained and chopped
½ teaspoon seasoned salt
2 cups shredded spinach leaves
6 eggs
¾ cup farmer cheese
Pinch of ground allspice

Heat olive oil in an 8-inch skillet or sauté pan over medium heat. Add onion, potatoes, and seasoned salt and sauté for 2 minutes. Stir in spinach and cook until it starts to wilt, about 2 minutes.

Lightly beat eggs in a medium bowl. Beat in cheese and allspice and pour over spinach mixture. Reduce heat and gently cook until eggs are set, about 7 minutes. Slide tortilla out of pan onto a serving dish.

MENU: Zucchini and tomato slices with tarragon vinegar. Crusty rolls. Orange sections with toasted coconut.

SERVINGS: Makes 4 servings.

Eggs Italiano

■ Breaking the egg into a cup prevents the yolk from breaking as it goes into the sauce. It's an extra step but worth the trouble.

1½ cups marinara sauce
4 large eggs
1 teaspoon chopped fresh oregano leaves or
　½ teaspoon dried
4 slices Italian bread, toasted
Freshly grated Parmesan cheese

Heat marinara sauce to boiling in a medium skillet over medium heat. Reduce heat so mixture simmers. Break 1 egg into a cup. Slip the egg from the cup into the sauce. Repeat with remaining eggs. Sprinkle chopped oregano over eggs. Cover and simmer for about 4 minutes or until whites are set.

Serve eggs over toast. Ladle on extra sauce. Pass Parmesan cheese.

MENU: Deli green bean salad. Marinated olives. Italian sesame-seed cookies.

SERVINGS: Makes 2 servings.

Mexican Scrambled Eggs

■ If you have a taste for hot foods, use hot ground chili powder.

8 large eggs
2 tablespoons milk
1 tablespoon chili powder
2 tablespoons corn oil
4 scallions, chopped

Lightly beat together eggs, milk, and chili powder in a medium bowl.

Heat oil in a 10-inch skillet over medium-high heat. Add scallions and cook until crisp-tender, about 1 minute. Add eggs and cook, stirring constantly, until just set.

MENU: Bakery corn muffins. Mexican-style stewed tomatoes. Chocolate pudding.

SERVINGS: Makes 4 servings.

Olé Omelet

■ Once I made chili that called for a hot chile unknown to me. The instructions said it was difficult to find this variety, especially in the Northeast. Whoever wrote the cookbook never visited New Jersey. I found the chile for my recipe in a little *bodega* in Perth Amboy, in the central part of the state.

The second editor's note said that if the chile were located, the cook should turn to page 9 of the cookbook for further instructions. Poppycock! What could page 9 tell an experienced cook like me? I set to work cutting up the hot chiles. Within seconds, my hands felt as if they were on fire. I was in agony!

If I had turned to page 9, it would have given me this simple instruction: Wear gloves. While the jalapeño chiles used here are not as potent as the little devils of my unfortunate encounter, they are not to be dismissed. Wear gloves if chopping them fresh, and be careful not to touch your eyes.

2 large eggs
2 tablespoons half-and-half
1 teaspoon fresh cilantro leaves, chopped
1 tablespoon butter
¼ cup shredded Monterey Jack cheese
1 small jalapeño chile, chopped
Salsa and sour cream (optional)

Beat together eggs, half-and-half, and cilantro in a small bowl.

Heat butter in 8-inch skillet over medium-high heat. When butter begins to brown, pour egg mixture into skillet. Slide skillet back and forth rapidly over heat and stir quickly with a fork to spread eggs continuously over bottom. Let stand a few seconds to lightly brown eggs.

Tilt skillet; run fork under edge of omelet, then jerk skillet sharply to loosen eggs from bottom. Sprinkle with cheese and chile.

Fold omelet to center. Slide omelet out of pan onto a plate. Serve with salsa and sour cream, if desired.

MENU: Bakery corn muffins. Deli three-bean salad. Apricot and nectarine slices topped with coconut.

SERVINGS: Makes 1 serving.

Deli Scramble

■ If I have a few eggs in my refrigerator, I have a meal—and a quick meal at that.

This is a scrambled-egg dish that always tastes a little different, because what goes into it depends a lot on what I have in the refrigerator. Maybe I find a bit of Cheddar, or half an onion, pepper, potato, tomato, salsa. Whatever's on hand goes into the frying pan. I advise anyone who makes deli scramble, so called because so often what goes in are remnants of leftover cold cuts and cheese—to add whatever they like. The only things I'd keep are the basics: butter, eggs, and milk. Then, let your leftovers be your guide. If cheese is among your finds, add it last, just before the eggs are cooked so it will melt but not burn in the pan.

I find a scrambled egg dish goes wonderfully well with crusty Italian bread, heated in the oven and topped with a little flavored olive oil or butter.

1 tablespoon butter
1 cup sliced mushrooms
1 cup diced salami
¼ cup chopped onion
8 large eggs
¼ cup milk
1 teaspoon dry mustard

Melt butter in a 10-inch skillet over medium heat. Add mushrooms, salami, and onion and cook until the mushrooms and onion are soft but not brown, about 3 minutes.

Meanwhile, beat together eggs, milk, and mustard in a medium bowl. Pour over vegetables and salami and cook, stirring constantly, until just set.

MENU: Citrus fruit salad. Crusty Italian bread. Bakery cheesecake.

SERVINGS: Makes 4 servings.

Nacho Eggs

■ Tortillas are the common bread of Mexico. They are unleavened, very flat rounds, something akin to a thin pancake or crepe. They are made from corn flour (masa) or wheat flour and can be found in supermarkets. Most non-Mexicans know them as the wrappers for burritos or tacos, but they're used in myriad dishes in Mexico—even soup.

I use them to add texture to a dish I call Nacho Eggs. It's a cross between a nacho appetizer and huevos rancheros (ranch eggs). It's a hearty, simple meal full of flavor. The fire from the diced jalapeño can be moderated to personal taste.

I don't use a lot of salt in my cooking, but this dish doesn't taste as good without it. For variation and color, I sometimes slice avocado around the dish.

8 corn tortillas
¼ cup canola oil
1 cup chopped onion
10 large eggs, beaten
1 teaspoon salt
3 tablespoons diced jalapeño chiles
8 ounces (2 cups) shredded Cheddar cheese
Taco sauce
Sour cream

Cut each tortilla into 12 wedges. Heat oil in a 10-inch skillet over medium-high heat. Add tortillas and fry until very crisp, stirring frequently.

Add onion and cook until crisp-tender, about 1 minute. Beat together eggs, salt, and chiles in a medium bowl. Pour over tortillas. Gently stir until eggs are set on the bottom and sides. Add cheese and stir to combine. Cook until cheese melts and eggs are firm.

Serve with taco sauce and sour cream.

MENU: Mixed greens tossed with chopped fresh cilantro leaves and favorite dressing. Rice pudding.

SERVINGS: Makes 5 or 6 servings.

Scrambled Eggs with Ham & Corn

■ Yes, you can make this dish with any of the egg substitutes available.

6 large eggs
¾ cup canned whole-kernel corn, drained
¼ cup diced cooked ham
2 scallions, finely chopped
½ teaspoon salt
⅛ teaspoon freshly ground black fresh
    pepper
2 tablespoons sunflower oil

Lightly beat eggs with a fork in a medium bowl. Stir in corn, ham, scallions, salt, and pepper.

Heat oil in an 8-inch skillet over medium-high heat. Pour in egg mixture. Cook, stirring slowly with a spatula, lifting and folding until all ingredients are well scrambled.

MENU: Toaster waffles with grape jelly. Fresh fruit cocktail.

SERVINGS: Makes 3 servings.

Huevos Rancheros

■ *Huevos rancheros* are a Mexican classic.

8 corn tortillas
1½ cups marinara sauce
½ teaspoon chili powder
3 tablespoons butter
½ cup finely chopped onion
3 green bell peppers, chopped
Salt
8 large eggs

Place tortillas, wrapped loosely in foil, in a 300F (150C) oven. Combine marinara sauce and chili powder in a 3-quart saucepan. Heat over low heat.

While tortillas warm and sauce heats, melt butter in a 10-inch skillet over medium heat. Add onion and bell peppers and stir-fry until soft and translucent, 5 minutes. Season with salt.

Break eggs over onion and peppers and fry until yolks are set.

Place warm tortillas on each of 4 plates. Spoon some sauce over tortillas. Top each serving with 2 eggs, some onion mixture, and another spoonful of sauce.

MENU: Bananas and strawberries.

SERVINGS: Makes 4 servings.

Tomato-Egg Dinner

■ I don't use cornstarch very often so it tends to get pushed to the back of the pantry shelf. It languishes there until I can no longer remember when I bought it, so I toss it. A great waste. Then I read that ¼ teaspoon of cornstarch per egg added before beating will make scrambled eggs seem richer and creamier. A ¼ teaspoon is not a great amount, but at least knowing I may need it keeps the cornstarch box to the front, and I'm not as likely to forget about it. And it really does make the eggs richer and creamier.

2 tablespoons butter
½ onion, chopped
2 tomatoes, cored and cut into chunks
½ teaspoon garlic salt
½ teaspoon cornstarch
2 to 3 large eggs
1 tablespoon chopped fresh parsley

Melt butter in a 10-inch skillet over medium heat. Add onion and cook until soft, about 5 minutes.

Increase heat to medium-high. Add tomatoes and garlic salt and simmer for 5 minutes, stirring occasionally, until liquid evaporates.

Beat together cornstarch and eggs with a fork in a small bowl. Add to tomato-onion mixture. Decrease heat to medium-low, cover skillet, and cook eggs until set, about 3 minutes. Sprinkle with fresh parsley.

MENU: Sourdough toast. Green grapes and Neufchâtel cheese cubes.

SERVINGS: Makes 2 or 3 servings.

Corn & Mushroom Scramble

■ Even before precut vegetables became widely available, this was an easy dish to make. Now with fresh sliced mushrooms at hand, this scramble is done in a dash. If you have whole mushrooms, dig out the egg slicer—the one with wire cutters. It will make quick work of slicing whole mushroom caps.

2 tablespoons butter
2 cups sliced mushrooms
1 cup canned or thawed frozen whole-kernel corn
½ cup diced green pepper
¼ cup diced red pepper
Salt and freshly ground black pepper
6 large eggs

Melt butter in a 10-inch skillet over medium heat. Add mushrooms and sauté until soft and moisture evaporates, about 5 minutes. Add corn, green and red pepper, and salt and pepper to taste. Cook for 3 minutes.

Whisk eggs in a medium-size bowl. Pour over vegetables. Stir frequently until eggs are set, about 3 minutes.

MENU: Bakery oatmeal muffins with blueberry jam. Carrot-raisin salad. Frozen vanilla yogurt.

SERVINGS: Makes 4 servings.

Chive-Cheese Scramble

■ You will not want to share this recipe with your cardiologist. It's a guilty pleasure. I give you permission to eat it once a year, but only if you promise not to take seconds.

1 (3-oz.) tub whipped chive cream cheese
¾ cup half-and-half
8 large eggs
Salt and freshly ground black pepper
Dash of cayenne pepper
2 tablespoons butter

Beat together cream cheese and half-and-half in a small bowl until well combined.

Add eggs and, using an electric mixer on low speed, beat until eggs are incorporated. Season with salt, black pepper, and cayenne.

Melt butter in a 12-inch skillet over medium heat. When butter sizzles, add egg mixture and stir constantly until eggs are set but soft.

MENU: Onion rolls. Thin slices of boiled ham with grainy mustard. Bakery chocolate cupcakes.

SERVINGS: Makes 4 servings.

Avocado Frittata

■ Frittatas are easier to serve than omelets because they aren't folded over. They cook slowly in a circular pan, so slicing them like a pizza or a pie makes it easier to bring a single serving from pan to plate.

2 tablespoons butter
2 medium zucchini, diced
1 cup sliced mushrooms
2 tablespoons chopped red onion
1 ripe avocado, seeded, peeled, and cut into cubes
½ teaspoon dried marjoram
4 large eggs
¼ cup milk
4 ounces (1 cup) grated Swiss cheese

Melt butter in a 12-inch skillet over medium heat. Add zucchini, mushrooms, and onion and sauté 3 to 4 minutes or until softened. Remove from heat; top with avocado and marjoram.

Beat eggs with milk in a small bowl until frothy. Pour over avocado in skillet, return to medium heat and cook until eggs are set, about 6 minutes. Top with cheese. Cover and cook for 1 to 2 minutes or until cheese begins to melt. Cut into wedges to serve.

MENU: Whole-wheat toast. Sliced smoked turkey on Romaine leaves. Fresh berries with vanilla yogurt.

SERVINGS: Makes 2 servings.

Eggs Fu Yung

■ Anyone who frequents Chinese restaurants has to be familiar with eggs fu yung, or maybe they've seen it spelled eggs foo yung. It's more a Chinese-American than an authentic Chinese dish. Basically it's scrambled eggs with Chinese vegetables, which is perfectly delicious, but I played a little with the contents, adding a few more American twists. Surimi or imitation crabmeat will work just fine.

6 large eggs
1 tablespoon water
2 cups bean sprouts
2 tablespoons minced scallions
1 tablespoon finely chopped canned bamboo
　shoots
1 teaspoon salt
½ teaspoon freshly ground black pepper
1 cup crabmeat, flaked
1 tablespoon canola oil
Soy sauce

Whisk eggs and water in a medium-sized bowl. Stir in sprouts, scallions, bamboo shoots, salt, pepper, and crabmeat.

Heat oil in an 8-inch skillet over medium heat. Add egg mixture, lower heat, and cover. Cook until eggs are set, about 5 minutes.

Serve with soy sauce.

MENU: Spinach salad with lemon vinaigrette. Bakery almond cookies.

SERVINGS: Makes 4 servings.

Jalapeño Frittata

■ The joy of eggs is that they can be made at the last minute, and made in minutes, and there's just no end to the varieties of fillings. Just look in the refrigerator: a little cheese, a little meat . . . let your imagination soar.

6 large eggs
2 tablespoons half-and-half
3 tablespoons butter
1⅓ cups (about 5 ounces) grated Monterey
　Jack cheese with chiles
6 pickled jalapeño chiles
4 pitted ripe olives
2 tablespoons chopped red onion
Sour cream

Preheat broiler. Whisk together eggs and half-and-half in a small bowl.

Melt 1½ tablespoons butter in a 10-inch cast-iron skillet over high heat until foamy. Add egg mixture, stir once with a fork, and cook until eggs are set, lifting edges to allow uncooked eggs to run underneath.

When eggs are set, sprinkle with ⅔ cup of the cheese. Place about 6 inches from source of heat and broil until cheese melts, about 1 minute. Cut frittata into 3 wedges, sliding each wedge onto a serving plate. Garnish with chiles, olives, onion, sour cream, and the remaining cheese.

MENU: Corn chips. Mango slices.

SERVINGS: Makes 3 servings.

Scrambled Eggs with Shrimp, Tomato, & Broccoli

■ One of the secrets of successfully scrambling eggs is to remove them from the source of heat about a minute before they're done. The heat of the pan and the eggs will finish the cooking without drying out the eggs from excessive heat.

4 large eggs
2 tablespoons soy sauce
1 teaspoon cornstarch
1 (6-oz.) can baby shrimp, drained
1 cup broccoli florets
1 teaspoon grated fresh ginger
1 tablespoon sherry
Salt and freshly ground black pepper
3 tablespoons peanut oil
1 shallot, minced
2 medium tomatoes, chopped and drained

Lightly beat eggs with soy sauce and cornstarch. Stir in shrimp, broccoli, ginger, sherry, salt, and pepper.

Heat oil in a 10-inch skillet or wok over medium heat. Add shallot and cook 30 seconds. Add egg mixture, stir, and turn. Sprinkle with tomatoes. Continue stirring until eggs have set.

MENU: Mandarin orange slices. Bakery sesame cookies.

SERVINGS: Makes 2 servings.

Snow Peas & Peanut Scramble

■ I love snow peas—the thin, crisp pea that's a common ingredient in stir-fries. The whole thing, pod and all, is edible. They have a bright, sharp flavor that lends balance to many recipes and, if not overcooked, develop a shiny, green color that makes any dish they're in doubly appealing. When buying snow peas, select only firm pods; limp or broken snow peas also taste limp and broken.

2 tablespoons peanut oil
½ pound snow peas, trimmed and washed
4 mushrooms, sliced
2 scallions, chopped
4 large eggs, lightly beaten
3 tablespoons soy sauce plus additional for serving
1 tablespoon grated ginger
2 tablespoons sherry
Salt
1 teaspoon sugar
1 teaspoon cornstarch
3 tablespoons unsalted peanuts, coarsely chopped

Heat oil in a 10-inch skillet or wok over medium heat. Add snow peas, mushroom slices, and scallions. Stir-fry for 2 minutes. Remove vegetables from pan with a slotted spoon. Keep warm.

Combine eggs, soy sauce, ginger, sherry, salt, sugar, and cornstarch. Pour into pan. Cook egg mixture over medium heat, stirring, until eggs are set, about 3 minutes. Transfer eggs to a plate, leaving a hole in the center. Place snow pea mixture in the center of eggs. Top with peanuts. Serve with additional soy sauce.

MENU: Rice cakes with apricot preserves. Bakery coconut macaroons.

SERVINGS: Makes 2 servings.

Eggs in Spring

■ In days of yore when knights errant roamed the world, dill was considered a magic herb and it was used in many potions. I can't vouch for its use in casting spells, except to say the smell of it makes any day a spring day for me. Although you can get the flavor of dill from its seeds or dried leaves, I prefer fresh, and because heat tends to destroy its flavor, always add it last.

6 large eggs, well beaten
¼ cup half-and-half
1 tablespoon white Worcestershire sauce
2 tablespoons butter
4 ounces (1 cup) grated Gruyère cheese
1 teaspoon snipped fresh dill

Beat together eggs, half-and-half, and Worcestershire sauce in a small bowl.

Melt butter in a 10-inch skillet over medium-low heat. Add egg mixture and tilt pan so that eggs cover the bottom in a smooth layer. Lift edges to let uncooked eggs run underneath. While center is still moist, sprinkle cheese over top and cook until cheese starts to melt. Sprinkle with dill. Fold over and cook 1 minute. Slide folded omelet onto a serving plate.

MENU: Potato rolls. Sliced, cold honey-baked ham. Strawberries with vanilla yogurt dusted with brown sugar.

SERVINGS: Makes 3 servings.

Salsa Eggs

■ Salsa came to the Northeast about twenty years ago. How did we ever live without it?

6 large eggs
2 tablespoons water
½ cup salsa
½ cup grated Monterey Jack cheese with chiles
4 toaster corn muffins, toasted
Picante sauce
Chili powder

Beat eggs in a medium bowl. Beat in water, salsa, and cheese.

Spray 4 microwave-safe individual soufflé dishes with nonstick cooking spray. Divide egg mixture evenly among the dishes. Cover with plastic wrap and cook two at a time in the microwave on MEDIUM power until set, about 7 minutes, turning once or twice.

Place corn muffin rounds on individual plates. Invert a soufflé dish over each round and lift off soufflé dishes (soufflé should drop away). Top with picante sauce and sprinkle with chili powder.

MENU: Chorizo sausage. Deli three-bean salad. Strawberry ice cream.

SERVINGS: Makes 4 servings.

Pasta

My family eats pasta. I can say that with some surety after having assembled all my recipes for this book. Pasta was a huge category. The reason why: EVERY-BODY in my family eats pasta. It is the one, surefire crowd pleaser. Hence I make it a lot because I like to see people eating good nutritious food.

Of course, there are some selfish reasons also. Pasta is fast, easy, and inexpensive. I tend to use refrigerated fresh pasta, which is not as inexpensive as dried pasta, because it saves time. Not all sauces go well with fresh because fresh tends to be more delicate and doesn't hold its shape as well as dried pasta. In the recipes that follow, fresh pasta is called for but all can be made with dried pasta if you don't mind waiting for the water to boil, and then waiting as long as 10 to 12 minutes for the pasta to cook. Quick-cooking dry varieties are angel hair and orzo, which will cook in boiling water in 2 to 4 minutes.

There are a few tips to shave off minutes from cooking time, if you decide to use dried pasta. For one, don't salt the water; it slows down the time it takes the water to reach the boiling point. Another is to cover the pot after adding the pasta. This will help the water return to a boil faster.

The variety of pasta available at supermarkets now is dazzling, and if you are fortunate enough to live near an Italian specialty market, the array is astounding. Each presents an opportunity to vary texture and taste, and some pasta shapes are designed to hold certain kinds of sauce.

Garlic Shrimp with Linguine & Lime

■ Shrimp and garlic are one of America's favorite flavor combinations.

1 (9-oz.) package refrigerated fresh linguine
2 tablespoons butter
1 tablespoon olive oil
1 small onion, sliced lengthwise
1 red bell pepper, chopped
2 large cloves garlic, minced
1 pound large shrimp, peeled and deveined
1 teaspoon crushed red pepper flakes
Juice of 1 lime

Cook pasta according to package directions. Drain pasta.

Meanwhile, heat butter and oil in a 12-inch skillet over medium heat. Add onion, bell pepper, and garlic. Cook, stirring occasionally, until vegetables are softened, about 2 minutes.

Add shrimp and stir-fry 2 minutes or until shrimp turn pink. Season with pepper flakes and lime juice. Toss with drained pasta.

MENU: Sesame bread sticks. Sliced papaya. Mixed melon slices.

SERVINGS: Makes 4 servings.

Shanghai Chicken Fettuccine

■ Hoisin sauce turns this tasty mixture into something exotic.

1 (9-oz.) package refrigerated fresh fettuccine
1 tablespoon olive oil
1 pound boneless, skinless chicken breast halves, cut into ¼-inch slices
1 (16-oz.) package frozen vegetables for stir-frying
1 cup sliced mushrooms
¼ cup hoisin sauce

Cook pasta according to package directions. Drain pasta.

Meanwhile, heat oil in a wok or 12-inch frying pan over medium-high heat. Add chicken; stir-fry 3 to 4 minutes. Add vegetables and mushrooms. Stir-fry about 3 minutes or until vegetables are crisp-tender. Stir in hoisin sauce. Bring to a boil; stir-fry 1 minute. Add drained pasta; toss and heat through, about 1 minute.

MENU: Marinated artichoke hearts. Lemon meringue pie.

SERVINGS: Makes 4 servings.

Linguine with Asparagus

■ Cooks in a hurry don't always want to take time to make a dish look pretty, but I recommend taking a few extra seconds to cut the asparagus on the diagonal. It makes a difference in the appearance of this dish.

1 (9-oz.) package refrigerated fresh linguine
6 asparagus spears, cut into 1-inch lengths on the diagonal
2 tablespoons butter
Generous grind of black pepper
2 tablespoons finely chopped fresh flat-leaf parsley
½ cup freshly grated Parmesan cheese

Cook pasta according to package directions. During last 2 minutes of cooking time, add asparagus to the pot. Drain, reserving 2 tablespoons of cooking liquid.

Return pasta and asparagus to pot. Add butter; toss to melt. Add reserved cooking liquid, pepper, and parsley. Toss to combine. Sprinkle with Parmesan cheese.

MENU: Garlic bagel chips. Field greens salad with mustard vinaigrette. Bakery cupcakes.

SERVINGS: Makes 4 servings.

Creamy Shrimp Fettuccine

■ Shrimp that has been deveined is available in some stores now. It costs a few pennies more but is well worth it, considering the time that's saved.

1 (9-oz.) package refrigerated fresh fettuccine
4 tablespoons butter
¾ pound medium shrimp, peeled and deveined
¾ cup sour cream
Juice of 1 lemon
Grated lemon peel
¼ cup minced fresh cilantro

Cook pasta according to package directions. Drain pasta.

Meanwhile, melt butter in a 10-inch skillet over medium-high heat. Add shrimp and stir-fry 2 minutes or until shrimp turn pink.

Add drained pasta to shrimp-and-butter mixture and toss to combine. Add sour cream, lemon juice, and lemon peel. Toss to combine and heat just until warm. Sprinkle with cilantro.

MENU: Hard rolls. Packaged Caesar salad. Bakery sticky buns.

SERVINGS: Makes 4 servings.

Spaghetti & Shrimp

■ The standard 9-ounce package of refrigerated fresh pasta yields 4 servings, but they are not generous servings, unless combined with other ingredients like the vegetables and seafood in this hearty dinner dish.

1 (9-oz.) package refrigerated fresh spaghetti
7 tablespoons olive oil
1 clove garlic, minced
½ teaspoon grated lemon peel
1 small zucchini, thinly sliced
1 medium tomato, chopped
1 pound medium shrimp, peeled and
   deveined
1 tablespoon fresh lemon juice
⅛ teaspoon cayenne pepper
1 tablespoon chopped fresh basil leaves

Cook pasta according to package directions.

Meanwhile, heat 6 tablespoons of the olive oil in a 12-inch skillet over medium heat. Add garlic and lemon peel; stir-fry 1 minute. Add zucchini, tomato, and shrimp; stir-fry 4 minutes or until shrimp turn pink. Sprinkle with lemon juice, cayenne, and basil.

Drain pasta and toss with remaining 1 tablespoon olive oil. Toss pasta with shrimp-and-vegetable mixture.

MENU: Deli fruit salad. French baguettes. Bakery devil's food cake.

SERVINGS: Makes 4 servings.

Hot Pepper Ravioli

■ Hot food lovers, do I have a pasta dish for you!

1 (9-oz.) package refrigerated fresh cheese
   ravioli
2 tablespoons extra-virgin olive oil
4 cloves garlic, minced
½ teaspoon crushed red pepper flakes
1 cup chopped sun-dried tomatoes in olive
   oil, drained
2 tablespoons grated Parmesan cheese
1 teaspoon chopped fresh basil leaves
1 cup spinach leaves, cut crosswise into
   ribbons

Cook ravioli according to package directions. Drain ravioli.

Meanwhile, in a 10-inch skillet over medium heat, warm oil, garlic, and pepper flakes for 2 minutes. Add tomatoes, Parmesan cheese, and basil and simmer 4 minutes. Stir in spinach and stir 1 minute.

Toss sauce with ravioli.

MENU: Sesame bread sticks with provolone. Peaches and raspberries.

SERVINGS: Makes 4 servings.

Scallops & Parsley Sauce

■ Every good Italian recipe that calls for parsley is specific in saying "flat leaf." Every good cook makes a point of stating that his or her best recipe uses parsley, "the kind with the flat leaves." It does have a stronger, coarser flavor than curly-leaf parsley, but curly-leaf parsley seems to grow better in my garden, and I think it looks prettier, too. This recipe is a rarity because it calls for curly-leaf parsley.

1 (9-oz.) package refrigerated fresh spaghetti
2 tablespoons butter
2 tablespoons olive oil
1¼ cups thinly sliced scallions
1 cup firmly packed chopped curly-leaf
    parsley leaves
¾ cup dry white wine
1 pound bay scallops, rinsed and patted dry
Salt and freshly ground black pepper

Cook pasta according to package directions. Drain pasta.

Meanwhile, heat butter and oil in heavy, large skillet over medium-high heat until butter is melted. Add scallions and ½ cup of the parsley and cook for 2 minutes or until scallions are softened, but not browned. Add wine; cook 2 minutes. Add scallops; reduce heat to low. Simmer, covered, 3 minutes or until scallops are opaque.

Stir in remaining parsley and season to taste with salt and pepper.

Pour over drained pasta; toss to mix.

MENU: Garlic bread. Red-leaf lettuce with sun-dried tomatoes in oil and fresh mozzarella cheese. Bakery apple pie.

SERVINGS: Makes 4 to 6 servings.

Pasta Puttanesca

■ Pasta is a low-calorie, low-fat food that provides important complex carbohydrates, and it's delicious. This classic pasta dish's name is translated as the "streetwalkers' pasta." According to the story of its creation, each lady of the night brought one ingredient.

1 (9-oz.) package refrigerated fresh spaghetti
1 tablespoon olive oil
3 cloves garlic, thinly sliced
¼ to ½ teaspoon crushed red pepper flakes
6 anchovy fillets, finely chopped
1 (6½-oz.) jar oil-cured ripe olives, pitted
1 tablespoon capers, rinsed and drained
3 large tomatoes, seeded and chopped
Salt and freshly ground black pepper

Cook pasta according to package directions. Drain pasta.

Meanwhile, heat oil in a 10-inch skillet over medium heat. Add garlic, pepper flakes, and anchovies; cook 1 minute. Add olives, capers, and tomatoes; cook 8 to 10 minutes, stirring occasionally, or until sauce thickens. Season with salt and pepper to taste.

Toss pasta with sauce.

MENU: Italian bread. Escarole with oil-and-vinegar dressing. Strawberry ice cream with fresh strawberries.

SERVINGS: Makes 4 servings.

Smoked Oysters & Fettuccine

■ Smoked oysters are something I keep in the cupboard just in case company drops by. Some cheese slices, some pepperoni slices, and crackers, and there's an elegant tray to present. No problem. One day, in desperation, I used them in a pasta sauce. Now I wouldn't dream of running out of smoked oysters.

1 (9-oz.) package refrigerated fresh
  fettuccine
1 tablespoon olive oil
2 cloves garlic, chopped
1 teaspoon grated fresh ginger
2 (3.75-oz.) cans smoked oysters, drained
2 tablespoons dry sherry
½ pound snow peas
2 tablespoons sesame seeds, toasted
2 scallions, chopped
1 teaspoon sesame oil

Cook pasta according to package directions. Drain pasta.

Meanwhile, heat olive oil in a 10-inch skillet or wok over medium-high heat. Add garlic, ginger, and oysters; stir-fry 1 minute or until oysters are heated through. Add sherry and snow peas; stir-fry 2 minutes.

Toss drained pasta with oyster sauce, sesame seeds, scallions, and sesame oil.

MENU: Garlic bread. Romaine lettuce leaves with garlic croutons and red-wine vinegar dressing. Bakery almond cookies.

SERVINGS: Makes 4 servings.

Angel Hair with Tiny Tomatoes

■ Cherry tomatoes are bright and pretty, and very easy to use in salads and pasta dishes. This pasta dish is perfect for a light and easy-to-make dinner.

1 (9-oz.) package refrigerated fresh angel
  hair pasta
2 tablespoons olive oil
2 cups sliced mushrooms
1 clove garlic, minced
4 cups cherry tomato halves
2 teaspoons chopped fresh basil leaves
1 cup (4 ounces) shredded mozzarella cheese
¼ cup grated Parmesan cheese

Cook pasta according to package directions. Drain pasta.

Meanwhile, heat oil in a 3-quart saucepan or Dutch oven over medium heat. Add mushrooms and garlic. Sauté until softened, about 4 minutes. Stir in tomatoes and basil. Cook, stirring occasionally, for 3 to 4 minutes or until thoroughly heated.

Add drained pasta and toss with sauce and mozzarella cheese. Sprinkle with Parmesan cheese.

MENU: Italian bread. Field greens salad with buttermilk dressing. Bakery brownies.

SERVINGS: Makes 4 servings.

Pasta & Prosciutto

■ *Prosciutto* is the Italian word for ham, but it refers to a ham that has been seasoned, salt cured, and air dried. It's available at gourmet Italian markets and most supermarket delis where it is sold in almost transparently thin slices.

I like it best simply eaten as is, but it also can be added at the last minute to cooked foods such as pastas or vegetables. Don't cook it longer than a minute or it'll toughen up.

1 (9-oz.) package refrigerated fresh fettuccine
⅓ cup olive oil
½ cup pignoli (pine) nuts, coarsely chopped
3 tablespoons minced fresh flat-leaf parsley
1 clove garlic, minced
½ pound prosciutto, chopped
Grated Parmesan cheese (optional)

Cook pasta according to package directions. Drain pasta.

Meanwhile, heat oil in a 12-inch skillet over medium-high heat. Add nuts, parsley, and garlic; sauté 3 to 4 minutes. Add prosciutto; sauté 1 minute.

Add drained pasta and toss until heated through. Serve immediately with Parmesan cheese, if desired.

MENU: Tomatoes vinaigrette. Italian bread. Fresh berries on fruit yogurt drizzled with a little honey.

SERVINGS: Makes 4 servings.

Scallops with Angel Hair

■ Angel hair pasta cooks in two minutes. Of course it takes water longer than that to boil so you have to count that into prep time, but a 9-ounce package of refrigerated fresh angel hair pasta does not require a vat of water. A large saucepan is big enough.

1 (9-oz.) package refrigerated fresh angel hair pasta
1 tablespoon olive oil
1 pound bay scallops, rinsed and patted dry
2 cloves garlic, minced
2 cups marinara sauce
1 tablespoon fresh lemon juice
⅛ teaspoon crushed red pepper flakes

Cook pasta according to package directions. Drain pasta.

Meanwhile, heat oil in a 10-inch skillet over medium-high heat. Add scallops and garlic; stir-fry for 3 minutes or until scallops are opaque. Stir in marinara sauce, lemon juice, and pepper flakes. Simmer 3 to 5 minutes or until heated through.

Toss pasta with sauce.

MENU: Italian bread. Endive and flat-leaf parsley salad. Bakery apple crumb cake.

SERVINGS: Makes 4 servings.

Vodka-Basil Fettucine

■ Vodka doesn't have any flavor of its own, but in this dish it softens the taste and helps meld the flavors of crushed red pepper flakes, tomato, and basil. The real star of the dish is the basil; it gives the most pronounced flavor. An easy way to cut the leaves into ribbons is to use a pair of kitchen scissors.

2 (9-oz.) packages refrigerated fresh spinach
   fettuccine
1 (28-oz.) can crushed tomatoes in puree
¼ cup vodka
1 to 2 teaspoons crushed red pepper flakes
1 cup fresh basil leaves, cut into thin ribbons
½ teaspoon salt

Cook pasta according to package directions. Drain pasta. Place in a serving bowl.

Meanwhile, combine tomatoes with puree, vodka, pepper flakes, basil, and salt in a 2-quart microwave-safe bowl. Microwave on HIGH for 3 minutes; stir. Microwave on HIGH for 2 to 3 minutes more or until heated through.

Add sauce to pasta and toss to combine.

MENU: Hot garlic bread. Packaged Caesar salad. Pear slices.

SERVINGS: Makes 6 servings.

Angel Hair with Garlic & Hot Pepper

■ This is a very garlicky, pungent pasta dish that's easy to make with virtually guaranteed results. The secret is to watch the garlic carefully. It needs to get soft, but not brown. Once it starts to brown, the flavor changes.

1 (12-oz.) package dried angel hair
   pasta
1 tablespoon olive oil
1 tablespoon thin garlic slices
½ teaspoon crushed red pepper flakes
2 tablespoons coarsely chopped fresh
   flat-leaf parsley

Cook the pasta according to package directions.

Meanwhile, heat oil in a 10-inch skillet over low heat until warm. Add the garlic and pepper flakes and cook, stirring, until garlic is soft, 3 to 5 minutes. Do not allow garlic to brown.

Ladle about ¼ cup of pasta cooking water into a large serving bowl. Add garlic-and-pepper-infused oil. Drain pasta and add to bowl. Toss pasta with sauce until thoroughly coated. Sprinkle with parsley.

MENU: Deli marinated mushrooms. Green salad with walnuts and favorite dressing. Grape halves tossed with grated coconut.

SERVINGS: Makes 4 servings.

Linguine with Roasted Bell Peppers

■ I'm a regular customer at the refrigerated fresh pasta case. Fresh pasta is delicious and it cooks very quickly, but it's also expensive. Dry pasta can be substituted, but it means taking a little more time.

1 (9-oz.) package refrigerated fresh linguine
1 (7-oz.) jar roasted red bell peppers, undrained
½ cup pitted ripe olives, halved
1 tablespoon olive oil
1 clove garlic, minced
1 teaspoon dried basil

Cook pasta according to package directions. Drain pasta; keep warm.

Meanwhile, slice bell peppers into strips. Place in a medium bowl along with remaining ingredients; toss to combine. Toss warm pasta with bell pepper mixture.

MENU: Bread sticks. Curly endive with freshly ground black pepper, oil, and vinegar. Melon cubes.

SERVINGS: Makes 4 servings.

Bean Ravioli

■ This is a popular dish at my house. The black and white beans give it special appeal and a big nutritional boost.

1 (9-oz.) package refrigerated fresh cheese ravioli
1 (14-oz.) jar chunky vegetable pasta sauce
1 (15-oz.) can black beans, drained
1 (15-oz.) can white kidney beans (cannellini), drained
½ cup shredded fresh Parmesan cheese

Cook ravioli according to package directions. Drain pasta; keep warm.

Meanwhile, combine pasta sauce with beans in a deep 12-inch skillet. Cook over medium heat until thoroughly heated.

Place cooked ravioli on a serving plate. Top with sauce. Sprinkle with Parmesan cheese.

MENU: Soft garlic bread sticks. Tossed green salad with creamy Italian dressing. Bakery apple turnovers.

SERVINGS: Makes 4 servings.

Almond Poppy-Seed Noodles

■ The main difference between noodles and pasta is that noodles usually contain eggs or egg yolks. Fettuccine is made with eggs. For some reason fresh commercially prepared fettuccine is usually not as good as dried fettuccine, but to its credit, it cooks fast.

1 (9-oz.) package refrigerated fresh fettuccine
¼ cup butter
½ cup slivered blanched almonds
2 tablespoons poppy seeds
1 tablespoon paprika

Cook pasta according to package directions. Drain pasta; keep warm.

Meanwhile, melt butter in a 10-inch frying pan. Add almonds and sauté until golden brown, about 2 minutes. Add poppy seeds and paprika; cook, stirring constantly, for 3 minutes. Toss with drained pasta.

MENU: Field greens salad with favorite dressing. Thin slices of Italian ham. Apple and pear slices with prepared caramel dip.

SERVINGS: Makes 4 to 6 servings.

Salmon with Couscous

■ Couscous looks like a grain, but it's really little balls of pasta. A boon to the cook who needs to get dinner on the table quickly is that instant couscous can be prepared in a matter of minutes. Like pasta, couscous is very versatile and accommodates many flavors.

1 tablespoon olive oil
½ cup sliced scallions
½ cup white wine
¼ cup fresh lime juice
Salt and freshly ground pepper
1 pound salmon fillets, rinsed and patted dry
½ cup water
½ cup uncooked instant couscous

Heat oil in a 10-inch skillet over medium-high heat. Add scallions; cook, stirring, 1 to 2 minutes.

Stir in wine, lime juice, salt, and pepper; bring to a boil. Reduce heat to medium-low. Add salmon, cover, and cook 7 to 8 minutes or until fish flakes with a fork. Remove scallions and salmon from skillet with a slotted spoon; keep warm.

Reserve ¼ cup cooking liquid; return liquid to skillet. Add water to reserved cooking liquid. Bring to a boil. Stir in couscous. Remove from heat. Cover; let stand 4 to 5 minutes or until liquid is absorbed.

Meanwhile, cut salmon into serving-size pieces. Serve salmon with scallions and couscous.

MENU: Deli carrot-raisin salad. Frozen vanilla yogurt.

SERVINGS: Makes 4 servings.

Pepperoni Pasta

■ I have a weakness for pepperoni, the Italian salami made with pork and beef and a lot of black and red peppers. Here's the best part: It's ready to eat. Just slice it and add it to whatever you like—scrambled eggs, pizza, or pasta.

1 (9-oz.) package refrigerated fresh spinach
   tortellini
¼ cup olive oil
1 large red onion, sliced
2 cloves garlic, minced
½ pound pepperoni, thinly sliced
2 medium red bell peppers, thinly sliced
1 (14-oz.) jar chunky pasta sauce
1 teaspoon dried basil

Cook pasta according to package directions. Drain pasta; keep warm.

Meanwhile, heat oil in a 10-inch skillet over medium heat. Add onion, garlic, pepperoni, and bell peppers; cook 5 minutes, stirring often.

Stir in sauce and basil. Cover and cook 4 minutes, stirring 2 to 3 times, or until bubbly. Uncover and cook 1 minute to thicken sauce slightly.

Serve pasta with sauce.

MENU: Garlic bagel chips. Romaine leaves with oil-and-vinegar dressing. Peppermint Patties candy.

SERVINGS: Makes 4 servings.

Tortellini with Artichoke Hearts

■ Tortellini is a stuffed pasta that comes from Bologna, Italy. They are little rounds, almost like belly buttons.

1 (9-oz.) package refrigerated fresh cheese-
   filled tortellini
1 (6½-oz.) jar marinated artichoke hearts,
   drained
2 tablespoons olive oil
3 cloves garlic, minced
¼ to ½ cup oil-packed sun-dried tomatoes,
   drained and cut into strips
½ cup white wine
1 teaspoon crushed red pepper flakes
Grated Romano cheese

Cook pasta according to package directions. Drain pasta. Place in a serving bowl.

Meanwhile, cut artichoke hearts into quarters.

Heat oil in a 12-inch skillet over medium-high heat. Add garlic and cook, stirring, until golden, about 2 minutes.

Reduce heat to low; add artichokes and tomatoes. Simmer 1 minute. Stir in wine and pepper flakes. Simmer 5 minutes, stirring occasionally.

Spoon sauce over pasta and toss to combine. Serve with grated cheese.

MENU: Bread sticks. Garden salad with green goddess dressing. Sliced kiwis and strawberries.

SERVINGS: Makes 4 servings.

Lemon-Pepper Pasta

■ Lemon-pepper seasoning is a good spice blend to keep in the spice rack. It enlivens the flavor of beef, seafood, chicken, and pasta.

1 (9-oz.) package refrigerated fresh angel hair pasta
3 tablespoons olive oil
2 cloves garlic, minced
½ cup chopped fresh basil
½ teaspoon lemon-pepper seasoning
½ cup grated Parmesan cheese

Cook pasta according to package directions. Drain pasta; keep warm.

Meanwhile, heat oil in a 12-inch nonstick skillet over medium-high heat. Add garlic and sauté until golden, about 2 minutes. Stir in basil and lemon-pepper seasoning. Add drained pasta and toss to combine. Sprinkle with cheese.

MENU: Heat-and-serve French-bread rolls. Thinly sliced prosciutto with fresh melon cubes on red-leaf lettuce leaves. Bakery pound cake with nondairy whipped topping and fresh berries.

SERVINGS: Makes 3 or 4 servings.

Summer Linguine

■ The tomatoes in this dish are not cooked, which means that they have to stand on their own flavor. Hence the best time to make this dish is when fresh tomatoes are at their peak.

1 (9-oz.) package refrigerated fresh linguine
¼ cup plus 1 tablespoon olive oil
½ cup chopped fresh basil leaves
4 vine-ripened tomatoes, chopped
2 cloves garlic, minced
Salt and freshly ground black pepper

Prepare pasta according to package directions; drain. Toss with 1 tablespoon of olive oil. Set aside in a colander.

Combine basil, tomatoes, garlic, and remaining oil in a large pasta serving bowl. Toss with pasta. Season with salt and pepper to taste.

MENU: Italian bread. Green salad with ranch dressing. Sliced fresh strawberries with vanilla ice cream.

SERVINGS: Makes 4 servings.

Zucchini Pasta

■ A lot of friends stopped growing zucchini because it's much too prolific. Now they simply buy what they need. Although the height of the growing season is summer, zucchini can be found in produce departments year-round.

1 (9-oz.) package refrigerated fresh cheese tortellini
1 medium zucchini, shredded
1 tablespoon olive oil
2 teaspoons finely chopped onion
2 cloves garlic, minced
1 medium tomato, diced
2 tablespoons chopped fresh basil
2 tablespoons grated Parmesan cheese

Cook pasta according to package directions. Drain pasta and place in a serving bowl.

Meanwhile, cook zucchini in hot oil in a 10-inch skillet over medium-high heat, stirring frequently, about 2 minutes. Reduce heat to medium. Add onion and garlic; cook 1 minute. Add tomato; cook, stirring, 45 seconds. Stir in basil.

Pour vegetable mixture over drained pasta and toss to mix. Add cheese and toss to combine.

MENU: Sesame bread sticks. Green salad with miniature shrimp tossed with creamy Italian dressing. Bakery lemon meringue pie.

SERVINGS: Makes 4 servings.

Pasta with Jersey Tomato Sauce

■ Being a Jersey girl, I'm naturally partial to Jersey tomatoes. Growing them is akin to religion in importance in the lives of home gardeners. They're ugly-looking, cracked on the top, sometimes gnarly, in improbable sizes, but fresh out of the garden on a hot August day, there's nothing more delicious. This dish can be made with any good, vine-ripened tomato, but if you want to sample it at its best come to the Garden State this summer.

1 (9-oz.) package refrigerated fresh linguine
1 tablespoon extra-virgin olive oil
1 medium onion, chopped
2 cloves garlic, minced
4 medium tomatoes, peeled and chopped (see Note, below)
½ teaspoon sugar
1 tablespoon fresh basil leaves, chopped
¼ cup white wine

Cook pasta according to package directions. Drain pasta and place in a serving bowl.

Meanwhile, in a 12-inch skillet, heat oil. Add onion and garlic and cook until softened, 2 minutes. Add remaining ingredients and simmer 10 to 12 minutes, stirring occasionally, or until slightly thickened.

Serve sauce over drained pasta.

MENU: Deli chicken salad on red-tipped lettuce leaves. Fresh peaches, fresh raspberries, and vanilla ice cream.

SERVINGS: Makes 4 servings.

NOTE
A quick way to peel a cored tomato is to hold it on a skewer or two-pronged fork over a gas flame, turning just until the skin splits, then pull off the shreds of the puckered skin.

Scallops & Pasta

■ Scallops are an ideal go-with for pasta. They cook in the blink of an eye and taste great in a creamy sauce. I use the little bay scallops that are popular on the East Coast, but larger sea scallops can be substituted. Just cut them in half or quarter them.

1 (9-oz.) package refrigerated fresh linguine
1 tablespoon butter
1 tablespoon olive oil
2 tablespoons finely chopped red onion
½ green bell pepper, finely chopped
½ red bell pepper, finely chopped
1 pound bay scallops, rinsed and patted dry
1 cup half-and-half

Cook pasta according to package directions. Drain pasta and place in a serving bowl.

Meanwhile, heat butter and oil in a 10-inch skillet over medium heat. Add onion; cook until softened, about 2 minutes, stirring occasionally. Add bell pepper and cook until soft, about 2 minutes.

Add scallops to the pan. Stir to combine and cook until opaque, about 1 minute. Stir in half-and-half and cook until half-and-half is slightly thickened, 3 to 4 minutes.

Pour sauce and scallops over drained pasta and toss to combine.

MENU: Italian bread. Sliced tomatoes on red-leaf lettuce with cucumber dressing. Bakery brownies.

SERVINGS: Makes 4 servings.

Spaghetti with Parsley Sauce

■ I remember a snide friend once commented that the only people who used parsley were home economists, and then just for decoration. What did she know? Parsley is full of aromatic flavor and nutrients. I always keep it on hand, stored like a bouquet in a juice glass full of water with a plastic bag loosely covering it. It seems to last forever as I snip and pinch off what I need.

1 (9-oz.) package refrigerated fresh spaghetti
3 tablespoons soy sauce
1½ teaspoons fresh lemon juice
½ cup olive oil
½ cup sunflower seeds
2 cups packed fresh parsley leaves
1 scallion, chopped
1 medium clove garlic, peeled

Cook pasta according to package directions. Drain pasta and place in a serving bowl.

Meanwhile, in a food processor or blender, combine soy sauce, lemon juice, ¼ cup of the olive oil, ¼ cup of the sunflower seeds, parsley, scallion, and garlic. Process until smooth. Gradually pour in remaining ¼ cup olive oil in a continuous stream until blended. Stir in remaining sunflower seeds.

Pour sauce over drained pasta and toss to combine.

MENU: Green salad with cucumber slices and blue-cheese dressing. Italian flat bread. Sesame cookies.

SERVINGS: Makes 4 servings.

Linguine with Hot Clam Sauce

■ The secret to success with shellfish is to add them at the very end so they don't over-cook and become tough. If fresh clams are not available, canned minced clams will work.

1 (9-oz.) package fresh refrigerated linguine
¼ cup olive oil
3 cloves garlic, finely chopped
3½ cups spicy tomato pasta sauce
1 pint shucked small fresh clams, drained and liquid reserved
1 teaspoon fresh parsley
Crushed red pepper flakes (optional)

Cook pasta according to package directions. Drain pasta.

Meanwhile, heat oil in a 3-quart saucepan over medium-high heat. Add garlic and sauté until golden. Stir in pasta sauce and clam liquid. Bring to a boil. Reduce heat and simmer sauce about 5 minutes. Stir in clams and parsley. Simmer for 3 to 4 minutes.

Toss sauce with drained pasta. Sprinkle with red pepper flakes, if using.

MENU: Crusty Italian bread. Cucumber slices and escarole dressed with red-wine vinegar and black pepper. Chocolate-coated ice cream squares.

SERVINGS: Makes 4 servings.

Vermicelli & Turkey with White Wine Sauce

■ I find a garlic press a useful kitchen gadget, but I've watched professional chefs do an equally efficient job by just smashing a clove with the broadside of a chef's knife.

1 (9-oz.) package refrigerated fresh vermicelli
2 tablespoons olive oil
1 clove garlic, finely chopped
1 medium onion, chopped
1 small green bell pepper, diced
1 pound ground turkey
1 cup white wine
2½ cups spaghetti sauce

Cook pasta according to package directions. Drain pasta and place in a serving bowl.

Meanwhile, heat oil in a 10-inch frying pan over medium heat. Add garlic, onion, and bell pepper; cook 2 minutes, stirring occasionally.

Increase heat to medium-high. Add turkey and cook, stirring with a wooden fork to break up meat, until no longer pink, about 8 minutes.

Reduce heat to medium. Pour in wine and cook, stirring, for about 2 minutes.

Stir in spaghetti sauce and bring to a boil, about 3 minutes. Serve over drained pasta.

MENU: Sesame bread sticks. Red-leaf lettuce with fresh mozzarella cheese cubes and favorite dressing. Bakery brownies.

SERVINGS: Makes 4 servings.

Camembert Angel Hair

■ Camembert is a famous French cow's milk cheese that is rich and creamy. It forms the basis of a wonderful and very quick-to-make sauce. When you buy Camembert, look for rounds that have a soft, fuzzy crust. Dry crusts tend to indicate age, and, with age, comes bitterness.

1 (9-oz.) package refrigerated fresh angel hair pasta
1 pound fresh cherry tomatoes, cut into wedges
1 cup packed fresh basil leaves
2 cloves garlic, chopped
8 ounces Camembert cheese, cut into small pieces

Cook pasta according to package directions.

Meanwhile, place tomatoes, basil, and garlic in a food processor or blender; pulse on and off until ingredients are coarsely chopped but not pureed. Combine mixture with cheese pieces in a large bowl.

Drain pasta and toss gently with cheese mixture until cheese melts.

MENU: Hot French bread. Packaged Caesar salad. Bakery sugar cookies.

SERVINGS: Makes 4 servings.

Gnocchi with Sauce Verde

■ Gnocchi are toothsome little dumplings that might contain ricotta cheese or potatoes. They're sold fresh in the refrigerated section. They are also frozen or dried, but the fresh ones cook the fastest.

1 (9-oz.) package refrigerated fresh gnocchi
1 cup tightly packed fresh flat-leaf parsley leaves
1 cup grated Parmesan cheese
½ cup walnuts
¼ cup extra-virgin olive oil
1 tablespoon chopped fresh basil
1 clove garlic, peeled

Cook gnocchi according to package directions. Drain gnocchi and place in a serving bowl.

Meanwhile, place remaining ingredients in a blender or food processor. Process 30 seconds or until smooth.

Serve sauce with drained gnocchi.

MENU: Endive leaves stuffed with deli seafood salad. Whole-wheat rolls. Bakery angel food cake with nondairy whipped topping and sliced strawberries.

SERVINGS: Makes 6 to 8 servings.

Curry with Couscous

■ Ground turkey has a pleasant, mild taste that goes well with many flavors. Paired here with curry and couscous, it's slightly exotic but thoroughly delicious.

1 tablespoon vegetable oil
1 pound ground turkey
½ cup chopped shallots
¼ cup chopped pecans
½ teaspoon curry powder
1 clove garlic, minced
2½ cups water
2 tablespoons butter
1 tablespoon chopped fresh parsley
¼ teaspoon salt
1½ cups instant couscous

Heat oil in a 10-inch skillet over medium-high heat. Add turkey and shallots and cook, breaking up turkey with a wooden fork, until no longer pink, about 6 minutes. Drain off fat.

Stir in pecans, curry powder, and garlic. Stir in water, butter, parsley, and salt. Bring to a boil. Stir in couscous; remove from heat. Cover and let stand 5 minutes or until liquid is absorbed. Fluff with a fork.

MENU: Endive and pear slices. Warm pita bread. Raspberry sherbet.

SERVINGS: Makes 4 servings.

Pasta & Cappicola

■ This is the best quick-cooking tip: Add the frozen peas to the boiling pasta water about 3 minutes before the pasta is finished cooking. You save a pan and the peas cook to perfection.

1 (9-oz.) package refrigerated fresh linguine
¾ cup frozen green peas
¼ cup butter
¼ cup olive oil
2 cloves garlic, minced
¼ pound cappicola (Italian ham) cut into
   ¼-inch strips
½ cup grated Parmesan cheese

Prepare pasta according to package directions, but add peas 3 minutes before pasta is finished cooking. Drain in a colander.

Wipe out pot and return to medium heat. Add butter and oil and heat until hot. Add garlic; cook for 1 minute. Remove from heat.

Add pasta and peas. Toss to coat with garlic, oil, and butter mixture. Add cappicola strips and Parmesan cheese. Toss to coat.

MENU: Romaine lettuce, topped with croutons and bottled Caesar salad dressing. Apricot halves filled with ricotta cheese.

SERVINGS: Makes 4 servings.

Angel-Hair Pasta with Fresh Tomatoes

■ This is a summer dish to make when tomatoes are at their peak. Don't make it with winter tomatoes. It will have no flavor.

1 (9-oz.) package refrigerated fresh angel-hair pasta
4 tablespoons olive oil
1 clove garlic, minced
2 cups diced tomatoes
2 teaspoons chopped fresh basil or ½ teaspoon dried
½ cup chicken broth
5 tablespoons grated Parmesan cheese

Prepare pasta according to package directions. Drain pasta.

Meanwhile, heat oil in a 10-inch skillet over medium-high heat; add garlic and cook for 1 minute. Add tomatoes and basil and cook for 3 minutes.

Add drained pasta to skillet and toss well to combine. Add chicken broth and toss well. Add Parmesan cheese and toss well.

MENU: Cantaloupe cubes and blueberries. Italian bread. Bakery sesame-seed cookies.

SERVINGS: Makes 4 or 5 servings.

Hot Garlic & Oil Pasta

■ I tend not to cook with extra-virgin olive oil because it imparts a strong, olive taste, which isn't bad but can be too powerful for a particular dish. But in this case, the oil flavor is very important to the sauce. Actually, it is the sauce.

1 (9-oz.) package refrigerated fresh fettuccine
⅔ cup extra-virgin olive oil
2 cloves garlic, finely minced
1 teaspoon salt
1 teaspoon crushed red pepper flakes

Prepare pasta according to package directions. Drain pasta and keep warm.

Meanwhile, heat oil in a 10-inch frying pan. Add garlic, salt, and pepper flakes. Cook over low heat about 3 minutes. Toss with drained pasta.

MENU: Dressed tomato slices and basil leaves with favorite dressing. Hard rolls. Fresh green and purple grapes.

SERVINGS: Makes 4 servings.

Tortellini with Sun-Dried Tomatoes

■ I regret all the years I lived before tasting sun-dried tomatoes. I love their intense flavor and now use them often in a variety of dishes, from pasta to stuffed chicken breasts. You can buy them dehydrated and rehydrate them as you need them, or just keep a small bottle of sun-dried tomatoes in oil on hand.

Asiago is an Italian cheese with a nutty flavor that when aged is grated like Parmesan.

1 (9-oz.) package refrigerated fresh tortellini
1 cup oil-packed sun-dried tomatoes
1 clove garlic, minced
3 tablespoons minced fresh basil
⅓ cup grated Parmesan cheese
⅓ cup grated Asiago cheese

Cook tortellini according to package directions. Drain, reserving ⅓ cup cooking water.

Meanwhile, drain tomatoes, reserving 2 tablespoons of their oil. Place the tomatoes and reserved oil in a food processor or blender and pulse until coarsely ground.

Place tomatoes in a 10-inch skillet, stir in garlic, and cook for 2 to 3 minutes. Remove from heat and set aside.

Mix together reserved cooking water, tomato mixture, and basil. Toss with drained tortellini. Add cheeses and toss again.

MENU: Deli green bean salad. Pear slices.

SERVINGS: Makes 4 servings.

Broccoli & Mushroom Spaghetti

■ The boiling water blanches the broccoli and mushrooms, keeping them slightly crunchy, bright, and firm.

1 (9-oz.) package refrigerated fresh spaghetti
1½ cups broccoli florets
¼ pound sliced mushrooms
Salt and freshly ground black pepper
¼ cup grated Parmesan cheese
1 tablespoon fresh lemon juice

Cook pasta according to package directions.

Meanwhile, place broccoli and mushrooms in a colander. Pour cooked pasta into the colander to drain. Place colander contents in a pasta bowl. Season with salt and pepper. Toss with cheese and lemon juice.

MENU: Hard rolls. Tossed salad with ranch dressing. Pear and apple slices.

SERVINGS: Makes 4 servings.

Lemon & Garlic Linguine

■ Fresh pasta has a shorter shelf life than dry pasta, so it's important to pay attention to freshness dates. I routinely buy fresh pasta when I shop once a week, at least two packages. My family will eat one, and probably the other (and if not I can freeze the pasta for later use), and I know I will have the ingredients for a speedy dish, like this, on hand.

1 (9-oz.) package refrigerated fresh linguine
¼ cup olive oil
3 cloves garlic, finely chopped
3 tablespoons fresh lemon juice
⅛ teaspoon freshly ground black pepper
¼ cup grated Parmesan cheese
¼ cup chopped fresh parsley

Cook pasta according to package directions. Drain pasta and place in a serving bowl.

Meanwhile, heat olive oil in a 10-inch skillet over medium-high heat. Add garlic and cook until golden, about 2 minutes. Add lemon juice and pepper. Reduce heat and simmer 1 minute more.

Add sauce to drained pasta and toss well. Add cheese and parsley and toss again.

MENU: Soft garlic bread sticks. Mixed greens with mandarin orange slices and thin slices of red onion. Bakery coconut cream pie.

SERVINGS: Makes 4 servings.

Scallops Fra Diavolo

■ *Fra diavolo* is a culinary term that, loosely translated, means "brother devil." Which is a poetic way of saying this dish is hot.

1 (9-oz.) package fresh linguine
¼ cup olive oil
1½ pounds bay scallops, rinsed and patted dry
1 cup chopped scallions
1 clove garlic, minced
4 tablespoons chopped fresh parsley
1 teaspoon chopped fresh oregano or ½ teaspoon dried
1 teaspoon crushed red pepper flakes
1 (14½-oz.) can chopped tomatoes in puree

Cook pasta according to package directions. Drain and place in a serving bowl.

Meanwhile, heat oil in a 10-inch skillet over medium-high heat. Add scallops. Cook until white, about 2 minutes. Add scallions and garlic; cook until translucent, about 2 minutes. Remove scallops and keep warm. Add parsley, oregano, pepper flakes, and tomatoes to skillet. Simmer for 5 minutes.

Add sauce and scallops to pasta and toss to coat.

MENU: Packaged Caesar salad. Apple slices drizzled with honey and lemon juice.

SERVINGS: Makes 4 or 5 servings.

Chicken Pasta

■ Shredded carrots are available now in refrigerated produce cases in neat little plastic bags. They keep in the refrigerator for several days and make a useful ingredient that can be added to many dishes without any hassle.

1 (9-oz.) package refrigerated fresh angel
  hair pasta
1 tablespoon vegetable oil
1 small onion, thinly sliced
2 cloves garlic, minced
1 roasted chicken breast, finely chopped
½ cup shredded carrot
3 tablespoons soy sauce
½ cup chicken broth
2 tablespoons finely chopped fresh parsley

Cook pasta according to package directions. Drain; rinse with cold water.

Meanwhile, heat oil in a 12-inch skillet or wok over medium-high heat. Add onion and garlic and cook until crisp-tender, about 1 minute. Add chicken, carrot, and soy sauce. Stir-fry for 2 minutes. Stir in pasta and broth. Heat through. Sprinkle with parsley.

MENU: Spinach salad with sliced strawberries and lemon vinaigrette. Nonfat chocolate ice cream.

SERVINGS: Makes 4 servings.

Sausage & Linguine

■ Have you checked the sausage cases lately? There's a whole new world of sausage products, low-fat, low-sodium, chicken, turkey . . . the variations are enormous and the taste is delicious. Any choice you make will be the right one for this dish.

1 (9-oz.) package refrigerated fresh linguine
2 teaspoons olive oil
½ pound turkey sausage, sliced
½ cup sliced scallions
2 cloves garlic, cut into slivers
½ pound sliced mushrooms
1½ cups tomato and mushroom pasta sauce

Cook pasta according to package directions. Drain pasta and place in a bowl.

Meanwhile, heat olive oil in a 12-inch skillet over medium heat. Add sausage slices, scallions, garlic, and mushrooms and sauté for about 5 minutes or until scallions are softened. Add pasta sauce and simmer for 5 more minutes.

Pour sauce over pasta and toss to combine.

MENU: Garlic bread. Packaged Caesar salad. Sliced mangoes and nonfat vanilla yogurt.

SERVINGS: Makes 4 servings.

Tortellini with Chicken & Broccoli

■ Broccoli is another often-used vegetable that I buy precut and ready for the pan. It never goes to waste, and it saves me a lot of time. In this dish, I cut the florets a bit more into smaller pieces than those that come in a package. It takes a few more minutes, but then it cooks more quickly—a worthwhile trade-off.

1 (9-oz.) package refrigerated fresh tortellini
2 tablespoons vegetable oil
1 cup chopped broccoli
⅓ cup chopped onion
2 cloves garlic, finely chopped
2 cups chopped cooked chicken
2 large tomatoes, chopped
⅓ cup grated Romano cheese

Cook pasta according to package directions. Drain and place in a serving bowl.

Meanwhile, heat oil in a 12-inch frying pan over medium heat. Add broccoli, onion, and garlic and sauté for about 8 minutes or until crisp-tender.

Stir in chicken and tomatoes. Cook, uncovered, about 3 minutes. Pour sauce over drained tortellini and toss to combine. Sprinkle with cheese.

MENU: Sesame bread sticks wrapped with paper-thin slices of prosciutto. Tossed salad with creamy Italian dressing. Nonfat strawberry yogurt with fresh strawberries.

SERVINGS: Makes 6 servings.

Pasta & Zucchini

■ A food processor will make easy work of slicing the zucchini. Scrub the vegetable first, but don't bother to peel—the skin is edible. The heat of the pasta water will blanch the zucchini.

1 (9-oz.) package refrigerated fresh angel hair pasta
1 zucchini, halved, then thinly sliced
4 tomatoes, cubed (about 3 cups)
3 tablespoons olive oil
1 tablespoon fresh oregano or 1½ teaspoons dried
1 tablespoon chopped fresh parsley

Cook pasta according to package directions.

Meanwhile, place zucchini in a colander. Drain pasta into colander over zucchini.

Toss pasta and zucchini with tomatoes, olive oil, oregano, and parsley.

MENU: Warm garlic bread. Arugula with creamy Italian dressing. Fresh peach halves tossed with flaked coconut and dusted with brown sugar.

SERVINGS: Makes 4 servings.

Tomato-Bacon Linguine

■ My favorite pasta dish takes a lot longer than 15 minutes to make—it's spaghetti and meat sauce the way my mother used to cook it. My second favorite pasta dish is this one, and it can be made in a snap.

1 (9-oz.) package refrigerated fresh linguine
3 to 4 slices bacon
¼ cup sliced scallions
2 tablespoons fresh chopped basil or 1 tablespoon dried
3 very ripe tomatoes, chopped
Salt and pepper to taste

Cook pasta according to package directions. Drain pasta and place in a serving bowl.

Meanwhile, cook bacon in microwave on HIGH 3 to 4 minutes or until crisp. Drain bacon on a paper towel, reserving 1 tablespoon of drippings.

Add drippings and scallions to a medium skillet; cook over medium heat until tender, about 3 minutes. While scallions cook, mix together basil and tomatoes. Add basil-tomato mix to skillet. Just heat through.

Toss sauce with drained linguine. Season with salt and pepper. Crumble bacon over linguine.

MENU: Warm Italian bread. Spinach salad with deli marinated mushrooms. Sliced plums sprinkled with port wine.

SERVINGS: Makes 4 servings.

Pesto Pasta with Salmon Steaks

■ I used to wait until summer when my own herb garden yielded enough fresh basil to make pesto sauce, but I've found that the small round plastic containers of fresh pesto that are usually sold side by side with refrigerated fresh pasta are quite good. The nice thing about this is, I can enjoy pesto year-round.

1 (9-oz.) package refrigerated fresh linguine
1 tablespoon olive oil
1 teaspoon fresh lemon juice
4 small salmon steaks, rinsed and patted dry
¾ cup pesto sauce (brought to room temperature)

Cook pasta according to package directions. Drain pasta and keep warm.

Meanwhile, mix olive oil and lemon juice. Brush salmon steaks with oil mixture.

Heat a heavy 10-inch skillet over medium heat. When hot, add oiled salmon steaks. Cook about 10 minutes, turning fish once.

Place fish on drained pasta. Spoon some pesto sauce over salmon steaks. Serve with remaining pesto on the side.

MENU: Warm Italian bread. Leaf lettuce with sliced radishes and red-wine-vinegar-and-oil salad dressing. Bakery carrot cake.

SERVINGS: Makes 4 servings.

Pasta with Scallops

■ I have several frying pans, and they get heavy use. Two 12-inchers have deep sides, which is good if I'm going to add additional ingredients like sauces. One has an enamel finish, which is great if I'm going to cook with acidic foods like tomatoes. I have two 10-inch skillets: One is heavy cast iron, which is great for uniform heat control and for dishes that will require a little time in the oven as well as on top of the stove. The other skillet, which is a more modern style, is half sauté pan, half skillet with heat conductors that do a good job at keeping a steady, even heat.

1 (9-oz.) package refrigerated fresh angel
   hair pasta
2 tablespoons olive oil
1½ pounds bay scallops, rinsed
2 tablespoons finely chopped garlic
1 cup julienned oil-packed sun-dried
   tomatoes, drained
Juice of ½ lemon
2 tablespoons unsalted butter
3 tablespoons chopped fresh flat-leaf parsley

Cook pasta according to package directions. Drain pasta.

Meanwhile, heat oil in a 10-inch skillet over medium-high heat. Add scallops and garlic. Cook until scallops are opaque, about 1 minute. Stir in sun-dried tomatoes. Cook 30 seconds more. Add lemon juice, butter, and parsley.

Toss sauce with drained pasta.

MENU: Sesame bread sticks. Tossed salad with favorite dressing. Bakery blueberry pie.

SERVINGS: Makes 4 servings.

Spinach Pasta

■ Coming up with different menus every day is challenging. Here are some guiding principles that help me:

· Vary flavors, colors, textures, and temperatures for contrast.
· Vary menus to suit the season.
· Begin with a main dish; then think about side dishes.
· Sometimes, for a little twist, I make a side dish the entree, as in spinach pasta, and use a salad—the antipasto platter—for serving meat and cheese.

1 (9-oz.) package refrigerated fresh linguine
½ cup vegetable oil
¼ cup butter
1 large onion, thinly sliced
2 cloves garlic, minced
1 (10-oz.) package frozen chopped spinach
1 teaspoon dried basil
½ teaspoon salt
½ cup grated Parmesan cheese, plus
   additional for serving

Prepare pasta according to package directions. Drain pasta and place in a serving bowl.

Meanwhile, heat oil and butter in a 10-inch skillet over medium heat. Add onion, garlic, and chopped spinach. Reduce heat and simmer, covered, for 10 minutes, stirring occasionally.

Stir in basil and salt. Cover; simmer 4 minutes more. Stir in Parmesan cheese.

Spoon over drained pasta. Serve with more Parmesan cheese on the side.

MENU: Antipasto platter (marinated artichokes, roasted peppers, ripe olives, provolone cheese, and prosciutto). Italian bread. Bakery apple crumb cake.

SERVINGS: Makes 4 to 6 servings.

Shells & Broccoli

■ I shop with a list of ingredients needed for various dishes I plan to cook, but the first place I head when I enter the store is the produce section, where the freshest and best can change my mind. For instance, recently a perfect broccoli bouquet—firm, compact, dark green, almost purple-green, clusters of small buds with tender, firm and not too thick stalks—convinced me to serve this dish for dinner.

1 pound dried small pasta shells
⅓ cup pignoli (pine) nuts
½ cup bottled roasted peppers, drained and
    chopped
⅓ cup olive oil
¼ cup grated Parmesan cheese
4 cups broccoli florets

Preheat oven to 350F (175C). Cook pasta according to package directions.

Meanwhile, toast nuts in the oven until golden, 6 to 8 minutes. Transfer to a large serving bowl. Stir in peppers, oil, and Parmesan cheese.

Place broccoli in a colander. Drain cooked pasta over the broccoli. (The hot water will blanch the broccoli.)

Add pasta and broccoli to pepper-and-oil mixture. Toss to combine. Serve immediately.

MENU: Whole-wheat bread sticks. Papaya and red-grapefruit slices sprinkled with lemon juice and sugar.

SERVINGS: Makes 4 or 5 servings.

Garlic Pasta

■ James Beard once commented that anyone who had pasta, olive oil, butter, and garlic in the kitchen need never go without good food. I heartily agree. Garlic pasta is a classic that can be prepared in minutes. I always have its ingredients on hand—I can't imagine a working kitchen without them.

Next time there's a stormy day, late meeting, or traffic delay, it's a good bet this is what I'll be cooking.

1 (9-oz.) package refrigerated fresh spaghetti
½ cup butter
½ cup extra-virgin olive oil
4 or 5 cloves garlic, minced
1 teaspoon salt
¼ teaspoon freshly ground black pepper
¼ teaspoon dried oregano (optional)
Grated Parmesan cheese to taste

Cook pasta according to package directions. Drain pasta and place in a bowl.

Melt the butter in a heavy 8-inch skillet over medium heat. Add the olive oil, garlic, salt, pepper, and oregano, if using. Cook, stirring, until garlic is lightly browned.

Toss sauce with drained pasta. Serve with grated cheese.

MENU: Italian bread. White beans, chopped tomatoes, and sliced mushrooms tossed with lemon vinaigrette. Raspberry sherbet with fresh berries.

SERVINGS: Makes 4 to 6 servings.

Chicken Livers & Ravioli

■ Chicken livers are inexpensive, nutritious, and versatile. They have a mild flavor, tender texture, and require little preparation, needing only some trimming before cooking. Trimming is a very important step to ensure good results in a chicken-liver dish. First cut away any green parts, which can be bitter after cooking. Next cut away any fat. Then find the connective tissue between the two halves of the liver and remove it as well as any veins. In most cases the livers should be cooked whole even if they are to be cut into smaller pieces later.

1 (9-oz.) package refrigerated fresh cheese-
   filled ravioli
3 tablespoons olive oil
8 ounces chicken livers, trimmed
4 scallions, thinly sliced
½ cup chopped fresh parsley
2 cloves garlic, minced
2 tablespoons unsalted butter
1 (14.5-oz.) can diced tomatoes, undrained

Cook ravioli according to package directions. Drain and place in a serving bowl.

Heat oil in a 12-inch skillet over medium-high heat. Add livers and cook until outsides are browned, about 3 minutes, turning once. Using a slotted spoon, transfer livers to cutting board. Reduce heat to medium-low. Add scallions, parsley, garlic, and butter; cook, stirring constantly, 2 minutes. Stir in tomatoes.

Coarsely chop livers, add to sauce, and pour over ravioli.

MENU: Deli marinated mushrooms. Ice-cream sandwiches.

SERVINGS: Makes 4 servings.

Shellfish Pasta

■ There's no guarantee of success when cleaning grit from shellfish. One method to get clams and mussels to expel sand is to cover them with clear seawater or a solution of 1 cup salt to 1 gallon of cool tap water. Allow to sit for 30 minutes, drain, and repeat the process several times. Then scrub shells with a stiff brush or plastic pot cleaner. This doesn't make for fast cooking, but it may add to the enjoyment of the shellfish.

1 (9-oz.) package refrigerated fresh linguine
1 (14.5-oz.) bottle pasta tomato sauce with
   basil
¼ teaspoon crushed red pepper flakes
1 pound mussels in shells, debearded and
   scrubbed
1 pound littleneck clams, scrubbed
⅓ cup finely chopped fresh parsley

Cook pasta according to package directions. Drain pasta and place in a serving bowl.

Meanwhile, simmer tomato sauce with red pepper flakes in a large saucepan over medium heat, about 3 minutes. Add the shellfish and bring to a boil. Cover and cook 5 minutes. Stir in parsley. Ladle shellfish and sauce over drained pasta, discarding any shellfish that do not open.

MENU: Crusty bread. Red-leaf lettuce with sun-dried tomatoes and Caesar salad dressing. Bakery sticky buns.

SERVINGS: Makes 4 servings.

Pasta for a Summer Night

■ As a culinary professional, I'm barred from entering cooking contests; nonetheless, if I could enter one, I'd like to take a shot at the Great Garlic! contest, an annual event that inspires garlic fans who call themselves "Lovers of the Stinking Rose." And the recipe I'd enter would be my Pasta for a Summer Night. It calls for four cloves of minced garlic, so it delivers a whopping, pungent taste. If, as researchers now say, garlic may have the potential to lower blood cholesterol, this dish will certainly be one you can eat to your heart's content.

1 (9-oz.) package refrigerated fresh spinach
   linguine
2 tablespoons butter
2 shallots, chopped
4 cloves garlic, minced
2 teaspoons fresh oregano or 1 teaspoon
   dried
½ pound boneless, skinless chicken chicken
   breast, rinsed and cut into 1½-inch pieces
1 cup sliced mushrooms
1 medium tomato, chopped

Cook pasta according to package directions. Drain pasta and place in a serving bowl.

Meanwhile, melt butter in a 12-inch skillet over medium-high heat. Add shallots, garlic, and oregano and cook for 2 minutes.

Add chicken. Stir-fry for 3 minutes. Add mushrooms. Reduce heat; cook, covered, 5 to 6 minutes or until chicken is no longer pink. Uncover, stir in tomato, and cook 1 to 2 minutes more or until liquid has evaporated.

Toss sauce with drained pasta.

MENU: Focaccia. Bibb lettuce with Russian dressing. Watermelon.

SERVINGS: Makes 4 servings.

Salad Bar Spaghetti

■ As I circled the salad bar of the supermarket where I shop, it occurred to me that right there before my eyes were all the fixings for pasta primavera—except the pasta, of course. Sliced mushrooms, raw onion rings, peppers, tomato, carrots, broccoli florets, and summer squash—the standard components. My pantry always has a supply of fresh garlic and pasta, so I was set.

1 (9-oz.) package refrigerated fresh spaghetti
2 to 3 tablespoons olive oil
½ cup finely chopped zucchini
1 cup sliced mushrooms
2 tablespoons finely chopped onion
2 cloves garlic, finely chopped
½ cup chopped green or red bell pepper
1 cup broccoli florets
½ cup cherry tomatoes or tomato wedges
1 egg, lightly whisked
2 tablespoons grated Parmesan cheese

Cook pasta according to package directions.

Heat oil in a 12-inch skillet over medium heat. Add zucchini, mushrooms, onion, garlic, bell pepper, and broccoli. Stir-fry for 5 minutes. Remove from heat.

Drain the pasta and return to hot pasta pan over heat and cook, tossing, until dry, about 2 minutes. Remove from heat, toss with egg and cheese to coat. Stir in tomatoes and stir-fried vegetables.

MENU: Deli chicken salad. Fruit salad with lemon yogurt dressing.

SERVINGS: Makes 4 servings.

Chicken Vermicelli

■ I'm serious about pasta cooking. After the pasta hits the hot water, I stir and stir to keep the pasta from sticking to itself or to the pot, and after the first five minutes of boiling, I start checking for doneness. Tender but chewy is how I like it. Once it's reached the desired stage, I dump it into a colander, drain it, and serve it. That's the right way. In my recipe for Chicken Vermicelli, I do it the easy way, so easy that my teenage children could be counted on to put this dish together.

1 pound ground chicken
1 medium onion, chopped
2 cloves garlic, minced
¼ teaspoon freshly ground black pepper
1 cup chicken broth
1 (6-oz.) can tomato paste
1 cup sliced mushrooms
6 ounces vermicelli, broken

Cook chicken, onion, garlic, and pepper in a 3-quart saucepan over medium heat, stirring frequently, until chicken is browned and onion is tender, about 6 minutes. Stir in chicken broth, tomato paste, and mushrooms.

Add vermicelli, a little at a time, stirring well after each addition. Cook, covered, over medium-low heat for 6 minutes or until vermicelli is tender.

MENU: Sesame bread sticks. Spinach salad with grapefruit bits. Bakery chocolate chip cookies.

SERVINGS: Makes 4 servings.

Herb Garden Spaghetti

■ My herb garden is my pride and joy. In spring when it's all planted, I wake up earlier than usual just to walk around it. I talk to sprouts, reprimand weeds, sniff the air for the wondrous perfume that hangs in the air— especially by the mint and basil. This little patch is the source of inspiration for many a meal. Fresh herbs are very common nowadays—even in the midst of winter I can find them in the supermarket. If the precise herbs listed here aren't available, feel free to substitute what you can find.

1 (9-oz.) package refrigerated fresh spaghetti
½ cup butter
½ cup olive oil
3 tablespoons fresh lemon juice
1 cup finely chopped fresh parsley
3 tablespoons finely chopped fresh mint leaves
3 tablespoons finely chopped fresh basil leaves
1 cup grated Parmesan cheese

Cook pasta according to package directions. Drain pasta and place in a serving bowl.

Heat oil and butter in a heavy 10-inch skillet over medium-high heat until mixture sizzles. Stir in lemon juice and herbs. Remove from heat.

Toss herb mixture and ½ cup Parmesan cheese with drained pasta. Serve hot with remaining cheese on the side.

MENU: Deli seafood salad. Bibb lettuce with blue-cheese dressing. Bakery cream puffs.

SERVINGS: Makes 4 servings.

Hot Linguine

■ My passion for hot food did not spring from tasting Southwestern cuisine or Mexican dishes. It came from our neighborhood pizzeria where shakers of crushed hot pepper flakes were on every table. To this day, I sprinkle crushed hot red pepper on my pizza. And in my kitchen, the spice I replenish most often (next to black pepper) is crushed red pepper flakes.

2 (9-oz.) package refrigerated fresh linguine
1 pound hot Italian sausage, cut into ½-inch pieces
1 large onion, chopped
1 medium green bell pepper, diced
1 clove garlic, minced
1 (28-oz.) jar pasta sauce
1 teaspoon crushed red pepper flakes
Grated Parmesan cheese

Cook pasta according to package directions. Drain pasta and place in a serving bowl.

Cook sausage, onion, bell pepper, and garlic in a 12-inch skillet over medium heat until sausage is completely cooked and no pink remains, about 10 minutes, stirring occasionally. Drain off fat. Add sauce and hot pepper flakes. Bring to a boil, stirring occasionally.

Serve over drained pasta. Sprinkle with cheese.

MENU: Garlic bread. Pear-and-endive salad. Sponge cake with vanilla yogurt.

SERVINGS: Makes 6 servings.

Pepper Spaghetti

■ Culinary artists have a palette of colors to work with when bell peppers are in the recipe. Green, red, chocolate, yellow, and orange are among the colors of peppers available at the supermarket where I shop. Cut up in salads or stir-fries, they not only taste delicious, they're bright and appealing to the eye. Peppers are interchangeable in recipes. They differ only slightly in taste, but a great deal in price. Green bell peppers are always the cheapest.

1 (9-oz.) package refrigerated fresh spaghetti
2 tablespoons olive oil
½ red bell pepper, cut into ¼-inch, lengthwise strips
½ yellow bell pepper, cut into ¼-inch, lengthwise strips
1 clove garlic, finely chopped
1 teaspoon fresh thyme or ⅛ teaspoon dried
Freshly ground black pepper
1 tablespoon grated Parmesan cheese

Cook pasta according to package directions.

Meanwhile, heat olive oil in a 10-inch skillet. Add the pepper strips and cook over medium heat, stirring occasionally, until the edges begin to brown, about 4 minutes.

Add the garlic and thyme, reduce heat to low, and stir-fry for 1 minute. Add a generous grinding of black pepper; set aside.

Ladle ¼ cup of pasta cooking water into a large bowl. Drain pasta. Add pasta to the bowl. Top with pepper mix and Parmesan cheese. Toss to combine.

MENU: Salad of dark greens with French dressing. Ice-cream sandwiches.

SERVINGS: Makes 4 servings.

Broccoli & Rotini

■ The first thing I tried to cook was a pancake. What came out of the pan looked like a doughy amoeba. It didn't taste good either, even with butter and syrup. I don't know what drove me back to the kitchen. I think I got married.

The hardest lesson to learn was confidence, and that came only with time and experience. I searched cookbooks for easy, foolproof recipes. With each success, I became bolder and happier about being in the kitchen. This recipe for broccoli and pasta is the kind of surefire dish that started me on my way to cooking for the sheer joy of it.

1 (9-oz.) package refrigerated fresh rotini
2 cups small broccoli florets
¾ cup milk
4 ounces (½ cup) cream cheese, at room
    temperature
1 tablespoon chopped red onion
1 tablespoon Dijon mustard

Cook pasta according to package directions.

Place broccoli in a colander. Drain cooked pasta over broccoli. (Boiling water will blanch the florets.)

Wipe out pasta pan; add milk, cream cheese, red onion, and mustard. Stir over low heat until cream cheese is melted, about 5 minutes. Toss sauce with broccoli and pasta.

MENU: Baby shrimp salad on Bibb lettuce leaves with creamy peppercorn dressing. Sesame bread sticks. Sliced pears.

SERVINGS: Makes 4 servings.

Green Bean Pasta

■ Chinese green beans look like green beans, only more so. Oddly enough, they belong to the same family as the black-eyed pea. They are perfect for stir-frying and braising, becoming chewy and firm in the process. The crunch is solid, not juicy, the taste less sweet than common green beans. They are known by other names—long bean, asparagus bean, yard-long bean, and, for those true fans, *dau gok*.

1 (9-oz.) package refrigerated fresh vermicelli
4 slices bacon, cut into 1-inch pieces
1 cup yard-long green beans, cut into thirds
3 scallions, thinly sliced

Cook vermicelli according to package directions. Drain.

Meanwhile, cook bacon in a microwave oven on HIGH about 4 minutes or until crisp. Drain on paper towels, reserving 2 teaspoons of drippings.

Add drippings to a 10-inch skillet over medium-high heat. Add beans and scallions to the pan and stir-fry for 2 to 3 minutes. Toss contents of pan with drained pasta. Crumble bacon on top.

MENU: Tossed salad with Russian dressing. Hard rolls. Bakery brownies à la mode.

SERVINGS: Makes 4 servings.

VARIATION
Substitute 2 teaspoons olive oil for the bacon fat.

Chinese Spaghetti

■ I didn't plan to call it Chinese Spaghetti. The reason it became Chinese Spaghetti was that it used to be impossible to find Asian foodstuffs in supermarkets. That's all changed, of course. But back in the old days when Asian noodles were a rarity, I substituted vermicelli. It worked out really well, and I've kind of gotten used to it.

The tricky part to the preparation of Chinese Spaghetti is that the pasta sauce for this dish is stir-fried. Anyone with experience with stir-frying knows that once the ingredients are cut, everything happens fast. So I cook the spaghetti first.

1 (9-oz.) package refrigerated fresh
   vermicelli
2 tablespoons vegetable oil
¾ cup chopped green bell pepper
1 clove garlic, chopped
1½ cups snow peas, trimmed
¾ cup red onion rings
½ cup canned sliced water chestnuts
2 teaspoons soy sauce
½ cup bean sprouts

Cook vermicelli according to package directions. Drain and place in serving bowl. Cover to keep warm.

Meanwhile, heat oil in a 12-inch skillet over medium-high heat. Add bell pepper, garlic, snow peas, onion, water chestnuts, and soy sauce. Stir-fry 3 to 4 minutes or until bell pepper is crisp-tender. Add bean sprouts and stir-fry 2 minutes longer or until heated through.

Spoon stir-fried vegetables over hot vermicelli.

MENU: Shredded iceberg lettuce and grated carrots tossed with Thousand Island dressing and topped with roasted peanuts. Pineapple spears with pineapple yogurt.

SERVINGS: Makes 3 or 4 servings.

Ravioli with Zucchini

■ Lighter meals not only cut calories, fat, and sugars, they cut time. For instance, skip a course—dessert. Stop screaming! Make dessert something for rare occasions. It'll seem extra-special during the times when it is served. If you must have something sweet, a piece of ripe fruit works great. For those who have to have baked goods, here's a quick one: Bake a batch of refrigerator biscuits or rolls, the kind that come from a tube or a can. They take just a few minutes, smell great, and taste good with a fruit spread or preserves. No, they are not as rich as double-chocolate fudge layer cake, but they're mighty satisfying.

1 (9-oz.) refrigerated fresh meat-filled ravioli
½ cup olive oil
1 clove garlic, minced
4 small zucchini, sliced into ¼-inch thick
   rounds
1 red bell pepper, chopped
¼ cup minced fresh basil
Salt and freshly ground black pepper

Cook ravioli according to package directions. Drain and place in a serving bowl.

Meanwhile, heat oil in a 12-inch skillet over medium-high heat. Add garlic; cook for 30 seconds. Add zucchini, bell pepper, basil, and salt to taste. Sauté vegetables, stirring occasionally, until they are tender, 5 to 7 minutes. Season with salt and black pepper to taste.

Ladle vegetables and all the oil on top of the ravioli.

MENU: Citrus salad sprinkled with shredded unsweetened coconut.

SERVINGS: Makes 4 to 6 servings.

Linguine with Tomato & Basil Sauce

■ There is a wealth of high-quality prepared ingredients currently available on supermarket shelves. Among the best selling are bottled pasta sauces. I'm partial to tomato-basil sauce, but I tend to doctor it a bit to freshen the flavors. Wine perks up this sauce.

1 (9-oz.) package refrigerated fresh linguine
2 tablespoons olive oil
1 cup chopped onion
3 cloves garlic, minced
2 cups sliced mushrooms
1 (14.5-oz.) jar tomato-basil pasta sauce
¼ cup dry red wine

Cook pasta according to package directions. Drain pasta and place in a serving bowl.

Heat oil in a 12-inch skillet over medium-high heat. Add onion and garlic and cook until onion is tender, about 3 minutes.

Add mushrooms. Cook for 5 minutes. Add pasta sauce and wine. Reduce heat to low and simmer, uncovered, 6 minutes.

Serve sauce over pasta.

MENU: Escarole with sliced cucumbers and oil-and-vinegar dressing. Garlic bread. Bakery sesame-seed cookies.

SERVINGS: Makes 4 servings.

Fettuccine & Vegetables

■ Sugar snap peas are a wondrous cross between snow peas and snap beans. Plump and sweet, they can be eaten raw and unhulled. They are so pretty that they make a wonderful addition to crudités. They're available fresh sometimes and frozen always in my supermarket. They seem to hold up after freezing. Although not as good as fresh, the frozen ones are still very good and easy to keep on hand.

1 (9-oz.) package refrigerated fresh fettuccine
1 cup sugar snap peas (see Note, below)
1 medium cucumber, seeded and chopped
2 scallions, thinly sliced
1½ teaspoons minced fresh dill
1 (12-oz.) carton ricotta cheese

Cook pasta according to package directions.
Meanwhile, place snap peas in a colander. Combine cucumber, scallions, dill, and ricotta cheese in a large bowl; mix well.
Drain cooked pasta over sugar snap peas. Toss warm pasta and peas with cucumber-ricotta cheese mixture until the pasta is thoroughly coated.

MENU: Bibb lettuce with blue-cheese dressing. Roasted deli chicken, sliced. Peach halves with toasted coconut.

SERVINGS: Makes 4 servings.

NOTE
Frozen sugar snap peas can be substituted, but they must be lightly steamed according to package directions.

Sausage & Noodles

■ Whenever anyone says "pasta," I think of spaghetti and all its cousins. I never think noodles. Noodles are technically pasta; what makes them different is the addition of eggs or egg yolks. There is a wide variety of noodles—ruffled, flat, thick, thin. You'll find them in many countries; there are noodle dishes from Eastern Europe, Italy, and Asia.

Sausage and Noodles is a dish with a lot of Old World flavors from cabbage, onion, and kielbasa. Thin noodles are the best to use for quick results.

3 cups thin noodles
2 tablespoons vegetable oil
1 pound kielbasa, cut into 1-inch rounds
4 cups coleslaw mix or 4 cups shredded cabbage and carrots
1 cup chopped onion
1 tablespoon butter

Cook noodles according to package directions.
Meanwhile, heat oil in a 12-inch skillet over medium-high heat. Add kielbasa rounds and cook until browned, about 3 minutes. Add coleslaw mix and onion and cook, stirring, until lightly browned, 6 minutes. Reduce heat, cover, and simmer 4 more minutes.
Drain noodles. Toss with butter in a large serving dish. Top with kielbasa-and-cabbage mixture.

MENU: Dark rye bread. Spinach salad with mushrooms and balsamic vinaigrette. Applesauce with raspberries.

SERVINGS: Makes 5 servings.

Pizza Pasta

■ Never underestimate the power of pizza. I made a pizza salad once and took it to a family picnic, where it was an instant hit. I know this because: a) It disappeared in no time; b) Everyone wanted the recipe; and c) It makes an appearance at every family gathering, and I don't make it. The best thing about this dish is that there are only three steps: cook the pasta, mix it with the other ingredients, and serve.

1 (9-oz.) package refrigerated fresh spaghetti
1 tablespoon olive oil
½ cup chopped onion
4 ounces sliced pepperoni, slices cut in half
1 (8-oz.) jar pizza sauce
4 ounces (1 cup) shredded mozzarella cheese
1 (8-oz.) carton ricotta cheese
1 tablespoon grated Parmesan cheese

Cook pasta according to package directions. Drain pasta and keep warm.

Meanwhile, heat oil in a 2-quart saucepan over medium heat. Add onion and pepperoni and cook, stirring, until onion is softened, about 2 minutes. Stir in pizza sauce. Cook until bubbly, about 2 minutes.

Mix together mozzarella and ricotta cheeses in a large pasta bowl or deep-sided serving dish.

Add drained pasta to cheese mixture and toss to mix well. Top with sauce. Sprinkle with Parmesan cheese.

MENU: Leaf lettuce with creamy Italian dressing. Fresh blueberries mixed with blueberry yogurt and spooned over angel food cake.

SERVINGS: Makes 4 servings.

Doctored Fettuccine Alfredo

■ "Doctoring" is a respectable tactic of the harried cook wherein he or she takes a convenience product and adds a few fresh ingredients to brighten the taste. Part of the ploy is silence. Confess to nothing. Chances are they'll never guess.

1 (9-oz.) package refrigerated fresh
  fettuccine
1 cup frozen green peas
1 cup chopped prosciutto
1 (26-oz.) jar creamy alfredo sauce

Prepare fettuccine according to package directions.

During last 5 minutes of cooking, add peas to boiling pasta water. Drain in a colander.

Combine ham and alfredo sauce in a pan. Stir to heat through, 2 minutes.

Add drained peas and pasta. Toss to combine. Transfer to a big pasta serving bowl.

MENU: Garlic bread. Deli olive salad. Vanilla pudding.

SERVINGS: Makes 4 servings.

Soups & Stews

It would be nice to have a big, old soup pot on the back burner bubbling away for hours with some aromatic brew. But who has time to watch the pot these days? Not all soups and stews need to be cooked all day, however. Let me show you the 15-minute way.

With high-quality convenience products blended with quick-cooking fresh foods, it is possible to produce divine, hearty dishes that can vie with the made-from-scratch, home-cooked variety. No kidding.

My personal favorite is a soup made from kielbasa, the famous spicy Polish sausage—a very high-flavor, smoky meat. Sautéed with garlic and onions, then bathed in some canned beef broth and a splash of red wine, it is mouthwatering. What's not to savor?

Not only are these one-pot dishes a boon to cooks facing a time crunch; they can also provide a meal that the whole family can enjoy.

Think of cooking a soup or a stew as building a house. Start with a good foundation—high-quality stocks or broth. Keep them in your pantry, and you are halfway to dinner. Then think of the endless variety of ingredients: beans, vegetables, quick-cooking noodles, hearty chopped greens, or mushrooms. A pinch of herbs, a squeeze of lemon—the possibilities are endless, and quick.

Pork with Noodles Soup

■ Dried angel hair pasta and thin noodles cook very quickly. Only 4 ounces of thin noodles are required for this recipe, so you don't need to heat a vat of water to cook them, which is what takes too much time.

1 tablespoon canola oil
½ pound boneless smoked pork chops, cut into narrow strips
1 (8-oz.) package coleslaw or 3 cups shredded cabbage
1 cup water
2 cups chicken broth
4 ounces fine egg noodles

Heat oil in a Dutch oven over high heat. Add pork strips and stir-fry about 2 minutes. Add coleslaw mix or cabbage and stir-fry for 3 minutes or until crisp-tender.

Add water and broth and bring to a full boil. Stir in noodles. Cover and cook for 8 to 9 minutes, stirring occasionally, or until noodles are tender.

MENU: Toasted rye bread. Applesauce. Bakery brownies.

SERVINGS: Makes 4 to 6 servings.

Lemony Bean Soup

■ This soup gets a refreshing flavor boost with the addition of lemon.

1 tablespoon olive oil
1 onion, chopped
1 (15-oz.) can red kidney beans, drained
6 cups beef broth
1 teaspoon salt
Juice of 1 lemon
¼ cup dry sherry
Garlic salt

Heat oil in a 5-quart saucepan or Dutch oven over medium heat. Add onion; sauté until soft, about 2 minutes. Add beans, broth, and salt. Simmer for 10 minutes.

Remove 1 cup of beans from pan and mash. Return mashed beans to pan. Stir in lemon juice and sherry. Simmer 1 minute.

Ladle into soup bowls. Sprinkle with garlic salt.

MENU: Mixed green salad with peppercorn salad dressing. Marble rye bread. Pineapple spears.

SERVINGS: Makes 4 servings.

Clam Noodle Soup

■ Memories of summer by the sea come with every spoonful of this delicious soup. For best results, select the tiniest littlenecks you can find.

1 (9-oz.) package refrigerated fresh
   fettuccine, cut into 2-inch-long strips
3 dozen littleneck clams, scrubbed
6 cloves garlic, minced
1 cup dry white wine
4 cups bottled clam juice
¼ teaspoon crushed red pepper flakes
¼ cup fresh parsley, minced

Cook pasta according to package directions.

Meanwhile, put clams, garlic, and wine in a 5-quart saucepan or Dutch oven. Bring to a boil over medium-high heat. Cover and simmer for 4 to 5 minutes or until clams have opened. Discard any unopened clams and remove clams from broth; set aside.

Add clam juice and pepper flakes to remaining broth in pan. Simmer 4 to 5 minutes. Add drained noodles. Remove from heat.

Ladle into soup bowls. Add clams in their shells. Sprinkle with parsley.

MENU: Rye crackers. Sliced-pear-and-spinach salad with poppy-seed dressing. Bakery blueberry muffins with strawberry jam.

SERVINGS: Makes 4 servings.

Zucchini Soup

■ A food processor will make quick work of shredding the zucchini. This is a good recipe to use up large zucchini, which tends not to be as tender as small zucchini.

4 bacon slices
3 cups milk
1 cup chicken broth
2 tablespoons finely chopped onion
1 teaspoon hot pepper sauce
1 cup shredded zucchini

Microwave bacon slices on HIGH 4 minutes. Drain on paper towels. Crumble and reserve.

Meanwhile, combine milk, broth, onion, and pepper sauce in a 5-quart saucepan or Dutch oven over medium heat. Bring to a simmer (do not boil); cook for 2 minutes. Stir in zucchini and simmer for 5 minutes or until onion is tender.

Ladle into soup bowls. Sprinkle with bacon.

MENU: Rice cakes spread with chive cream cheese. Citrus sections.

SERVINGS: Makes 4 servings.

Tortellini Soup

■ The frozen foods section of the supermarket is a treasure trove of helpful products for quick meals. I'm not speaking of frozen TV dinners; I'm talking about basic ingredients—for instance, the plastic bags full of frozen cheese- and meat-filled pasta like tortellini and ravioli. They're great to keep on hand as the basis for many fast meals.

1 cup frozen cheese tortellini
1 clove garlic, minced
2 cups chicken broth
1 (14.5-oz.) can crushed tomatoes in puree
1 teaspoon dried oregano
2 tablespoons grated Parmesan cheese

Combine tortellini, garlic, and broth in a 5-quart saucepan or Dutch oven. Bring to a boil over medium-high heat. Reduce heat and simmer for 6 minutes. Stir in tomatoes and oregano. Simmer for 5 minutes or until tortellini are tender.

Ladle into soup bowls. Sprinkle Parmesan cheese over each serving.

MENU: Bread sticks. Thin slices of cappicola (Italian ham). Angel food cake with cherry pie filling on top.

SERVINGS: Makes 4 servings.

Garlic Soup

■ You'd think with so much garlic this soup would be overpowering, but it isn't. Cooking the garlic this way makes it very tame and mellow.

¼ cup minced garlic
1 teaspoon white pepper
½ teaspoon dried thyme
1 bay leaf
5 cups vegetable broth
2 slices pumpernickel bread, toasted
4 teaspoons extra-virgin olive oil

Combine garlic, pepper, thyme, bay leaf, and broth in a 5-quart saucepan or Dutch oven. Bring to a boil over medium-high heat. Cover, reduce heat, and simmer for 6 minutes.

Crumble toasted bread into the soup. Return to a boil; cook 1 minute.

Ladle into soup bowls. Drizzle 1 teaspoon oil over each serving.

MENU: Pilot or other crackers. Tossed salad with cherry tomatoes and Russian dressing. Sliced peaches.

SERVINGS: Makes 4 servings.

Bourbon Black Bean Soup

■ This a soup for grown-ups only, because one of the ingredients is bourbon. If you're serving this soup to children, skip the bourbon.

1 (15-oz.) can black beans, drained
2 cups beef broth
1 tablespoon bourbon
⅛ teaspoon ground nutmeg
4 very thin lemon rounds
2 tablespoons minced red onion

Combine beans, broth, and bourbon in a 5-quart saucepan or Dutch oven. Mix well and bring to a boil over medium-high heat. Stir in nutmeg. Reduce heat and simmer 5 minutes.

Place a lemon slice in each of 4 soup bowls. Ladle soup over lemon. Garnish each serving with minced red onion.

MENU: Bakery pineapple muffins. Deli seafood salad on Romaine leaves. Canned pear halves drizzled with chocolate sauce.

SERVINGS: Makes 4 servings.

Tomato-Yogurt Soup

■ This is a refreshing cold soup for summer. Fresh garden tomatoes provide the pizzazz.

1 large cucumber, seeded, peeled, and cut into chunks
2 tablespoons balsamic vinegar
1 teaspoon seasoned salt
1 clove garlic, pressed
3 medium vine-ripened tomatoes, quartered
4 scallions, chopped
2 cups plain yogurt

Combine cucumber, vinegar, salt, garlic, tomatoes, and scallions in a food processor or blender. Process 1 minute or until finely chopped. Pour into a large bowl. Stir in yogurt until well blended.

MENU: Norwegian flat bread. Fruit salad.

SERVINGS: Makes 4 servings.

Lemon Soup

■ This recipe is inspired by the classic Greek soup made with lemon juice. The reason you stir in the eggs and lemon juice with hot broth before returning it to the pan is to keep the eggs from cooking in clumps.

2 cups shredded cooked chicken
4 cups chicken broth
⅓ cup quick-cooking rice
3 eggs
1 tablespoons fresh lemon juice

Combine chicken, broth, and rice in a 5-quart saucepan or Dutch oven. Cover and cook over medium heat until rice is tender, about 10 minutes. In a large bowl, whisk together eggs; whisk in lemon juice.

Slowly blend half of hot chicken broth mixture into egg mixture. Add egg mixture to remaining broth mixture in saucepan. Cook, stirring, over low heat until combined. Do not boil.

MENU: Pita pockets stuffed with tomato, cucumber, and feta cheese. Honey grahams.

SERVINGS: Makes 4 servings.

Ocean Deep Soup

■ Prepared fish broth is hard to find for some reason. One store in my area sells fish broth cubes like chicken broth cubes and beef broth cubes. If it's not available in your area, substitute Clamato juice or bottled clam juice.

6 cups fish broth
1 cup dry white wine
1 *each* red and yellow bell peppers, cut into thin strips
3 large ripe tomatoes, chopped
1 clove garlic, finely chopped
¾ pound haddock fillets, rinsed and cut into chunks

Combine broth and wine in a 5-quart saucepan or Dutch oven. Bring to a boil over medium heat. Add bell peppers, tomatoes, and garlic. Reduce heat and simmer 4 minutes.

Add fish chunks. Cover and simmer 7 minutes or until fish is cooked through.

MENU: Saltines. Melon-and-berry salad. Angel food cake with nondairy whipped topping.

SERVINGS: Makes 6 servings.

Fresh Mushroom Soup

■ There are a lot of variations on mushroom soup. This one is unusual because it's made in the microwave. Buy the mushrooms already sliced.

1 tablespoon butter
2 tablespoons chopped scallions
3 ounces sliced mushrooms
1 cup chicken broth
½ cup half-and-half
Dash of white pepper

Place butter, scallions, and mushrooms in a 2-cup microwave-safe measuring cup. Cover and microwave on HIGH until scallions are tender, 1 to 1½ minutes.

Stir in chicken broth; cover and microwave on HIGH 2 minutes, stirring once. Stir in half-and-half and microwave on HIGH until hot, 30 to 60 seconds. Season with white pepper.

MENU: Potato rolls. Sliced fresh fruit.

SERVINGS: Makes 2 servings.

Mushroom Noodle Soup

■ This is a hearty mushroom soup with an Asian touch.

2 (14.5-oz.) cans chicken broth
1 cup sliced mushrooms
1 small green bell pepper, chopped
½ cup sugar snap peas
1 teaspoon dried rosemary
1 teaspoon soy sauce
½ (6-oz.) package ramen noodles with
    seasoning packet

Mix all ingredients except noodles in a 3-quart saucepan over medium heat. Simmer about 3 minutes.

Add noodles with contents of seasoning packet. Bring to a boil. Reduce heat and simmer 3 minutes or until noodles are tender, stirring occasionally.

MENU: Rice crackers. Spinach salad with marinated mushrooms. Refrigerated orange gelatin.

SERVINGS: Makes 4 servings.

Cucumber-Chicken Soup

■ Cucumbers are one of my favorite salad vegetables. I love their cool taste and appetizing crunch. They don't get cooked very often, although they can be. Try them in this easy soup.

6 cups chicken broth
1 cup chopped cooked chicken
1 large cucumber, peeled, seeded, and cut into thin slices
½ cup sour cream
Dill sprigs, chopped

Combine chicken broth and chicken in a 2-quart saucepan over medium-high heat. Bring to a simmer. Stir in cucumber. Heat until bubbly.

Ladle into soup bowls. Float a dollop of sour cream on each bowl. Sprinkle with dill.

MENU: Toasted whole-wheat rolls. Fruit salad. Bakery raisin cookies.

SERVINGS: Makes 4 servings.

Chicken Oodles of Noodles Soup

■ I use fresh fettuccine as the noodles in my chicken noodle soup. They cook quickly.

1 quart chicken broth
¼ teaspoon dried dill weed
1 tablespoon chopped onion
½ cup chopped cooked chicken
⅓ cup refrigerated fresh fettuccine
1 tablespoon fresh flat-leaf parsley, chopped

Place broth and dill in a 5-quart saucepan or Dutch oven. Bring to a boil over medium-high heat.

Stir in onion, chicken, fettuccine, and parsley. Return to a boil. Reduce heat and simmer until noodles are tender, about 5 minutes.

MENU: Chowder crackers. Celery and carrot sticks. Bakery chocolate-chocolate chip cookies.

SERVINGS: Makes 4 to 6 servings.

Chicken Spinach Soup

■ I use cooked chicken breast in this recipe, but dark meat will work just fine.

1 (1-lb.) whole roasted chicken breast
½ teaspoon cornstarch
8 ounces fresh spinach, stems removed
4 cups chicken broth
3 thin slices fresh ginger
1 teaspoon salt

Remove bones and skin from chicken; shred meat. Toss meat with cornstarch. Tear spinach into bite-size pieces.

Bring chicken broth and ginger to a boil in a 5-quart saucepan or Dutch oven over medium-high heat. Stir in chicken; bring to a boil.

Stir in spinach and salt; bring to a boil. Reduce heat and simmer 2 minutes.

MENU: Bagel crisps. Apples with caramel dipping sauce.

SERVINGS: Makes 6 servings.

Cream of Tomato Soup

■ In my childhood, cream of tomato soup out of the can was the food I selected most often when I was starting to feel better after a bout of the flu or a cold. Don't wait to get sick to enjoy this fresh version.

2 tablespoons extra-virgin olive oil
¾ cup chopped onion
1 cup chicken broth
2 teaspoons hot Hungarian paprika
4 cups diced tomatoes
1 teaspoon sea salt
1 cup half-and-half

Heat oil in a 5-quart saucepan or Dutch oven over medium heat. Add onion and sauté until softened, about 3 minutes. Add chicken broth and paprika. Bring to a boil; add tomatoes and salt. Simmer until tomatoes are soft, about 8 minutes.

Place half of the tomatoes and liquid in a food processor or blender and process until smooth.

Return pureed tomatoes to soup. Stir in half-and-half. Heat until hot, but do not boil.

MENU: Black-pepper crackers. Green salad with lemon vinaigrette. Blueberries sprinkled with sugar.

SERVINGS: Makes 4 servings.

Chorizo Black Bean Soup

■ Chorizo is the spicy Spanish sausage that is now widely available. I use it here to deliver a flavor spike to black bean soup.

1 (15-oz.) can black beans, drained
1 (11-oz.) can condensed black bean soup
1⅓ cups water
1 cup diced cooked chorizo sausage
Salsa

Combine all ingredients, except salsa, in a 3-quart saucepan. Simmer over medium heat until hot, about 5 minutes.

Ladle into soup bowls. Top each serving with a spoonful of salsa.

MENU: Portuguese bread. Slices of white cheese. Butter cookies.

SERVINGS: Makes 4 servings.

Red Beans & Rice

■ This is just an opinion: Home-cooked dried beans are better than canned dried beans. This is reality: Canned beans may not be as good as home-cooked beans, but they are a whole lot quicker, which in my book, makes them good enough.

So when a recipe calls for dried beans, I get out the can opener. Here are a few things I've learned about how to switch one for the other.

· Use twice the amount of canned beans, since dried beans double in volume when cooked.
· If the recipe calls for water, make sure it's not for soaking. Dried beans have to be soaked; canned ones don't.
· Even if water is a legitimate ingredient, you'll probably need much less of it if substituting canned beans.
· Reduce cooking time. As a general rule of thumb, you'll need a half to one hour less if the beans are used in a stew or a soup. I cook the meats and vegetables until tender, then add the canned beans for the last 10 minutes.

This recipe for red beans and rice—a southern Louisiana dish—is a breeze to make.

Instant rice
2 tablespoons canola oil
1 cup chopped onions
⅔ cup chopped green bell pepper
2 large cloves garlic, minced
1 (15-oz.) can kidney beans, drained
½ pound smoked kielbasa or andouille
    sausage, cut into thin rounds
1 bay leaf

Prepare enough rice according to package directions to yield 4 cups after cooking.

Meanwhile, heat oil in a 10-inch skillet. Add onions, bell pepper, and garlic and sauté until onions are tender, about 3 minutes. Stir in beans, sausage, and bay leaf; simmer 10 minutes. Remove bay leaf.

Serve bean mixture over rice.

MENU: Lettuce and sliced tomatoes drizzled with oil-and-vinegar dressing. Bakery bran muffins. Cantaloupe slices.

SERVINGS: Makes 4 servings.

Island Black Bean Stew

■ Black beans are a kitchen staple in the Caribbean. The most famous dish is Cuban black bean soup. But this black bean stew may have it beat.

1 tablespoon corn oil
1 large yellow bell pepper, chopped
1 clove garlic, minced
1 large onion, chopped
1 (15-oz.) can black beans, undrained
¼ teaspoon dried sage
Salt and freshly ground black pepper
½ teaspoon dried thyme
3 tablespoons cider vinegar

Heat oil in a 5-quart saucepan or Dutch oven over medium-high heat. Add bell pepper, garlic, and onion and sauté until vegetables begin to soften, about 3 minutes.

Add beans, sage, salt, black pepper, and thyme. Reduce heat, cover, and simmer for 7 minutes, adding a little water if necessary to keep beans from scorching. Stir in vinegar. Cook 1 minute.

MENU: Whole-wheat crackers. Mango sorbet.

SERVINGS: Makes 6 servings.

Bean Tortilla Soup

■ I've never found two people to agree on a recipe for tortilla soup. You'd think that such a simple, easy soup would not be a source of controversy, but a friend who was raised in Mexico swore she'd never speak to me again because I added beans to the recipe. Then she tried it.

2 tablespoons corn oil
2 cloves garlic, crushed
4 corn tortillas, cut into 1 × ¼-inch strips
1 medium onion, thinly sliced
1 jalapeño chile, seeded and diced
4 cups chicken broth
1 (15-oz.) can red kidney beans, drained
Chili powder
4 lime wedges

Heat 1 tablespoon of the oil in a 5-quart saucepan or Dutch oven over medium-high heat. Add garlic and fry until garlic begins to brown, about 1 minute. Remove garlic with a slotted spoon and discard. Add tortilla strips and cook, turning often, until light brown, about 2 minutes. Remove from pan and drain on paper towels.

Add remaining 1 tablespoon of oil to the pan. Add onion and chile and sauté, stirring often, until onion begins to brown, about 2 minutes. Add chicken broth and beans and bring to a boil, about 4 minutes.

Divide tortilla strips among 4 soup bowls. Ladle soup over tortilla strips. Sprinkle with chili powder. Serve with lime wedges.

MENU: Lettuce-and-tomato salad with ranch dressing. Chocolate ice cream with fudge topping.

SERVINGS: Makes 4 servings.

Tomato, Avocado, & Crab Soup

■ This is a soup to make when you are lucky enough to find avocados ready to eat, or have one that needs to be used. Jicama (see page 247) stays crunchy even after cooking.

1 tablespoon olive oil
¼ cup julienned jicama
1 (11-oz.) can condensed tomato bisque
   soup plus 1 soup can water
1 medium avocado, diced
2 teaspoons fresh lemon juice
½ cup cooked crabmeat or imitation
   crabmeat

Heat oil in a 2-quart saucepan over medium heat. Add jicama and sauté about 1 minute.

Add remaining ingredients. Bring to a boil. Reduce heat and simmer about 4 minutes.

MENU: Whole-wheat crackers. Cream-cheese scallion spread. Citrus sections.

SERVINGS: Makes 4 servings.

Mexican Soup

■ There is a class of recipes I call "the dumps" because they usually mean little more work than dumping ingredients in a pan and heating. Bless 'em.

2 tablespoons canola oil
2 medium onions, chopped
2 green bell peppers, chopped
1 (8-oz.) jar taco sauce
1 (4-oz.) can green chiles
2 (10-¾-oz.) cans condensed chicken broth
2 (11-oz.) cans whole-kernel corn, drained
Cayenne pepper
6 tablespoons shredded Monterey Jack
   cheese

Heat oil in a 5-quart saucepan or Dutch oven over medium-high heat. Add onions and bell peppers and sauté, stirring occasionally, until soft, about 4 minutes.

Add taco sauce, chiles, chicken broth, and corn. Stir to mix. Simmer, uncovered, for 10 minutes.

Ladle into soup bowls. Give each bowl a dash of cayenne and 1 tablespoon of cheese.

MENU: Corn chips with bean dip. Banana and strawberry slices tossed with banana non-fat yogurt.

SERVINGS: Makes 6 servings.

Cucumber-Dill Soup

■ This is a cold soup for a lazy summer day. Garnish it with fresh dill sprigs.

3 medium cucumbers
1 tablespoon chopped fresh dill
1 clove garlic, minced
1 teaspoon extra-virgin olive oil
3 cups plain nonfat yogurt
Salt and freshly ground black pepper

Peel, seed, and cut up cucumbers. Process in a food processor or blender until coarsely chopped, about 10 seconds. Add dill, garlic, and oil. Process 10 seconds.

Transfer cucumber mixture to a large bowl. Stir in yogurt. Season to taste with salt and pepper.

MENU: Whole-wheat crackers. Deli green bean salad. Fruit cup.

SERVINGS: Makes 4 servings.

Alphabet Noodle Soup

■ This is a soup that delighted my children when they were young. They were so happy with the letters that they never noticed they were eating vegetables!

½ pound ground beef
3 cups beef broth
3 cups vegetable juice, such as V8
¾ cup water
¼ teaspoon dried thyme
1 teaspoon Worcestershire sauce
1½ cups mixed frozen vegetables
⅔ cup alphabet macaroni

Cook beef in a 5-quart saucepan or Dutch oven over medium-high heat until browned, about 3 minutes, stirring to break up beef. Drain off fat.

Add broth, vegetable juice, water, thyme, and Worcestershire sauce. Bring to a boil. Add vegetables and macaroni. Reduce heat and simmer, covered, for 8 to 10 minutes or until pasta is tender.

MENU: Bakery corn muffins with apple butter. Radishes with kosher salt for dipping. Coffee ice cream drizzled with honey.

SERVINGS: Makes 6 servings.

Pantry Bean Soup

■ This soup is made from kitchen staples. Corned beef from the deli is best, but even canned corned beef will make a good soup.

1 tablespoon canola oil
1 onion, chopped
½ stalk celery, chopped
5 cups beef broth
1 (15-oz.) can red kidney beans, drained
1 cup chopped cooked or canned corned beef
1 cup fresh, frozen, or canned whole-kernel corn

Heat oil in 5-quart saucepan or Dutch oven over medium heat. Add onion and celery and cook, stirring occasionally, 2 minutes.

Add broth and remaining ingredients. Bring to a boil, then reduce heat and simmer, covered, for about 10 minutes.

MENU: Bagel chips. Ice-cream sandwiches.

SERVINGS: Makes 6 servings.

Cucumber Soup with Tomatoes

■ This is a seasonal soup to make when tomatoes are bright red, juicy, and noticeably fragrant. Once you buy them, plan to use them within a few days. Don't put them into the refrigerator—cold temperatures destroy their flavor.

4 medium cucumbers
2 cups tomato juice or Clamato juice
1 cup chopped tomatoes
¼ cup fresh lemon juice
¼ teaspoon freshly ground black pepper

Peel the cucumbers and quarter lengthwise. Remove the seeds with the tip of a spoon. Puree 2 of the cucumbers with tomato or Clamato juice in a blender or food processor.

Pour the cucumber puree into a 3-quart saucepan. Cook over medium heat until hot. Thinly slice the remaining 2 cucumbers. Add to the pan along with the chopped tomatoes, lemon juice, and pepper. Cook, stirring gently, until combined and thoroughly heated.

MENU: Pita bread stuffed with bean sprouts, tofu cubes, and thin slices of red onion, topped with ranch dressing. Peach slices with candied ginger.

SERVINGS: Makes 4 to 6 servings.

Onion & Cheese Soup

■ An easy way to peel a large onion is to cut a small slice off the top and root ends. Then hold the onion under warm running water and pull the skin off.

2 tablespoons butter
1 cup chopped onion
2 tablespoons instant flour (see Note, page 33)
6 cups half-and-half
Salt and freshly ground black pepper
2 cups (8 ounces) grated sharp Cheddar cheese

Melt butter in a 10-inch frying pan over medium heat. Add onion and cook until softened, about 2 minutes. Stir in flour and cook, stirring constantly, until blended. Gradually stir in half-and-half and cook, stirring constantly, until thickened.

Adjust heat so mixture is just below boiling. Season with salt and pepper. Stir in cheese and cook, stirring, until cheese melts.

MENU: Rye crackers. Watercress and endive salad. Orange slices.

SERVINGS: Makes 2 quarts.

Egg Drop Soup

■ To save time, I use canned chicken broth as a soup base. It's important to read soup can labels when shopping. Some soups are ready-to-serve, which means they're already diluted; others are condensed, which means you'll need to add water or milk.

5 cups chicken broth
2 eggs
1 teaspoon chopped fresh cilantro
Freshly ground black pepper
Few drops of white Worcestershire sauce

Pour broth into a 3-quart saucepan and bring to a boil over high heat.

Meanwhile, beat eggs until frothy in a small bowl. Add cilantro, pepper, and Worcestershire sauce. Beat to combine.

Reduce heat to medium. Drizzle egg mixture into liquid, stirring quickly; cook about 30 seconds. Remove from heat.

MENU: Rice cakes with chive cream cheese and bean spouts. Toasted pound cake topped with chocolate ice cream.

SERVINGS: Makes 5 servings.

Scallop Soup

■ Clam juice makes a great base for a fish soup, although it tends to be too salty if not diluted.

3 cups bottled clam juice
1 cup water
6 scallions, thinly sliced

1 red bell pepper, diced
½ pound bay scallops, rinsed and halved
2 tablespoons chopped fresh flat-leaf
    parsley

Heat clam juice and water in a 2-quart saucepan over medium heat, about 4 minutes. Add scallions and bell pepper and simmer 5 minutes or until tender.

Add scallops and cook 3 minutes or until scallops are opaque. Garnish with parsley.

MENU: Garlic bagel chips. Bagged Italian salad with creamy Italian dressing. Pink grapefruit slices drizzled with honey.

SERVINGS: Makes 4 servings.

Tomato-Cabbage Soup

■ Bagged coleslaw mix has become an important staple in my kitchen. I use it for coleslaw, of course, but it's also good in stews and soups.

⅗ (1-lb.) package (about 4 cups) coleslaw
    mix or shredded cabbage
¼ cup chopped onion
1½ cups water
¼ teaspoon hot Hungarian paprika
2 (14.5-oz.) cans stewed tomatoes

Combine coleslaw mix, onion, water, and paprika in a 3-quart saucepan. Bring to a boil. Reduce heat and simmer, covered, for 5 minutes or until cabbage is crisp-tender.

Stir in tomatoes. Using a wooden spoon, break up tomatoes in the pan until there are no large chunks. Cover, return soup to a simmer, and cook for 6 to 8 minutes more.

MENU: Rye bread. Bakery apple turnovers.

SERVINGS: Makes 6 servings.

Sauerkraut Soup

■ The most important difference between canned sauerkraut and fresh sauerkraut sold in plastic packages in refrigerated dairy cases is that fresh is crunchier.

1 (16-oz.) package fresh sauerkraut
1 tablespoon vegetable oil
1 small onion, chopped
2 teaspoons paprika
4 cups water
1 (15-oz.) can kidney beans, drained

Drain sauerkraut in a colander.

Heat oil in a 5-quart saucepan or Dutch oven over medium heat. Add onion and cook, stirring, 2 minutes or until wilted.

Stir in paprika. Add sauerkraut and water. Reduce heat and simmer, uncovered, for about 8 minutes, stirring occasionally.

Add beans and simmer 5 minutes.

MENU: Pumpernickel bread, toasted. Deli potato salad. Apple and pear slices.

SERVINGS: Makes 4 servings.

Leek & Mushroom Soup

■ I keep canned chicken broth in the pantry. Not only is it a time saver; it's also a very tasty convenience product. I add a few fresh ingredients to give it a boost, however—chopped carrots, onion, or fresh herbs. In this case, fresh ginger and scallions make a big difference in taste.

4 cups chicken broth (see Note, below)
2 thin slices fresh ginger
2 scallions, cut into 2-inch pieces
1 tablespoon olive oil
2 small leeks, split and sliced into ⅛-inch slivers
¼ pound sliced fresh mushrooms

Combine broth, ginger, and scallions in a large Dutch oven. Bring to a boil; reduce heat, cover, and simmer.

Meanwhile, heat olive oil in a 10-inch sauté or frying pan over medium heat. Add leeks and stir-fry for about 2 minutes. Add mushrooms and sauté 2 minutes. Add leeks, mushrooms, and oil to soup. Simmer for 5 more minutes or until vegetables are tender.

MENU: Rye crackers. Beet-and-orange salad. Tapioca pudding.

SERVINGS: Makes 4 servings.

NOTE
Vegetable broth can be substituted for chicken broth.

Bean Soup

■ Keep your pantry stocked with canned beans—they're a real lifesaver. They can be added to salads, stews, and soups. They not only taste great; they also give a big nutrition boost. Canned beans tend to be a bit salty. It helps to drain them and rinse them with cold water before adding to the pot.

2 tablespoons olive oil
1 large onion, finely chopped
1 large clove garlic, minced
4 cups vegetable broth
1 (15-oz.) can red beans, drained
¼ cup dry sherry (optional)
Sliced scallions

Heat oil in a 5-quart saucepan or Dutch oven over medium-high heat. Add onion and garlic and cook, stirring occasionally, until softened, about 2 minutes.

Add broth and beans. Simmer 5 minutes. Process 2 cups of bean-and-broth mixture in a food processor or blender until smooth. Return pureed beans to saucepan. Add sherry, if using, and heat until hot.

Ladle into bowls. Garnish with scallions.

MENU: Water crackers. Deli marinated mushrooms on endive. Tapioca pudding with mandarin orange slices.

SERVINGS: Makes 4 to 6 servings.

Fish Stew

■ Do you use your microwave only to reheat leftovers? You're wasting a really wonderful tool for creating delicious dinners. A microwave oven doesn't do the best job for cooking meat and chicken, but vegetables and fish are superb microwaved.

¾ cup sliced celery
1¼ cups bottled clam juice
1 (14-oz.) jar marinara sauce
¾ pound catfish chunks, rinsed
½ pound scallops, rinsed
½ pound medium shrimp, peeled and deveined

Combine celery and ¼ cup of the clam juice in a 3-quart, microwave-safe casserole dish. Cover with lid; microwave on HIGH 2 minutes, stirring once.

Stir in sauce and remaining clam juice. Cover; microwave on HIGH 5 minutes, stirring once.

Add catfish, scallops, and shrimp. Cover; microwave on HIGH 7 minutes or until catfish is opaque.

MENU: Saltines. Apple slices with prepared caramel dip.

SERVINGS: Makes 4 servings.

Corn Chowder

■ This is a really creamy soup that doesn't have cream. The creaminess comes from the cream-style corn.

1 tablespoon butter
1 tablespoon instant flour (see Note, page 33)
½ teaspoon grated onion
Dash of white pepper
1 cup milk
1 (8½-oz.) can cream-style corn
1 (8-oz.) can whole-kernel corn, drained
2 tablespoons crumbled cooked bacon or Real Bacon Bits

Melt butter in a 2-quart medium saucepan over medium heat. Stir in flour, onion, and pepper. Cook, stirring constantly, until well blended. Add milk all at once. Cook, stirring constantly, until thickened, 1 to 2 minutes.

Stir in creamed corn and whole-kernel corn. Heat until hot, stirring.

Ladle into bowls. Garnish each bowl with bacon bits.

MENU: Norwegian flat bread. Carrot sticks, celery sticks, and cucumber spears. Apple slices dusted with brown sugar.

SERVINGS: Makes 2 servings.

Kielbasa Soup

■ Kielbasa, sometimes called Polish sausage, is a smoked sausage, sometimes made of pork, though beef can be added. It comes in chunky links (about 2 inches thick) and is usually sold precooked, though small butcher shops may also sell it fresh.

2 teaspoons canola oil
2 large onions, chopped
4 to 6 cloves garlic, minced
1 pound kielbasa, sliced into ½-inch rounds and the rounds sliced into quarters
6 cups beef broth
¼ cup dry red wine
Freshly ground black pepper

Heat oil in a 5-quart saucepan or Dutch oven over medium heat. Add onions and cook until golden, about 5 minutes. Add the garlic and cook until onions turn a light brown, about 2 minutes. Add the kielbasa slices and cook, turning often, for about 5 minutes.

Add broth and wine and bring to a boil. Reduce heat and simmer, uncovered, for 2 minutes.

Ladle into bowls. Sprinkle with pepper.

MENU: Deli coleslaw. Muenster cheese with multigrain crackers. Toasted pound cake with vanilla ice cream.

SERVINGS: Makes 4 servings.

Oyster Pan Roast

■ I love this New England dish for dinner on a lazy late Sunday afternoon—preferably when there's snow on the ground and the sun is just setting. This dish is comforting, probably because it is loaded with cream and butter. So you don't want to eat it every day, but as an occasional treat, it can't be beat.

6 tablespoons butter
1 shallot, minced
½ stalk celery, minced
¾ cup heavy cream
24 shucked oysters, drained, liquor reserved
2 tablespoons white wine
¼ teaspoon hot pepper sauce
2 teaspoons fresh thyme or ¾ teaspoon dried
4 thick slices sourdough bread, toasted

Melt butter in a 12-inch frying pan over medium-low heat. Add shallot and celery and cook for about 1 minute or until softened.

Stir in cream, oyster liquor, wine, hot pepper sauce, thyme, and oysters. Bring to a simmer and cook until edges of oysters just curl, about 2 minutes. Remove from heat.

Place sourdough bread in soup bowls; ladle oysters and liquid over the bread.

MENU: Chopped romaine lettuce with French dressing. Pear slices tossed with a sprinkle of lemon juice, sugar, and chopped dried cranberries.

SERVINGS: Makes 4 servings.

Escarole & Pasta Soup

■ Endive was making me crazy. When the supermarket scanner registered "chicory" and I thought I had purchased escarole, I knew it was time to track down the truth about these bitter greens. Here's what I learned—escarole is one of three types of endive, which is often confused with its cousin, chicory. They belong to the same botanical family.

I don't have a problem picking out Belgian endive, the compact little aristocrat of the family. But curly endive, found in loose heads of lacy, green-rimmed outer leaves that curl at the tips, and escarole, which has broad, slightly curved, pale green leaves with a milder flavor than either Belgian or curly endive, are ringers for chicory.

½ cup small pasta shells
2 (14½-oz.) cans chicken broth with enough
   water to equal 4 cups
1 cup sliced mushrooms
½ pound escarole, torn into 2-inch pieces
Lemon-pepper seasoning

Cook shells according to package directions; drain in a colander. Rinse with cold water; set aside.

Meanwhile, bring chicken broth to a boil in a 5-quart saucepan or Dutch oven over medium-high heat. Add mushrooms. Reduce heat to medium and simmer 5 minutes.

Gradually add escarole to simmering broth, stirring. Cook 5 minutes. Stir in cooked pasta. Sprinkle with lemon-pepper seasoning and heat until hot.

MENU: Honey-baked ham and brie on pumpernickel-raisin bread. Lemon yogurt swirled with chopped nuts.

SERVINGS: Makes 4 to 6 servings.

Salmon Chowder

■ The word *chowder* originally referred to a thick, rich fisherman's soup containing seafood, but now it refers to any thick, rich soup with chunks of ingredients. With that much liberty, the possibilities are limitless, hence Salmon Chowder—salmon for the traditional, the cucumber, scallions, dill, and sour cream to comply with the thick-and-rich requirement. For the nutrition-conscious, I've prepared this recipe using fat-free sour cream.

1 tablespoon butter
½ cup chopped cucumber
2 tablespoons chopped scallion
¼ teaspoon chopped fresh dill
1 (10¾-oz.) can condensed cream of celery
   soup
⅓ cup fat-free sour cream
1 cup water
1 (6-oz.) can boneless salmon, drained and
   flaked

Melt butter in a 5-quart saucepan or Dutch oven over medium heat. Add cucumber, scallion, and dill. Cook until tender, about 2 minutes.

Stir in soup and sour cream; gradually stir in water and salmon. Cook over medium heat, stirring occasionally, until hot—without boiling, or the sour cream will curdle—about 5 minutes.

MENU: Crusty whole-wheat bread. Fresh fruit cup with lemon sherbet.

SERVINGS: Makes 4 servings.

Senegalese Soup

■ Curry powder is widely used in Indian cooking, but the kind available on spice shelves in American supermarkets is a pale shadow of the curry powder used in authentic Indian kitchens. There, curry powder is made fresh each day and varies dramatically depending on the region and the cook.

Curry powder is a pulverized blend of up to 20 spices, herbs, and seeds. Among those most commonly used are cardamom, chiles, cinnamon, cloves, coriander, cumin, fennel seed, fenugreek, mace, nutmeg, red and black peppers, poppy and sesame seeds, saffron, tamarind, and turmeric.

I devised my Senegalese soup using the supermarket kind of curry powder. It has much to commend it and the ability to deliver a powerful flavor punch in an instant.

2 tablespoons butter
1½ tablespoons all-purpose flour
2 teaspoons curry powder
3 cups chicken broth
2 egg yolks
½ cup half-and-half
1 roasted chicken breast, meat removed from the bone and shredded into small pieces
⅓ cup plain yogurt

Melt butter in a 5-quart saucepan or Dutch oven over medium heat. Stir in flour and curry powder. Stir in chicken broth and bring to a boil over medium-high heat. Remove from heat.

Beat together egg yolks with half-and-half in a medium bowl. Pour egg mixture in a thin stream into the broth mixture, stirring constantly.

Add chicken to the soup. Return soup to medium heat and cook without boiling, stirring occasionally, for about 5 minutes.

Remove from heat. Stir in yogurt.

MENU: Cucumber sticks and apple wedges. Pita chips. Mango slices.

SERVINGS: Makes 4 servings.

Cabbage Kielbasa Soup

■ Kielbasa is a lot more versatile than many people think. It can be grilled, broiled, and used in casseroles. For a fast supper, I often make this soup that cooks in a New York minute but gives the flavor of a slow-cooked peasant soup.

1 tablespoon canola oil
½ pound kielbasa, cut into ½-inch pieces
1 small head cabbage, coarsely chopped
1 medium onion, sliced
4 carrots, thinly sliced
2½ quarts (10 cups) chicken broth

Heat oil in a 5-quart saucepan or Dutch oven over medium-high heat. Add kielbasa and cook until browned, about 2 minutes. Remove kielbasa with a slotted spoon. Keep warm. Drain all but 2 tablespoons of drippings from the pan.

Add cabbage, onion, and carrots to drippings; cook over medium heat until lightly browned, about 7 minutes. Add chicken broth. Cover; simmer 5 minutes or until vegetables are tender.

Add sausage; cook until hot, about 1 minute.

MENU: Pumpernickel bread. Spinach-mushroom salad with poppy-seed dressing. Bakery apple turnovers.

SERVINGS: Makes 6 servings.

Baby Food Soup

■ Some years ago, when my children were way past the Pablum stage, I came across a baby food company's cookbook that used baby food as an ingredient in dishes for grown-ups. Long out of the habit of buying those little glass jars of pureed fruits, vegetables, and meats, I didn't see much use for the book. I wish I'd held onto it. I didn't realize that grandparents—I'm one now—kept baby food in their kitchens. But because baby food didn't get eaten as quickly as it did when there were infants in the house full-time, I found ways to use it within a month or two of purchase.

My granddaughter is past the Pablum stage now, but I became quite partial to the soup I made from her favorite baby food vegetable—carrots.

Lest anyone think this a bit strange, let me defend my use of baby food. It is nutritious, usually contains no added salt, has no artificial coloring, and it has a pleasant natural flavor and pretty color.

1 quart (4 cups) chicken broth
4 (4-oz.) jars baby food carrots or any
   pureed baby food vegetable
⅔ cup half-and-half
1 tablespoon minced fresh flat-leaf parsley

Heat chicken broth in a 2-quart saucepan over medium heat for about 2 minutes. Stir in baby food carrots, blending until smooth. Bring to a boil.

Reduce heat and stir in half-and-half. Cook until hot but do not boil, about 1 minute.

Ladle into soup bowls. Sprinkle with minced parsley.

MENU: Toasted sourdough bread. Garden salad with sliced radishes and cucumbers. Chocolate-covered doughnuts.

SERVINGS: Makes 6 servings.

Crab Soup

■ Instead of recounting disasters, I'll simply provide the correct information about making this soup.

· Lesson 1. To help prevent curdling, always add acidic ingredients (such as tomatoes or lemon juice) to a milk base, rather than vice versa. A little whipping cream also will help.
· Lesson 2. If you overheat a soup containing milk products and it curdles, simply strain it into a blender jar and process until smooth. Don't fill the blender more than two-thirds full with a hot liquid, be sure to put the lid on the container, and always begin blending at low speed.
· Lesson 3. When keeping a cream- or milk-based soup warm—or if reheating it—do so in a double boiler. It'll prevent scorching.
· Lesson 4. If reheating in a microwave oven, cover the soup loosely with waxed paper or plastic wrap. Thick soups tend to explode when heated quickly.

There now, you're on your own.

2 cups milk
¼ teaspoon ground mace
2 pieces lemon peel
1½ cups (about 12 ounces) crabmeat, drained and cartilage removed
¼ cup butter
2 cups half-and-half
2 teaspoons sherry

Combine milk, mace, and lemon peel in a 2-quart saucepan over medium heat. Bring to a simmer and cook for 2 to 3 minutes.

Stir in crabmeat, butter, and half-and-half. Cook until hot but do not boil, about 5 minutes.

Remove soup from heat. Stir in sherry.

MENU: Iceberg lettuce with Russian dressing. Strawberries and pineapple.

SERVINGS: Makes 5 or 6 servings.

Cold Yogurt Soup

■ To me, low-fat and nonfat yogurt simply don't have what food scientists call a good "mouth feel." I cannot make the leap to low fat or nonfat even though I could be saving as much as 11 grams of fat and 90 calories per cup. If you prefer to substitute the low-fat or nonfat yogurt in the recipe for cold yogurt soup, be my guest.

1 cup finely chopped cooked chicken
1 teaspoon fresh lemon juice
¾ teaspoon minced fresh dill
⅛ teaspoon garlic salt
2 to 3 cups plain yogurt
1 small cucumber, peeled, seeded, and diced
⅓ cup chopped celery
3 tablespoons thinly sliced scallion

Place chicken, lemon juice, dill, and garlic salt in a small bowl.

Place yogurt in a medium bowl. Stir with a fork or whisk until smooth and creamy. Stir chicken mixture, cucumber, celery, and scallion into yogurt. Pour soup into bowls.

MENU: Sesame-seed flat bread. Carrot sticks. Mixed berries tossed with coconut.

SERVINGS: Makes 4 servings.

Red Pepper Soup

■ This recipe for Red Pepper Soup calls for roasted peppers, but I'm not going to explain how to roast the peppers. It's very easy once mastered, but it takes time. Roasted red bell peppers come in several size jars (they even come already chopped) and recently, my supermarket deli started selling them fresh roasted, which is another quick, easy, if more expensive, option.

2 tablespoons olive oil
1 small red onion, chopped
1 (2-oz.) jar roasted and chopped red bell peppers, drained
1 (28-oz.) can crushed tomatoes in puree
¼ cup red wine
6 to 8 shredded fresh basil leaves
1 cup vegetable juice, such as V8

Heat oil in a 5-quart saucepan or Dutch oven over medium-high heat. Add onion and cook, stirring occasionally, until softened, about 2 minutes.

Add bell peppers and tomatoes. Blend in wine and basil. Bring to a boil. Reduce heat, cover, and simmer for 10 minutes. Stir in vegetable juice; simmer for 2 minutes.

MENU: Deli chicken salad. Toasted sourdough bread. Lemon ice.

SERVINGS: Makes 5 servings.

Tomato Bisque

■ One of the best tools for speedy cooking is a food processor. It can make speedy work of any cutting job. It works well here, in chopping up the tomatoes for a soup that is best made at the height of the summer growing season.

4 vine-ripened tomatoes
1 cup buttermilk
1 (12-oz.) can vegetable juice, such as V8
1 tablespoon fresh basil, chopped, plus additional for garnish (optional)
Salt and freshly ground black pepper

Peel and chop tomatoes very fine either by hand or in a food processor.

Place all ingredients into a large bowl. Stir until well blended. Garnish with more basil, if desired.

MENU: Pita bread pockets filled with roast beef, sharp Cheddar cheese, and lettuce. Watermelon.

SERVINGS: Makes 4 servings.

Halibut Stew

■ I cook a lot of fish in my home because I love it and because fresh fish is easy to buy and quick to cook. This recipe for halibut stew is a speedy dish that takes a helping hand from some high-quality convenience products.

3 slices bacon
1 tablespoon canola oil
1 cup chopped onion
2 (10¾-oz.) cans condensed cream of potato soup
2 cups milk
1 (14.5-oz.) can stewed tomatoes
1 (10-oz.) package frozen mixed vegetables
1 (8-oz.) can whole-kernel corn, drained
1 pound halibut steak, rinsed and cut into chunks

Microwave bacon on HIGH for 3 minutes. Drain bacon on absorbent paper towels; crumble.

Meanwhile, heat oil in a 5-quart saucepan or Dutch oven over medium-high heat. Add onion and cook until softened, about 3 minutes.

Add soup, milk, tomatoes, mixed vegetables, and corn. Heat, stirring occasionally, until the stew comes to a simmer, about 3 minutes. Add fish, and simmer until fish flakes, 5 to 6 minutes.

Ladle into bowls. Sprinkle with bacon.

MENU: Focaccia. Fruit-topped angel food cake.

SERVINGS: Makes 6 servings.

Spinach & Leek Soup

■ Savoring a good friend's homemade soup, I lamented how hard it was to find time to make a lovely slow-cooked meal.

"It's hard for me, too!" my friend snapped. Seems we working women don't want anyone inferring that we dawdle in the kitchen.

"But this is great soup," I protested.

"Mixes," she said, laughing.

"Get out!" I said.

1½ cups water
2 (4-oz.) jars baby food spinach
1 (2.4-oz.) package leek soup mix
2 cups half-and-half
2 tablespoons finely chopped fresh dill or 1 teaspoon dried

Combine water, baby food spinach, and soup mix in a saucepan and stir well. Bring to a boil over medium-high heat. Reduce heat and cook 2 minutes. Add half-and-half and dill; cook until hot, but do not boil, about 2 minutes.

Serve garnished with additional dill, if desired.

MENU: Crusty country bread. Fig bars.

SERVINGS: Makes 4 servings.

Lobster Stew

■ One summer during a weekend sail along the Maine coast, a sudden storm forced us to seek safe harbor at a small island fishing village. The inhabitants took us under their protective wings, inviting us ashore for cribbage —a game taken seriously there—and dinner, which consisted of lobster stew eaten at a card table set up in a small living room in a seaside cottage. The best!

Lobster is more common there than chicken is in most places. Unfortunately, I can't afford lobster often, but when the price is right, I serve this wonderful stew.

2 tablespoons unsalted butter
2 cups cooked lobster meat
1 cup milk
1 cup heavy cream
Salt and freshly ground black pepper
2 tablespoons minced fresh chives

Melt butter in a 2-quart saucepan over low heat. Add lobster meat and cook for 2 minutes.

Add milk and cream and heat until hot but not boiling, about 5 minutes. Season with salt and pepper to taste. Add chives and serve.

MENU: Dinner rolls. Deli coleslaw. Chocolate pudding with nondairy whipped topping.

SERVINGS: Makes 2 servings.

Creole Peanut Butter Soup

■ People who live anywhere but in the South flinch at the mention of peanut butter soup. But those who live there, once lived there, or visited there seriously intent on sampling the local cooking are forever changed. Peanut butter soup is a mellow, delicious, and thoroughly satisfying dinner. This version takes some flavor notes—celery salt and tomato— from the cooking of southern Louisiana.

2 tablespoons peanut oil
1 medium onion, minced
1 tablespoon instant flour (see Note, page 33)
½ teaspoon celery salt
½ cup smooth peanut butter
2 cups milk
2 cups tomato juice
Chopped fresh parsley

Heat peanut oil in a 5-quart saucepan or Dutch oven over medium-high heat. Add onion and sauté until softened, about 2 minutes.

Stir in flour and celery salt until blended. Stir in peanut butter. Stir in milk. Cook, stirring constantly, until thickened, about 8 minutes. Add juice and bring just to a boil.

Spoon into bowls. Sprinkle with parsley.

MENU: Deli chicken salad in pita bread. Bakery peach turnovers.

SERVINGS: Makes 4 servings.

Corn & Summer Squash Soup

■ This soup comes right out of summer. If you have any time to spend at the height of the corn season, make this luscious soup with fresh corn cut off the cob. But if it's rush-hour cooking you must do, high-quality canned corn will yield good results.

1 tablespoon butter
1 onion, diced
2 cloves garlic, minced
3 small yellow summer squash, grated
1 (11-oz.) can whole-kernel corn, drained
2 medium plum tomatoes, seeded and diced
2 tablespoons shredded fresh basil
2½ cups chicken broth
1 cup half-and-half
Freshly ground black pepper

Melt butter in a 5-quart saucepan or Dutch oven over medium heat. Add onion and garlic and sauté until softened, 2 minutes.

Add grated squash and cook 2 minutes, stirring constantly. Stir in corn, tomatoes, basil, and chicken broth. Bring to a boil over medium heat. Reduce heat and simmer 5 minutes.

Stir in half-and-half. Season with pepper. Cook, stirring, until hot but do not boil, about 2 minutes.

MENU: Corn muffins with strawberry jam. Plums.

SERVINGS: Makes 6 servings.

Three-Bean Stew

■ Legume lovers will adore this easy-to-assemble dish that is loaded with healthful, tasty beans.

3 tablespoons canola oil
1 pound mushrooms, sliced
2 cloves garlic, minced
½ cup shredded carrots
¼ cup chopped fresh flat-leaf parsley
½ teaspoon coarsely ground black pepper
1 (15-oz.) can Great Northern beans, drained
1 (15-oz.) can pinto beans, drained
1 (15-oz.) can red kidney beans, drained
2 (14.5-oz.) can stewed tomatoes
½ cup red onion, minced

Heat oil in a 5-quart saucepan or Dutch oven over medium-high heat. Add mushrooms and sauté 2 minutes, stirring occasionally. Add garlic, carrots, parsley, and pepper and sauté 1 minute.

Add beans and stewed tomatoes with juice. Bring to a simmer; cook 10 minutes.

Ladle into soup bowls. Divide minced onions among the bowls.

MENU: Multigrain bread. Green salad with Russian dressing. Frozen chocolate yogurt.

SERVINGS: Makes 8 servings.

Curried Tomato Soup

■ This soup is a real rush-hour boon. It takes very little time to assemble and even less time to cook, yet the flavors are rich and full.

1 (14.5-oz.) crushed tomatoes in puree
1 teaspoon grated fresh ginger
1 tablespoon olive oil
2 tablespoons minced fresh flat-leaf parsley
1 tablespoon tarragon vinegar
¼ cup chopped chives
1 large clove garlic, minced
1 teaspoon curry powder

Combine all ingredients in a 3-quart saucepan. Bring to a simmer. Cover partially and simmer for 4 minutes or until hot.

MENU: Pita bread stuffed with tuna salad. Mango slices with crystallized ginger.

SERVINGS: Makes 2 to 3 servings.

Polish Pea Soup

■ This is a quick soup filled with Old World flavors.

1 tablespoon canola oil
1 large onion, chopped
1 pound kielbasa, cut into 1-inch rounds
2 (19-oz.) cans split-pea soup
1 (15-oz.) can whole potatoes, drained and diced

Heat oil in a 5-quart saucepan or Dutch oven over medium heat. Add onion and kielbasa and cook, stirring, until onion is softened, about 3 minutes.

Add soup and potatoes. Reduce heat, cover, and simmer for 10 minutes.

MENU: Pumpernickel bread. Cucumber slices in sour cream sprinkled with dill. Peach ice cream.

SERVINGS: Makes 6 servings.

Vegetable Beef Soup

■ Soups are wonderful, nourishing meals. Would that I had time to simmer a soup all day on the back burner of the stove, but I've found some shortcuts that result in delicious meals.

2 tablespoons canola oil
1 large onion, coarsely chopped
1 large clove garlic, minced
2 (14½-oz.) cans beef broth
1 (14.5-oz.) can crushed tomatoes in puree
1 small zucchini, sliced into thin rounds,
   then quartered
1 cup shredded carrots
Sea salt to taste
1 teaspoon dried thyme
Freshly ground black pepper
Seasoned croutons

Heat oil in a 5-quart saucepan or Dutch oven over medium heat. Add onion and garlic and sauté until onion is softened, about 2 minutes.

Add broth, tomatoes, zucchini, carrots, salt, thyme, and pepper. Reduce heat, cover, and simmer 10 minutes.

Ladle into soup bowls. Top with croutons.

MENU: Focaccia bread. Melon slices.

SERVINGS: Makes 4 to 6 servings.

Bean Vegetable Soup

■ Beans are an excellent source of fiber. They are also inexpensive. This hearty soup is one way to get more beans into your diet.

2 teaspoons olive oil
1 small onion, chopped
2 cloves garlic, minced
1 (15-oz.) can red kidney beans, drained
6 cups chicken broth
1 teaspoon dried marjoram
½ teaspoon sea salt
¼ teaspoon dried sage
¼ cup shredded carrots
1 stalk celery, thinly sliced
¼ cup chopped fresh flat-leaf parsley
1 medium tomato, chopped

Heat oil in a 5-quart saucepan or Dutch oven over medium heat. Add onion and garlic and sauté until onion is softened, about 2 minutes.

Add beans, chicken broth, marjoram, salt, sage, carrots, and celery. Increase heat to medium-high. Simmer, uncovered, for 8 minutes.

Remove a cup of soup and puree in a food processor or blender. Stir pureed mixture back into remaining soup. Stir in parsley and tomato. Heat until hot, stirring occasionally.

MENU: Soft pretzels with mustard dip. Pineapple nonfat yogurt.

SERVINGS: Makes 6 servings.

Main-Dish Salads

Main-dish salads became a relative newcomer to my cooking repertoire after I enjoyed such meals in restaurants. They seem the best of all possible worlds: the harmonious combination of leafy vegetables, meat, and a delectable salad dressing. All else that's needed is a crusty, chewy slice of bread.

And the beauty of it is that composing such a dish requires little time, although a healthy dose of inspiration and imagination can help. Little touches like Neufchâtel cheese cut into cubes and dipped into toasted sesame seeds add visual appeal and tangy taste. Sugar-coated walnuts tossed over the top instead of croutons provide lovely crunch and a bit of sweetness.

Although main-dish salads can be served year-round, the height of summer is truly their season. This is when there is a profusion of glorious, locally grown produce—vegetables, herbs, fruit—in their perfection.

Salads are also a wonderful way to take advantage of the wide range and nutritious benefits associated with greens like arugula, romaine, spinach, and radicchio. I especially love Bibb lettuce because it has such a buttery, silky feel on the tongue.

Dressings also offer boundless variety. Although I'm partial to vinaigrettes, there are creamier dressings to suit other tastes.

Think of it: wonderful meals and very little cooking!

Broccoli Salad

■ Just about every ingredient in this salad can be purchased already cut up and ready to be combined. But if you are starting with broccoli with stalks, keep the stalks, blanch them for 1 minute, and freeze. They can be used in soups and stews on another day.

2 cups broccoli florets
2 tablespoons water
2 cups sliced mushrooms
2 cups coarsely chopped red cabbage
½ cup ranch dressing
2 ounces Colby cheese, cubed
2 ounces Muenster cheese, cubed
1 cup cherry tomatoes, halved

Combine broccoli and 2 tablespoons water in a 1-quart microwave-safe casserole. Cover and microwave on HIGH power for 1 minute. Rinse under cold water and drain.

Combine broccoli, mushrooms, cabbage, and dressing in a large salad bowl. Toss gently to coat. Add cheese cubes and tomato halves and toss to combine.

MENU: Garlic bagel chips. Plum slices topped with lemon yogurt and dusted with cinnamon.

SERVINGS: Makes 5 servings.

Artichoke Pasta Salad

■ There's a seemingly long list of ingredients for this dish, but very little to do but combine them and enjoy them.

1 (9-oz.) package refrigerated fresh
   fettuccine, cut in half
1 (6-oz.) jar marinated artichoke hearts
¾ cup sliced ripe olives
1 cup broccoli florets
2 large tomatoes, diced
4 ounces sharp Cheddar cheese, diced
½ pound smoked salmon, thinly sliced
1¼ cups vinaigrette

Cook pasta according to package directions. Drain and rinse with cold water.

Meanwhile, combine artichoke hearts, olives, broccoli, and tomatoes in a large serving bowl. Combine with pasta. Toss with cheese, smoked salmon, and vinaigrette.

MENU: Sesame bread sticks with thin slices of prosciutto. Fresh blueberries with nonfat sour cream.

SERVINGS: Makes 5 servings.

Italian Bean Salad

■ Unfortunately most provolone cheese is factory made in America with few of the fine characteristics of the real stuff. Real provolone is aromatic, with a yellowish rind and a firm, light yellow interior that darkens with age. If you live near a good Italian market, stop in to get what you need to make this salad.

½ cup pepperoni slices, quartered
1 small red onion, very thinly sliced
1 (15-oz.) can red kidney beans, drained
1 (15-oz.) can white kidney beans
    (cannellini), drained
2 ounces provolone cheese, sliced into
    matchstick-size strips
1 tomato, cut into wedges
¼ cup pitted ripe olives, sliced
½ cup Italian salad dressing

Toss together all ingredients, except dressing, in a large salad bowl. Pour dressing over all and toss to combine.

MENU: Crusty Italian bread. Bakery cookies.

SERVINGS: Makes 4 servings.

Pasta with Salad Sauce

■ Is this a hot pasta salad or pasta with a non-cook sauce? You decide.

1 (9-oz.) package refrigerated fresh linguine
1 small clove garlic, mashed
½ teaspoon salt
¼ cup red-wine vinegar vinaigrette
1 tablespoon chopped fresh basil
4 cups diced tomatoes
⅓ cup diced red onion
½ cup sliced mushrooms
½ cup freshly grated Parmesan cheese

Cook pasta according to package directions. Drain.

Meanwhile, combine garlic and salt in a medium bowl. Stir in vinaigrette and basil. Add tomatoes, onion, and mushrooms and toss to combine.

Add cheese to hot pasta and toss to combine. Add pasta mixture to tomato mixture and toss to combine.

MENU: Hard rolls. Biscotti.

SERVINGS: Makes 4 servings.

Dinner & Lunch Bean Salad

■ I make a double batch of this salad, saving half to serve as a lunch at work for a few days.

¼ cup extra-virgin olive oil
1 tablespoon fresh lemon juice
Salt and freshly ground black pepper
¼ cup sliced scallions
2 tablespoons chopped fresh flat-leaf parsley
1 (15-oz.) can Great Northern beans, drained
1 large tomato, seeded and chopped
Romaine lettuce leaves

Combine oil, lemon juice, salt, pepper, scallions, and parsley in a medium bowl. Add beans and tomato and toss gently to combine.

Arrange lettuce leaves on 4 plates. Top with bean mixture.

MENU: Garlic bagel chips. Melon slices with raspberries.

SERVINGS: Makes 4 servings.

Steak & Arugula Salad

■ Arugula leaves and balsamic vinegar give this steak salad a special twist. Arugula is a salad green that looks like a cross between mustard greens and radish leaves. Young leaves have a pungent, peppery taste.

1 (8-oz.) New York strip steak, trimmed of fat
4 tablespoons Italian salad dressing, plus extra for serving
Freshly ground black pepper
4 cups arugula leaves, trimmed, washed, and dried
2 tablespoons balsamic vinegar

Preheat broiler. Marinate steak in salad dressing for 5 minutes. Drain steak and discard dressing. Place steak on a broiler pan rack. Broil about 10 minutes, turning, for medium or to desired degree of doneness. Sprinkle with black pepper and cut into ¼-inch strips. Set aside.

Toss arugula with vinegar. Top with steak slices. Serve additional Italian salad dressing on the side.

MENU: Thin sliced Italian bread. Deli new-potato salad. Pound cake with nondairy whipped topping and fresh strawberries.

SERVINGS: Makes 4 servings.

Citrus Chicken Salad

■ There's a little grapefruit tree in the side yard of my vacation home in Florida. We're usually there in the fall when it is heavily laden with bright yellow globes. I've become proficient at grapefruit cookery because I'm determined that none of this wondrous bounty of a healthful food will go to waste. This takes a little more work if you start with the whole fruit, but bottled grapefruit sections make this salad an easy job.

2 cups fresh or bottled grapefruit sections, drained
½ cup sliced canned water chestnuts, drained
1 (2-oz.) jar sliced pimientos, drained
2 cups cubed cooked chicken
⅔ cup light mayonnaise
3 tablespoons chopped scallions
Sea salt
4 cups torn romaine lettuce
2 cups torn escarole
12 kalamata olives

Cut grapefruit sections in half. Combine in a salad bowl with water chestnuts, pimientos, chicken, mayonnaise, scallions, and salt to taste.

Divide greens among 4 serving plates. Arrange chicken mixture on top. Garnish with olives.

MENU: Rye crackers. Strawberry frozen yogurt.

SERVINGS: Makes 4 servings.

Chinese Slaw

■ This is a big, beautiful salad that should come to the table in a deep salad bowl. Toss dramatically at the table for extra effect.

1 (1-lb.) package (about 5 cups) coleslaw mix
½ cup canned sliced bamboo shoots, drained
1 cup mandarin orange segments, drained
½ red bell pepper, cut into thin bite-size strips
1 small red onion, thinly sliced and separated into rings
2 tablespoons snipped fresh cilantro leaves
¼ cup orange juice
1 tablespoon rice-wine vinegar
2 teaspoons soy sauce
1 teaspoon sesame oil
2 tablespoons chopped cashews

Combine coleslaw mix, bamboo shoots, orange segments, bell pepper, onion, and cilantro in a large salad bowl.

In a small jar with a tight-fitting lid, shake together orange juice, vinegar, soy sauce, and sesame oil. Pour dressing over coleslaw mixture. Toss lightly to coat. Sprinkle with cashews.

MENU: Sesame rice cakes spread with natural peanut butter. Cantaloupe wedges.

SERVINGS: Makes 4 servings.

Grilled Seafood Salad

■ A lot has been written about the healthful benefits of seafood. But how much should you eat? Recent studies have indicated that one or two fish dishes a week may help prevent heart disease. This grilled seafood salad is easy medicine to take.

1½ pounds halibut, rinsed, patted dry, and
   cut into 1½-inch cubes
½ cup fresh lemon juice
1 tablespoon olive oil
⅛ teaspoon dried oregano
1 clove garlic, minced
2 cups torn spinach
2 cups torn romaine lettuce
1 red onion, cut into wedges
1 cup cherry tomato halves
Cucumber salad dressing

Preheat broiler. Place fish in a shallow glass baking dish. Combine lemon juice, olive oil, oregano, and garlic. Pour over fish. Set aside 5 minutes.

With a slotted turner, remove fish from marinade and place on a broiler pan rack that has been sprayed with nonstick cooking spray. Broil 4 inches from source of heat for 8 minutes, turning once and basting with marinade, or until fish flakes when tested with a fork.

Meanwhile, mix together spinach and lettuce in a medium bowl. Divide among 4 serving plates. Top with cooked fish, onion wedges, and cherry tomatoes. Serve with cucumber salad dressing on the side.

MENU: Crusty French bread. Bakery cherry pie.

SERVINGS: Makes 4 to 6 servings.

Corn & Tuna Salad

■ Never, never run out of canned tuna! White albacore packed in spring water is best for salads.

2 (6-oz.) cans white albacore tuna packed in
   water, drained
1 (11-oz.) can whole-kernel corn, drained
¾ cup lemon vinaigrette, plus additional for
   serving
3 tablespoons chopped fresh flat-leaf parsley
½ teaspoon hot pepper sauce
2 tomatoes, chopped
¼ cup shredded carrots
4 cups torn red-leaf lettuce leaves
2 cups assorted field greens
½ cup thinly sliced scallions

Combine tuna, corn, vinaigrette, parsley, hot pepper sauce, tomatoes, and carrots in a large bowl.

Mix together lettuce and greens in a medium bowl. Divide among 4 to 6 plates. Arrange tuna mixture on greens. Sprinkle with scallions. Serve with additional lemon vinaigrette on the side.

MENU: Norwegian flat bread with nonfat scallion cream cheese spread. Pineapple spears dusted with brown sugar.

SERVINGS: Makes 4 to 6 servings.

Fruit & Vegetable Medley Salad

■ My niece loves to make salads. She sees it as an art form, mixing taste, texture, color. She liked this simple go-together.

6 cups torn salad greens
1 small red onion, thinly sliced and separated into rings
1 (11-oz.) can mandarin orange segments, drained
1 cup sugar snap peas, sliced into 1-inch lengths
½ cup sliced mushrooms
French dressing

Toss together greens, onion, oranges, peas, and mushrooms in a large bowl. Serve with French dressing on the side.

MENU: Focaccia spread with ricotta cheese and chopped sun-dried tomatoes. Green and purple grapes.

Chicken Salad with Yogurt Dressing

■ This is a great main-dish salad to serve on a hot, steamy day when you don't want to work in the kitchen. Rotisserie chicken comes to the rescue again.

½ cup low-fat lemon yogurt
1 tablespoon finely chopped fresh flat-leaf parsley
3 tablespoons milk
2 cups torn red-leaf lettuce
2 cups torn romaine lettuce
2 cups cubed cooked chicken
1 cup bean sprouts, rinsed and drained
1 cup broccoli florets
¼ cup thinly sliced red bell pepper

Combine yogurt, parsley, and milk in a small bowl. Set aside.

Toss together remaining ingredients in a large salad bowl. Serve with yogurt dressing on the side.

MENU: Whole-wheat crackers. Grapefruit sections.

SERVINGS: Makes 4 servings.

Stir-Fry Salad

■ This is a great dish for making a little bit of meat go a long way. For best results, cut the beef into very thin strips, against the grain. If the meat is frozen, the slicing goes all the easier. Remember, high heat is what makes a stir-fry fast and tasty.

About ½ (9-oz.) package refrigerated fresh spaghetti
2 tablespoons water

2 tablespoons orange juice

2 tablespoons soy sauce

¾ pound beef top round, cut into paper-thin
slices

2 tablespoons rice wine vinegar

1 teaspoon sesame oil

¼ teaspoon crushed red pepper flakes

1 garlic clove, minced

1 tablespoon corn oil

2 cups cauliflowerets, chopped

1 small red bell pepper, chopped

4 cups crosswise sliced Napa (Chinese)
cabbage

⅓ cup chopped scallions

Cook spaghetti according to package
directions.

Meanwhile, combine water, 1 tablespoon
of the orange juice, and 1 tablespoon of the
soy sauce in a medium bowl. Stir in beef
slices.

In another small bowl, combine remaining
soy sauce and orange juice, vinegar, sesame
oil, pepper flakes, and garlic to make a dressing. Set aside.

Heat corn oil in a 12-inch skillet or wok
over high heat. Add beef strips and stir-fry 2
minutes. Add cauliflower and bell pepper and
stir-fry 2 minutes or until beef is brown and
vegetables are crisp-tender. Remove from
heat.

Combine beef mixture, drained spaghetti,
cabbage, and scallions in a large serving bowl.
Pour dressing over all. Toss lightly.

MENU: Sesame rice cakes. Orange slices and
flaked coconut.

SERVINGS: Makes 4 to 6 servings.

Middle Eastern Salad

■ Mint is a popular herb in Middle Eastern
cookery. Despite all the other wonderful,
healthful ingredients in this main-dish salad,
it's the mint you will remember.

1 (15-oz.) can white kidney beans
(cannellini), drained

1 medium onion, chopped

1 cup cherry tomato halves

1 medium cucumber, peeled, seeded, and
diced

½ cup chopped fresh flat-leaf parsley

1 tablespoons chopped fresh mint

¼ cup extra-virgin olive oil

¼ cup fresh lemon juice

Salt and freshly ground black pepper

Romaine lettuce leaves

Combine beans, onion, tomatoes, cucumber, parsley, and mint in a medium bowl. Beat
together olive oil, lemon juice, salt, and pepper in a small bowl. Pour over bean mixture
and toss to coat thoroughly.

Line 4 salad plates with lettuce. Divide
bean mixture among plates.

MENU: Pita bread. Fresh figs sprinkled with
freshly ground black pepper.

SERVINGS: Makes 4 servings.

Parmesan-Basil Vegetable Salad

■ Precut vegetables give you a head start in making this tasty salad.

2 tablespoons chopped fresh basil
2 cloves garlic, finely chopped
2 cups broccoli florets
1½ cups cauliflowerets
1 medium zucchini, cut into ½-inch rounds, then quartered
1 medium yellow summer squash, cut into ½-inch rounds, then quartered
2 medium carrots, thinly sliced
1 red onion, thinly sliced and separated into rings
1 cup creamy Parmesan cheese salad dressing

Combine all ingredients in a large salad bowl and toss to coat with dressing.

MENU: Deli grilled chicken sandwiches. Potato chips. Blueberries with cream.

SERVINGS: Makes 6 servings.

Bean & Tuna Salad

■ Many people rinse canned beans thinking they are eliminating all the salt. Rinsing will help take away some of the salt used in processing, but not all.

1 (19-oz.) can Great Northern beans, drained
1 (6-oz.) can white albacore tuna packed in water, drained
1 cup broccoli florets
⅔ cup mustard vinaigrette
Leaf lettuce
4 cherry tomatoes, halved

Combine beans, tuna, and broccoli in a large bowl. Add dressing and turn carefully to coat.

Line 4 salad plates with leaf lettuce. Divide tuna mixture over lettuce. Garnish with cherry tomato halves.

MENU: Stone-ground wheat crackers. Deli marinated mushrooms. Peach slices with candied ginger slices.

SERVINGS: Makes 4 servings.

Black Bean Salad

■ This is one of the prettiest salads to bring to the table. *Jicama* is a large root vegetable with a brown skin and sweet, crunchy white flesh. Peel before using.

1 (11-oz.) can whole-kernel corn, drained
1 cup diced jicama
1 medium tomato, chopped
1 (15-oz.) can black beans, rinsed and
  drained
1 scallion, sliced
¼ cup red-wine vinegar and oil salad
  dressing
½ teaspoon chili powder
Romaine lettuce leaves

Toss together corn, jicama, tomato, black beans, and scallion in a medium bowl.

Mix together wine and vinegar dressing and chili powder in a small bowl. Pour over corn and bean mixture and toss to combine.

Line 5 salad plates with lettuce leaves. Divide salad over lettuce.

MENU: Mango and papaya slices. Cinnamon graham crackers spread with grape jam.

SERVINGS: Makes 5 servings.

Swiss Salad

■ Garbanzos are also called chickpeas or ceci. They're meaty and delicious. Usually they're found in Mediterranean and Middle Eastern cooking and in some Mexican dishes and western and southwestern food. I'm taking them north.

1 cup canned garbanzo beans, drained
2 large slices Swiss cheese, cut into julienne
  strips
3 tablespoons finely chopped parsley
2 tablespoons finely chopped red onion
3 tablespoons olive oil
1 tablespoon fresh lemon juice
½ teaspoon garlic salt

Combine beans, Swiss cheese, parsley, and red onion in a medium bowl. Set aside.

Combine oil, lemon juice, and garlic salt in a small bowl. Beat together with a fork or whisk. Pour over cheese mixture and toss to coat.

MENU: Deli marinated mushrooms. Toasted whole-wheat rolls. Watermelon.

SERVINGS: Makes 4 servings.

Warm Bean & Tuna Salad

■ I love olive oil and consume a lot of it, but I don't use it in every dish because there are some dishes that require a bland oil that won't compete with the flavors I want to emphasize. In this dish, a fruity extra-virgin olive oil is perfect.

1 tablespoon extra-virgin olive oil
1 small onion, chopped
1 clove garlic, chopped
1 (15-oz.) can Great Northern beans, drained
1 tablespoon fresh parsley, chopped
¼ cup mustard vinaigrette
Leaf lettuce
1 (6-oz.) can white albacore tuna packed in water, drained

Heat oil in a saucepan over medium heat. Add onion and garlic. Cook 2 minutes or until softened.

Add beans and parsley. Cook 4 minutes over low heat, stirring occasionally, or until hot. Transfer contents of saucepan to a bowl. Pour vinaigrette over beans and gently mix.

Line 4 salad plates with lettuce leaves. Spoon bean mixture over lettuce. Divide tuna chunks over bean mixture.

MENU: Whole-wheat toast. Green and purple grapes.

SERVINGS: Makes 4 servings.

Tossed Tuna Salad

■ I know that canned tuna has no reputation among fine cooks. I know that grilled fresh tuna and canned tuna are worlds apart in flavor and texture. Still, I've thrown together many a meal with canned tuna. During warm weather months, it is especially helpful because it requires no cooking. It can turn a simple salad into a pleasing entree. I prefer the solid white tuna packed in water. I like its meaty texture and pretty, light appearance.

About ½ cup plain low-fat yogurt
3 tablespoons chili sauce, such as Heinz
8 cups torn romaine lettuce
1 (6-oz.) can white albacore tuna packed in water, drained
1 small red onion, sliced and separated into rings
½ cup sliced ripe olives
1 jalapeño chile, chopped

For the dressing, stir together yogurt and chili sauce to desired consistency in a small bowl.

Combine lettuce, tuna, onion, olives, and chile in a large bowl. Pour dressing over all and toss to coat.

MENU: Bakery corn muffins. Red and green grapes.

SERVINGS: Makes 4 servings.

Tuna Garden Salad

■ I hate to think that my life is ordered by vegetables, but in the summer, the number of zucchini and tomatoes that come into my home courtesy of avid gardening neighbors and friends is astounding.

2 cups cubed zucchini cubes
2 cups cubed tomatoes
1 (6-oz.) can white albacore tuna packed in
    water, drained
1½ teaspoons chopped fresh dill
¼ cup thinly sliced scallions
⅛ teaspoon freshly ground black pepper
2 tablespoons fresh lime juice
Red-leaf lettuce leaves

    Combine zucchini, tomatoes, and tuna in a medium bowl. Sprinkle with dill, scallions, pepper, and lime juice. Toss well.
    Line 4 salad plates with lettuce leaves. Spoon tuna mixture over lettuce.

MENU: Toasted bakery bran muffins. Vanilla frozen yogurt sprinkled with crushed pistachio nuts.

SERVINGS: Makes 4 servings.

Hot Cabbage Salad

■ Cabbage is one of the most important vegetables in my kitchen. To those unfamiliar with using cabbage except in classic dishes like *pot-au-feu* and *choucroute garni*, it possesses a light and almost creamy texture and taste when carefully sautéed.

4 slices thick bacon, diced
4 tablespoons red-wine vinegar and oil salad
    dressing
2 to 3 scallions, finely chopped
⅘ (1-lb.) package (about 4 cups) coleslaw mix
1 (4-oz.) package garlic-and-herb cream
    cheese
Freshly ground black pepper
Chopped fresh parsley

    Microwave the bacon on HIGH for 4 minutes. Drain on paper towels.
    Meanwhile, heat 3 tablespoons of the salad dressing in a 12-inch skillet over medium heat. Add the scallions and cook until limp and translucent, about 1 minute.
    Add coleslaw mix, increase heat to high, and stir-fry until cabbage begins to wilt, about 4 minutes. Add bacon and remaining dressing.
    Divide the cabbage between 2 large dinner plates. Cut the cheese in half and center each half in the hot cabbage.
    Grind pepper over all and sprinkle with fresh parsley.

MENU: Sourdough bread. Chunky applesauce dusted with cinnamon.

SERVINGS: Makes 2 servings.

Blue Cheese Steak Salad

■ I have become a vinaigrette person. There was a time when I could not say no to blue cheese salad dressing, a time when Russian looked pretty good, and ranch was irresistible. Now, I pass them by. I have come to love the taste of a well-made vinaigrette so much that the heavier salad dressings—even those with "low-fat" and "no-fat" labels—hold no interest for me.

3 cups mixed salad greens (such as watercress, romaine, butter, or red-leaf lettuce)
½ pound cooked roast beef, sliced
2 ounces blue cheese, crumbled
¼ cup sliced scallions
½ cup mustard vinaigrette (see Note, below)

Divide salad greens between 2 plates.
Arrange roast beef slices on top. Sprinkle blue cheese and scallions over beef. Serve with dressing.

MENU: Thick slices of pumpernickel bread, toasted. Gingerbread squares with nondairy whipped topping.

SERVINGS: Makes 2 servings.

NOTE
Vinaigrettes are extremely easy to make at home—just whisk together 2 tablespoons wine vinegar or strained fresh lemon juice and 6 tablespoons olive oil, and season to taste. I like to add a teaspoon of Dijon mustard to the basic blend. I use it to dress this steak salad because it seems perfect for the greens and only lightly coats the meat. If you prefer, bottled mustard vinaigrette also works well.

Spinach, Tuna, & Shrimp Salad

■ Tuna salad sandwiches are a favorite lunch in my home, but sometimes, when the weather is hot and I don't feel like cooking, this spinach and tuna salad is a dinnertime blessing.

5 cups torn spinach leaves
1 (6-oz.) can white albacore tuna packed in water, drained and broken into chunks
1 (5-oz.) can baby shrimp, drained
1 small cucumber, peeled and thinly sliced
4 radishes, thinly sliced
Mustard vinaigrette

Toss together spinach, tuna, shrimp, cucumber, and radishes in a large salad bowl.
Serve in individual salad bowls with vinaigrette on the side.

MENU: Herbed French bread. Bakery blueberry turnovers.

SERVINGS: Makes 4 servings.

Black Bean & Chicken Salad

■ Keep a supply of canned beans on your pantry shelves—red beans, white beans, black beans, pinto beans, pigeon peas. They can be used in everything from soups to salads, providing good nutrition, good flavor, and good texture. Black beans, the popular cooking bean of Mexico and the Caribbean, star in this main-dish salad.

1 (15-oz.) can black beans, drained
1 (8-oz.) can whole-kernel corn, drained
2 cups halved cherry tomatoes
1 medium green bell pepper, chopped
4 scallions, thinly sliced
⅓ cup olive oil
⅓ cup steak sauce
3 tablespoons red-wine vinegar
2 to 3 tablespoons honey
2 cloves garlic, minced
2 tablespoons chopped fresh cilantro
¼ teaspoon dried oregano leaves, crushed
Leaf lettuce
3 cups sliced cooked chicken

Combine beans, corn, tomatoes, bell pepper, and scallions in a large bowl. Cover and set aside.

In a jar with a tight-fitting lid, combine oil, steak sauce, vinegar, honey, garlic, cilantro, and oregano. Shake vigorously until thoroughly blended.

Pour ⅔ of dressing over vegetable mixture and toss gently to coat.

Line 4 plates with leaf lettuce. Spoon vegetable mixture onto lettuce. Arrange chicken on top. Drizzle with remaining dressing.

MENU: Seasoned corn chips with salsa. Pineapple spears and strawberries.

SERVINGS: Makes 4 servings.

Cabbage & Cheese Salad

■ White or purple cabbage will work in this recipe, but the purple cabbage gives the dish a very appealing look.

1 (8-oz.) package shredded red cabbage
  (about 3 cups)
½ pound gouda cheese, cut into cubes
1 (8-oz.) can sliced water chestnuts, drained
¼ pound honey-roasted ham, cut into thin
  strips
3 tablespoons extra-virgin olive oil
3 tablespoons fresh lemon juice
2 tablespoons chopped fresh flat-leaf parsley
Salt and freshly ground pepper

Combine cabbage, cheese, water chestnuts, and ham in a large bowl.

Whisk together olive oil, lemon juice, parsley, salt, and pepper to taste in a small bowl. Toss dressing with cabbage mixture to coat.

MENU: Pumpernickel bread. Bakery apple turnovers.

SERVINGS: Makes 4 servings.

Cantonese Chicken Salad

■ Where I shop, Chinese cabbage is called "Napa" cabbage. It's available year-round in most markets. It has a thinner leaf than other cabbages, and it's also very tender, crisp, juicy, and mild. It can be cooked, but it's also delicious raw in salads.

5 cups torn Napa cabbage
½ cup shredded carrots
½ cup scallions, finely chopped
3 cups coarsely chopped cooked chicken
¼ cup soy sauce
⅓ cup rice-wine vinegar
2 tablespoons toasted sesame seeds
2 teaspoons sugar
1 teaspoon grated fresh ginger
2 tablespoons minced fresh cilantro

Combine cabbage, carrots, scallions, and chicken in a large bowl. Set aside.

In a jar with a tight-fitting lid, combine soy sauce, vinegar, sesame seeds, sugar, and ginger. Shake well until sugar dissolves. Pour over vegetables and chicken and toss to coat. Sprinkle with cilantro.

MENU: Chinese noodles with duck sauce. Bakery cake.

SERVINGS: Makes 4 servings.

Pepperoni Pasta Salad

■ Tortellini are little nuggets of pasta stuffed with meat or cheese. They're a meal in themselves but, combined with some savory ingredients, they're the basis for a hearty main-dish salad.

1 (9-oz.) package refrigerated fresh cheese-filled tortellini
6 ounces sliced pepperoni
½ cup oil-packed sun-dried tomatoes, drained and cut into strips
½ yellow bell pepper, cut into thin strips
¼ cup chopped red onion
½ cup red-wine vinegar and oil salad dressing
Red-leaf lettuce leaves

Cook pasta according to package directions.

Meanwhile, cut each slice of pepperoni into 4 wedges; combine with sun-dried tomatoes, bell pepper, onion, and salad dressing in a medium bowl. Add drained pasta and toss lightly to coat.

Line 4 plates with lettuce leaves. Spoon pasta mixture onto center of plate.

MENU: Italian bread. Lemon sorbet.

SERVINGS: Makes 4 servings.

Chicken & Pear Salad

■ Slicing a pear for salad requires a little care. The area around the pit can be quite gritty, so take care to cut it away.

6 tablespoons olive oil
3 cups coarsely chopped cooked chicken
½ cup pecan pieces
Salt and freshly ground black pepper
4 scallions, thinly sliced
2 tablespoons rice-wine vinegar
2 pears, cored and sliced
8 cups chopped romaine lettuce
¼ cup crumbled feta cheese

Heat 2 tablespoons of the oil in a 10-inch skillet over medium-high heat. Add chicken and pecans and sauté until chicken is heated through, about 2 minutes. Remove chicken and pecans with a slotted spoon. Keep warm in a large salad bowl. Season with salt and pepper to taste.

Add scallions to skillet and cook until translucent, about 1 minute. Add vinegar and bring to a boil, scraping up bits from the bottom of skillet.

Remove pan from burner; whisk in remaining 4 tablespoons oil. Add pears and stir gently to coat.

Add pear mixture to chicken mixture and toss to combine. Serve on a bed of romaine and garnish with feta cheese.

MENU: Toasted English muffins. Ice-cream sandwiches.

SERVINGS: Makes 4 servings.

Warm Chicken & Almond Salad

■ It was happy news when researchers found that nuts, although high in fat, are high in the kind of fat that is healthy for us. That isn't license to consume vats of nuts, but it is good reason to consume them in moderation as part of a healthful diet. I sprinkle this salad with a healthy amount of sliced almonds for a wonderful taste and great crunch.

8 cups mixed field greens
¼ cup fresh cilantro leaves
¼ cup thinly sliced scallions
4 nectarines
3 cups coarsely sliced cooked chicken
¼ cup sliced almonds, toasted
Cucumber salad dressing

Arrange field greens on 4 serving plates. Sprinkle with cilantro. Top with scallions.

Slice nectarines into wedges and arrange on plates with greens. Top greens with chicken. Sprinkle chicken with toasted almonds. Serve with salad dressing on the side.

MENU: Whole-grain rolls. Raspberry sherbet with fancy cookies.

SERVINGS: Makes 4 servings.

Scallop & Cauliflower Salad

■ Scallops cook very quickly—in 1 to 3 minutes—and like other kinds of seafood will toughen if cooked too long. That's the last thing we want to do.

2 cups cauliflowerets
2 small red bell peppers, cut into strips
1 cup sliced mushrooms
1 cup Russian salad dressing
1 tablespoon butter
1 pound sea scallops, rinsed and patted dry
8 cups mixed salad greens

Combine cauliflowerets, bell pepper, mushrooms and salad dressing in a large bowl. Cover and set aside.

Melt butter in a 10-inch skillet over medium-high heat. Add scallops and cook 3 minutes or until opaque. Drain scallops.

Arrange salad greens on 4 plates. Spoon reserved vegetable mixture over greens. Divide scallops among the plates.

MENU: Potato rolls. Tropical fruit compote.

SERVINGS: Makes 4 servings.

Honey Chicken Salad

■ This tasty salad was inspired by an American classic—Waldorf salad—which was created at the famous Waldorf-Astoria Hotel in New York City. It's usually made with celery, apples, and walnuts tossed with mayonnaise. I took out the mayo and added some chicken to make a heartier, healthier dinner salad.

¼ cup honey
2 tablespoons Dijon mustard
⅓ cup fresh lemon juice
¼ cup olive oil
12 dried dates, sliced
2 cups cubed cooked chicken
2 Granny Smith or McIntosh apples, cored and diced
1 cup diced celery
⅓ cup chopped walnuts
Lettuce leaves

Stir together honey, mustard, lemon juice, and olive oil in a large bowl. Add dates. Let stand 5 minutes. Add chicken and toss lightly. Add apples, celery, and walnuts and toss to combine.

Line 6 plates with lettuce leaves. Divide apple mixture among the plates.

MENU: Whole-wheat rolls. Pumpkin pie.

SERVINGS: Makes 6 servings.

Corn & Chicken Salad

■ Have you taken a closer look at the seasoning mixes now available in the spice aisles at supermarkets? There are all manner of enticing seasoned salt and seasoned pepper blends. There are mixes especially for chicken, beef, and pork, for the barbecue, and for meat loaf. I could go on and on. I used one specifically designed for chicken for this salad, but feel free to choose what appeals to you—you can't go wrong—or make a combination of seasoning ingredients by mixing a few spices and herbs that you have on hand.

3 cups coarsely chopped cooked chicken
1 (11-oz.) can whole-kernel corn, drained
½ cup sliced green bell pepper
½ cup sliced celery
4 tomatoes, seeded and chopped
¼ cup mayonnaise
2 tablespoons fresh lemon juice
1 teaspoon seasoned salt
Romaine lettuce leaves

Combine chicken, corn, bell pepper, celery, and tomatoes in a large bowl.

Mix together mayonnaise, lemon juice, and seasoned salt in a small bowl. Toss with chicken and vegetable mixture.

Line 6 dishes with lettuce leaves. Divide chicken salad among the plates.

MENU: Oatmeal bread. Fruit salad drizzled with honey.

SERVINGS: Makes 6 servings.

Warm Chicken Salad

■ A warm salad is really a one-dish meal—quick, easy to prepare, and easy to clean up. The best part is that it can be delicious and nourishing.

4 boneless, skinless chicken breast halves, rinsed and patted dry
1 (15-oz.) can black beans, drained and rinsed
1 small red onion, chopped
Oil and vinegar dressing
1 (11-oz.) can whole-kernel corn, drained
2 tablespoons chopped red bell pepper
2 tablespoons chopped fresh cilantro
Red-leaf lettuce leaves
1 cup cherry tomatoes, halved

Place chicken on a broiler rack that has been sprayed with nonstick cooking spray. Broil 4 inches from the source of heat for 6 minutes. Turn and broil 6 minutes more or until both sides are browned.

Meanwhile, combine beans, onion, and ¼ cup of dressing in a medium bowl. Set aside.

Combine corn, bell pepper, and cilantro in another bowl. Set aside.

Place lettuce leaves on 4 plates. Slice chicken cutlets and divide among the plates. Complete plates with portions of bean mixture, corn mixture, and cherry tomatoes. Serve with additional oil and vinegar dressing.

MENU: Corn chips. Orange slices with pomegranate seeds and grated coconut.

SERVINGS: Makes 4 servings.

Chicken Asparagus Salad

■ Asparagus is available year-round, but the tiny, pencil-thin spears of asparagus that I use in this salad are best in early spring.

2 cups coarsely sliced cooked chicken
½ pound very thin asparagus spears, cut in half
1 (8¾-oz.) can baby corn, drained and rinsed
2 tablespoons soy sauce
½ cup rice vinegar (see Note, below)
¼ cup peanut oil
½ teaspoon sesame oil
Dash of black pepper
Spinach leaves
3 small tomatoes, chopped
½ cup sliced mushrooms

Place chicken, asparagus, and corn in a medium bowl. In another bowl, combine soy sauce, vinegar, peanut and sesame oils, and pepper. Toss ¼ cup of vinegar mixture with chicken, asparagus, and corn. Set aside for 5 minutes.

Meanwhile, line 4 plates with spinach leaves. Drain chicken-corn mixture. Arrange on top of spinach. Garnish plates with tomatoes and mushrooms. Serve with remaining soy-vinegar dressing.

MENU: Sesame-seed rice cakes. Bakery banana cream pie.

SERVINGS: Makes 4 servings.

NOTE
Rice vinegar is generally available in supermarkets. It is a milder vinegar than the very astringent white vinegar it resembles. If you can't find it, substitute white-wine vinegar.

Greek Isles Tuna Salad

■ Feta, the classic Greek cheese, is white, crumbly, and very salty. It has a rich, tangy flavor that adds just the right touch to a satisfying main-dish salad. It is sold in packages as well as in jars, packed in its own salty brine.

¼ pound green beans
3 tablespoons water
1 (12-oz.) can white albacore tuna packed in water, drained
1 (15-oz.) can Great Northern beans, drained, rinsed
1 large tomato, chopped
12 ripe Greek olives
¼ cup crumbled feta cheese
Snipped fresh chives
Lemon vinaigrette

Place green beans and 3 tablespoons water in a microwave-safe dish. Microwave on HIGH for 4 minutes or until crisp-tender. Drain. Rinse with cold water and drain.

Place tuna in center of a serving platter.

Arrange green beans, Great Northern beans, tomato, and olives around tuna. Sprinkle with feta cheese and chives. Serve with lemon vinaigrette.

MENU: Soft bread sticks. Vanilla ice cream with cherry pie filling.

SERVINGS: Makes 4 to 6 servings.

Warm London Broil Salad

■ The cut of meat sold as London broil is cut from the beef flank, round, or even sirloin, depending on your part of the country. In my area it is from the round. It's a real bargain, sometimes costing less per pound than chicken or even hot dogs. It's not a naturally tender cut, but cooked and carved right, it can be. I broil it rare and then cut it diagonally into thin slices so my carving knife does the work of cutting through any tough fibers. The secret here is broiling to rare, then cutting it thin and on the bias.

1¼ pounds London broil steak
Salt and freshly ground black pepper
¼ pound sugar snap peas
3 tablespoons water
Bibb lettuce leaves
1 medium red onion, sliced into thin rings
1 large tomato, sliced into eighths
Mustard vinaigrette

Place steak on a broiler pan rack that has been sprayed with nonstick cooking spray. Broil 5 minutes. Turn and broil 4 minutes for rare or to desired degree of doneness. Season with salt and pepper to taste.

Place peas and 3 tablespoons water in a microwave-safe dish. Microwave on HIGH for 4 minutes or until crisp-tender. Drain.

Slice steak diagonally across grain into thin slices.

Line a serving platter with lettuce leaves. Arrange steak slices in center. Surround with snap peas, onion, and tomato wedges. Serve with mustard vinaigrette on the side.

MENU: Deli-style potato chips. Melon slices.

SERVINGS: Makes 4 or 5 servings.

Shrimp Salad

■ It took food manufacturers some time to work things out, but there are finally some very good tasting nonfat and low-fat mayonnaises. If desired, feel free to substitute your favorite for the regular mayonnaise called for in this salad.

1 pound large cooked shrimp, peeled and halved crosswise
1 firm ripe avocado, peeled, pitted, and diced
¼ cup sliced canned water chestnuts
½ cup shredded carrots
2 scallions, chopped
½ cup salsa
¼ cup mayonnaise
2 tablespoons chopped fresh flat-leaf parsley
2 teaspoons fresh lime juice
Salt and freshly ground black pepper
Leaf lettuce

Combine shrimp, avocado, water chestnuts, carrots, and scallions in a large bowl. Set aside.

Combine salsa, mayonnaise, parsley, and lime juice in a small bowl. Toss with shrimp mixture. Season with salt and pepper.

Line 4 plates with lettuce leaves. Divide shrimp salad among plates.

MENU: Warm tortillas. Bakery peanut butter cookies.

SERVINGS: Makes 4 servings.

Italian Steak Salad

■ I keep wedges of Parmesan cheese in the refrigerator along with shredded Parmesan. I like to use shavings from the wedge when I'm serving a salad. It looks very appetizing on top of dark greens.

1 to 1¼ pound London broil (top round steak)
1 tablespoon garlic-pepper spice blend
1 bunch escarole, torn into bite-size pieces
1 cup seasoned garlic croutons
1 cup cherry tomatoes, halved
½ cup freshly shaved Parmesan cheese, plus additional for serving
½ cup Italian salad dressing

Preheat broiler. Season steak with spice blend. Place steak on a broiler pan rack that has been sprayed with nonstick cooking spray. Broil 5 minutes. Turn and broil 4 minutes for rare or to desired degree of doneness. Thinly slice beef across the grain.

Toss together escarole, croutons, tomatoes, Parmesan cheese, and dressing in a large bowl.

Divide salad among 4 plates. Top with beef slices. Serve with additional slivers of Parmesan cheese.

MENU: Garlic bread sticks. Neapolitan ice cream.

SERVINGS: Makes 4 servings.

Sesame Chicken Salad

■ Sesame seeds have a nutty, slightly sweet flavor that intensifies with toasting. There are several ways to toast sesame seeds—in the oven, on top of the stove, but the quickest is in the microwave. Just place sesame seeds in a small microwave-safe bowl and microwave them, uncovered, on HIGH 1 to 2 minutes, stirring every 30 seconds until golden brown.

⅓ cup peanut oil
¼ cup rice-wine vinegar
1 tablespoon sesame seeds, toasted
1 teaspoon sesame oil
½ teaspoon sugar
6 cups chopped romaine lettuce
1 (8-oz.) can sliced water chestnuts, drained
½ cup shredded carrots
1 cup thinly sliced zucchini
1 (7-oz.) jar baby corn, drained
2 cups coarsely chopped cooked chicken breast

Combine peanut oil, vinegar, sesame seeds, sesame oil, and sugar in a jar with tight-fitting lid. Set aside.

Combine lettuce, water chestnuts, carrots, zucchini, and baby corn in a large salad bowl. Shake peanut-sesame oil mixture well and pour over vegetable mixture. Toss to coat.

Divide salad among 4 serving plates. Top with chicken.

MENU: Bakery oat-bran muffins. Lime sherbet with fresh fruit.

SERVINGS: Makes 6 servings.

Chicken Fruit Salad

■ The only time-consuming chore in putting this tasty salad together is slicing the grapes. Take consolation in the fact that there couldn't be an easier job and the delicious fresh taste is worth the extra effort.

3 cups coarsely chopped cooked chicken
¾ cup sliced green seedless grapes
1 (11-oz.) can mandarin orange segments, drained
1 (8-oz.) can sliced water chestnuts, drained
½ cup mayonnaise
1 tablespoon fresh lemon juice
1 teaspoon sugar
Mixed salad greens

Combine chicken, grapes, mandarin orange segments, and water chestnuts in a large bowl.

Mix together mayonnaise, lemon juice, and sugar in a small bowl. Pour mayonnaise mixture over chicken mixture and toss to coat.

Divide salad greens among 4 plates. Top with chicken salad.

MENU: Bagel chips. Chocolate pudding with nondairy whipped topping.

SERVINGS: Makes 4 servings.

Tarragon Chicken Salad

■ I use cantaloupe in this recipe, but honeydew, or any similar melon will work as well. Melons are sweet and flavorful, yet very low in calories, and most are good sources of vitamin C and potassium.

¾ cup low-fat sour cream
¼ cup low-fat mayonnaise
2 tablespoons chopped fresh tarragon or 2 teaspoons dried
4 cups chopped cooked chicken
2 cups cantaloupe cubes
Red-leaf lettuce
¼ cup walnuts

Combine sour cream, mayonnaise, and tarragon in a large bowl. Add chicken and cantaloupe and toss to coat.

Line a serving platter with lettuce leaves. Spoon salad onto lettuce. Sprinkle with walnuts.

MENU: Pita bread. Bakery brownies.

SERVINGS: Makes 4 servings.

Warm Vegetable & Pasta Salad

■ There are some dishes that require vegetables to be blanched before adding them to other ingredients. To blanch: Bring water to a boil in a pot, add the vegetables, boil for 1 minute, and drain. In this dish, both the asparagus and the sugar snap peas need to be blanched. Here's what I did to save time: I cooked the pasta and during the last minute of cooking, I added the vegetables to the boiling pasta water. Pasta and vegetables are drained together in a colander, rinsed with cold water, and *voilà*—everything's ready to be tossed with the other ingredients for this warm pasta salad.

1 (9-oz.) package refrigerated fresh linguine
1 pound asparagus, cut into 4-inch pieces
½ pound sugar snap peas
½ cup mayonnaise
¼ cup plain yogurt
2 tablespoons fresh lemon juice
Dash of lemon-pepper seasoning
¼ cup finely diced red onion
1 medium red bell pepper, coarsely chopped

Cook pasta according to package directions. During last minute of cooking, add asparagus and peas to pasta. Drain in a colander. Rinse with cold water.

While pasta cooks, combine mayonnaise, yogurt, lemon juice, and lemon-pepper seasoning in a small bowl. Set aside.

Combine pasta, asparagus, and snap peas with red onion and bell pepper in a large bowl.

Stir in mayonnaise mixture and toss to coat.

MENU: Pizza-flavored crackers. Strawberries drizzled with chocolate syrup.

SERVINGS: Makes 4 servings.

Smoked Whitefish Salad

■ Smoked fish is a convenience food. Far better than anything out of a can or the freezer, the rich flavor of smoked fish makes for great eating without having to do any cooking. The deli counter at supermarkets usually has several varieties of smoked fish. Among them are smoked whitefish and smoked chub, a member of the whitefish family. These fish, from the Great Lakes area and the lakes of Canada, have excellent-flavored flesh that is firm but creamy.

½ pound smoked whitefish
1 (15-oz.) can whole potatoes, drained and sliced
¼ pound green beans, cut into 1½-inch lengths, lightly steamed
½ cup thinly sliced red onion
¼ cup chopped fresh parsley
⅓ cup Thousand Island dressing
4 red-leaf lettuce leaves

Flake fish into bite-size pieces. Combine potatoes and green beans in a large bowl. Add fish, onion, and parsley. Add Thousand Island dressing and mix gently to coat.

Place lettuce leaves on 4 plates. Divide salad over the lettuce.

MENU: Ripe olives. Poppy-seed rolls. Pumpkin pie.

SERVINGS: Makes 4 servings.

VARIATION
Although I favor whitefish, this main-dish salad is worth making with sablefish or smoked salmon—although smoked salmon is much more expensive.

Greek Salad

■ Greek salad is one of the most often ordered salads from the deli that delivers lunch to our office. It's really not a difficult salad to make. Like most Mediterranean fare, it is simple and direct.

1 large garlic clove, peeled
1 small head Boston lettuce, torn into bite-size pieces
2 ounces feta cheese, crumbled
2 teaspoons extra-virgin olive oil
3 plum tomatoes, quartered
1 large cucumber, peeled, seeded, and diced
10 small ripe olives, pitted and diced
2 tablespoons red-wine vinegar
Coarsely ground black pepper
1 teaspoon chopped fresh oregano

Rub a salad bowl with the peeled garlic. Discard. Add lettuce to bowl.

Combine feta cheese and oil in another bowl. Add tomatoes, cucumbers, and olives and gently toss with the feta cheese. Add vinegar, pepper, and oregano and add to lettuce. Toss and serve.

MENU: Pita bread. Bakery honey cake.

SERVINGS: Makes 4 servings.

Beef & Napa Cabbage Salad

■ Beef salads are enormously popular. The thing I like about them is that just a little bit of beef seems like a great big meal—that's because of all the vegetables that go with it.

½ pound sliced cooked roast beef
2 cups cherry tomatoes, halved
½ large red bell pepper, cut into julienne strips
2 cups shredded Napa cabbage
1 cup bean sprouts, rinsed and drained
½ cup mustard vinaigrette

Combine beef, tomatoes, bell pepper, cabbage, and bean sprouts in a large bowl. Pour dressing over salad and toss gently to coat.

MENU: Focaccia bread. Peach ice cream with fresh peach slices.

SERVINGS: Makes 4 servings.

Chicory Salad

■ Chicory is that pretty, spiny-looking green you see in supermarkets. It has a strong taste, but not as strong as other bitter greens.

2 small heads chicory, chopped
1 tomato, chopped
1 (5-oz.) can baby shrimp, drained
Juice of 1 lemon
1 clove garlic, minced
½ cup mustard vinaigrette
¼ cup chopped red onion

Place chicory in a large salad bowl.

Toss tomato and shrimp with lemon juice in a medium bowl. Add garlic, vinaigrette, and onion and toss to combine. Pour vinaigrette mixture over chicory and toss to combine.

MENU: Salt-free saltines. Deli three-bean salad. Mango slices.

SERVINGS: Makes 4 servings.

Fig & Feta Salad

■ Fresh figs are a seasonal delight. If you've never tasted them, you have a wonderful surprise in store.

6 ounces feta cheese, cut into cubes
6 fresh figs, cut lengthwise into halves
¼ cup kalamata olives

¼ cup orange juice
4 tablespoons olive oil and balsamic vinegar salad dressing
2 tablespoons chopped fresh flat-leaf parsley
Romaine lettuce leaves

Combine cheese, figs, and olives in a medium bowl.

In a small jar with a tight-fitting lid, shake together orange juice, salad dressing, and parsley. Pour dressing over cheese-fig mixture, tossing lightly to coat.

Arrange lettuce leaves on 4 plates. Top with cheese-fig mixture.

MENU: Pita bread. Bakery lemon cookies.

SERVINGS: Makes 4 servings.

Summer Bean Salad

■ The radishes in this dish deliver a nice, bright bite. Although radishes come without tops in plastic bags, I think the bunches with the greens still on taste fresher.

1 (15-oz.) can red kidney beans, drained
2 medium cucumbers, peeled and sliced into ¼-inch rounds
1 cup sliced celery
1 cup sliced radishes
1 teaspoon salt
½ cup Russian dressing

Place all ingredients in a salad bowl and toss to combine.

MENU: Black-pepper crackers with alfalfa sprouts. Melon slices.

SERVINGS: Makes 6 servings.

Daikon Salad

■ Daikon is a large white radish from Asia with a sweet fresh flavor.

1 medium daikon, sliced thinly on the
    diagonal (2 cups)
1 cup sliced mushrooms
¼ cup sliced scallions
2 tablespoons rice-wine vinegar
1 tablespoon sunflower oil
1 tablespoon soy sauce
1 teaspoon grated fresh ginger
½ teaspoon sesame oil
¼ teaspoon sea salt
6 Bibb lettuce leaves
1 teaspoon sesame seeds

Combine daikon, mushrooms, and scallions in a large bowl.

Whisk together vinegar, oil, soy sauce, ginger, sesame oil, and salt in a small bowl. Pour over daikon mixture and toss to coat.

Line 6 plates with lettuce leaves. Divide daikon mixture over lettuce. Sprinkle sesame seeds on top of salads.

MENU: Spinach salad with tofu cubes. Rice crackers. Tangerines.

SERVINGS: Makes 6 servings.

Couscous Salad

■ You'll find prepared pesto sauce in the refrigerated cases where fresh pasta is sold. It saves a lot of time and delivers superb flavor.

Instant couscous
1 cup canned white kidney beans
    (cannellini), rinsed and drained
½ cup pesto
3 tablespoons fresh lemon juice
¼ cup chopped red onion
1 medium tomato, seeded and chopped
1 cup celery slices

Prepare couscous according to package directions for 6 servings.

Combine cooked couscous with remaining ingredients in a large bowl and toss to mix.

MENU: Flat bread. Fresh figs.

SERVINGS: Makes 6 servings.

White Bean Salad

■ White bean salad is simple to prepare and dramatic to present. Its natural colors and flavors always make it a hit. I prefer cannellini beans, but any white bean will do.

2 (15-oz.) cans white kidney beans
  (cannellini), drained
½ cup sugar
1 teaspoon sea salt
½ teaspoon coarsely ground black pepper
⅓ cup tarragon vinegar
¾ cup extra-virgin olive oil
1 yellow bell pepper, chopped
½ cup chopped red bell pepper
½ cup chopped fresh parsley leaves

Combine all ingredients in a large bowl and toss gently.

MENU: Red-leaf lettuce leaves with sun-dried tomato vinaigrette. Norwegian flat bread. Melon slices.

SERVINGS: Makes 8 servings.

Bean & Olive Salad

■ Green olives stuffed with pimiento are a handy condiment to have. I buy jars of them already chopped for a quick addition to salads, chicken, meat, or fish.

1 (15-oz.) can white kidney beans
  (cannellini), drained
½ cup chopped pimiento-stuffed green
  olives
½ cup chopped red onion
1 cup cherry tomatoes, halved
⅓ cup chopped fresh flat-leaf parsley
3 tablespoons fresh lemon juice
1 teaspoon chopped fresh oregano
1 teaspoon fresh thyme
2 tablespoons extra-virgin olive oil

Combine all ingredients in a large bowl and toss gently.

MENU: Sesame rice cakes. Fresh figs.

SERVINGS: Makes 4 servings.

Vegetable Entrees

I'm not a vegetarian but a lot of readers of *The Record*, the newspaper where I work, are. Because of their interest I've turned my hand toward developing vegetable entrees. I confess, it was not a task I originally relished, but exploring the possibilities of vegetable dishes has been something of an epiphany for me.

I tended to think of vegetables as solitary side dishes that added variety and nutritious compounds or as ingredients in a animal-protein dish—like a chicken stir-fry.

The logical thing to try was making dishes I really enjoyed, sans the meat. The chicken stir-fry had pea pods, bean sprouts, onions, and a soy-based sauce. Take out the chicken, and it was still tasty, but not satisfying—the kind of thing I could get used to but why have to get used to something? What did the chicken provide that could be replaced with a vegetable substitute? For one thing, I liked its chewiness. I added white kidney beans. Better. I threw in some cashews not just for crunchiness but for flavor. I liked it. I served it over brown rice for another flavor boost.

I believe in success. It gives you courage to continue, so I did, and I've found dozens of ways to make interesting, complex, and speedy dishes without meat. I make them now not because I want to cut back on meat, not because they are inexpensive, or more healthful, but because they're so delicious. Some are so good, I will take time to brag, I serve them to my carnivorous husband, who never says, "Is that all there is? I'm still hungry."

Stewed Garbanzos

■ Half the fun of making this dish is saying its name: stewed gar-BAN-zos. Garbanzos are also known as chickpeas.

2 tablespoons olive oil
2 bunches scallions, chopped
3 cloves garlic, minced
2 (15-oz.) cans garbanzo beans, drained
1 (14.5-oz.) can crushed tomatoes in puree
1 tablespoon minced fresh cilantro
½ teaspoon dried oregano

Heat oil in a 5-quart saucepan or Dutch oven over medium heat. Add scallions and sauté until translucent, about 2 minutes. Add garlic and sauté until golden, about 2 minutes. Add beans, tomatoes, cilantro, and oregano.

Cover and simmer over low heat for 10 minutes to heat through and blend flavors.

MENU: Whole-wheat crackers. Lemonade. Fresh blueberries.

SERVINGS: Makes 4 servings.

Vegetable Sauté

■ This vegetable mélange requires only a few ingredients, but they deliver a powerhouse of flavor.

1 tablespoon olive oil
1 medium onion, chopped
3 medium zucchini, peeled and cut into quarters
1 tomato, chopped
1 tablespoon soy sauce
1 teaspoon chopped fresh basil leaves

Heat oil in a 12-inch skillet over high heat. Add onion and sauté 1 minute. Add zucchini and stir-fry 3 minutes. Stir in tomato, soy sauce, and basil. Stir-fry 4 minutes or until vegetables are crisp-tender.

MENU: Norwegian flat bread. Melon slices.

SERVINGS: Makes 6 servings.

White Bean & Tomato Mélange

■ White kidney beans make a pretty contrast to the red tomatoes in this hearty dinner in a dish.

1½ teaspoons olive oil
1 medium onion, chopped
1 clove garlic, minced
6 fresh plum tomatoes, seeded and chopped
1 (15-oz.) can white kidney beans
   (cannellini), drained
½ teaspoon hot pepper sauce
½ teaspoon salt
1 tablespoon chopped fresh cilantro

Heat oil in a 10-inch skillet over medium-high heat. Add onion and garlic and stir-fry until onion softens, about 2 minutes. Add tomatoes and stir-fry for 2 minutes.

Add beans, hot pepper sauce, and salt and stir-fry 2 minutes. Reduce heat, cover, and simmer 2 minutes for flavors to blend.

Remove from heat. Stir in cilantro and serve.

MENU: Corn chips. Apple slices with peanut butter dip.

SERVINGS: Makes 4 servings.

Green Beans, Indian Style

■ This is a slightly exotic dish that's pretty enough and tasty enough to serve at a party.

2 tablespoons olive oil
1 teaspoon mustard seeds
1 medium onion, chopped
½ cup thinly sliced carrots
1 pound green beans, trimmed and sliced
   into 1-inch pieces
¼ teaspoon salt
1 teaspoon ground coriander
⅛ teaspoon ground ginger
2 tablespoons fresh lemon juice

Heat olive oil in a 10-inch skillet over medium-high heat. Stir in mustard seeds and sauté 30 seconds or until seeds start to pop. Stir in onion, carrots, and beans and stir-fry 5 minutes or until vegetables are crisp-tender.

Stir in salt, coriander, and ginger. Reduce heat, cover, and simmer for 8 minutes or until vegetables are tender.

Stir in lemon juice and serve.

MENU: Pita bread. Sliced tomatoes with cucumber dressing. Orange slices dusted with toasted coconut.

SERVINGS: Makes 4 servings.

Cucumbers & Tomato Skillet

■ I can't get enough of garden-fresh cucumbers. When I make this dish, I serve it with cucumber water. That's in a pitcher which I fill about ¼ full with thin slices of cucumber, and then fill to the top with spring water. Let it sit a few minutes, and pour into tumblers with ice cubes. It's the most refreshing beverage you'll ever drink.

2 tablespoons olive oil
2 medium cucumbers, cut into 1-inch pieces
1 medium onion, sliced and separated into rings
4 medium tomatoes, cut into wedges
1 tablespoon chopped fresh dill

Heat oil in a 10-inch skillet over medium heat. Add cucumbers and onion and sauté 5 minutes, stirring frequently, until cucumbers are crisp-tender.

Stir in tomatoes. Cook, stirring occasionally, just until tomatoes are heated through. Sprinkle with dill.

MENU: Popcorn or rice cakes. Pear slices with green grape halves.

SERVINGS: Makes 6 servings.

Curried Vegetables

■ This dish offers hearty flavors that stick to the ribs.

2 tablespoons olive oil
1 large onion, coarsely chopped
1 cup sliced celery
1 cup shredded carrots
1 small red bell pepper, thinly sliced
1 small green bell pepper, thinly sliced
1 small zucchini, thinly sliced
½ teaspoon curry powder
2 tomatoes, diced
Pinch of sugar
¼ teaspoon fresh lemon juice

Heat oil in 12-inch skillet over medium-high heat. Add onion and stir-fry 3 minutes. Add celery and carrots and stir-fry 3 minutes.

Add bell peppers and zucchini and stir-fry until vegetables are crisp-tender, about 3 minutes.

Add curry powder and tomatoes and heat 1 minute. Add sugar and lemon juice, toss to combine, and serve.

MENU: Rice cakes. Fresh fruit salad.

SERVINGS: Makes 6 servings.

Stir-Fried Sugar Snap Peas & Cucumbers

■ Who would have dreamed a vegetable dish could be so satisfying? The sugar snap peas give it an especially fine taste.

2 tablespoons peanut oil
1 small onion, chopped
¼ teaspoon crushed red pepper flakes
1 cucumber, peeled, halved, seeded, and
   sliced into ¼-inch slices
1 pound sugar snap peas, trimmed
1 tablespoon cider vinegar
1 teaspoon chopped fresh ginger

Heat oil in a 10-inch skillet over medium-high heat. Stir in onion and stir-fry 2 minutes. Add crushed red pepper and stir-fry 5 seconds.

Add cucumber and stir-fry 1 minute. Add snap peas and stir-fry 2 minutes or until vegetables are crisp-tender. Stir in vinegar and ginger and serve.

MENU: Onion rings. Pineapple spears with sliced strawberries.

SERVINGS: Makes 4 servings.

Corn & Lima Beans

■ We know corn and lima beans as succotash, but this combination is a stew, hearty and worth serving as a main course.

1 tablespoon olive oil
1 onion, chopped
2 cloves garlic, mashed
¼ teaspoon freshly ground black pepper
1 teaspoon dried tarragon
1 (11-oz.) can whole-kernel corn, drained
1 cup canned or frozen green lima beans,
   drained

Heat oil in a 3-quart saucepan over medium heat. Add onion and garlic and sauté 3 minutes.

Add pepper and tarragon and cook 1 minute. Stir in corn and limas; cook 4 minutes over low heat or until heated through.

MENU: Canned potato sticks. Watermelon slices.

SERVINGS: Makes 4 servings.

Spicy Veggies

■ This is a sweet, spicy mixture of vegetables with raisins as the surprise ingredient.

2 tablespoons olive oil
2 medium carrots, sliced
1 large onion, chopped
1 large red bell pepper, cut into ¾-inch
   pieces
2 cloves garlic, minced
½ cup raisins
1 teaspoon ground cumin
¼ teaspoon ground turmeric
¼ teaspoon ground cinnamon
1 small zucchini, sliced into ¼-inch rounds
1 (15-oz.) can garbanzo beans, drained
2 tablespoons chopped fresh flat-leaf parsley

Heat oil in a 12-inch nonstick skillet over medium-high heat. Add carrots, onion, bell pepper, and garlic and stir-fry 4 minutes.

Stir in remaining ingredients, except parsley. Stir-fry 5 minutes, or until zucchini is tender. Sprinkle with parsley.

MENU: Deli potato salad. Sliced nectarines.

SERVINGS: Makes 5 servings.

Stir-Fried Cauliflower & Sweet Peppers

■ Cauliflower fans will love this colorful stir-fry.

2 tablespoons peanut oil
2 (1-inch) rounds fresh ginger
1 pound cauliflowerets
1 large red bell pepper, cut into thin strips
½ teaspoon white Worcestershire sauce
½ cup carrot juice

Heat oil in a 10-inch skillet or wok over high heat. Add ginger and stir-fry 10 seconds.

Add cauliflowerets and pepper strips and stir-fry 1 minute. Add Worcestershire sauce and stir-fry 1 minute.

Add carrot juice. Cover pan, reduce heat, and simmer 5 minutes.

MENU: Norwegian flat bread. Banana slices with papaya spears.

SERVINGS: Makes 4 servings.

Tofu Stir-Fry

■ A lot of people turn up their noses at tofu. They shouldn't. It is an excellent source of protein and can be amazingly versatile.

2 tablespoons canola oil
1 teaspoon minced fresh ginger
1 medium onion, chopped
¾ cup snow peas, trimmed and cut in half lengthwise
⅓ cup stir-fry sauce
4 cherry tomatoes, halved
1 pound tofu, drained well and cut into ½-inch cubes

Heat oil in a 10-inch skillet or wok over high heat. Add ginger and stir-fry 30 seconds. Add onion and stir-fry 2 minutes. Add snow peas and stir-fry 1 minute.

Add stir-fry sauce, tomatoes, and tofu. Gently stir to coat tofu and vegetables with sauce. Reduce heat and cook only until tomatoes and tofu are heated through, about 1 minute.

MENU: Rice cakes. Sliced peaches sprinkled with vanilla sugar.

SERVINGS: Makes 4 servings.

Stir-Fried Vegetables & Peanuts

■ I love the look of this dish with all the shiny, bright, and appealing vegetables, most of which can be purchased precut. In a pinch, I've used a bag of frozen stir-fry vegetable combination. These never turn out with as much flavor and verve as fresh vegetables, but when you're in a hurry, the frozen mixes do speed things along. The very best part of this dish is the crunchy texture that comes from the roasted peanuts.

¾ cup vegetable juice, such as V8
2 tablespoons soy sauce
2 teaspoons cornstarch
2 teaspoons grated fresh ginger
1 clove garlic, minced
2 tablespoons peanut oil
1 cup sliced carrots
1 cup sliced broccoli florets
½ cup sliced celery
½ cup sliced red bell pepper
4 scallions, sliced into 1-inch strips
1 (11-oz.) can mandarin orange segments, drained
¼ cup dry-roasted peanuts, chopped

Mix together juice, soy sauce, cornstarch, ginger, and garlic in a small bowl. Set aside.

Heat oil in a wok or 12-inch skillet over medium-high heat. Add carrots, broccoli, celery, bell pepper, and scallions and stir-fry 3 to 4 minutes or until crisp-tender.

Stir mandarin oranges and peanuts into vegetables and pour reserved juice mixture over all.

Cook, stirring constantly, 2 to 3 minutes or until mixture is thickened and thoroughly heated through.

MENU: Deli sesame or other prepared noodles with shredded cucumber. Asian pear slices with mint leaves.

SERVINGS: Makes 6 servings.

Vegetable Stew

■ This vegetable stew is packed with good nutrition, and it only takes a few minutes to make.

2 cups vegetable juice, such as V8
2 tomatoes, quartered
1 medium zucchini, sliced into ½-inch
  rounds
1 cup sugar snap peas
1 cup frozen white shoepeg corn
2 celery stalks, sliced
Seasoned salt
1 small onion, sliced

Combine all ingredients in a 5-quart saucepan or Dutch oven over medium-high heat. Bring to a boil. Reduce heat, cover, and simmer 10 minutes or until vegetables are tender.

MENU: Norwegian flat bread spread with bean dip. Fruit salad.

SERVINGS: Makes 4 servings.

Vegetable Skillet Supper

■ I'm not a big fan of instant rice, but there are times when it comes in handy. Using instant rice in this dish makes a complete vegetarian meal in a matter of minutes.

1 cup instant rice
2 tablespoons canola oil
1 medium onion, chopped
2 cloves garlic, minced
1 medium zucchini, chopped
1 medium red bell pepper, chopped
½ teaspoon dried marjoram
Freshly ground black pepper
2 medium tomatoes, coarsely chopped
1 (15-oz.) can white kidney beans
  (cannellini), drained
Seasoned salt

Prepare rice according to package directions.

Meanwhile, heat oil in a 12-inch skillet over medium-high heat. Add onion and garlic and stir-fry until onion is tender, about 2 minutes. Add zucchini, bell pepper, marjoram, and black pepper to taste. Stir-fry until vegetables are crisp-tender, about 5 minutes.

Stir in tomatoes and beans. Cover and cook until heated through, about 3 minutes. Add seasoned salt to taste.

Spoon hot cooked rice onto a serving platter. Top with vegetable mixture.

MENU: Bananas sprinkled with lemon juice and brown sugar.

SERVINGS: Makes 7 servings.

Southwestern Stir-Fry

■ Remember when chopping jalapeño chiles to take care not to touch your eyes. The natural oils that create a delightful culinary burn on the tongue cause extreme pain when they come in contact with the delicate membranes of the eyes.

2 tablespoons corn oil
¾ cup coarsely chopped onion
¾ cup coarsely chopped green bell pepper
1 jalapeño chile, seeded and chopped
1 clove garlic, minced
1 tablespoon chili powder
½ teaspoon ground cumin
3 cups diced yellow summer squash
1½ cups cherry tomato halves
1 (11-oz.) can corn with bell peppers, drained
Freshly ground black pepper

Heat oil in a 12-inch skillet or wok over high heat. Add onion, bell pepper, jalapeño, and garlic and stir-fry until onion is tender, about 2 minutes.

Add chili powder and cumin and stir-fry 30 seconds. Reduce heat to low. Add squash and tomatoes. Cover and simmer 6 minutes or until squash is tender. Stir in corn and simmer 1 minute. Season with black pepper to taste.

MENU: Warm flour tortillas. Citrus salad. Bakery cherry pie.

SERVINGS: Makes 4 servings.

Asparagus Stir-Fry

■ Asparagus has become a year-round vegetable, but the cheapest and best asparagus comes to market in the spring.

1 bunch (about 1½ pounds) fresh asparagus
3 tablespoons peanut oil
2 tablespoons fresh lemon juice
½ teaspoon salt
¼ teaspoon freshly ground black pepper
1 tablespoon chopped walnuts
Lemon wedges

Wash asparagus well under cold running water. Cut off tips and reserve. Cut stalks diagonally into slices about ¼ inch thick and 1 inch long.

Heat oil in large skillet or wok. Add sliced stalks and stir-fry 4 to 5 minutes or just until crisp-tender. Add tips and stir-fry 2 to 3 minutes longer. Stir in lemon juice, salt, and pepper and stir-fry 30 seconds.

Spoon asparagus into a heated serving dish. Sprinkle with walnuts. Garnish plate with lemon wedges.

MENU: Toasted pita bread. Deli marinated mushrooms. Fresh sliced strawberries sprinkled with sugar.

SERVINGS: Makes 4 servings.

Eggplant Neapolitan

■ Eggplants absorb a lot of oil when they are fried, so you have to keep adding as you go. To minimize the amount of oil used, I fry eggplant slices in a nonstick frying pan.

1 medium eggplant
1 cup Italian-flavored fine bread crumbs
3 tablespoons olive oil
½ pound thinly sliced mozzarella cheese
1¼ to 1½ cups chunky pasta sauce
2 tablespoons chopped flat-leaf parsley

Cut eggplant crosswise into ½-inch slices.

Dip eggplant into bread crumbs to coat. Heat 1 tablespoon of the oil in a 12-inch skillet over medium-high heat. Add eggplant and fry until golden, about 10 minutes, adding more oil as needed.

Top eggplant slices with mozzarella cheese. Spoon sauce over eggplant slices. Cover, reduce heat, and cook until cheese melts, about 5 minutes. Sprinkle with parsley.

MENU: Romaine and endive salad. Garlic bread sticks. Bakery angel food cake with nondairy whipped topping.

SERVINGS: Makes 4 servings.

Salad Bar Stir-Fry

■ God bless salad bars. Before the era of precut vegetables, the salad bar was a savior. I still use them in a pinch.

1 tablespoon sesame oil
2 tablespoons canola oil
1 cup sliced celery
2 cloves garlic, minced
1 cup sliced mushrooms
1 cup thinly sliced scallions
1 cup green bell pepper strips
1 cup red bell pepper strips
½ cup stir-fry sauce

Heat oils in a 12-inch frying pan or wok over high heat. Add celery, garlic, and mushrooms and stir-fry for 2 minutes. Add scallions and both green and red bell pepper strips and stir-fry until crisp-tender, 2 to 3 minutes. Stir in stir-fry sauce and cook until heated through. Serve immediately.

MENU: Deli sesame or other prepared noodles. Pineapple spears.

SERVINGS: Makes 4 servings.

Hot Black Beans

■ Black beans get a real flavor boost with this simple preparation that borrows some fire from jalapeño chiles.

1 tablespoon canola oil
1 cup chopped plum tomatoes
2 bunches scallions, chopped
2 (15-oz.) cans black beans, drained
½ cup beer
⅓ cup chopped fresh cilantro
¼ cup seeded, chopped jalapeño chiles

Heat oil in a 10-inch skillet over medium-low heat. Add tomatoes and scallions and sauté for 2 minutes. Add remaining ingredients; stir, and simmer, covered over low heat for 10 minutes.

MENU: Ranch-style corn chips and green salsa. Strawberry frozen yogurt.

SERVINGS: Makes 4 to 6 servings.

Green Bean & Tomato Stew

■ One of the few green vegetables I could get my children to eat was fresh green beans. They'd turn their noises up at canned or frozen. They'd spirit handfuls of fresh beans away to eat raw for a snack. Delighted, I bought extra.

3 cups green beans, cut into 1-inch pieces
¼ cup water
¼ cup olive oil
½ cup chopped red onion
1 clove garlic, minced
1 cup sliced mushrooms
4 medium plum tomatoes, chopped
2 tablespoons minced fresh flat-leaf parsley

Place beans and water in a microwave-safe dish. Microwave on HIGH for 5 minutes or until crisp-tender.

Meanwhile, heat oil in a 10-inch skillet over medium heat. Add onion and garlic and sauté for 4 minutes or until tender.

Stir in beans with cooking liquid, mushrooms, and tomatoes. Bring to a boil, reduce heat, and simmer about 4 minutes. Stir in parsley.

MENU: Sesame-seed rice cakes. Cantaloupe cubes with sliced cherries.

SERVINGS: Makes 4 to 6 servings.

German Cabbage

■ Fresh cabbage has a lovely mild and mellow taste when it is cooked quickly. Cook it too long, though, and the heat will cause the cabbage to free an enzyme that breaks down to release hydrogen sulfide—the characteristic odor of rotten eggs. We 15-minute chefs never worry about that.

⅓ cup carrot juice
⅓ cup dry white wine
1 (1-lb.) package coleslaw mix or about 5 cups shredded cabbage
1 onion, thinly sliced
1 Granny Smith apple, peeled and thinly sliced
1 teaspoon caraway seeds

Combine juice and wine in a 5-quart saucepan or Dutch oven over medium-high heat. Bring to a boil.

Meanwhile, toss together coleslaw mix, onion, apple, and caraway seeds. Add to juice mixture. Cover, reduce heat, and simmer 10 to 12 minutes or until vegetables are crisp-tender.

MENU: Pumpernickel bread. Strawberry gelatin.

SERVINGS: Makes 6 servings.

Brussels Sprouts & Carrots

■ Fresh Brussels sprouts are like miniature cabbages, but they have a unique flavor that is reminiscent of nuts. They're generally sold in 10-ounce containers. Don't buy packages with sprouts that have yellow leaves or brown spots. They're way past their prime.

2 tablespoons water
½ teaspoon sea salt
2 teaspoons fresh thyme
10 ounces fresh Brussels sprouts
6 baby carrots
1 celery stalk, sliced
¼ cup mustard vinaigrette

Combine water, salt, thyme, Brussels sprouts, carrots, and celery in a 1-quart microwave-safe casserole dish. Cover and microwave on HIGH 4 minutes. Stir and microwave 4 to 5 minutes or until vegetables are crisp-tender. Drain and let stand 2 minutes.

Place vinaigrette in a microwave-safe measuring cup and cook on HIGH for 30 seconds. Drizzle over vegetables.

MENU: Wheat crackers with bean dip. Grapes.

SERVINGS: Makes 4 servings.

Carrots & Cauliflower

■ Bags of carrots that have been peeled and cut down to baby size are sold in supermarkets now, making carrots an easy vegetable to use. I've noticed these same bags at co-workers' desks in my office. In addition to being used in cooking, they've become a popular snack to be eaten raw.

6 baby carrots
½ pound cauliflowerets
2 tablespoons olive oil
½ teaspoon sea salt
⅛ teaspoon dried dill weed

Place all ingredients in a 1-quart microwave-safe casserole. Cover and microwave on HIGH 4 minutes. Stir and microwave 4 to 5 minutes or until vegetables are crisp-tender. Let stand 5 minutes.

MENU: Rice cakes spread with bean dip. Frozen juice bars.

SERVINGS: Makes 4 servings.

Herbed Squash

■ This dish is best in summer, but it can be prepared year-round since squash can be found any month of the year. Zucchini can be used instead. The dish won't be as colorful, but it will taste just fine.

2 tablespoons canola oil
2 medium zucchini, thinly sliced
1 medium yellow summer squash, thinly sliced
1 clove garlic, minced
2 teaspoons fresh oregano or 1 teaspoon dried
1 teaspoon chopped fresh basil or ½ teaspoon dried
Salt and freshly ground black pepper
1 cup cherry tomatoes, halved

Heat oil in a 12-inch skillet or wok over medium-high heat. Add zucchini, summer squash, garlic, oregano, basil, salt, and pepper. Stir-fry 2 minutes. Reduce heat, cover, and simmer for 5 minutes.

Remove lid, increase heat to medium-high, and cook until pan liquids evaporate, about 3 minutes. Stir in tomatoes and heat through, 1 minute.

MENU: Rice cakes with tofu spread and bean sprouts. Mango and papaya wedges.

SERVINGS: Makes 4 servings.

Ratatouille

■ This is a 15-minute version of the usually long-cooking vegetable stew. The speed secret is the friendly microwave oven.

1 medium eggplant, peeled and cut into ½-inch cubes
1 medium onion, thinly sliced and separated into rings
1 green bell pepper, thinly sliced
1 large clove garlic, minced
¼ cup olive oil
1 medium zucchini, thinly sliced
2 teaspoons chopped fresh basil
1½ teaspoons fresh thyme or ¾ teaspoon dried
1 teaspoon sea salt
2 large plum tomatoes, chopped

Combine eggplant, onion, bell pepper, garlic, and oil in a 3-quart microwave-safe casserole. Cover and microwave on HIGH 4 minutes. Stir and microwave 4 minutes or until onion and bell pepper are tender.

Add zucchini, basil, thyme, and salt. Microwave, covered, on HIGH until eggplant and zucchini are tender, 5 minutes. Stir in chopped tomato. Let stand 2 minutes.

MENU: Deli pasta salad. Purple and green grapes.

SERVINGS: Makes 6 servings.

Green Bean Stir-Fry

■ If you are fortunate enough to live near a good Asian market you won't have any problem finding Chinese long beans. They look like regular green beans on steroids. The taste is sweeter and more delectable. Regular garden-fresh green beans are a good substitute.

½ cup vegetable juice, such as V8
1 teaspoon minced fresh ginger
1 clove garlic, minced
1 scallion, thinly sliced
1 pound yard-long beans, cut crosswise into thirds, or green beans, trimmed and cut into half lengthwise
⅓ cup canned water chestnuts, sliced
1 teaspoon soy sauce

Bring juice, ginger, garlic, and scallion to a boil in a 10-inch frying pan or a wok over high heat. Add beans, water chestnuts, and soy sauce. Cover and reduce heat to medium and cook 4 to 5 minutes.

Uncover, increase heat to high, and stir-fry until liquid is evaporated, about 3 minutes.

MENU: Vegetable crackers. Pineapple spears.

SERVINGS: Makes 4 servings.

Quick Baked Beans

■ When I lived in Boston during my student days, I was shocked to discover that many people ate baked beans for breakfast on Sunday morning. These were the beans that were left over from a traditional New England Saturday night dinner that always included Boston baked beans that were cooked in the oven for hours. Sorry, I can't face beans at breakfast, but this hurry-up version of baked beans works for me almost any night.

1 (15-oz.) can vegetarian baked beans, undrained
3 tablespoons chopped onion
¼ cup ketchup
2 tablespoons granulated brown sugar
½ teaspoon sea salt
½ teaspoon dry mustard

Combine all ingredients in a 2-quart saucepan over medium heat. Bring to a boil. Reduce heat and simmer 10 minutes.

MENU: Boston brown bread. Fresh fruit compote.

SERVINGS: Makes 4 servings.

Lemony Lima Beans

■ One of the hardest tasks a parent has is teaching children an appreciation for lima beans. I persevered, knowing that someday they would thank me. I never forced my children to eat anything, but I did insist that a spoonful of every dish that was brought to the table be put on every plate. They were encouraged to take a taste. This tactic worked for just about everything but limas and Brussels sprouts. I never got a thank you, but I still say they don't know what they're missing.

1 (10-oz.) package frozen lima beans
1 tablespoon olive oil
2 tablespoons chopped fresh parsley
1 medium onion, chopped
½ teaspoon sugar
1 teaspoon fresh lemon juice

Add beans and a little water to a 1-quart microwave-safe casserole. Cover and microwave on HIGH 4 minutes. Stir and microwave an additional 4 minutes. Drain.

Stir in remaining ingredients. Cover and cook on MEDIUM-HIGH for 2 minutes. Let stand 5 minutes before serving.

MENU: Whole-wheat crackers. Green salad with reduced-calorie cucumber dressing. Papaya slices.

SERVINGS: Makes 4 servings.

Polenta with Mushrooms & Salsa

■ Polenta can now be found in the refrigerated cases in most supermarkets. Polenta, for those who have not sampled it, is essentially cornmeal mush, Italian style. The prepared polenta is sold in a plastic tube—much like breakfast sausage, which makes for easy slicing into rounds. These rounds can be pan-fried or grilled and then topped with a savory sauce.

3 teaspoons olive oil
4 (1-inch) thick rounds prepared polenta
½ cup sliced mushrooms
¾ cup salsa
1 tablespoon chopped fresh cilantro

Heat 1 teaspoon of the oil in a 10-inch skillet over medium heat. Add polenta rounds and brown evenly on both sides, about 4 minutes, turning once. Remove from pan. Keep warm.

Heat remaining 2 teaspoons oil in skillet. Add mushrooms and sauté for 5 minutes. Add salsa and cook until heated through, 1 minute.

Top polenta slices with mushroom mixture and sprinkle with cilantro.

MENU: Escarole with red-wine vinegar and oil and coarsely ground black pepper. Pear slices with golden raisins splashed with pineapple juice.

SERVINGS: Makes 4 servings.

Vegetarian Chili

■ I experimented for a long time to find a satisfying chili that didn't have meat in it. I was finally happy with this recipe which includes fresh mushrooms. The mushrooms provide a wonderful texture that will make the most devoted carnivore forget about beef.

1 tablespoon corn oil
1 pound sliced mushrooms
3 medium onions, chopped
2 cloves garlic, minced
2 jalapeño chiles, seeded and chopped or
   ½ cup canned, chopped chili peppers
2 tablespoons chili powder or ground New
   Mexico chiles
2 teaspoons ground cumin
1 teaspoon dried oregano
1 (14.5-oz.) can Mexican-style stewed
   tomatoes
2 (15-oz.) cans red kidney beans, drained

Heat oil in a 5-quart saucepan or Dutch oven over medium heat. Add mushrooms and cook 1 minute. Add onions, garlic, and chiles and cook 2 minutes or until soft.

Stir in chili powder, cumin, oregano, tomatoes, and beans. Simmer 10 minutes.

MENU: Corn chips. Cucumber slices with ranch dressing. Apple slices sprinkled with lemon juice and granulated brown sugar.

SERVINGS: Makes 6 servings.

In a Pinch Stir-Fry

■ At work one day, I realized that I would not have time to stop at the supermarket on my way home. I did a quick mental inventory of my pantry shelves, which I can always count on for basic ingredients, but the refrigerator produce bins were empty and I hate to serve a meal without something fresh. A stroke of genius! The office lunchroom has a salad bar, why not get the fresh ingredients for a quick stir-fry there?

2 tablespoons hoisin sauce
1 tablespoon rice-wine vinegar
1 tablespoon cornstarch
1 clove garlic, minced
4 teaspoons peanut oil
½ cup prepared sesame noodles (see Note, opposite)
1 large red onion, chopped
½ cup sliced mushrooms
1 red bell pepper, cut into thin slices
1 cup broccoli florets
½ teaspoon sesame seeds

Combine hoisin sauce, vinegar, cornstarch, and garlic in a small bowl. Set aside.

Heat 1 teaspoon of the oil in a 10-inch skillet or wok over medium heat. Add noodles and stir-fry until heated through, about 1 minute. Remove from pan and set aside.

Heat remaining oil in skillet over medium-high heat. Add onion and stir-fry until soft, about 2 minutes. Add mushrooms, bell pepper, and broccoli. Stir-fry until vegetables are crisp-tender, about 2 minutes.

Pour the hoisin sauce mixture over the vegetables and stir-fry until thickened and shiny, about 4 minutes. Add the noodles and sesame seeds and toss to combine.

MENU: Chow mein noodles with duck sauce. Banana slices splashed with rum and coconut.

SERVINGS: Makes 4 servings.

NOTE
If prepared sesame noodles are not available, 4 ounces of cooked, refrigerated fresh spaghetti tossed with 1 tablespoon of soy sauce can be substituted.

Couscous with Cashews

■ Great looks and delicious taste are not the only elements of a great dish. There needs to be a satisfying texture, too. This dish has cashews that provide delightful crunch.

Instant couscous
1 tablespoon peanut oil
1 cup sliced celery
2 scallions, halved and sliced into ½-inch pieces
1 cup sugar snap peas (see Note, page 283)
1 teaspoon fresh marjoram or ½ teaspoon dried
⅛ teaspoon cayenne pepper
¼ cup chopped cashews
¼ cup chopped fresh parsley

Prepare couscous according to package directions to yield 2 cups after cooking.

Meanwhile, heat oil in a 10-inch skillet or wok over medium-high heat. Add celery and scallions and stir-fry until soft, about 2 minutes. Add snap peas, marjoram, and cayenne. Stir-fry for 5 minutes or until vegetables are crisp-tender. Remove from heat and stir in cashews and parsley. Spoon over warm couscous.

MENU: Torn romaine leaves with lemon vinaigrette. Mixed berries dusted with powdered sugar.

SERVINGS: Makes 4 servings.

NOTE

Frozen snap peas can be used, but they should be held under running water to separate. Proceed as directed but increase cooking time to 8 minutes.

Corn with Peppers

■ I don't buy a lot of canned goods, preferring fresh foods in most cases, but there are some items in the canned foods aisle that I find indispensable. Among those are canned tomatoes in all forms, canned corn, and canned beans. Canned corn stars in this dish.

1 (11-oz.) can whole-kernel corn, drained
1 teaspoon apple cider vinegar
2 teaspoons corn oil
1 clove garlic, minced
4 scallions, thinly sliced
¼-inch slice fresh ginger, peeled and shredded
1 red bell pepper, cut into ¼ inch slivers
1 small jalapeño chile, seeded and diced
1 tablespoon fresh cilantro leaves, chopped

Place corn in a medium bowl. Sprinkle with vinegar.

Heat oil in a 10-inch skillet over medium heat. Add garlic, scallions, and ginger and stir-fry 2 minutes. Add bell pepper and jalapeño and stir-fry 1 minute.

Stir in corn and sprinkle with cilantro. Cook until heated through.

MENU: Whole-wheat rolls. Cucumber spears. Ruby red grapefruit sections.

SERVINGS: Makes 4 servings.

Green Bean & Mushroom Stir-Fry

■ It's not hard to find dinner inspiration these days. In only a matter of minutes, almost any vegetable can be steamed or stir-fried to tender-crisp perfection. I'll take stir-fry. Stir-frying seems to take a little longer because everything has to be cut into uniform pieces to ensure even cooking times, but the time is made up in quick cooking once the vegetables are in the wok or frying pan. Don't let the lack of a wok deter you from stir-frying. To tell the truth, I think a frying pan works better on American stoves because the pan is closer to the flame, allowing it to get hotter.

1 tablespoon canola oil
⅔ cup whole almonds
½ pound green beans, trimmed and cut into
    1-inch pieces
4 scallions, cut into ½-inch slices
1 cup sliced mushrooms
2 tablespoons soy sauce
1 garlic clove, minced

Heat oil in large skillet or wok over medium-high heat. Add almonds and stir-fry until lightly toasted, about 1 minute.

Add green beans, scallions, and mushrooms and stir-fry until crisp-tender, about 4 minutes.

Combine soy sauce and garlic in a small bowl; stir into vegetable mixture. Serve immediately.

MENU: Rice cakes and guava paste. Fresh peaches with fresh peach ice cream.

SERVINGS: Makes 4 servings.

Green Beans & Sautéed Mushrooms

■ Mushrooms provide a thick, hearty taste to this simple vegetable mélange.

2 tablespoons olive oil
1 pound sliced mushrooms
1 pound green beans, trimmed and cut in
    half lengthwise
1 teaspoon Dijon mustard
1½ tablespoons fresh lemon juice
Salt and freshly ground black pepper

Heat oil in a 10-inch skillet over medium heat. Add mushrooms and cook for 5 minutes. Add beans, cover pan, and simmer until crisp-tender, about 5 minutes.

Meanwhile, in a large bowl, combine mustard, lemon juice, salt, and pepper. Add mushroom-and-bean mixture and toss well. Serve immediately.

MENU: Rye crackers. Iceberg lettuce with creamy Italian dressing. Red and green seedless grapes.

SERVINGS: Makes 4 servings.

Index

15–Minute Chicken Molé, 110
Alfredo sauce
  Doctored Fettuccine Alfredo, 205
Almonds
  Almond Poppy-Seed Noodles, 181
  Green Bean & Mushroom Stir-Fry, 284
  Raisin-Almond Chicken, 112
  Red Pepper Stir-Fry, 123
  Scallops Amandine, 99
  Sole Amandine, 73
  Warm Chicken & Almond Salad, 253
Alphabet Noodle Soup, 220
Anchovies
  Pasta Puttanesca, 176
  Red Snapper with Anchovies, 66
Angel-Hair Pasta with Fresh Tomatoes,
  189
Angel Hair with Garlic & Hot Pepper, 179
Angel Hair with Tiny Tomatoes, 177
Any-Day Chicken, 105
Apple jelly
  Apple-Wine Chicken, 135
  Braised Pork Chops, 32
Apple juice
  Apple-Dapple Chicken, 106
  Ham Skillet, 35
Apples
  Chicken with Apples, 138
  German Cabbage, 277
  German Sausage & Red Cabbage Skillet,
    38
  Ham Steaks with Cabbage & Apples, 38
  Honey Chicken Salad, 254
  Knockwurst Boiled Dinner, 18
  Oktoberfest Turkey Burgers, 149
  Stir-Fried Apples & Chicken, 108
Apricot chutney
  India Eggs, 159
Apricot jam
  Ham Steak, 36
Apricot preserves
  Dipper's Chicken, 138
Apricots
  Salmon in Apricot Sauce, 60
  Sherry Chicken, 115
  Winter Pork with Fruit, 31
Armenian Patties, 40
Artichoke bottoms
  Hearts & Sole, 72
Artichoke hearts
  Artichoke Pasta Salad, 239
  Tortellini with Artichoke Hearts, 182

Arugula
  Steak & Arugula Salad, 241
Asian Beef Stir-Fry, 10
Asparagus
  Asparagus Stir-Fry, 274
  Beef with Asparagus, 11
  Chicken Asparagus Salad, 256
  Linguine with Asparagus, 174
  Warm Vegetable & Pasta Salad, 260
Avocados
  Crab Salad with Mushrooms, 95
  Shrimp Salad, 257
  Tomato, Avocado, & Crab Soup, 219
  Viva Beef Salad, 16
Avocado Frittata, 166

Baby food
  Baby Food Soup, 229
  Spinach & Leek Soup, 232
Bacon
  Corn Chowder, 225
  Green Bean Pasta, 201
  Halibut Stew, 232
  Hot Cabbage Salad, 249
  Lamb Patties, 43
  Tomato-Bacon Linguine, 194
  Zucchini Soup, 210
Baking mix
  Beer-Battered Shrimp, 89
Balsamic Beef, 4
Bamboo shoots
  Chinese Slaw, 242
  Eggs Fu Yung, 167
Barbecue sauce
  Down-Mexico-Way Chicken, 136
  Red-Wine Barbecued Chicken, 135
  Spicy Lamb Chops, 41
Barbecue spice
  Down & Dirty Shrimp, 91
Basil
  Basil Chicken, 132
  Camembert Angel Hair, 187
  Corn & Summer Squash Soup, 234
  Herb Garden Spaghetti, 199
  Lemon-Basil Halibut, 55
  Lemon-Pepper Pasta, 183
  Pasta with Jersey Tomato Sauce, 184
  Ravioli with Zucchini, 202–203
  Summer Linguine, 183
  Tomato-Bacon Linguine, 194
  Tortellini with Sun-Dried Tomatoes, 190
  Vodka-Basil Fettucine, 179

Bavarian Dinner, 35
Bean sprouts
  Beef & Napa Cabbage Salad, 261
  Chicken Salad with Yogurt Dressing, 244
  Chinese Spaghetti, 202
  Eggs Fu Yung, 167
  Turkey Chow Mein, 155
Beans
  Bean & Olive Salad, 264
  Bean & Tuna Salad, 246
  Bean Ravioli, 180
  Bean Soup, 224
  Bean Tortilla Soup, 218
  Bean Vegetable Soup, 236
  Black Bean & Chicken Salad, 250–251
  Black Bean Salad, 247
  Bourbon Black Bean Soup, 212
  Chicken & Bean Burritos, 140
  Chili con Pollo, 137
  Chorizo Black Bean Soup, 217
  Corn & Lima Beans, 270
  Couscous Salad, 263
  Dinner & Lunch Bean Salad, 241
  Greek Isles Tuna Salad, 256
  Green Bean & Mushroom Stir-Fry, 284
  Green Bean & Tomato Stew, 276
  Green Bean Pasta, 201
  Green Bean Stir-Fry, 279
  Green Beans & Sautéed Mushrooms, 284
  Green Beans, Indian Style, 268
  Hot Black Beans, 276
  Italian Bean Salad, 239
  Lemony Bean Soup, 209
  Lemony Lima Beans, 280
  Middle Eastern Salad, 245
  Pantry Bean Soup, 221
  Quick Baked Beans, 280
  Red Beans & Rice, 217
  Sauerkraut Soup, 223
  Smoked Whitefish Salad, 260
  Spicy Veggies, 271
  Spur-of-the-Moment Chili, 15
  Stewed Garbanzos, 267
  Summer Bean Salad, 262
  Swiss Salad, 247
  Three-Bean Stew, 234
  Vegetable Skillet Supper, 273
  Vegetarian Chili, 281
  Warm Bean & Tuna Salad, 248
  Warm Chicken Salad, 255
  White Bean & Tomato Mélange, 268
  White Bean Salad, 264

Beef & Veal, 1–22
Beef, cooked
    Beef Fajitas, 12
    Beef & Napa Cabbage Salad, 261
Beef, corned
    Pantry Bean Soup, 221
    Red Flannel Hash, 12
Beef, ground
    Beef with Cabbage, 17
    Beef with Cabbage & Carrots, 16
    Hamburger Skillet, 17
    Sautéed Beef with Onions, 14–15
    Sesame Burgers, 15
    Spur-of-the-Moment Chili, 15
    Viva Beef Salad, 16
Beef gravy
    Meatballs with Burgundy Sauce, 14
Beef steak
    Asian Beef Stir-Fry, 10
    Beef, Pepper, & Onion Stir-Fry, 11
    Beef Stir-Fry, 3
    Beef with Asparagus, 11
    Beef with Leeks & Mushrooms, 10
    Blue Cheese Steak Salad, 250
    Chili Steak, 6
    Garden Steak, 7
    Great Steaks with Mushroom Topping, 4
    Grillades, 5
    Italian Steak Salad, 258
    Lemon Flank Steak, 9
    Pepper Steak, 9
    Spicy Minute Steaks, 6
    Steak & Arugula Salad, 241
    Steak Bourguignonne, 8
    Three-Pepper Steak, 7
    Stir-Fry Salad, 244
    Warm London Broil Salad, 257
Beef tenderloin
    Beef Sauté, 8
    Deviled Steak, 5
    Balsamic Beef, 4
Beer
    Bavarian Dinner, 35
    Beer-Battered Shrimp, 89
    Hot Black Beans, 276
    Kielbasa with Cabbage, 19
Beets
    Red Flannel Hash, 12
Belgian endive
    Beef Sauté, 8
Bell peppers
    Asian Beef Stir-Fry, 10
    Beef Fajitas, 12
    Beef, Pepper, & Onion Stir-Fry, 11
    Black Bean & Chicken Salad, 250–251
    Cajun Chicken, 122
    Chicken & Peppers, 129
    Chicken Italiano, 107
    Chinese Spaghetti, 202
    Cod, Asian Style, 48
    Corn & Chicken Salad, 255
    Corn & Mushroom Scramble, 165
    Corn with Peppers, 283
    Curried Vegetables, 269
    Down-Mexico Chicken, 136
    Halibut Ragu, 56
    Honeyed Pork Stir-Fry, 27
    Hot Linguine, 200
    Hotcha Halibut, 57

Huevos Rancheros, 164
Island Black Bean Stew, 218
Lettuce Stir-Fry, 94
Linguine with Roasted Bell Peppers, 180
Mexican Soup, 219
Mushroom Noodle Soup, 214
Ocean Deep Soup, 213
Pepper Spaghetti, 200
Pepper Steak, 9
Pepperoni Pasta, 182
Peppers with Sole, 70
Pork & Black Bean Sauce, 29
Pork Chops with Peppers, 30
Ratatouille, 279
Ravioli with Zucchini, 202–203
Red Beans & Rice, 217
Red Pepper Cod, 49
Red Pepper Soup, 231
Red Pepper Stir-Fry, 123
Salad Bar Spaghetti, 198
Salad Bar Stir-Fry, 275
Scallop & Cauliflower Salad, 254
Scallop Soup, 222–223
Scallops & Pasta, 185
Scallops & Peppers, 100
Shells & Broccoli, 196
Shrimp Casserole, 91
Southwestern Stir-Fry, 274
Spanish Clams, 81
Spicy Veggies, 271
Stir-Fried Cauliflower & Sweet Peppers, 271
Stir-Fried Chicken Burritos, 109
Stir-Fry Salad, 244
Sweet & Sour Chicken, 119
Three-Pepper Steak, 7
Turkey Cutlets with Sun-Dried Tomatoes,
    149
Warm Vegetable & Pasta Salad, 260
White Bean Salad, 264
Thyme Shrimp & Broccoli Stir-Fry, 85
Vegetable Skillet Supper, 273
Vermicelli & Turkey with White Wine Sauce,
    186
Black Bean & Chicken Salad, 250–251
Black Bean Salad, 247
Black bean paste
    Chinese Burgers, 34
Black bean sauce
    Pork & Black Bean Sauce, 29
Black bean sauce
    Turkey Stir-Fry with Tofu, 155
Black bean soup
    Chorizo Black Bean Soup, 217
Blue Cheese Steak Salad, 250
Bourbon Black Bean Soup, 212
Braised Pork Chops, 32
Bread crumbs
    Broiled Lemon Sole, 73
    Citrus Fish, 72
    Eggplant Neapolitan, 275
    Limey Fillets, 50
    Scallops Dijon, 101
    Sole with Lemon Sauce, 70
    Turkey Tenderloins Dijon, 145
Broccoli
    Artichoke Pasta Salad, 239
    Bean & Tuna Salad, 246
    Beef Stir-Fry, 3
    In a Pinch Stir-Fry, 282

Broccoli & Mushroom Spaghetti, 190
Broccoli & Rotini, 201
Broccoli Salad, 239
Chicken Salad with Yogurt Dressing, 244
Chicken with Broccoli, 116
Chili-Chicken Stir-Fry, 120
Parmesan-Basil Vegetable Salad, 246
Salad Bar Spaghetti, 198
Scrambled Eggs with Shrimp, Tomato, &
    Broccoli, 168
Shells & Broccoli, 196
Stir-Fried Vegetables & Peanuts, 272
Thyme Shrimp & Broccoli Stir-Fry, 85
Tortellini with Chicken & Broccoli, 193
Broiled Lemon Sole, 73
Broiled Salmon Steaks, 61
Broiled Scallops, 98
Broiled Turkey Tenderloins, 145
Broiled Whitefish, 77
Browned Pork with Capers, 31
Brussels Sprouts & Carrots, 277
Buffalo Drumsticks, 134
Burgers
    Chinese Burgers, 34
    Oktoberfest Turkey Burgers, 149
    Sesame Burgers, 15
    Teriyaki Burgers, 153
Buttermilk
    Tomato Bisque, 231

Cabbage
    Beef & Napa Cabbage Salad, 261
    Beef with Cabbage & Carrots, 16
    Broccoli Salad, 239
    Cabbage & Cheese Salad, 251
    Cabbage Kielbasa Soup, 228–229
    Cantonese Chicken Salad, 252
    German Sausage & Red Cabbage Skillet, 38
    Honeyed Pork Stir-Fry, 27
    Kielbasa with Cabbage, 19
    Knockwurst Boiled Dinner, 18
    One-Dish German Dinner, 34
    Stir-Fry Salad, 244
Cajun Chicken, 122
Camembert Angel Hair, 187
Cantaloupe
    Tarragon Chicken Salad, 259
Capers
    Pork with Capers, 31
    Chicken in Caper Sauce, 105
    Clams with Scallions & Parsley, 81
    Pasta Puttanesca, 176
    Trout with Caper Sauce, 76
Carrots
    Parmesan-Basil Vegetable Salad, 246
    Bavarian Dinner, 35
    Beef with Cabbage & Carrots, 16
    Brussels Sprouts & Carrots, 277
    Cabbage Kielbasa Soup, 228–229
    Cantonese Chicken Salad, 252
    Carrots & Cauliflower, 278
    Chicken Pasta, 192
    Corn & Tuna Salad, 243
    Curried Vegetables, 269
    Easy Chicken Supper, 111
    Green Beans, Indian Style, 268
    Hot Chicken Salad, 141
    Knockwurst Boiled Dinner, 18
    Sesame Chicken Salad, 258

Shrimp Salad, 257
Spicy Veggies, 271
Stir-Fried Vegetables & Peanuts, 272
Vegetable Beef Soup, 236
Cashews
Chili-Chicken Stir-Fry, 120
Chinese Slaw, 242
Couscous with Cashews, 282–283
Hot, Hot Chicken with Cashews, 112
Catfish
Deviled Catfish, 47
Fish Stew, 225
Pecan Catfish, 47
Cauliflower
Carrots & Cauliflower, 278
Parmesan-Basil Vegetable Salad, 246
Scallop & Cauliflower Salad, 254
Stir-Fried Cauliflower & Sweet Peppers, 271
Stir-Fry Salad, 244
Celery
Bean Vegetable Soup, 236
Corn & Chicken Salad, 255
Couscous Salad, 263
Couscous with Cashews, 282–283
Curried Vegetables, 269
Fish Stew, 225
Honey Chicken Salad, 254
Salad Bar Stir-Fry, 275
Stir-Fried Vegetables & Peanuts, 272
Summer Bean Salad, 262
Turkey Chow Mein, 155
Vegetable Stew, 273
Celery soup
Salmon Chowder, 227
Cheese
Angel-Hair Pasta with Fresh Tomatoes, 189
Angel Hair with Tiny Tomatoes, 177
Artichoke Pasta Salad, 239
Avocado Frittata, 166
Bean Ravioli, 180
Blue Cheese Steak Salad, 250
Broccoli & Mushroom Spaghetti, 190
Broccoli & Rotini, 201
Broccoli Salad, 239
Cabbage & Cheese Salad, 251
Camembert Angel Hair, 187
Chicken & Bean Burritos, 140
Chicken & Eggplant Italiano, 137
Chicken & Spinach Italiano, 133
Chicken Italiano, 107
Chicken Mozzarella, 139
Chicken Parmesan, 114
Chicken Quesadillas, 141
Chili con Pollo, 137
Chili-Topped Potatoes, 3
Chive-Cheese Scramble, 166
Eggplant Neapolitan, 275
Eggs in Spring, 169
Eggs Italiano, 161
Fettuccine & Vegetables, 204
Fig & Feta Salad, 262
Florentine Frittata, 160
Gnocchi with Sauce Verde, 187
Greek Isles Tuna Salad, 256
Greek Salad, 261
Gruyére Omelet, 159
Herb Garden Spaghetti, 199
Hot Pepper Ravioli, 175
Italian Bean Salad, 239

Italian Steak Salad, 258
Jalapeño Frittata, 167
Kraut Brats, 18–19
Lemon & Garlic Linguine, 191
Lemon-Pepper Pasta, 183
Linguine with Asparagus, 174
Mexican Rice & Turkey, 154
Mexican Soup, 219
Mexican Turkey, 146
Nacho Eggs, 163
Oktoberfest Turkey Burgers, 149
Olé Omelet, 162
Onion & Cheese Soup, 222
Pasta & Cappicola, 188
Pasta with Salad Sauce, 240
Pizza Pasta, 205
Salmon on Leeks, 62
Salsa Chicken, 131
Salsa Eggs, 169
Sardine Raclette, 64
Shells & Broccoli, 196
Shrimp Quesadilla, 92
Spanish Rice, 153
Spanish Tortilla, 160
Spinach Pasta, 195
Summer Chicken, 127
Swiss Salad, 247
Tomato & Cheese Fillets, 65
Tortellini with Chicken & Broccoli, 193
Tortellini with Sun-Dried Tomatoes, 190
Turkey & Chanterelles, 150
Turkey Pizza, 148
Veal with Prosciutto, 20
Viva Beef Salad, 16
Zucchini Pasta, 184
Chicken, 103–142
Chicken breasts
15-Minute Chicken Molé, 110
Any-Day Chicken, 105
Apple-Dapple Chicken, 106
Cajun Chicken, 122
Chicken & Olives, 115
Chicken & Peppers, 129
Chicken & Zucchini, 121
Chicken Cacciatore, 113
Chicken from the Orient, 127
Chicken Italiano, 107
Chicken Parmesan, 114
Chicken Piccata, 113
Chicken Stir-Fry, 116
Chicken with Broccoli, 116
Chicken with Mushrooms, 125
Chicken with Zinfandel Baste, 118
Chili Chicken, 124
Chili Chicken Stir-Fry, 120
Chinese Barbecued Chicken, 121
Curried Chicken, 129
Deviled Chicken, 111
Easy Chicken Supper, 111
Five-Spice Chicken with Walnuts, 118
Garlic Chicken, 123
Garlic Lovers' Chicken, 110
Guilty Chicken in Mushroom Sauce, 128
Herbed Chicken with Lemon, 130
Herbed Chicken, 125
Honeyed Chicken, 114
Hot, Hot Chicken with Cashews, 112
Lemon Chicken, 124
Macadamia Chicken, 107

Maple Chicken, 108
Mediterranean Chicken, 130
Orange Chicken Salad, 117
Orange-Onion Chicken with Couscous, 106
Pasta for a Summer Night, 198
Raisin-Almond Chicken, 112
Red Pepper Stir-Fry, 123
Salsa Chicken, 131
Shanghai Chicken Fettuccine, 173
Spicy Chicken with Hoisin Sauce, 131
Spicy Yogurt Chicken, 128
Stir-Fried Apples & Chicken, 108
Stir-Fried Chicken Burritos, 109
Summer Chicken, 127
Sweet & Sour Chicken, 119
Tarragon Chicken, 122
Teriyaki Honey Chicken, 117
Warm Chicken Salad, 255
Zesty Lemon Chicken, 120
Chicken, cooked
Black Bean & Chicken Salad, 251
Cantonese Chicken Salad, 252
Chicken & Bean Burritos, 140
Chicken & Pear Salad, 253
Chicken Asparagus Salad, 256
Chicken Fruit Salad, 259
Chicken Oodles of Noodles Soup, 215
Chicken Pasta, 192
Chicken Quesadillas, 141
Chicken Salad with Yogurt Dressing, 244
Chicken Spinach Soup, 216
Citrus Chicken Salad, 242
Cold Yogurt Soup, 230
Corn & Chicken Salad, 255
Creamed Chicken, 140
Cucumber-Chicken Soup, 215
Honey Chicken Salad, 254
Hot & Spicy Chicken, 142
Hot Chicken Salad, 141
Lemon Soup, 213
Senegalese Soup, 228
Sesame Chicken Salad, 258
Tarragon Chicken Salad, 259
Tortellini with Chicken & Broccoli, 193
Warm Chicken & Almond Salad, 253
Chicken drumsticks
Buffalo Drumsticks, 134
Red-Wine Barbecued Chicken, 135
Chicken, ground
Chicken & Eggplant Italiano, 137
Chicken Vermicelli, 199
Chicken with Apples, 138
Chili con Pollo, 137
Chicken gravy
Raisin-Almond Chicken, 112
Chicken Livers & Ravioli, 197
Chicken nuggets
Chicken Tidbits with Pineapple Sauce, 139
Dipper's Chicken, 138
Chicken patties
Chicken Mozzarella, 139
Chicken thighs
Apple-Wine Chicken, 135
Basil Chicken, 132
Chicken & Spinach Italiano, 133
Down-Mexico Chicken, 136
Hot Sherried Chicken Thighs, 133
Hungarian Chicken Thighs, 132

Chicken thighs (continued)
    Lime-Soy Chicken, 134
    Sunshine-Glazed Chicken Thighs, 136
Chicory Salad, 262
Chiles
    Bean Tortilla Soup, 218
    Chinese Hot Clams, 82
    Corn with Peppers, 283
    Down-Mexico Chicken, 136
    Hot Black Beans, 276
    Jalapeño Frittata, 167
    Mexican Rice & Turkey, 154
    Mexican Soup, 219
    Nacho Eggs, 163
    Olé Omelet, 162
    Tossed Tuna Salad, 248
    Southwestern Stir-Fry, 274
    Vegetarian Chili, 281
Chili Chicken, 124
Chili con Pollo, 137
Chili oil
    Chili-Chicken Stir-Fry, 120
Chili paste
    Sichuan Scallops, 96
Chili Steak, 6
Chili
    Chili con Pollo, 137
    Spur-of-the-Moment Chili, 15
    Vegetarian Chili, 281
Chili-Topped Potatoes, 3
    Chili-Topped Potatoes, 3
Chinese Barbecued Chicken, 121
Chinese Burgers, 34
Chinese Hot Clams, 82
Chinese Pork Chops, 27
Chinese Slaw, 242
Chinese Spaghetti, 202
Chives
    Chive-Cheese Scramble, 166
    Curried Tomato Soup, 235
    Flounder with Chives, 53
    Salmon with Chive Butter, 60
Chorizo Black Bean Soup, 217
Cilantro
    Cilantro Scallops, 97
    Creamy Shrimp Fettuccine, 174
    Flounder with Cilantro Butter, 52
    Flounder with Cilantro Sauce, 51
    Meatballs with Cilantro Dipping Sauce, 13
Citrus Chicken Salad, 242
Citrus Fish, 72
Clam juice
    Clam Noodle Soup, 210
    Fish Stew, 225
    Scallop Soup, 222–223
    Thyme Shrimp & Broccoli Stir-Fry, 85
Clams
    Chinese Hot Clams, 82
    Clam Noodle Soup, 210
    Clams Italiano, 82
    Clams with Scallions & Parsley, 81
    Linguine with Hot Clam Sauce, 186
    Shellfish Pasta, 197
    Spanish Clams, 81
Cocoa powder
    15–Minute Chicken Molé, 110
Cod
    Cod with Parsley Butter, 48
    Cod, Asian Style, 48

Garlic Lovers' Cod, 49
Greek Fish, 50
Limey Fillets, 50
Red Pepper Cod, 49
Coffee
    Ham with Red-Eye Gravy, 36–37
Cold Yogurt Soup, 230
Coleslaw mix
    Beef with Cabbage, 17
    Chinese Slaw, 242
    German Cabbage, 277
    Ham Skillet, 35
    Ham Steaks with Cabbage & Apples, 38
    Hot Cabbage Salad, 249
    Hot Chicken Salad, 141
    Pork with Noodles Soup, 209
    Sausage & Noodles, 204
    Tomato-Cabbage Soup, 223
Corn
    Black Bean & Chicken Salad, 250–251
    Black Bean Salad, 247
    Chicken Asparagus Salad, 256
    Corn & Lima Beans, 270
    Corn & Mushroom Scramble, 165
    Corn & Summer Squash Soup, 234
    Corn & Tuna Salad, 243
    Corn Chowder, 225
    Corn with Peppers, 283
    Halibut Stew, 232
    Ham Steak, 36
    Mexican Rice & Turkey, 154
    Mexican Soup, 219
    Pantry Bean Soup, 221
    Scrambled Eggs with Ham & Corn, 164
    Sesame Chicken Salad, 258
    Southern Ham & Vegetable Dinner, 39
    Southwestern Stir-Fry, 274
    Vegetable Stew, 273
    Warm Chicken Salad, 255
Couscous
    Couscous Salad, 263
    Couscous with Cashews, 282–283
    Curry Couscous, 188
    Orange-Onion Chicken with Couscous, 106
    Salmon with Couscous, 181
Crab
    Crab Imperial, 95
    Crab Salad with Mushrooms, 95
    Crab Soup, 230
    Eggs Fu Yung, 167
    Tarragon Crab, 94
    Tomato, Avocado, & Crab Soup, 219
Cream of Tomato Soup, 216
Creamed Chicken, 140
Cream
    Flounder with Cilantro Sauce, 51
    Lobster Stew, 233
    Oyster Pan Roast, 226
Creamy Shrimp Fettuccine, 174
Creole Peanut Butter Soup, 233
Cucumbers
    Cold Yogurt Soup, 230
    Cucumber-Chicken Soup, 215
    Cucumber Soup with Tomatoes, 221
    Cucumbers & Tomato Skillet, 269
    Cucumber-Dill Soup, 220
    Fettuccine & Vegetables, 204
    Greek Salad, 261
    Middle Eastern Salad, 245

Salmon Chowder, 227
Salmon with Cucumber Sauce, 59
Spinach, Tuna, & Shrimp Salad, 250
Stir-Fried Sugar Snap Peas & Cucumbers, 270
Summer Bean Salad, 262
Tomato-Yogurt Soup, 212
Curry powder
    Curried Chicken, 129
    Curried Flounder, 53
    Curried Shrimp, 88
    Curried Tomato Soup, 235
    Curried Turkey, 148
    Curried Vegetables, 269
    Curry Couscous, 188
    Senegalese Soup, 228

Daikon Salad, 263
Dates
    Honey Chicken Salad, 254
Deli Scramble, 162
Deviled Catfish, 47
Deviled Chicken, 111
Deviled Steak, 5
Dill
    Cucumber-Dill Soup, 220
    Cucumbers & Tomato Skillet, 269
    Eggs in Spring, 169
    Mustard & Dill-Basted Salmon, 59
    Trout with Dill, 75
    Tuna Garden Salad, 249
Dinner & Lunch Bean Salad, 241
Dipper's Chicken, 138
Doctored Fettuccine Alfredo, 205
Down & Dirty Shrimp, 91
Down-Mexico Chicken, 136

Easy Chicken Supper, 111
Eggplant
    Chicken & Eggplant Italiano, 137
    Eggplant Neapolitan, 275
    Garden Steak, 7
    Ratatouille, 279
Egg safety, 157
Eggs, 157–169
Eggs, scrambled
    Chive-Cheese Scramble, 166
    Corn & Mushroom Scramble, 165
    Deli Scramble, 162
    Mexican Scrambled Eggs, 161
    Scrambled Eggs with Ham & Corn, 164
    Scrambled Eggs with Shrimp, Tomato, &
        Broccoli, 168
    Shrimp Egg Scramble, 93
    Snow Peas & Peanut Scramble, 168
End-of-Summer Stir-Fry, 146
Escarole
    Escarole & Pasta Soup, 227
    Italian Steak Salad, 258

Fennel
    Mahi-Mahi in Fennel Sauce, 57
    Trout with Fennel, 75
Fettuccine & Vegetables, 204
Fig & Feta Salad, 262
Fish broth
    Ocean Deep Soup, 213
Fish Mexicano, 54
Fish Stew, 225
Fish, 45–77

Fish (*See* individual species)
Five-spice powder
  Five-Spice Chicken with Walnuts, 118
  Five-Spice Snapper, 69
Florentine Frittata, 160
Flounder
  Curried Flounder, 53
  Flounder with Chives, 53
  Flounder with Cilantro Butter, 52
  Flounder with Cilantro Sauce, 51
  Marjoram-Scented Flounder Fillets, 52
  Sunshine Fish, 51
Fresh Mushroom Soup, 214
Frittatas
  Avocado Frittata, 166
  Florentine Frittata, 160
  Jalapeño Frittata, 167
Fruit & Vegetable Medley Salad, 244
Fusion Sausages, 37

Garlic
  Angel Hair with Garlic & Hot Pepper, 179
  Garlic & Rosemary Veal Chops, 21
  Garlic Chicken, 123
  Garlic-Lemon Fillets, 69
  Garlic Lovers' Chicken, 110
  Garlic Lovers' Cod, 49
  Garlic Pasta, 196
  Garlic Shrimp, 86
  Garlic Shrimp with Linguine & Lime, 173
  Garlic Soup, 211
  Hot Garlic & Oil Pasta, 189
  Lemon & Garlic Linguine, 191
  Shrimp Scampi, 87
  Sichuan Scallops, 96
  Steamed Mussels & Herbs, 84
German Cabbage, 277
German Sausage & Red Cabbage Skillet, 38
Ginger
  Chicken Spinach Soup, 216
  Chinese Burgers, 34
  Ginger Scallops, 97
  Ginger Shrimp, 94
  Hot Sherried Chicken Thighs, 133
  Hot, Hot Chicken with Cashews, 112
  Orange-Ginger Lamb Chops, 42
  Pineapple Swordfish, 74
  Pork with Orange Sauce, 28
  Scented Lamb Chops, 39
  Sichuan Scallops, 96
  Snow Peas & Peanut Scramble, 168
  Winter Pork with Fruit, 31
Gnocchi with Sauce Verde, 187
Golden Shrimp, 86
Grape jelly
  German Sausage & Red Cabbage Skillet, 38
Grapefruit
  Citrus Chicken Salad, 242
Grapes
  Chicken Fruit Salad, 259
Great Steaks with Mushroom Topping, 4
Greek Fish, 50
Greek Isles Tuna Salad, 256
Greek Salad, 261
Green Bean & Tomato Stew, 276
Green Bean Pasta, 201
Green Bean Stir-Fry, 279
Green Beans & Sautéed Mushrooms, 284
Green Beans, Indian Style, 268

Green Fish, 71
Grillades, 5
Grilled Seafood Salad, 243
Gruyére Omelet, 159
Guilty Chicken in Mushroom Sauce, 128

Haddock
  Fish Mexicano, 54
  Haddock with Olives, 54
  Ocean Deep Soup, 213
Half-and-half
  Baby Food Soup, 229
  Chive-Cheese Scramble, 166
  Corn & Summer Squash Soup, 234
  Crab Soup, 230
  Eggs in Spring, 169
  Fresh Mushroom Soup, 214
  Olé Omelet, 162
  Onion & Cheese Soup, 222
  Scallops & Pasta, 185
  Senegalese Soup, 228
  Spinach & Leek Soup, 232
  Turkey & Chanterelles, 150
Halibut
  Grilled Seafood Salad, 243
  Halibut Broil, 55
  Halibut in Wine, 56
  Halibut Ragu, 56
  Halibut Stew, 232
  Lemon-Basil Halibut, 55
  Southwestern Halibut, 57
Ham
  Cabbage & Cheese Salad, 251
  Garlic Shrimp, 86
  Ham Skillet, 35
  Ham Steak, 36
  Ham Steaks with Cabbage & Apples, 38
  Ham with Red-Eye Gravy, 36–37
  Scrambled Eggs with Ham & Corn, 164
  Southern Ham & Vegetable Dinner, 39
  Spanish Clams, 81
Hamburger Skillet, 17
Hawaiian Lamb Chops, 42
Herb Garden Spaghetti, 199
Herbal Turkey Patties, 154
Herbed Chicken, 125
Herbed Chicken with Lemon, 130
Herbed Squash, 278
Hoisin sauce
  Chicken from the Orient, 127
  Chinese Barbecued Chicken, 121
  Chinese Pork Chops, 27
  In a Pinch Stir-Fry, 282
  Shanghai Chicken Fettuccine, 173
  Spicy Chicken with Hoisin Sauce, 131
Honey
  Curried Turkey, 148
  Honey Chicken Salad, 254
  Honeyed Chicken, 114
  Honeyed Pork Stir-Fry, 27
  Sunshine-Glazed Chicken Thighs, 136
Horseradish
  Chicken Tidbits with Pineapple Sauce, 139
  Chicken with Broccoli, 116
  Deviled Catfish, 47
  Dipper's Chicken, 138
  Mandarin Chicken, 126
Hot & Spicy Chicken, 142

Hot Black Beans, 276
Hot Cabbage Salad, 249
Hot Chicken Salad, 141
Hot Garlic & Oil Pasta, 189
Hot Linguine, 200
Hot Pepper Ravioli, 175
Hot Sherried Chicken Thighs, 133
Hot Shrimp, 92–93
Hot, Hot Chicken with Cashews, 112
Huevos Rancheros, 164
Hungarian Chicken Thighs, 132

In a Pinch Stir-Fry, 282
India Eggs, 159
Island Black Bean Stew, 218
Italian Bean Salad, 239
Italian Steak Salad, 258

Jalapeño Frittata, 167
Jicama
  Black Bean Salad, 247
  Tomato, Avocado, & Crab Soup, 219

Kielbasa Soup, 226
Kielbasa with Cabbage, 19
Knockwurst Boiled Dinner, 18
Kraut Brats, 18–19

Lamb chops
  Hawaiian Lamb Chops, 42
  Lamb with Yogurt Mint Sauce, 41
  Lemon & Garlic Lamb Chops, 40
  Orange-Ginger Lamb Chops, 42
  Scented Lamb Chops, 39
  Spicy Lamb Chops, 41
  Thyme Lamb Chops, 43
Lamb, ground
  Armenian Patties, 40
  Lamb Patties, 43
Leek soup mix
  Spinach & Leek Soup, 232
Leeks
  Beef with Leeks & Mushrooms, 10
  Leek & Mushroom Soup, 224
  Salmon on Leeks, 62
Lemon
  Broiled Lemon Sole, 73
  Broiled Whitefish, 77
  Cucumber Soup with Tomatoes, 221
  Down & Dirty Shrimp, 91
  Garlic-Lemon Fillets, 69
  Ginger Scallops, 97
  Greek Fish, 50
  Grilled Seafood Salad, 243
  Herbed Chicken with Lemon, 130
  Lemon & Garlic Lamb Chops, 40
  Lemon & Garlic Linguine, 191
  Lemon-Basil Halibut, 55
  Lemon Chicken, 124
  Lemon Flank Steak, 9
  Lemon-Nut Pork Chops, 26
  Lemon-Pepper Pasta, 183
  Lemon Soup, 213
  Lemon Teriyaki Salmon, 63
  Marjoram-Scented Flounder Fillets, 52
  Sherry Shrimp, 87
  Sole Amandine, 73
  Sole with Lemon Sauce, 70
  Soy-Lemon Pork Chops, 28

Lemon (*continued*)
  Sunshine Fish, 51
  Turkey Piquant, 152
Lemony Bean Soup, 209
Lemony Lima Beans, 280
Zesty Lemon Chicken, 120
Lime
  Fish Mexicano, 54
  Lime-Cumin Pork Chops, 26
  Limey Fillets, 50
  Salmon with Couscous, 181
  Salmon with Salsa, 58
  Lime-Soy Chicken, 134
Linguine with Asparagus, 174
Linguine with Hot Clam Sauce, 186
Linguine with Roasted Bell Peppers, 180
Linguine with Tomato & Basil Sauce, 203
Lobster Stew, 233

Macadamia nuts
  Lemon-Nut Pork Chops, 26
  Macadamia Chicken, 107
Mahi-Mahi in Fennel Sauce, 57
Main-Dish Salads, 237–264
Mandarin Chicken, 126
Maple syrup
  Maple Chicken, 108
Marinara sauce
  Chicken Mozzarella, 139
  Clams Italiano, 82
  Eggs Italiano, 161
  Fish Stew, 225
  Huevos Rancheros, 164
  Mediterranean Snapper, 67
  Mediterranean Turkey with Olives, 151
  Red Snapper with Anchovies, 66
  Scallops with Angel Hair, 178
  Sole in Tomato Sauce, 74
  Turkey & Peppers, Italian Style, 152
Marjoram-Scented Flounder Fillets, 52
Meatballs & Ravioli, 13
Meatballs with Burgundy Sauce, 14
Meatballs with Cilantro Dipping Sauce, 13
Mediterranean Chicken, 130
Mediterranean Snapper, 67
Mediterranean Turkey with Olives, 151
Mexican Rice & Turkey, 154
Mexican Scrambled Eggs, 161
Mexican Soup, 219
Mexican Turkey, 146
Middle Eastern Salad, 245
Mint
  Herb Garden Spaghetti, 199
  Lamb with Yogurt Mint Sauce, 41
  Middle Eastern Salad, 245
Mixed vegetables
  Alphabet Noodle Soup, 220
  Hamburger Skillet, 17
Mushroom gravy
  Steak Bourguignonne, 8
Mushrooms
  Angel Hair with Tiny Tomatoes, 177
  Asian Beef Stir-Fry, 10
  Avocado Frittata, 166
  Beef with Leeks & Mushrooms, 10
  Broccoli & Mushroom Spaghetti, 190
  Broccoli Salad, 239
  Chicken Asparagus Salad, 256
  Chicken Stir-Fry, 116

Chicken Vermicelli, 199
Chicken with Mushrooms, 125
Corn & Mushroom Scramble, 165
Crab Salad with Mushrooms, 95
Daikon Salad, 263
Deli Scramble, 162
Escarole & Pasta Soup, 227
Florentine Frittata, 160
Fresh Mushroom Soup, 214
Fruit & Vegetable Medley Salad, 244
Garden-Style Tuna Steak, 76
Great Steaks with Mushroom Topping, 4
Green Bean & Mushroom Stir-Fry, 284
Green Bean & Tomato Stew, 276
Green Beans & Sautéed Mushrooms, 284
Guilty Chicken in Mushroom Sauce, 128
In a Pinch Stir-Fry, 282
Leek & Mushroom Soup, 224
Linguine with Tomato & Basil Sauce,
  203
Meatballs with Burgundy Sauce, 14
Mushroom Noodle Soup, 214
Pasta for a Summer Night, 198
Pasta with Salad Sauce, 240
Peppers with Sole, 70
Polenta with Mushrooms & Salsa, 281
Red Pepper Cod, 49
Salad Bar Spaghetti, 198
Salad Bar Stir-Fry, 275
Sausage & Linguine, 192
Sautéed Beef with Onions, 14–15
Scallop & Cauliflower Salad, 254
Shrimp Casserole, 91
Snow Peas & Peanut Scramble, 168
Tarragon Chicken, 122
Tarragon Veal, 20
Three-Bean Stew, 234
Three-Pepper Steak, 7
Turkey & Chanterelles, 150
Turkey Chow Mein, 155
Turkey Cutlets with Sun-Dried Tomatoes,
  149
Turkey Pizza, 148
Veal Marsala, 19
Vegetarian Chili, 281
Zesty Lemon Chicken, 120
Mussels
  Mussels Mariniére, 85
  Mussels Steamed in Wine, 83
  Mussels with Mustard Sauce, 84
  Shellfish Pasta, 197
  Steamed Mussels & Herbs, 84
Mustard seeds
  Green Beans, Indian Style, 268
Mustard
  Broccoli & Rotini, 201
  Deviled Catfish, 47
  Deviled Chicken, 111
  Dipper's Chicken, 138
  Hawaiian Lamb Chops, 42
  Hungarian Chicken Thighs, 132
  Mussels with Mustard Sauce, 84
  Mustard & Dill-Basted Salmon, 59
  Mustard Scrod, 66
  Pecan Catfish, 47
  Pork with Orange Sauce, 28
  Scallops Dijon, 101
  Scallops with Lemon Mustard, 96
  Spicy Minute Steaks, 6

Turkey Tenderloins Dijon, 145
Veal with Onions, 21

Nacho Eggs, 163
Nectarines
  Warm Chicken & Almond Salad, 253
Noodles
  Beef Stir-Fry, 3
  Chicken Oodles of Noodles Soup, 215
  In a Pinch Stir-Fry, 282
  Mushroom Noodle Soup, 214
  Pork with Noodles Soup, 209

Ocean Deep Soup, 213
Okra
  Southern Ham & Vegetable Dinner, 39
Oktoberfest Turkey Burgers, 149
Olé Omelet, 162
Olives
  Artichoke Pasta Salad, 239
  Bean & Olive Salad, 264
  Chicken & Olives, 115
  Chicken Parmesan, 114
  Citrus Chicken Salad, 242
  Fig & Feta Salad, 262
  Greek Fish, 50
  Greek Isles Tuna Salad, 256
  Greek Salad, 261
  Haddock with Olives, 54
  Italian Bean Salad, 239
  Jalapeño Frittata, 167
  Linguine with Roasted Bell Peppers, 180
  Mediterranean Turkey with Olives, 151
  Pasta Puttanesca, 176
Omelets
  Eggs in Spring, 169
  Gruyére Omelet, 159
  India Eggs, 159
  Olé Omelet, 162
  Spanish Tortilla, 160
One-Dish German Dinner, 34
Onions
  Beef Fajitas, 12
  Beef, Pepper, & Onion Stir-Fry, 11
  Cabbage Kielbasa Soup, 228–229
  Cajun Chicken, 122
  Chicken Stir-Fry, 116
  Chili Steak, 6
  Chinese Spaghetti, 202
  Curried Vegetables, 269
  Easy Chicken Supper, 111
  End-of-Summer Stir-Fry, 146
  Garden Steak, 7
  Grillades, 5
  Grilled Seafood Salad, 243
  Halibut Ragu, 56
  Ham Skillet, 35
  Ham Steak, 36
  Hot Linguine, 200
  In a Pinch Stir-Fry, 282
  Island Black Bean Stew, 218
  Kielbasa Soup, 226
  Marjoram-Scented Flounder Fillets, 52
  Mexican Soup, 219
  Nacho Eggs, 163
  Onion & Cheese Soup, 222
  Parmesan-Basil Vegetable Salad, 246
  Pepperoni Pasta, 182
  Pork Chops & Red Onions, 32

Red Beans & Rice, 217
Salad Bar Stir-Fry, 275
Sausage & Noodles, 204
Sautéed Beef with Onions, 14–15
Scallops Fra Diavolo, 191
Southwestern Stir-Fry, 274
Spanish Clams, 81
Spicy Veggies, 271
Spur-of-the-Moment Chili, 15
Steak Bourguignonne, 8
Sunshine Fish, 51
Veal with Onions, 21
Vegetable Beef Soup, 236
Vegetable Sauté, 267
Vegetarian Chili, 281
Warm London Broil Salad, 257
Orange juice
　Chicken Tidbits with Pineapple Sauce,
　　139
　Curried Chicken, 129
　Honeyed Chicken, 114
　Mandarin Chicken, 126
　Orange-Ginger Lamb Chops, 42
　Orange-Onion Chicken with Couscous,
　　106
　Pork with Orange Sauce, 28
　Quick Turkey à L' Orange, 150
　Salmon in Apricot Sauce, 60
　Scented Lamb Chops, 39
　Sunshine Fish, 51
　Sunshine-Glazed Chicken Thighs, 136
Orange marmalade
　Hawaiian Lamb Chops, 42
　Mandarin Chicken, 126
　Orange-Onion Chicken with Couscous,
　　106
Oranges
　Chicken Fruit Salad, 259
　Chinese Slaw, 242
　Fruit & Vegetable Medley Salad, 244
　Mandarin Chicken, 126
　Orange Chicken Salad, 117
　Orange-Scented Salmon, 61
　Stir-Fried Vegetables & Peanuts, 272
Oysters
　Oyster Pan Roast, 226
　Smoked Oysters & Fettuccine, 177

Pantry Bean Soup, 221
Parmesan-Basil Vegetable Salad, 246
Parsley
　Gnocchi with Sauce Verde, 187
　Herb Garden Spaghetti, 199
　Middle Eastern Salad, 245
　Parsley Scallops, 100
　Scallops & Parsley Sauce, 176
　Scallops Provençal, 98
　Spaghetti with Parsley Sauce, 185
　White Bean Salad, 264
Pasta & Cappicola, 188
Pasta & Prosciutto, 178
Pasta & Zucchini, 193
Pasta for a Summer Night, 198
Pasta Puttanesca, 176
Pasta with Jersey Tomato Sauce, 184
Pasta with Salad Sauce, 240
Pasta with Scallops, 195
Shellfish Pasta, 197
Pasta, 171–205

Pasta
　Meatballs & Ravioli, 13
　Pepperoni Pasta Salad, 252
　Warm Vegetable & Pasta Salad, 260
Pasta sauce
　Bean Ravioli, 180
　Chicken & Zucchini, 121
　Eggplant Neapolitan, 275
　Hot Linguine, 200
　Linguine with Hot Clam Sauce, 186
　Meatballs & Ravioli, 13
　Pepperoni Pasta, 182
　Sausage & Linguine, 192
　Spanish Rice, 153
Peanut butter
　Creole Peanut Butter Soup, 233
Peanuts
　Snow Peas & Peanut Scramble, 168
　Stir-Fried Vegetables & Peanuts, 272
Peas
　Doctored Fettuccine Alfredo, 205
　Pasta & Cappicola, 188
　Pork & Black Bean Sauce, 29
Pears
　Chicken & Pear Salad, 253
Pecans
　Curried Turkey with Couscous, 188
　Pecan Catfish, 47
Pepper Spaghetti, 200
Pepper Steak, 9
Peppered Pork, 33
Pepperoni
　Italian Bean Salad, 239
　Pepperoni Pasta Salad, 252
　Pepperoni Pasta, 182
　Pizza Pasta, 205
Peppers with Sole, 70
Pesto
　Couscous Salad, 263
　Pesto Pasta with Salmon Steaks, 194
Pickapeppa sauce
　Shrimp with Rosemary, 90
Pimientos
　Citrus Chicken Salad, 242
　Crab Imperial, 95
　Spanish Rice, 153
Pine nuts
　Pasta & Prosciutto, 178
　Shells & Broccoli, 196
Pineapple
　Hawaiian Lamb Chops, 42
　Honeyed Pork Stir-Fry, 27
　Macadamia Chicken, 107
　Pineapple Swordfish, 74
　Sweet & Sour Chicken, 119
Pineapple jelly
　Chicken Tidbits with Pineapple Sauce,
　　139
Pineapple juice
　Halibut Broil, 55
Pizza Pasta, 205
Pizza sauce
　Pizza Pasta, 205
　Pizza, 148
Pizza
　Turkey Pizza, 148
Poached Red Snapper, 68
Polenta with Mushrooms & Salsa, 281
Polish Pea Soup, 235

Poppy seeds
　Almond Poppy-Seed Noodles, 181
Pork & Lamb, 23–43
Pork chops
　Braised Pork Chops, 32
　Chinese Pork Chops, 27
　Lemon-Nut Pork Chops, 26
　Lime-Cumin Pork Chops, 26
　One-Dish German Dinner, 34
　Peppered Pork, 33
　Pork Chops & Red Onions, 32
　Pork Chops with Gravy, 33
　Pork Chops with Peppers, 30
　Pork Chops with Piquant Sauce, 25
　Pork with Noodles Soup, 209
　Rum Pork Chops, 30
　Soy-Lemon Pork Chops, 28
　Teriyaki Pork Chops, 25
Pork, ground
　Chinese Burgers, 34
Pork tenderloin
　Browned Pork with Capers, 31
　Honeyed Pork Stir-Fry, 27
　Pork & Black Bean Sauce, 29
　Pork with Orange Sauce, 28
　Teutonic Pork Tenderloin, 29
Pork tenderloin
　Pork with Noodles Soup, 209
　Chili-Topped Potatoes, 3
　Hearts & Sole, 72
Potatoes
　Knockwurst Boiled Dinner, 18
　Polish Pea Soup, 235
　Red Flannel Hash, 12
　Sardine Raclette, 64
　Smoked Whitefish Salad, 260
　Spanish Tortilla, 160
　Steak Bourguignonne, 8
Prosciutto
　Chicken Italiano, 107
　Doctored Fettuccine Alfredo, 205
　Pasta & Prosciutto, 178
　Veal with Prosciutto, 20

Quesadillas
　Chicken Quesadillas, 141
　Shrimp Quesadilla, 92
Quick Baked Beans, 280
Quick Turkey à L' Orange, 150

Radishes
　Daikon Salad, 263
　Spinach, Tuna, & Shrimp Salad, 250
　Summer Bean Salad, 262
Raisins
　Curried Flounder, 53
　Raisin-Almond Chicken, 112
　Spicy Veggies, 271
　Winter Pork with Fruit, 31
Ratatouille, 279
Ravioli with Zucchini, 202–203
Red Beans & Rice, 217
Red Flannel Hash, 12
Red Pepper Cod, 49
Red Pepper Soup, 231
Red Pepper Stir-Fry, 123
Red Snapper Fillets, 68
Red Snapper with Anchovies, 66
Red-Wine Barbecued Chicken, 135

Rice
  Lemon Soup, 213
  Mexican Rice & Turkey, 154
  Quick Turkey à L' Orange, 150
  Red Beans & Rice, 217
  Scallops with Lime Sauce, 99
  Spanish Rice, 153
  Vegetable Skillet Supper, 273
Rum
  Raisin-Almond Chicken, 112
  Rum Pork Chops, 30

Sage Turkey, 148
Salad Bar Spaghetti, 198
Salad Bar Stir-Fry, 275
Salads, Main-Dish, 237–264
Salads
  Crab Salad with Mushrooms, 95
  Viva Beef Salad, 16
Salami
  Deli Scramble, 162
Salmon
  Artichoke Pasta Salad, 239
  Broiled Salmon Steaks, 61
  Lemon Teriyaki Salmon, 63
  Mustard & Dill-Basted Salmon, 59
  Orange-Scented Salmon, 61
  Pesto Pasta with Salmon Steaks, 194
  Salmon Chowder, 227
  Salmon in Apricot Sauce, 60
  Salmon on Leeks, 62
  Salmon Teriyaki, 58
  Salmon with Chive Butter, 60
  Salmon with Couscous, 181
  Salmon with Cucumber Sauce, 59
  Salmon with Ginger Glaze, 63
  Salmon with Salsa, 58
  Sesame Salmon, 62
Salsa
  15-Minute Chicken Molé, 110
  Fish Mexicano, 54
  Garlic Chicken, 123
  Mexican Rice & Turkey, 154
  Polenta with Mushrooms & Salsa, 281
  Red Snapper Fillets, 68
  Salmon with Salsa, 58
  Salsa Chicken, 131
  Salsa Eggs, 169
  Shrimp Qesadilla, 92
  Shrimp Salad, 257
  Southwestern Halibut, 57
Sardine Raclette, 64
Sauerkraut
  Bavarian Dinner, 35
  Kraut Brats, 18–19
  Sauerkraut Soup, 223
Sausage
  Bavarian Dinner, 35
  Cabbage Kielbasa Soup, 228–229
  Chorizo Black Bean Soup, 217
  Fusion Sausages, 37
  German Sausage & Red Cabbage Skillet, 38
  Hot Linguine, 200
  Kielbasa Soup, 226
  Kielbasa with Cabbage, 19
  Knockwurst Boiled Dinner, 18

Kraut Brats, 18–19
Sausage & Linguine, 192
Sausage & Noodles, 204
Sautéed Beef with Onions, 14–15
Scallops
  Broiled Scallops, 98
  Cilantro Scallops, 97
  Fish Stew, 225
  Ginger Scallops, 97
  Parsley Scallops, 100
  Pasta with Scallops, 195
  Scallop & Cauliflower Salad, 254
  Scallop Soup, 222–223
  Scallops & Parsley Sauce, 176
  Scallops & Pasta, 185
  Scallops & Peppers, 100
  Scallops Amandine, 99
  Scallops Dijon, 101
  Scallops Fra Diavolo, 191
  Scallops Provençal, 98
  Scallops with Angel Hair, 178
  Scallops with Lemon Mustard, 96
  Scallops with Lime Sauce, 99
  Sichuan Scallops, 96
Scented Lamb Chops, 39
Scrambled Eggs with Shrimp, Tomato, & Broccoli, 168
Scrod
  Mustard Scrod, 66
  Scrod with Tarragon, 65
Senegalese Soup, 228
Sesame oil
  Chinese Hot Clams, 82
  Cod, Asian Style, 48
  Five-Spice Chicken with Walnuts, 118
  Hot, Hot Chicken with Cashews, 112
  Sesame Salmon, 62
  Smoked Oysters & Fettuccine, 177
Sesame seeds
  Cantonese Chicken Salad, 252
  Sesame Burgers, 15
  Sesame Chicken Salad, 258
  Sesame Salmon, 62
  Smoked Oysters & Fettuccine, 177
Shallots
  Chicken with Mushrooms, 125
  Pasta for a Summer Night, 198
Shanghai Chicken Fettuccine, 173
Shellfish, 79–101
Shells & Broccoli, 196
Sherry Chicken, 115
Sherry Shrimp, 87
Sherry Turkey, 147
Shrimp
  Beer-Battered Shrimp, 89
  Chicken Scampi, 126
  Chicory Salad, 262
  Creamy Shrimp Fettuccine, 174
  Curried Shrimp, 88
  Down & Dirty Shrimp, 91
  Fish Stew, 225
  Garlic Shrimp, 86
  Garlic Shrimp with Linguine & Lime, 173
  Hot Shrimp, 92–93
  Lettuce Stir-Fry, 94
  Scrambled Eggs with Shrimp, Tomato, & Broccoli, 168
  Sherry Shrimp, 87

Shrimp Casserole, 91
Shrimp Egg Scramble, 93
Shrimp Quesadilla, 92
Shrimp Salad, 257
Shrimp Scampi, 87
Shrimp with Rosemary, 90
Spaghetti & Shrimp, 175
Spinach, Tuna, & Shrimp Salad, 250
Tequila Shrimp, 88
Thyme Shrimp & Broccoli Stir-Fry, 85
Sichuan Scallops, 96
Smoked Oysters & Fettuccine, 177
Smoked Whitefish Salad, 260
Snapper
  Five-Spice Snapper, 69
  Garlic-Lemon Fillets, 69
  Mediterranean Snapper, 67
  Poached Red Snapper, 68
  Red Snapper Fillets, 68
  Red Snapper with Anchovies, 66
  Tomato Snapper, 67
Snow peas
  Chinese Spaghetti, 202
  Smoked Oysters & Fettuccine, 177
  Snow Peas & Peanut Scramble, 168
  Stir-Fried Apples & Chicken, 108
  Tofu Stir-Fry, 272
Sole
  Broiled Lemon Sole, 73
  Citrus Fish, 72
  Green Fish, 71
  Hearts & Sole, 72
  Peppers with Sole, 70
  Sole Amandine, 73
  Sole in Tomato Sauce, 74
  Sole Vinaigrette, 71
  Sole with Lemon Sauce, 70
Soups & Stews, 207–236
Sour cream
  Chicken with Broccoli, 116
  Creamy Shrimp Fettuccine, 174
  Cucumber-Chicken Soup, 215
  Guilty Chicken in Mushroom Sauce, 128
  Mexican Turkey, 146
  Mussels with Mustard Sauce, 84
  Salmon Chowder, 227
  Tarragon Chicken Salad, 259
Southern Ham & Vegetable Dinner, 39
Southwestern Halibut, 57
Southwestern Stir-Fry, 274
Soy-Lemon Pork Chops, 28
Spaghetti & Shrimp, 175
Spaghetti with Parsley Sauce, 185
Spaghetti sauce
  Chicken & Eggplant Italiano, 137
  Chicken Cacciatore, 113
  Chicken Parmesan, 114
  Hot & Spicy Chicken, 142
  Vermicelli & Turkey with White Wine Sauce, 186
Spanish Clams, 81
Spanish Rice, 153
Spanish Tortilla, 160
Spicy Chicken with Hoisin Sauce, 131
Spicy Lamb Chops, 41
Spicy Minute Steaks, 6
Spicy Veggies, 271
Spicy Yogurt Chicken, 128

292

Spinach
    Chicken & Spinach Italiano, 133
    Chicken Spinach Soup, 216
    Florentine Frittata, 160
    Greek Fish, 50
    Grilled Seafood Salad, 243
    Hot Pepper Ravioli, 175
    Spanish Tortilla, 160
    Spinach & Leek Soup, 232
    Spinach Pasta, 195
    Spinach, Tuna, & Shrimp Salad, 250
Split-pea soup
    Polish Pea Soup, 235
Spur-of-the-Moment Chili, 15
Steak & Arugula Salad, 241
Steak Bourguignonne, 8
Steak sauce
    Beef Stir-Fry, 3
    Black Bean & Chicken Salad, 250–251
    Halibut Broil, 55
Steamed Mussels & Herbs, 84
Stewed Garbanzos, 267
Stir-Fried Apples & Chicken, 108
Stir-Fried Cauliflower & Sweet Peppers, 271
Stir-Fried Vegetables & Peanuts, 272
Stir-Fry Salad, 244
Stir-fry sauce
    Chili-Chicken Stir-Fry, 120
    End-of-Summer Stir-Fry, 146
    Pork & Black Bean Sauce, 29
    Red Pepper Cod, 49
    Salad Bar Stir-Fry, 275
    Tofu Stir-Fry, 272
Stuffing mix
    Ham Steak, 36
Sugar snap peas
    Couscous with Cashews, 282–283
    Fettuccine & Vegetables, 204
    Fruit & Vegetable Medley Salad, 244
    Mushroom Noodle Soup, 214
    Stir-Fried Sugar Snap Peas & Cucumbers, 270
    Vegetable Stew, 273
    Warm London Broil Salad, 257
    Warm Vegetable & Pasta Salad, 260
Summer Bean Salad, 262
Summer Chicken, 127
Summer Linguine, 183
Summer Squash
    Corn & Summer Squash Soup, 234
    Herbed Squash, 278
    Hot Chicken Salad, 141
    Parmesan-Basil Vegetable Salad, 246
Sunflower seeds
    Spaghetti with Parsley Sauce, 185
Sunshine Fish, 51
Sunshine-Glazed Chicken Thighs, 136
Sweet and sour sauce
    Sweet & Sour Chicken, 119
Swiss Salad, 247
Swordfish
    Pineapple Swordfish, 74

Taco sauce
    Chicken & Bean Burritos, 140
    Mexican Soup, 219
    Viva Beef Salad, 16
Tarragon Chicken, 122
Tarragon Chicken Salad, 259
Tarragon Crab, 94

Tarragon Veal, 20
Tartar sauce
    Citrus Fish, 72
    Limey Fillets, 50
Tequila Shrimp, 88
Teriyaki sauce
    Fusion Sausages, 37
    Lemon Teriyaki Salmon, 63
    Salmon Teriyaki, 58
    Sesame Salmon, 62
    Teriyaki Honey Chicken, 117
    Teriyaki Pork Chops, 25
Teutonic Pork Tenderloin, 29
Three-Pepper Steak, 7
Thyme Lamb Chops, 43
Thyme Shrimp & Broccoli Stir-Fry, 85
Thyme Veal Chops, 22
Tofu
    Tofu Stir-Fry, 272
    Turkey Stir-Fry with Tofu, 155
Tomato bisque soup
    Tomato, Avocado, & Crab Soup, 219
Tomato juice
    Creole Peanut Butter Soup, 233
    Cucumber Soup with Tomatoes, 221
Tomato paste
    Chicken Vermicelli, 199
Tomato puree
    Spur-of-the-Moment Chili, 15
Tomato sauce
    15–Minute Chicken Molé, 110
Tomatoes (fresh and canned)
    Angel Hair with Tiny Tomatoes, 177
    Angel-Hair Pasta with Fresh Tomatoes, 189
    Artichoke Pasta Salad, 239
    Asian Beef Stir-Fry, 10
    Bean & Olive Salad, 264
    Black Bean Salad, 247
    Beef & Napa Cabbage Salad, 261
    Beef Sauté, 8
    Black Bean & Chicken Salad, 250–251
    Broccoli Salad, 239
    Cajun Chicken, 122
    Camembert Angel Hair, 187
    Chicken & Olives, 115
    Chicken Asparagus Salad, 256
    Chicken Italiano, 107
    Chicken Livers & Ravioli, 197
    Chili con Pollo, 137
    Corn & Summer Squash Soup, 234
    Corn & Tuna Salad, 243
    Cream of Tomato Soup, 216
    Cucumber Soup with Tomatoes, 221
    Cucumbers & Tomato Skillet, 269
    Curried Tomato Soup, 235
    Curried Vegetables, 269
    Dinner & Lunch Bean Salad, 241
    Garden-Style Tuna Steak, 76
    Garden Steak, 7
    Greek Salad, 261
    Green Bean & Tomato Stew, 276
    Green Fish, 71
    Grillades, 5
    Grilled Seafood Salad, 243
    Halibut Ragu, 56
    Hamburger Skillet, 17
    Herbed Squash, 278
    Hot Black Beans, 276

    Italian Steak Salad, 258
    Middle Eastern Salad, 245
    Ocean Deep Soup, 213
    Pasta & Zucchini, 193
    Pasta Puttanesca, 176
    Pasta with Jersey Tomato Sauce, 184
    Pasta with Salad Sauce, 240
    Ratatouille, 279
    Red Pepper Soup, 231
    Scallops Fra Diavolo, 191
    Scrambled Eggs with Shrimp, Tomato, & Broccoli, 168
    Shrimp Casserole, 91
    Southern Ham & Vegetable Dinner, 39
    Southwestern Stir-Fry, 274
    Spaghetti & Shrimp, 175
    Stewed Garbanzos, 267
    Stir-Fried Chicken Burritos, 109
    Summer Chicken, 127
    Summer Linguine, 183
    Three-Bean Stew, 234
    Tomato & Cheese Fillets, 65
    Tomato Bisque, 231
    Tomato Snapper, 67
    Tomato-Bacon Linguine, 194
    Tomato-Cabbage Soup, 223
    Tomato-Egg Dinner, 165
    Tomato-Yogurt Soup, 212
    Tortellini Soup, 211
    Tortellini with Chicken & Broccoli, 193
    Tuna Garden Salad, 249
    Turkey & Peppers, Italian Style, 152
    Veal Cutlets with Tomato Sauce, 22
    Vegetable Beef Soup, 236
    Vegetable Skillet Supper, 273
    Vegetable Stew, 273
    Vegetarian Chili, 281
    Vodka-Basil Fettucine, 179
    Warm Chicken Salad, 255
    Warm London Broil Salad, 257
    White Bean & Tomato Mélange, 268
Tomatoes, sun-dried
    Hot Pepper Ravioli, 175
    Pasta with Scallops, 195
    Pepperoni Pasta Salad, 252
    Tortellini with Artichoke Hearts, 182
    Tortellini with Sun-Dried Tomatoes, 190
    Turkey Cutlets with Sun-Dried Tomatoes, 149
Tortellini Soup, 211
Tortellini with Artichoke Hearts, 182
Tortellini with Chicken & Broccoli, 193
Tortellini with Sun-Dried Tomatoes, 190
Tortillas
    Bean Tortilla Soup, 218
    Beef Fajitas, 12
    Chicken & Bean Burritos, 140
    Chicken Quesadillas, 141
    Huevos Rancheros, 164
    Shrimp Quesadilla, 92
    Stir-Fried Chicken Burritos, 109
Tossed Tuna Salad, 248
Trout
    Trout with Caper Sauce, 76
    Trout with Dill, 75
    Trout with Fennel, 75
Tuna
    Bean & Tuna Salad, 246
    Corn & Tuna Salad, 243

Tuna *(continued)*
    Garden-Style Tuna Steak, 76
    Greek Isles Tuna Salad, 256
    Spinach, Tuna, & Shrimp Salad, 250
    Tossed Tuna Salad, 248
    Tuna Garden Salad, 249
    Warm Bean & Tuna Salad, 248
Turkey, 143–155
Turkey, cooked
    Turkey Pizza, 148
Turkey cutlets
    End-of-Summer Stir-Fry, 146
    Sage Turkey, 148
    Sherry Turkey, 147
    Turkey Cutlets with Sun-Dried Tomatoes, 149
Turkey fillets
    Mexican Turkey, 146
Turkey, ground
    Curry Couscous, 188
    Herbal Turkey Patties, 154
    Oktoberfest Turkey Burgers, 149
    Spanish Rice, 153
    Teriyaki Burgers, 153
    Turkey Chow Mein, 155
    Turkey Stir-Fry with Tofu, 155
    Vermicelli & Turkey with White Wine Sauce, 186
Turkey tenderloins
    Broiled Turkey Tenderloins, 145
    Curried Turkey, 148
    Mediterranean Turkey with Olives, 151
    Quick Turkey à L' Orange, 150
    Turkey & Chanterelles, 150
    Turkey & Peppers, Italian Style, 152
    Turkey Piquant, 152
    Turkey Tenderloins Dijon, 145

Veal
    Garlic & Rosemary Veal Chops, 21
    Tarragon Veal, 20
    Thyme Veal Chops, 22
    Veal Cutlets with Tomato Sauce, 22
    Veal Marsala, 19
    Veal with Onions, 21
    Veal with Prosciutto, 20
Vegetable Beef Soup, 236
Vegetable broth
    Bean Soup, 224
Vegetable Entrees, 265–284
Vegetable juice
    Alphabet Noodle Soup, 220
    Green Bean Stir-Fry, 279
    Red Pepper Soup, 231
    Stir-Fried Vegetables & Peanuts, 272
    Tomato Bisque, 231
Vegetable Sauté, 267
Vegetable Stew, 273
Vegetarian Chili, 281

Vermicelli & Turkey with White Wine Sauce, 186
Viva Beef Salad, 16
Vodka-Basil Fettucine, 179

Walnuts
    Asparagus Stir-Fry, 274
    Chicken with Walnuts, 109
    Five-Spice Chicken with Walnuts, 118
    Gnocchi with Sauce Verde, 187
    Honey Chicken Salad, 254
    Tarragon Chicken Salad, 259
Warm Bean & Tuna Salad, 248
Warm Chicken & Almond Salad, 253
Warm Chicken Salad, 255
Warm London Broil Salad, 257
Warm Vegetable & Pasta Salad, 260
Water chestnuts
    Cabbage & Cheese Salad, 251
    Chicken Fruit Salad, 259
    Chinese Spaghetti, 202
    Citrus Chicken Salad, 242
    Green Bean Stir-Fry, 279
    Sesame Chicken Salad, 258
    Shrimp Salad, 257
    Stir-Fried Apples & Chicken, 108
    Teriyaki Burgers, 153
Watercress
    Green Fish, 71
White Bean & Tomato Mélange, 268
White Bean Salad, 264
Whitefish
    Broiled Whitefish, 77
    Smoked Whitefish Salad, 260
Wine
    Apple-Wine Chicken, 135
    Browned Pork with Capers, 31
    Chicken Piccata, 113
    Chicken Stir-Fry, 116
    Chicken with Mushrooms, 125
    Chicken with Zinfandel Baste, 118
    Chili Steak, 6
    Clam Noodle Soup, 210
    Clams Italiano, 82
    Clams with Scallions & Parsley, 81
    Garden-Style Tuna Steak, 76
    German Cabbage, 277
    Halibut in Wine, 56
    Hot Sherried Chicken Thighs, 133
    Kielbasa Soup, 226
    Lemony Bean Soup, 209
    Lime-Cumin Pork Chops, 26
    Linguine with Tomato & Basil Sauce, 203
    Mussels Mariniére, 85
    Mussels Steamed in Wine, 83
    Mussels with Mustard Sauce, 84
    Ocean Deep Soup, 213

Quick Turkey à L' Orange, 150
Red-Wine Barbecued Chicken, 135
Salmon on Leeks, 62
Salmon with Couscous, 181
Scallops & Parsley Sauce, 176
Scallops with Lemon Mustard, 96
Sherry Chicken, 115
Sherry Shrimp, 87
Sherry Turkey, 147
Shrimp Casserole, 91
Shrimp Scampi, 87
Spanish Clams, 81
Steak Bourguignonne, 8
Steamed Mussels & Herbs, 84
Teriyaki Honey Chicken, 117
Tortellini with Artichoke Hearts, 182
Veal Marsala, 19
Vermicelli & Turkey with White Wine Sauce, 186
Winter Pork with Fruit, 31

Yogurt
    Armenian Patties, 40
    Chicken Salad with Yogurt Dressing, 244
    Cold Yogurt Soup, 230
    Cucumber-Dill Soup, 220
    Lamb with Yogurt Mint Sauce, 41
    Meatballs with Cilantro Dipping Sauce, 13
    Salmon with Cucumber Sauce, 59
    Sautéed Beef with Onions, 14–15
    Senegalese Soup, 228
    Spicy Yogurt Chicken, 128
    Tomato-Yogurt Soup, 212
    Tossed Tuna Salad, 248

Zesty Lemon Chicken, 120
Zucchini
    Avocado Frittata, 166
    Chicken & Zucchini, 121
    Chicken Cacciatore, 113
    Curried Vegetables, 269
    Herbed Squash, 278
    Parmesan-Basil Vegetable Salad, 246
    Pasta & Zucchini, 193
    Pork & Black Bean Sauce, 29
    Ratatouille, 279
    Ravioli with Zucchini, 202–203
    Salad Bar Spaghetti, 198
    Sesame Chicken Salad, 258
    Spaghetti & Shrimp, 175
    Spicy Veggies, 271
    Tuna Garden Salad, 249
    Vegetable Beef Soup, 236
    Vegetable Sauté, 267
    Vegetable Skillet Supper, 273
    Vegetable Stew, 273
    Zucchini Pasta, 184
    Zucchini Soup, 210

About the Author

Patricia Mack is Food Editor for *The Record*, in Hackensack, New Jersey, and also contributes to the Lifestyle and Health sections. She has received five awards from the Association of Food Journalists and numerous other writing awards, including an award in accuracy in health reporting. Patricia Mack has appeared on Fox Five's *Good Day New York*, the Television Food Network's *In Food Today*, ABC Eyewitness News, and Comcast's *Family Matters*.